The Croat Question

The Croat Question

Partisan Politics in the Formation of the Yugoslav Socialist State

Jill A. Irvine

with a Foreword by Ivo Banac

Westview Press

BOULDER • SAN FRANCISCO • OXFORD

Published in 1993 in the United States of America by Westview Press, Inc., 5500 Central Avenue, Boulder, Colorado 80301-2877, and in the United Kingdom by Westview Press, 36 Lonsdale Road, Summertown, Oxford OX2 7EW

Library of Congress Cataloging-in-Publication Data
Irvine, Jill A.
  The Croat Question: partisan politics in the formation of the Yugoslav socialist state / by Jill A. Irvine
      p.   cm.
  Includes bibliographical references and index.
  ISBN 0-8133-8542-3
  1. Yugoslavia—Politics and government—1945- .   2. Yugoslavia—
Politics and government—1918–1945.   3. Yugoslavia—Ethnic
relations.   4. Nationalism—Yugoslavia.   I. Title
DR1302.I78   1993
949.702—dc20   92-27252
                                                                          CIP

Printed and bound in the United States of America

The paper used in this publication meets the requirements of the American National Standard for Permanence of Paper for Printed Library Materials Z39.48-1984.

10   9   8   7   6   5   4   3   2   1

To my mother,
Martha Emery Streu

and to the memory of
Ivan Jelić and Fikreta Jelić-Butić

Contents

Foreword

Ivo Banac

Any review of literature on post-1945 Yugoslavia will surely document the limits of social science research. With few exceptions, the practitioners in the field had no firm grasp of South Slavic developments, the nature of the Yugoslav revolution, or Tito's polity and its internal underpinnings. The reasons for the vast failure are varied. My hunch is that they are both empirical and methodological. The vast majority of Yugoslav specialists never dealt with real evidence, had no grasp of the nuances of South Slavic cultures, and frequently depended on irrelevant and derivative models for their analyses. Research restrictions were only partially to blame. Even at the worst of times shrewd researchers were able to get at the evidence. But instead of reading the *New York Times* and *Radio Free Europe Reports*, instead of depending on subjective interviews, it was necessary to pursue vastly more interesting topics than the study of bureaucratic structures and regime fantasies ("self-management"). It was necessary, too, to develop the instincts of an investigative reporter.

The importance of Jill Irvine's monograph on the Croatian Communist movement during the Second World War has everything to do with her determination to go against the conventions of her guild. Instead of studying the various "federal crises" of late Titoism, she went to the root of the nationality question in Partisan Croatia, the land in which the Communists scored their greatest successes and where they had to confront the intractable Croat question, the chief political problem of both royal and Communist Yugoslavia. Moreover, instead of relying on various latter-day reinterpretations, she drew her evidence from the archival collections of the Communist Party of Croatia and the Land Antifascist Council of People's Liberation of Croatia, the chief political and representative institutions of the insurgent movement. In studying the record of Croat and Serb Communists, their mutual relations, and evolving ideas on Croatia's role in the new Yugoslav federation, she has produced an intricate picture of people and circumstances that does not fit the paperboard legend of the Yugoslav war. Although I do not share all of Jill Irvine's conclusions, I am convinced that her work is indispensable for an understanding of Croatia, Yugoslavia, and all of their discontents.

The career of Andrija Hebrang, the Croat Communist leader who dominates Irvine's book, is a paradigm of her larger concerns. Hebrang was a Communist of Slavonian peasant origin and joined the party in the 1920s. The great writer Miroslav Krežla nicknamed him "Potato Baron" because Hebrang occasionally financed party activities by borrowing money from his mother, a vegetable vender at the Zagreb farmer's market. Hebrang's revolutionary instincts were honed in the period of Comintern support for the independence of Croatia (1924-1935), a proposition that sustained Croat Communists even when they were obliged to switch to the new Yugoslav federalist belief. The tension between two types of collectivism—class-based and national—was the chief dilemma of Hebrang's leadership, as was the perspective of a Communist minority in a country dominated by a peasant-based national movement that called itself the Croat Peasant Party.

The advantages of Communist activism and discipline were frequently offset by a freely offered—but occasionally troubled—loyalty to Stalin and Tito, who stood on the highest rungs of the Communist hierarchical ladder. Their angles of vision were different. Stalin suspended the Comintern's revolutionary program in order to safeguard the Grand Alliance, which was essential for Soviet state interests. Tito suspended the unquestioning loyalty to Stalin in order to safeguard the Communist domination over the Partisan movement, which was essential for Yugoslav revolutionary interests. Hebrang stood midway between these contending imperatives. He practiced a restricted version of an alliance with Croat non-Communists but also constrained the Communist domination over the Partisan base. His approach was that of a self-limiting Popular Front.

Although concerned primarily with the Communists, Jill Irvine also assesses the wider political terrain of wartime Croatia. Fully aware of Yugoslavia's fragility, she has detected all the ideational and political antecedents to its demise in the 1990s. Although this book is not an introduction to the problems of the post-Yugoslav Balkans, there is a certain unmistakable air of déjà vu about the issues and situations that are discussed. But there are also vast differences between the 1940s and 1990s. The Communist movement reconstructed Yugoslavia in the course of the war. It is possible to argue that the edifice would have been firmer had the concerns of Croat and other non-Serb Communists prevailed in the early days of Communist power. The Communists, ever faithful to Leninist voluntarism, preferred to think that their unity guaranteed the strength of the edifice. This chicken-or-egg dilemma need not concern us. But it does matter that the national question, more than any other single concern, ultimately undermined Communist unity. With the collapse of the Communist party, Yugoslavia was no longer possible. Non-Communist compulsion was no alternative.

Preface

I have been interested in the national question in Yugoslavia for almost as long as I can remember, beginning with my first trip to Yugoslavia in 1972. As an American with no family ties to this part of the world, I was deeply fascinated by the way in which national identities and passions had influenced the history of this area; the nationalist violence and turmoil of the Second World War were especially perplexing and compelling to me. On my frequent subsequent visits to the country, and during my two year stay as a Fulbright Scholar from 1978 to 1980, I thought and talked about this subject with many Yugoslavs, though our conversations were sometimes constrained by political events. My conversations with scholars, politicians and ordinary citizens from all regions of the country convinced me that even in Communist Yugoslavia the national question remained the key to understanding the workings of the polity.

Several years later as a graduate student at Harvard University, I decided to write my dissertation about communism and the national question in Yugoslavia, focusing particularly on the events in Croatia during the Second World War. To me, questions concerning the way in which the national question had influenced the process of creating the Yugoslav Socialist state were of particular significance, not only for gaining a better understanding of its formative period but also for understanding its subsequent development. I decided to focus on the Croat question because it lay at the heart of national conflict in Yugoslavia; Tito and other Communist leaders were convinced that resolving the Croat question was the key to their success in gaining and maintaining political power. Despite its importance, however, there was no detailed study in English on the Communists' approach to the Croat question. Among the aspects of this question that had not been considered in the Yugoslav or western scholarly literature on the subject was the role of Andrija Hebrang, the central figure of the Partisan movement in Croatia and of this book. The character of what I call his federalist state-building strategy is essential to understanding the framework of the state established by the Communist-led Partisan movement and the fissures that appeared within it.

The bulk of my research for this book was conducted between 1985 and 1987 when I was in Yugoslavia on a combined Fulbright-IREX Award. My archival materials were drawn primarily from the excellent collection at the Institute for the History of the Workers' Movement of Croatia. This was an exciting time to be researching this topic in Yugoslavia, as scholars increasingly turned their attention to a critical reappraisal of the Partisan period. Many questions which had previously been taboo became the subject of research and discussion, reflecting the expansion of debate in Yugoslav society. Numerous scholars at the institute and at other institutions displayed enormous interest in this project and gave me a great deal of help.

Although this book reflects much of the thinking and research I did during that stay in Yugoslavia, it has been substantially enlarged and rewritten. The dramatic and tragic events of the past three years have required much rethinking of the significance and legacy of the Communists' approach to the national question in Yugoslavia. As the conflict escalated among Yugoslavia's national groups, and as they returned increasingly to the tensions and even the terminology from the Second World War, I became more convinced than ever that understanding the Partisans' approach to the Croat question was essential to understanding the disintegration of the Yugoslav state. Consequently, I added a new chapter (chapter six), which is intended to be more ruminative in character, in which I trace important connections between the legacy of the Partisan period and the current conflicts.

When I first started writing about the national conflict in Yugoslavia during the Second World War, I could never have imagined that such violence would erupt again. It has been particularly painful to be working on a manuscript about the wartime period during the past several years, as many of the old hostilities among Yugoslavia's national groups have reappeared. I finish the book with the fervent hope that a more enduring solution to the national question can be achieved in the aftermath of the current strife.

•   •   •   •   •   •

I would like to thank the many people who have helped me as I have worked on this book. I am indebted to Adam Ulam for his support during the difficult early stages of this project. As director of the Russian Research Center, Professor Ulam provided me with a congenial and stimulating place to work, for which I am grateful. Special thanks to Ivo Banac for his guidance and encouragement throughout this project; his scholarship and dedication have been a constant source of inspiration to me. I also must thank Ellen Comisso, Mark Beissinger, Susan Woodward and Aleksa Djilas for their advice and comments on portions of this book. Robin Remington, Robert Cox, Mark Branden, Jeff Rubin and Carol Lilly gave me valuable comments and suggestions on later drafts of the manuscript. My thanks to Dragan Milivojević and Erich Frankland for their editorial assistance. For his excellent maps and production skills, I extend my deepest thanks to Ronald Halterman.

Numerous friends and family members have given me practical advice as well as moral support as I have written this book. I would like to thank Aaron Friedberg, Sarah Gardner, Jane Katz, Susan Meigs, Ethan Nadelmann, Susan Nardone, Emmy Norris, Kay Paul, Gabe Schoenfeld, Nick Zeigler and especially Alice Stanton for their generous assistance. My special thanks to Hatsy Thompson for her love and encouragement and for her expert editorial eye. Olga Zeilborg Irvine, Tom Irvine, Sadi Irvine Delaney, and Herb and Martha Streu gave me a great deal of the enthusiasm with which I began this project and, most importantly, the determination to complete it.

This book would not have been possible without the generous assistance of numerous Yugoslavs who shared with me their personal experiences and extensive knowledge of this subject. I would like to thank Dušan Bilandžić for his official sponsorship of this project during my stay in Yugoslavia. Eugen Pusić nurtured and guided my interest in Yugoslavia for many years, for which I am grateful. I am especially grateful to the late Ivan Jelić for his scholarly advice and guidance; his interest and encouragement during the past several years meant a great deal to me. The Institute for the History of the Workers' Movement of Croatia in Zagreb, where I conducted most of my research, offered not only a rich and well organized archival collection but a wonderful collegial environment. Countless conversations over coffee with associates at the Institute made this a much better book, although my colleagues are not to be held accountable for the opinions expressed here in any way. This book could not have been written without the help of Alenka Čičin-Šain, who taught me so much about Yugoslavia and myself and who was always ready to get me out of a jam.

I am indebted also to the various institutions that provided financial support for the research and writing of this book. The International Research and Exchanges Board and the Fulbright Commission both funded my research in Yugoslavia in 1985. A Radcliffe Grant for Graduate Women also provided financial assistance for my trip in 1987. In 1988 and 1989, a grant from the American Council of Learned Societies allowed me to work fulltime on this project. I am indebted to the

University of Oklahoma for its generous support during this past year of writing.

Finally, I would like to thank my husband, Ronald Halterman, for his support for this book. Ron has helped me in too many ways to list here; for his love and encouragement I am profoundly grateful. Our children, Andrew and Julie, who were born in the later stages of this project, have provided a welcome distraction from its more difficult moments and a delightful reminder of the truly important things in life.

Jill A. Irvine

Introduction

This book investigates the impact of nationalism on the formation and development of the Communist state in Yugoslavia and its legacy for post-Communist change. In particular, it examines the way in which the Communist Party of Yugoslavia (CPY) approached the Croat question as it remade the state from 1941-1945. Yugoslavia today, like the other states of Central and Eastern Europe and the former Soviet Union, is undergoing another round of state-making in which the entire future order of the state has been thrown into question. Conflicts about the Croat question are at the heart of this process (which has so far claimed thousands of lives), as Yugoslavia's national groups seek to redefine the way in which this question was resolved by the CPY during the Second World War. How, for example, should the borders between independent Serbian and Croatian political units or states be drawn? What should be the status of the approximately six hundred thousand Serbs residing in Croatia? What should be the relationship between Serbs and Croats and their brethren living across the border in Bosnia and Hercegovina? The way in which these questions were answered by the Communist-led Partisan movement during the Second World War is now being challenged by all major political groups in Yugoslavia. Whether and how they succeed are questions for future study; what they are fighting against is the focus of this one.

The Croat question, or the question of how to achieve Croat aspirations for statehood, has been the most serious political problem in the Yugoslav state since its inception. Croats and Serbs, who joined together with several other national groups to form the Yugoslav state in 1918, had clearly defined national identities and movements and frequently mutually exclusive national goals. Although these two groups possessed great linguistic and ethnic similarities, they had different political traditions and experiences—the mostly Catholic Croats had been part of the Austro-Hungarian Empire while the Orthodox Serbs lived under Ottoman rule. Serbs generally desired a unitary state; by virtue of their independent statehood before the First World War and the support they received from the Allies, they were able to establish a centralized political order which they dominated in the interwar period. Croats, who were the largest national group in Yugoslavia after the Serbs, greatly resented their subordinate political status; the majority of Croats desired greater political autonomy, either in a federal Yugoslavia or a separate Croatian state. The large numbers of Serbs residing within Croatia's traditional borders and the mixed population of Serbs and Croats inhabiting Bosnia and Hercegovina, however, meant that drawing boundaries between the two groups was extremely difficult. Conflict between these two nations threatened the very survival of the interwar Yugoslav state and led to the outbreak of civil violence during the Second World War.

Numerous studies of Yugoslavia have treated the complicated events and political rivalries of the Second World War.[1] Several of these works examine the CPY's nationalities policy during this period.[2] However, there has been no detailed study in English of the CPY's policy toward Croatia; explaining this policy is essential to understanding the development of the Yugoslav state after 1945 and its more recent dissolution. During the war, Communist leaders fought over important aspects of how the Croat question would be resolved in the new party-state. There were disagreements over Serb and Croat claims to Bosnia-Hercegovina and the way in which to draw the borders of the republics. Communists struggled over the status of Serbs in Croatia and their relations to Serbs in other republics. Most importantly, Communist leaders fought over the character of the new Yugoslav federalism and how much real autonomy it would provide Croatia and the other republics. Although party leaders declared these questions resolved in 1945, they continued to struggle over them in the postwar period. After Tito's death in 1980, these ques-

---

1. For example, see Jozo Tomasevich, *The Chetniks, War and Revolution in Yugoslavia, 1941-1945* (Stanford: Stanford University Press, 1975); Wayne Vucinich (ed.), *Contemporary Yugoslavia, Twenty Years of Socialist Experiment* (Berkeley: University of California Press, 1969); Matteo Milazzo, *The Chetnik Movement and the Yugoslav Resistance* (Baltimore and London: Johns Hopkins University Press, 1975); Stephen Clissold, *Whirlwind* (London: Cresset Press, 1949); Walter R. Roberts, *Tito, Mihailović and the Allies, 1941-1945* (New Brunswick: Rutgers University Press, 1973).

2. For a discussion of CPY nationalities policy during the war see Paul Shoup, *Communism and the Yugoslav National Question* (New York and London: Columbia University Press, 1968); Chalmers Johnson, *Peasant Nationalism and Communist Power* (Stanford: Stanford University Press, 1962); Walker Connor, *The National Question in Marxist-Leninist Theory and Strategy* (Princeton: Princeton University Press, 1984).

tions resurfaced as the most important and contentious political issues in the Yugoslav state.

In examining the CPY's approach to the Croat question, I demonstrate how Croat national sentiment caused Communist Party of Croatia (CPC) leader Andrija Hebrang to modify the CPY's "Bolshevik" state-building strategy. The Bolshevik strategy, which was patterned closely after the Soviet experience, featured a highly centralized state covered by a veneer of federal institutions. In contrast, the "federalist" strategy adopted by Hebrang in 1943-1944 sought maximum political autonomy for the Communist Party of Croatia and the institutions it created. Convinced that he must appeal more effectively to Croat national sentiment, Hebrang attempted to give Communist support for Croatian autonomy more credence by endowing the new federal institutions with some real power. Hebrang's emphasis on Croatian institutions and concerns ultimately brought him into conflict with Tito, who was not prepared to tolerate such autonomy in the party or the state it sought to create. Consequently, Tito removed Hebrang in 1944 and imposed the Bolshevik solution to the Croat question: federalization of the government in theory but strict centralization of the party and state in practice. I then show how the struggle over these two visions of the party-state continued to affect the postwar political development of the Yugoslav Socialist state. When the process of political and economic reform was initiated in the 1960s, the distribution of power between the central and regional party organizations resurfaced as the main point of contention among party leaders, and led to the unraveling of the Yugoslav Communist system.

Hebrang is an extremely controversial figure in Yugoslav historiography and has been the subject of much inaccurate speculation. After he was denounced as an Ustasha, Nazi, and Cominform spy, Hebrang's wartime activities were omitted or obscured in most historical accounts of this period. Western treatments of him have also been sparse. Yet an examination of his role is crucial to understanding the CPY's efforts to build a new party-state during the war and the legacy of the Communist approach to the national question. I argue that the main source of Hebrang's conflict with Tito and other members of the CPY Politburo was not simply, as previous western scholars have suggested, a personal rivalry between two powerful Communist leaders.[3] Nor was it due to Hebrang's anti-Serb chauvinism or his commitment to political pluralism, as his Yugoslav opponents and proponents claim.[4] Rather, it was his

---

3. For example, see Shoup, *Communism and the Yugoslav National Question.*

4. For the former view see *Drugi kongres Komunističke partije Hrvatske* (Zagreb, 1949), 71-72. For the latter view see Ivan Supek, *Crown Witness against Hebrang,*

federalist state-building strategy which, if it had succeeded, would have resulted in a very different state than the one that ultimately emerged after the war.

In examining the Communist Party's state-building efforts in the Yugoslav context, this book speaks to the broader discussion on comparative state-building. A number of recent works on state-building have proposed new lines of inquiry which inform some basic questions of this study. I will argue, however, using the Yugoslav case as an example, that these works do not treat adequately the role of nationalism in the formation and development of the state. Consequently, they are unable to account theoretically for the relationship between social mobilization and institutional change in Yugoslavia and other multinational states. Defined as a political doctrine and movement aimed at gaining or exercising state power, nationalism is crucial to understanding the impact of social forces upon state transformation.[5] While I share the emphasis these works place on the role of the state and state-building elites in social and political upheaval, I argue that it is impossible to understand this role without examining how these elites define the relationship between nation and state.

There are two main reasons why the literature on state-building has failed to take nationalism fully into account. The first has to do with the way in which many of these works understand the role of nationalism in the process of state formation, which they base upon the West European experience. Scholars observing state-building in Western Europe have generally emphasized the positive impact of nationalism.[6] As Charles

---

(Chicago: Markanton Press, 1983). For a more balanced picture of Hebrang see Ivo Banac, *With Stalin against Tito, Cominformist Splits in Yugoslav Communism* (Ithaca, New York: Cornell University Press, 1988).

5. John Breuilly and others have pointed out that nationalism makes "eminent sense" in the situations produced by the modern state, which declares itself the legitimate dispenser of political and economic demands. As the state expands its functions and capabilities, power over the state apparatus becomes the crucial goal of national movements. (John Breuilly, *Nationalism and the State*, New York: St. Martin's Press, 1982). Nationalism in this sense is a movement with explicitly state-building goals; how it achieves them will shape the evolution of the state. See also Joseph Rothschild, *Ethnopolitics; a Conceptual Framework* (New York: Columbia University Press, 1981).

6. This ethnocentric view of the role nationalism plays in the state-building process is reinforced by what may be termed the "historical theories" of nationalism which have dominated research on this question in the past several decades. These theories generally view nationalism in Western Europe as the original, benign form of this phenomenon and its appearance elsewhere as a poor or dis-

Tilly points out, nation-building in Western Europe usually succeeded state-building and reinforced the strength of the state.[7] As state organs expanded their activity in the seventeenth and eighteenth centuries, they exerted pressure downward to create a cohesive community. Unification along linguistic lines strengthened this sense of community and produced a self-conscious national awareness. When nationalism emerged as a political ideology after the French revolution, it reinforced this congruence of nation and state.

Nationalism, however, has played a very different role in the state-building process elsewhere. For example, in nineteenth-century Eastern Europe, nation-building often meant state destroying, since the growth of nationalist sentiment among their constituent national groups undermined Eastern Europe's three multinational empires.[8] The national demands of Croats, Czechs and other Slavs contributed greatly to the demise of the Habsburg state during the First World War. By failing to account for the different effects of nationalism on the state-building process, the literature on state-building does not explore fully situations in

---

torted imitation, with ultimately destructive effects. For example, Elie Kedourie in his study on nationalism argues that, although nationalism was originally linked with notions of popular sovereignty and political liberalism, it shed these characteristics as it spread to other parts of the world. According to his theory, nationalism assumed a distorted form in Eastern Europe, transmogrified by German romanticism as it made its way east into an anti-liberal, integral form (*Nationalism*, New York: Frederick A. Praeger, 1960). Hugh Trevor-Roper similarly emphasizes the essentially derivative character of East European nationalism. According to him, the East European intelligentsia borrowed its images and concepts from nationalism in the west. This poor imitation of historic nationalism, what he calls "secondary nationalism," had a more destructive impact than its progenitor (*Man and Events, Historical Essays by Hugh Trevor-Roper*, New York: Octagon Books, 1976). In Seton-Watson's terms, the difference is between old and new nations; in Western Europe nationalism arose out of already formed nations, whereas in the east, nations were created by nationalism (*Nationalism and Communism*, New York: Frederick A. Praeger, 1965).

7. Charles Tilly, *The Formation of National States in Western Europe* (Princeton, New Jersey: Princeton University Press, 1975).

8. Chlebowczyk, a Polish historian, explains the different effect of nationalism in Eastern Europe by the reversed order of state and nation building. In contrast to Western Europe, in Eastern Europe linguistic unification and the formation of national consciousness preceded the formation of modern state structures. See Jozef Chlebowczyk, *On Small and Young Nations in Europe: Nation Forming Processes in Ethnic Borderlands in East Central Europe* (Warsaw, 1980).

which the population is not nationally homogeneous.[9] Nor does it account for situations in which the rise of nationalism does not automatically reinforce the process of centralization, which these works view as essential to state-building.[10] For state-builders in multinational societies, the difficult problem of integration cannot always be resolved by centralization. In many cases, rulers have been faced with the necessity of adopting federal structures that allow for the decentralization of political power to national groups (or to regions where certain national groups are dominant) while maintaining a unified and effective state.[11] The battle between Serbs and Croats over whether and what kind of fed-

---

9. Much of the literature on political modernization adopts a similar view of nationalism based on its function in Western democracies. For these authors, nationalism is essential for creating the system of values necessary to reinforce democratic political structures because by drawing on the past it creates new social and plitical loyalties centered on the modern state (Gabriel Almond and Sidney Verba, *The Civic Culture; Political Attitudes and Democracy in Five Nations*, Princeton University Press, 1963; Karl Deutsch, *Nationalism and Social Communication; an Inquiry into the Foundations of Nationality*, Cambridge, MIT Press, 1962; David Lerner, *The Passing of Traditional Society: Modernizing the Middle East*, Glencoe, Illinois, The Free Press, 1958). This postulate is too broad, however, to be of use in the comparative study of political development; it ignores the numerous varieties of nationalism and the purposes to which they can be put in reinforcing or undermining the state.

10. For example, Tilly sees centralization as an important component of the acquisition of "stateness" which is essential for the successful formation of the modern state. See Tilly, *The Formation of National States in Western Europe*, Introduction. Or to take the more functionalist definition of state-building offered by Su-Hoon Lee, the state increases its extractive, incorporative and coercive abilities in the process of state-building. See Su-Hoon Lee, *State-Building in the Contemporary Third World* (Westview Press, Boulder, 1988).

11. Despite its importance, the study of federalism has been long out of fashion, caught in the no-man's-land of institutional description, and it is frequently dismissed as too broad to be a useful tool of analysis. Its absence is particularly striking in the recent research on states and state-building, which views centralization as an inexorable fact of modern political life. Yet, an examination of federalism offers a useful way of investigating the relationship between state and society, even in Communist countries. Federalism is an essential part of the modern state-building arsenal and should be considered a significant factor in the study of state-building activities of political elites. For the best recent work on federalism see Daniel J. Elazar, *Exploring Federalism*. See also Daniel J. Elazar (ed.), *Federalism and Political Integration* (New York and London: Lanham, 1984); and William J. Riker, *Federalism, Origin, Operation and Significance* (Boston and Toronto: Little Brown & Company, 1964).

eral structures to adopt has been the main focus of Yugoslav political life since 1918 and has had a fundamental impact on the development of the Yugoslav state.

The second way in which the literature on state-building does not treat nationalism adequately is its tendency to view class relations as the most important category for understanding the relation between state and society. Although these works argue for the relative autonomy of state from society, they remain primarily concerned with the relation between the state and the dominant social class.[12] Several works from what might be labeled the comparative historical perspective on state-building argue that alliances among classes are the most significant determinant of state structures.[13] According to them, these alliances are determined by the character of their commercial relations. Yet nationalism can be crucial in forging alliances among classes whose economic interests are in conflict.[14] For example, the Communist Party of Yugoslavia was able to unite a wide segment of the population in the

---

12. Nicos Poulantzas first argued for the "relative autonomy" of the state from capitalist interests. According to him, the state occasionally acts against the interests of specific capitalists and cannot therefore be considered the mere product or tool of the ruling class. Nicos Poulantzas, "The Problem of the Capitalist State," *New Left Review* 58 (1969): 67-78. If a strictly materialist interpretation of the state is abandoned, the question then becomes what forces of change are political structures subject to? Many of the questions Poulantzas poses concerning the relationship between state and class could also be asked about the relationship between state and nation. How, for example, do we know that the state is dominated by particular national groups? When does it act in their interest? What is the intersection of nation and class and how does this influence state actions? What role does nationalism play in revolutionary upheaval?

13. The authors from this perspective employ a form of comparative historical method to map out historical sequences and patterns of state formation. Focusing largely though not exclusively on Western Europe, they attempt to identify the factors facilitating the emergence of the modern state and the variations in its features. For example see Barrington Moore Jr., *The Origins of Dictatorship and Democracy: Lord and Peasant in the Making of the Modern World* (Boston: Beacon Press, 1966), Perry Anderson, *Lineages of the Absolutist State* (London: Verso, 1979), Gregory Luebbert, *Liberalism, Fascism, or Social Democracy: Social Classes and the Political Origins of the Regimes of Interwar Europe.* (New York: Oxford University Press, 1991).

14. For example, Samuel Huntington argues convincingly that most successful peasant revolutions have occurred when the threat of external invasion creates the conditions for an alliance between the urban intelligentsia and middle classes and the rural peasantry. Samuel Huntington, *Political Order in Changing Societies* (New Haven: Yale University Press, 1968).

Partisan movement by appealing to national as well as class interests. Many works on state-building similarly view social mobilization as a function of economic factors. Yet social mobilization in the last two centuries has occurred frequently along national as well as class lines. For example, in Eastern Europe peasants were equally likely to be mobilized into politics by national groups and parties, such as the Croat Peasant Party, as by class-based organizations.

By focusing almost exclusively on social mobilization along class lines, the literature on state building often ignores how nationalism affects the state-building activities of political elites. For example, authors from what might be labeled the "statist" perspective on state building emphasize that the activities of political elites (who are independent of particular social classes or groups) are most important for understanding the process of state-building.[15] But they do not consider the ways in which elites are constrained in their choices of strategies by nationalist sentiments and goals. Revolutionary leaders are not free, as these writers suggest, to pursue singlemindedly their state-building aims, but are often fettered by the national demands of various groups. Yugoslav Communists were constrained by the national sentiments of Croats (and other national groups) in their efforts to build a unitary state; attempting to respond to this sentiment led to strife over which state-building strategy to adopt. After the revolution, political leaders in or out of power may use a host of techniques to manage national conflict and accommodate nationalist demands to their state-building goals. A variety of factors such as their ideology and organizational resources, the history of the country's political institutions, the character of the indigenous national movements, or the pattern of national dominance in society may

---

15. The works from this perspective stress the importance of the state as an independent force in political life. The question it asks is why and how certain elites manage to seize and remake the state while others fail miserably. According to this perspective, the success of political leaders in gaining power and remaking the state is contingent on their ability to create new state structures that more effectively achieve the interests of the state, such as economic modernization or political centralization. For example, see Theda Skocpol, *States and Social Revolution* (Cambridge, England: Cambridge University Press, 1979); Peter B. Evans, Dietrich Reuschemeyer and Theda Skocpol, *Bringing the State Back In*, (Cambridge and New York: Cambridge University Press, 1985); Charles Bright and Susan Harding, *State-Making and Social Movements* (Ann Arbor: The University of Michigan Press, 1984); Ellen Trumberger, "A Theory of Elite Revolutions," *Studies in Comparative International Development* (Fall 1972): 191-201; Youseff Cohen, "The Paradoxical Nature of State-Making: The Violent Creation of Order," *American Political Science Review* (December 1981): 901-910.

prompt them to choose a particular strategy of balancing these two tasks, and their strategies may vary at different points in time.[16] In Yugoslavia after 1945, Communist leaders attempted to accommodate the decentralizing thrust of Croat sentiments to the centralizing thrust of their state-building goals (and Serb national sentiments) by adopting first the Bolshevik strategy of state-building, then the federalist strategy, and finally an uneasy compromise between the two.

The main contention of this work is that it is essential to consider the effects of nationalism on the state-building process. From the viewpoint of the state, there are various questions which might be raised. How, for example, does the manner in which national identity is reflected in the institutional framework of the state affect its performance and stability? How do we know whether a state is dominated by a particular national group and when does it act in its interest? What techniques do political leaders use to manage national conflicts and how do these affect their state-building goals? From the viewpoint of society, there is an equal number of questions which might be asked. What, for example, are the varieties of national movements and national ideologies and how do their demands affect the activities and development of the state? What is the intersection of nation and class and how does it influence state actions? When does national conflict result in a major transformation of the state?

While these questions must be answered in order to gain a more complete understanding of the effects of nationalism on the state-building process, I do not hope to address them all here. Rather, in investigating this problem, I will focus on the the ways in which nationalism influences the state-building strategies of Communist elites. There are at least two good reasons for approaching the question in this way. First, it is important for precision; focusing on actors forces us to be concrete and specific. Since the state and nationalism are both abstractions, the best way to discuss the relationship between them is to look at real institutions, groups, and participants who interact. Literature on the state often confusingly talks about the actions of the state without specifying exactly

---

16. For example, political leaders may opt for federal or consociational elements of government to achieve their aims. Or they may attempt to manage national conflict by allocating privileges to certain groups by recruiting them into various branches of the state apparatus, such as the army or bureaucracy. See Cynthia Enloe's study of how political elites distribute political privileges in the military and bureaucracy in order to regulate ethnic conflict. Cynthia Enloe, *Police, Military and Ethnicity: Foundations of State Power* (New Brunswick, New Jersey: Transaction Books, 1980).

who is doing the acting; focusing on particular state-building elites can avoid this problem. Secondly, formulating the study in this way best captures the salient feature of the Yugoslav case where Communist leaders pursued different strategies for building new state structures. Since Communists have paid close attention to creating new political institutions wherever they have come to power, my approach will best lend itself to comparative analysis.

Few attempts have been made to delineate the activities of state-building elites. In his study of the Kuomintang's state-building efforts in China, Robert Bedeski defines these activities as encompassing the spheres of force, power and authority.[17] First, state-builders must firmly establish military control over their territory; then they must institutionalize the instruments of rule, including a government, bureaucracy, and administrative apparatus; and finally, they must legitimize themselves through a new normative order. This scheme, while useful, places too much emphasis on the consecutive nature of these activities. CPY leaders created new political structures at the same time they built an army and gained military control over the country. They did not wait until the new government had been established to form a new normative order, but cast themselves as the founders of a new order in their attempt to galvanize popular support. The CPY's state-building activities during the war can be divided roughly into two periods: the period of mobilization from 1941 to 1943 (chapters three and four) and the period of institutionalization from 1943 to 1945 (chapters four and five). Although these processes cannot be neatly separated, they do possess certain distinct features. In the first period, the CPY laid the foundations for its state-building activities by (1) mobilizing popular support, (2) expanding the party organization and extending its links with the population, (3) building an army to defend its political gains and (4) establishing political structures in the localities. In the second period, the CPY began to institutionalize federal political structures and to create the framework of a new party-state.

In examining how nationalism affected the state-building activities of Yugoslav Communists, I will consider the dilemmas that nationalism created for them and the way in which they responded. How did Croat national sentiment affect the strategy Communist leaders adopted? And how, in turn, did this strategy affect the state structures that emerged during the war? I will pay particular attention to the federal elements in the Communists' state-building strategy, the problems they were in-

---

17. Robert E. Bedeski, *State-Building in Modern China: the Kuomintang in the Prewar Period* (Berkeley: The University of California Press, 1981).

tended to resolve, and their effectiveness. In addressing these questions, I demonstrate how Communists' state-building efforts were fundamentally shaped by the political aims of the Croat national movement.

Until the failure of communism in 1989, Communists were frequently characterized as successful state builders. Scholars argued that a key to their success was their ability to manage national conflict while building a more centralized, modern state. Writers on political development such as Richard Lowenthal and many since him emphasized the connection between Communist parties which assumed power in economically underdeveloped countries and their ability to create a state apparatus capable of executing rapid modernization.[18] Writers on state-building have also made this point.[19] With their centralizing and modernizing ideology, their ability to concentrate the means of coercion in their hands, and their ability to mobilize large segments of the population to achieve developmental goals, Communist parties were seen as the most effective state-builders for backward agrarian societies with weak state structures. In his book on political development, Samuel Huntington pointed out that the key to the success of Communist parties was not their ideological appeal but their highly developed state-building skills.[20] According to him, the determinant of a state's stability and strength is its capacity to develop an institutional structure commensurate with its level of economic development. Communists' ability to create a highly inclusive and controlled form of political participation accounted largely for their success in gaining and maintaining power and often rendered them more effective than leaders of national movements in building and controlling new political institutions.[21] In short, Communists' ability to deflect and channel nationalist pressures enabled them to launch the process of industrialization and political centralization that had eluded

---

18. Richard Lowenthal, "Development versus Utopia in Communist Policy," in Chalmers Johnson (ed.), *Change in Communist Systems* (Stanford: Stanford University Press, 1970).

19. See Theda Skocpol, *States and Social Revolution*.

20. Huntington, *Political Order in Changing Societies*.

21. Kenneth Jowitt made a similar point in his book on revolutionary elites in Romania. He argued that nationalists were less successful state-builders because they were constrained by societal forces which Communist leaders, by virtue of their ideology and organizational structure, were free to ignore; once in power nationalists were more likely to adopt a reformist strategy of state-building while their Communist counterparts chose the "more effective" course of revolutionary change. Kenneth Jowitt, *Revolutionary Breakthrough and National Development* (Berkeley: University of California Press, 1971).

their predecessors in the interwar period, who had been divided over the national question.

As these writers have suggested, Communists possessed some advantages as state-builders. But they were not impervious to societal forces such as nationalism in their efforts to create new political structures.[22] The political demands of national movements frequently interfered with Communists' state-building strategies and goals and ultimately undermined their achievements in this realm. Nationalism posed two major problems for the state-building aims of Communists: first, how to win the support of national movements when Communists opposed their political aspirations for greater political autonomy or separate nation-states; and secondly, once in power, how to reconcile the political demands of national movements with a Communist state-building strategy of rapid centralization. In a multinational state, Communists were forced to reconcile the decentralizing demands of national groups with the centralizing thrust of their state-building activities.

The first problem elicited a variety of responses, from the Austro-Marxist support for cultural autonomy to the Bolshevik policy of self-determination. Though Soviet Communists advocated self-determination, what this policy meant concerning particular states or political groups was subject to frequent changes. As chapter two will illustrate, Communists faced enormous difficulties in competing for popular support with nationalist parties such as the Croat Peasant Party. They could call for the break-up of the state, which was the only decentralizing strategy that did not require the cooptation of the nationalist party, but in so doing they risked confrontations with the political authorities that could sap their strength and alienate more moderate supporters. Or they could pursue a Popular Front strategy with the aim of subverting the nationalist party or coopting its members, and risk being subsumed or diluted by the stronger nationalist party. Communists' attention when attempting to seize power in Yugoslavia and elsewhere was directed at resolving this difficult problem.

The second problem of how to reconcile the decentralizing demands of national groups with political centralization proved even more difficult for Communists. The Bolsheviks, who were the first to grapple with this problem after they came to power in 1917, adopted a state-building

---

22. For example, in his study of state building in China, Franz Schurmann demonstrates how the administrative apparatus established by the CPC differed significantly from the Bolshevik model, due in large part to cultural differences between the two countries. Franz Schurmann, *Ideology and Organization in Communist China* (Berkeley: University of California Press, 1968).

strategy that balanced federal elements with a highly unified party. Although the state was organized along federal lines, it was subject to powerful unitary pressures. This pattern of state-making was largely adopted by Communist parties as they came to power elsewhere, especially in multinational countries. The Bolshevik state-building strategy can be roughly summarized as follows: (1) Communists supported a territorial federal system which attempted to reduce nationalist discontent by appearing to respond to national aspirations for political autonomy. In the Soviet polity this federal system included a constitutional endorsement of a formal division of powers between the federal government and the governments of the federal units, a bicameral legislature, and an administrative system organized along federal lines into all-union, union-republic, and republic ministries. (2) Communists endorsed a nationalities policy which advocated cultural autonomy. (3) The Communist party maintained a monopoly of political power. The highly unified party, organized according to the principle of democratic centralism, ensured that there was no significant federal division of power in the Soviet state. Although the party leadership supported the development of national cadres, these regional leaders were subject to central party control. (4) The Communist party was committed to implementing a command economy which reinforced the centralist aspects of the state.[23]

In contrast to the Bolshevik strategy, the federalist strategy formulated by Communists in Croatia during the Second World War responded to nationalism by decentralizing political power to regional party authorities. In effect, it was based upon a federal Communist Party. As chapter three will illustrate, Croats were unwilling to join a movement that did not address their aspirations for statehood. Consequently, the Communist Party of Croatia under Hebrang sought to build political institutions that would provide a real measure of autonomy to Croatia without undermining the basis of one-party rule. This federalist strategy fundamentally restructured the relation between nation and state con-

---

23. Elements two and four of this state-building strategy did not remain constant. For example, a policy of Russification and the suppression of cultural autonomy was adopted during much of the Stalinist era. Similarly, the alternative developmental strategy embraced by the New Economic Policy and during subsequent periods of reform sought to decentralize the highly centralized Soviet economy. Nevertheless, the most important aspects of the way in which the Bolshevik state-building strategy responded to nationalist pressures remained the same; its federal elements, which were designed to fulfill national aspirations for political autonomy, were counterbalanced by a highly centralized party.

tained in the Bolshevik strategy. Although the CPY rejected the federalist strategy in 1945, it embraced this strategy again as a model of decentralization when the regime attempted to introduce economic reforms in the 1960s.

The federalizing strategy adopted by the CPC under Hebrang in 1944 and the League of Communists of Croatia (LCC) in 1971 can be summarized as follows: (1) Regional party elites developed a power base in their own republics. (2) Regional leaders sought to increase their decision-making autonomy by augmenting the power of regional party and state organs. (3) Regional elites responded to regional interests first. They were sensitive to the demands of the national movement in their area and preoccupied with the political party or organization identified with this movement. They designed their state-building strategy, based on a combination of coercion and cooptation, with this party in mind. (4) Regional party leaders struggled with party leaders from other federal units over national concerns, especially over the question of disputed territory between them. (5) Regional elites came into conflict with central party leaders who pursued a centralizing state-building strategy. (6) The national minority in the republic, in this case the Serbs, questioned the commitment of regional party leaders to protecting their interests and appealed to central party authorities to bolster their position. (7) Regional elites attempted to keep economic resources in their own regions and to maximize the resources they received from the center.

When LCC reformers adopted this federalist strategy in 1971, they attempted to provide it with legitimacy by appealing to its roots in the Communist revolution. However, the LCC emphasis on Croat interests and its tolerance of public discussion of these interests led to the outbreak of nationalist activities which the Communist Party could not control. Consequently, Tito removed the popular republic leaders and replaced them with leaders less responsive to the nationalist sentiments and aspirations of the populace. Nevertheless, he could not prevent regional leaders from reacting to these pressures after his death. After 1980, the political system became paralyzed by the conflicting interests of the League of Communists of Yugoslavia's (LCY) several republic parties and deadlocked over the question of how to distribute power between central and republic authorities. This conflict and its resulting political paralysis contributed significantly to the collapse of the Yugoslav party-state.

In summary, this book aims to accomplish two main tasks. First, it provides a detailed analysis of how the Croat question influenced the formation and development of the Yugoslav state. In doing this, it aims to provide a clearer understanding of the collapse of communism and the forces leading to the break-up of Yugoslavia. Secondly, this book aims to turn the discussion of state-building to a closer examination of nationalism. The current round of state-making in Eastern Europe and the former Soviet Union can only be understood by taking into account the way in which nationalism affects the construction of new political institutions and the transition to market economies. By investigating the way in which Communist leaders responded to the forces of nationalism in Yugoslavia, this study reveals how nationalism undermined the state-building efforts of Communist elites, and the legacy of this failure for their non-Communist successors.

The book consists of six chapters. In chapter one, I examine the roots of the Croat question in Yugoslavia. I trace the source of conflict between Serbs and Croats to differences in their national ideologies and to the circumstances of political unification in 1918. I then show how Serb leaders' failure to resolve the Croat question by adopting a federal order undermined their efforts to build a stable political order during the interwar period. I argue that the main Croat political party, the Croat Peasant Party (CPP), also contributed to the weakening of the state by failing to support the establishment of a federal system when it gained considerable autonomy in 1939. Chapter two treats the CPY's approach to the Croat question in the interwar period. This period witnessed a factional struggle in the party that I argue is attributable primarily not to Comintern intervention, but instead to serious disagreement among Yugoslav Communists about Croatian statehood. I then show how these disagreement carried over into the Second World War. Chapters three, four, and five treat the period from 1941-1945. Chapter three looks at how Croat nationalism affected the process of political mobilization at the beginning of the war and how this in turn influenced the contending state-building strategies adopted by Communist elites (chapter four). I argue that the CPY's failure to elicit Croat support caused CPC leader Andrija Hebrang to adopt an alternative state-building strategy that responded more directly to Croat national aims. Chapter five details the efforts of Communist leaders in the last year of the war to centralize the party and new state structures and to eradicate the autonomous power of non-Communist Croat elites. Chapter six treats political developments in Yugoslavia since the Second World War. I argue that Hebrang's federalist state-building strategy prefigured the decentralizing reforms championed by Communists in Croatia from the mid-sixties to 1971. In the last part of chapter six I consider the role these ideas and leaders have played in state-building developments since Tito's death in 1980.

1

The Roots of the Croat Question

In 1918, the Kingdom of Serbs, Croats and Slovenes was created out of the diverse regions of the South Slav lands. It was the most complicated of the states created after the First World War, combining numerous peoples and political units. Before the war, Bosnia and Hercegovina had been annexed by the Habsburgs. Slovenia and Dalmatia were administered by the Austrian half of the Habsburg Empire, while Croatia-Slavonia, which retained a semi-autonomous status, was administered by the Hungarian half. Vojvodina was part of the latter. The Independent Kingdoms of Montenegro and Serbia also joined the Yugoslav state.[1] Although the new South Slav state was lauded at Versailles as a paragon of the principle of self-determination, it was soon racked by conflict among its constituent groups, especially Serbs and Croats. Croat leaders had voted enthusiastically for unconditional union with Serbia and Montenegro, but they quickly became disillusioned with centralized arrangement of the new state. The ensuing conflict between Serbs and Croats over the shape of the Yugoslav state, which was the defining feature of Yugoslav political life for most of its existence, can be traced to differences in their national ideologies and the circumstances of their political unification.

The Formation of National Ideologies

The formation of Serb and Croat national movements began in the early nineteenth century when the ideas of the French revolution and the German romantic period stirred the nations of Eastern Europe and

---

1. The breakdown of the population according to national identity, taken from the census of 1921, is roughly as follows: Serbs (including Montenegrins) 43%, Croats 23%, Slovenes 8.5%, Macedonians 5%, Bosnians 6%, other 14.5%. Joseph Rothschild, *East Central Europe between the Two World Wars* (Seattle, London: University of Washington Press: 1974), 202-203.

prompted their search for cultural and political identities.[2] Although
Serbs and Croats shared many common linguistic and ethnic characteristics, their national movements were molded by different historical experiences. They also had different religious identities; while Croats were
Roman Catholic, Serbs embraced the Orthodox faith. Serbs and Croats
drew on distinctive experiences of medieval statehood in forming their
political identity, and their political classes retained a strong consciousness of this past. Moreover, in the intervening centuries they were subject
to different occupying powers, the Croats to Austrian and Hungarian
authority and the Serbs to Ottoman dominion. While Serbs established
an independent kingdom in the first part of the nineteenth century,
Croatia remained part of the Austro-Hungarian Monarchy during this
period of national awakening. Thus despite their proximity and similarity, the particular characteristics of these nations and their political experiences produced very different national ideologies.

Croat national leaders faced several problems in building a national
movement. Their biggest challenge was to create a sense of unity out of
the diverse regions that comprised the Triune Kingdom: Dalmatia,
Slavonia and Croatia proper (the area around Zagreb that was usually
termed inner Croatia, or Banska Hrvatska [Banate Croatia] at the beginning of the nineteenth century). Dalmatia, which comprised the heart of
the Croatian medieval kingdom, had been subject to strong Venetian
influence in the intervening centuries; in 1797 it fell under Habsburg
administration. Slavonia and inner Croatia had looked primarily to
Hungary and then to Austria after the demise of the Croatian medieval
kingdom; portions of their territories were also occupied by the
Ottomans. Croatia's marked regional flavor was expressed in a variety of
dialects: the kajkavian dialect spoken in the Zagreb region, the čajkavian
in parts of the Croatian Littoral and Dalmatia, and the štokavian dialect
everywhere else.

The Military Frontier (Vojna krajina), first established by the
Habsburgs in the early sixteenth century, further fractured Croatia's cultural and political unity.[3] This crescent-shaped area along the borders

---

2. For a discussion of how these ideas affected the formation of national
movements in Eastern Europe see Elie Kedourie, *Nationalism* (London, 1961). For
a discussion of the formation of Serb and Croat national movements see Ivo
Banac, *The National Question in Yugoslavia, Orogins, History, Politics* (Ithaca, New
York: Cornell University Press, 1984).

3. For a thorough history of the Military Frontier see Gunther Erich
Rothenberg, *The Austrian Military Border in Croatia, 1522-1747* (Urbana, Illinois:
University of Illinois Press, 1960).

with Serbia and Bosnia was created as a military buffer when the Turks came within striking distance of Habsburg lands.[4] The mainly Orthodox refugees driven into Croatia by the Turkish advance were given land in exchange for military service; this policy of colonization was later extended to the local Roman Catholic population. Several large waves of migration thereafter gave this region a definite Serb majority.[5] When Croatia came under Austrian dominion, the Habsburg king received the authority to appoint general officers to command the border region with full authority over civil and military affairs, removing this area from the jurisdiction of Croat civil authorities.[6] The repeated attempts of the Croatian Estates and governor, or Ban, to extent their authority into this region met with little success until the mid-nineteenth century.[7] At this time, Hungarians began to campaign for the eradification of the Military Frontier, which they saw as a Habsburg encroachment on their sphere of influence. The Habsburgs, who worried that the colonists might support nationalist uprisings, particularly in Bosnia, also began to look towards its eventual dismantlement.

During the nineteenth century, Serbs and Croats in this region began to struggle with the question of their national identities. Although there was a long tradition of cooperation among Serb and Croat colonists, the Military Frontier also proved fertile ground for the more exclusivist strands of Serb and Croat national movements. Before 1848, many Serbs in the Military Frontier were infected by Illyrianist ideas, and they wished to see this area returned to the Triune Kingdom. By the mid-nineteenth century, however, they began to gravitate more toward the Serb national movement, and they became increasingly alienated from Croat national aims. As Croats sought to bring this region under the control of the Croatian Parliament, or Sabor, a rancorous debate erupted about whether the population of the Military Frontier could be considered part

---

4. There were initially two military districts. The Karlovac Border stretched from the coast to the Sava River. The Slavonian or Varaždin Border encompassed the area from the Sava to the Drava Rivers. A third border region was added in the 1690s in the area between the Kupa and Una rivers.

5. Colonists were given grants of land and relieved of manorial obligations. They were also permitted to retain a share of booty from the enemy. While they were subject to the ultimate control of the Habsburgs, they were authorized to elect their own leaders. The mainly Orthodox Serbs were also granted freedom of worship.

6. The third military district remained subject to the control of the Croatian Ban.

7. The colonists, or *graničari*, were usually loyal to the Emperor since they saw their status as greatly preferable to that of the serfs.

of the Croat nation. After the Military Frontier was incorporated into
Croatia in 1881, Serbs comprised almost twenty-five percent of Croatia's
population.[8] At the urging of the Orthodox bishops, the Sabor officially
recognized the existence of the Serb nation on Croatian territory. Many
Croats continued to fear Serbia's claims to this territory, however, and to
deny the existence of a separate Serb nation in the Triune Kingdom.[9] By
the end of the century, as Hungarian authorities pursued a policy of
fomenting conflict between Serbs and Croats in Croatia, pressure by
Croats for the assimilation of these Serbs grew.[10] Tensions over the status
of this area preoccupied both the Serb and Croat national movements,
and they were to become a permanent feature of the new Yugoslav state
established in 1918.

In addition to the regional diversity of the Triune Kingdom, there
were also a large number of Croats living outside its borders, especially
in Bosnia and Hercegovina. According to the Habsburg census, in 1910
there were 434,061 Croats living in Bosnia and Hercegovina, or twenty-
three percent of their population.[11] Orthodox Serbs comprised forty-
three percent of the population and Muslims thirty-two percent. Bosnia,
which was an independent kingdom in medieval times, had developed a

---

8. The Serbs in this area were also called *prečani* Serbs, meaning "beyond" the
Sava, Danube and Una rivers to the north. Serbs in Serbia proper were known as
Srbijanci. Prečani Serbs comprise approximately one fifth the total population of
Serbs.

9. As one scholar describes these fears: "While the area was indispensible to a
Croatian state, its annexation by Serbia would be disastrous for the Croatian
position in their historic lands. Because of the Miltary Frontier with its high concentration of Serbs, the danger existed that should Serbia ever succeed in carrying through the Greater Serbian program of uniting all her people, Croatia would
lose her claims to Bosnia-Hercegovina and much of her southern lands in the
Military Frontier. In fact, by seizing the Lika region in southwestern Croatia,
which had a large Serbian population, Serbia could drive a wedge between
Croatia and Dalmatia. Should this happen it would be inevitable that the rest of
Croatian territories would eventually be absorbed by the neighboring states."
Barbara and Charles Jelavich, *The Establishment of the Balkan National States*
(Seattle, Washington: University of Washington Press, 1977), 254.

10. This policy reached its apogee under Károly Khuen-Hédeváry, who was
Ban of Croatia from 1883 to 1903. Khuen-Hédeváry adopted a divide-and-rule
policy and he attempted to secure the political loyalty of Serbs by making concessions concerning the Orthodox religion, the Cyrillic alphabet and political autonomy.

11. This census was calculated according to religion. See Robert J. Donia, *Islam
under the Double Eagle: The Muslims of Bosnia and Hercegovina, 1878-1914* (New
York: Columbia University Press, 1981).

distinctive character under Ottoman occupation in the intervening centuries when a substantial portion of its population had converted to Islam. Although these Muslims did not yet possess a distinct national identity, they did not generally consider themselves to be Serbs or Croats. When the Serb and Croat national movements were formed in the nineteenth century, they began to make strong and competing claims to this area. Most Croats envisioned a Croat political unit encompassing this area, either inside or outside the Habsburg state; the Habsburg acquisition of Bosnia and Hercegovina in 1887 strengthened these claims. Serbs wished to annex this area. After the turn of the century, both Serbs and Croats in Bosnia and Hercegovina formed political parties which were used to further their national aims.[12] Muslims formed the Muslim National Organization (MNO) which worked for the achievement of cultural autonomy.

In addition to Bosnia, there were also a substantial number of Croats living in Vojvodina.[13] This area consisted of the three districts of Baranja, Bačka and the Banat in what was traditionally Hungarian territory.[14] It was populated mainly by Serb Orthodox refugees from the Turks; there were also a substantial number of Croats in the western districts. After 1848, Bačka and the Banat were formed into an autonomous Serb Vojvodina. However, both Serbs and Croats wished to join it to their political units. The Ban of Croatia, Josip Jelačić, argued for the creation of an Illyrian state within the Habsburg Empire that would include inner Croatia, Slavonia, Dalmatia and the Serb districts of south Hungary. Serb elites, many of whom originated from this area, also hoped to join

---

12. The Serb National Organization was formed in 1907; the Croat National Society was formed in 1908; and in 1910 the Croat Catholic Association was established. The Muslim National Organization (MNO) was established in 1906. For the formation of political parties in Bosnia and Hercegovina see Donia, *ibid.*, chapter 7.

13. According to the Austrian census of 1910, there were 7,000 Croats in Vojvodina. But many Croats considered the number to be higher because the Slavs known as Bunjevci, settled mainly around Subotica, appear to have migrated to this area from Bosnia and Dalmatia in the seventeenth century. According to this census, the Bunjevci, together with another ethnic group, the Šokci, numbered 63,000 in Vojvodina. See Stephen Clissold, *A Short History of Yugoslavia* (Cambridge, England: Cambridge University Press, 1966), 154-155.

14. In 1690, the Habsburg Emperor Leopold invited massive migration into Hungarian territory. He granted the Serb migrants recognition as an Orthodox nation in Hungary and the right to elect their own leaders or *vojvoda*. Although the Hungarian Diet rejected this political autonomy for the Serbs, the name of *vojvoda* stuck to this territory.

Vojvodina to the newly formed Serbian Kingdom. Although it never caused as much friction between Serbs and Croats as Bosnia and Hercegovina did, political control of Vojvodina also became a source of tension in the new Yugoslav state.

In their efforts to define the Croat nation in the face of this regional diversity, the element most frequently stressed in Croat national ideologies was political nationhood and the theory of Croat state right. Since several dialects were spoken in the Croatian lands, language was an unclear criterion for defining the Croat nation, especially since Serbs held that štokavian was an exclusively Serb idiom. Additionally, in matters of religion, the Catholicism of most Croats did not necessarily reinforce Croat nationhood. Whereas in Serbia the autocephalous Orthodox Church reinforced Serbian political institutions, in Croatia the universalist Catholic Church provided no such support.

Emphasizing Croatia's medieval statehood provided Croats with the broadest definition of their nation: all people residing in the Triune Kingdom, regardless of language and religious affiliation, belonged to the Croat political nation. Leaders of the Croat national movement such as Ante Starčević emphasized the legal continuity of the Croatian state since the formation of the medieval kingdom in the tenth century. According to him, Croatia had retained its autonomous political rights when it had signed the *Pacta Conventa* with Hungary in 1091, by which Croats recognized the Hungarian ruler as king in exchange for the king's commitment to respect Croat rights and privileges.[15] When Ferdinand was crowned king of Hungary and Croatia in 1527, the *Pacta Conventa* had remained in effect and these privileges were retained. Starčević and his followers maintained that the Croat nation, by freely choosing the Habsburg dynasty, had executed a legal contract between two juridical persons, a contract that could be legally revoked.[16]

Invoking state right proved useful in asserting prerogatives against the Habsburgs, who were much swayed by formalist arguments.[17] It often interfered, however, with another crucial aspect of Croat national

---

15. Croatia retained its own Sabor, a partly independent military organization and separate taxation and currency.

16. For an evaluation of Starčević's arguments concerning Croatian state right see Mario S. Spalatin, "The Croatian Nationalism of Ante Starčević, 1845-1871," *Journal of Croatian Studies* XVI (1975), 94-100.

17. In the mid-nineteenth century, the self-rule of various political units in Austria was widely discussed. The privileges of political autonomy based on history, known as state right, were accepted by the October Diploma. The Magyars succeeded in realizing their political goals in 1867 by basing their arguments on state right. See *ibid*, 97.

aims: political arrangements with other South Slavs which would protect Croats from Habsburg and Hungarian encroachments and later from Italian and German threats. Croat claims on the numerous Serbs residing within Croatia's borders clashed with Serb national aims, which sought to reunite them to the Serbian state. South Slav political unity and Croatian state right were two conflicting strands of Croat national ideology.[18]

In the mid-nineteenth century, Croat leaders endorsed a variety of ideas for transforming their national goals into political realities. These myriad strategies reflected the complexities of political life in this area as Croats struggled to define their relations with Hungary, Austria and with other South Slavs, especially Serbs. In the previous several decades, Croatia's political autonomy had been severely reduced, first by Austria's centralizing reforms and then by Magyar nationalism. After their help in putting down the revolt of 1848 in Hungary, Croats looked in vain for their political reward. Inner Croatia and Slavonia were established as an Austrian crown land separate from Hungary but subject to equally fierce centralizing pressures from Vienna. In 1868, these territories again fell under Hungarian purview and, though the Croatian Sabor possessed some autonomous powers, Croat national expressions were severely restricted.[19]

Among the multitude of schemes for regaining Croatia's traditional autonomy and achieving its national goals, at least three major approaches emerged: the South Slav federalist approach advocated by the Illyrian Movement and later by Bishop Josip Juraj Strossmayer and Franjo Rački, the independent state approach espoused by Ante Starčević and Eugen Kvaternik, and the Yugoslav, unitarist variant which emerged at the end of the century and was advocated most fervently by Svetozar Pribićević. All of these approaches desired the unification of Croatian lands and the restoration of political rights, but they embraced very different notions of how to define the relation between the Croat nation and the state.

The Illyrian Movement, started by the poet and publicist Ljudevit Gaj, was primarily cultural and linguistic, but it also addressed political matters.[20] It was formed in 1835 with the official blessing of Vienna which

---

18. See Banac, *The National Question in Yugoslavia*, 70-115.

19. The Sabor retained control over internal affairs. The Parliament in Pest determined foreign policy and economic and trade matters. The Croatian Ban continued to be appointed by the prime minister of Hungary.

20. For a treatment of Gaj's work see Elinor Murray Despalatović, *Ljudevit Gaj and the Illyrian Movement* (New York: Columbia University Press, 1975). See also

saw it as a useful counter to Hungarian nationalism. Gaj and his followers chose the Illyrian appellation, a reference to the Illyrian provinces
established by Napoleon in 1809, in order to stress the common heritage
of South Slavs.[21] They saw their main task as paving the way for Slavic
solidarity by delineating a common language and orthography.
Although Gaj and many of his followers spoke the kajkavian dialect, they
encouraged the use of the štokavian dialect, believing this would foster
greater cooperation and unity among South Slavs. Ultimately, they
hoped to establish an Illyrian community of all South Slavs in the
Habsburg Empire under one language, though they remained loyal to
the Habsburgs in the meantime. Nevertheless, some Illyrianists had more
immediate political goals. Gaj's follower, the perhaps more astute Count
Janko Drašković, argued for a more explicitly political understanding of
Illyrianism. In his *Disertacija* written in 1832, Drašković called for the
reinstatement of the Triune Kingdom with control over the Military
Frontier, Rijeka, Slavonia and Bosnia, and the establishment of Croatian
as an official language. When the Illyrian party adopted its political
platform in 1843 (and changed its name to the National Party), it called
for the unification of Croatian lands and the extension of the power of
the Sabor to Slavonia and Dalmatia. The Yugoslavism (*jugoslavenstvo*)
strand advocated by the Bishop Strossmayer and the National Party
arose in the 1840's out of the Illyrian Movement. Attempting to counter
the absolutist centralization carried out from Vienna, Strossmayer
championed South Slav unity and launched a movement for educational
and cultural revival.[22] Like Gaj, Strossmayer believed that language
formed the basis of culture and that, therefore, Serbs and Croats possessed one "soul." For him, a universal national culture embracing all
South Slavs was a precondition for their national existence. Together

---

Wayne S. Vucinich, "Croatian Illyrianism: Its Background and Genesis," in
Stanley Winters and Joseph Held eds., *Intellectual and Social Developments in the
Habsburg Empire from Marie Teresa to World War I* (New York: Columbia
University Press, 1975).

21. They also sought to avoid using the terms Croat and Croatian because they
were associated at that time with Magyarophiles. The Illyrian Provinces established by Napoleon in 1809 included Carinthia, Carniola, Gorz, Istria, part of
Croatia, Dalmatia, and Ragusa. They were incorporated as an integral part of the
French Empire until 1815.

22. For a discussion of Strossmayer see: Mirijana Gross, "On the Integration of
the Croatian Nation: A Case Study in Nation Building," *East European Quarterly*
15 (2) (1981) : 209-225; Pedro Ramet, "From Strossmayer to Stepinac: Croatian
National Ideology and Catholicism," *Canadian Review of Studies in Nationalism* 12
(1) (1979): 123-137; Banac, *The National Question in Yugoslavia*, 89-92.

with his close associate, the historian (and priest) Franjo Rački, Strossmayer founded several important cultural and educational institutes such as the Yugoslav Academy of Sciences and Art at Zagreb in 1867. Strossmayer believed that the different religious loyalties of Serbs and Croats had been especially harmful to their unity, and worked for the reorganization of the Catholic Church along national lines in order to bring Serbs into its fold.

Strossmayer and the National Party championed the unification of Slovenes, Croats, and Serbs in an autonomous unit in the Habsburg Monarchy.[23] Nevertheless, they ultimately hoped for a separate federal state that included Serbia and Montenegro. In 1867, Strossmayer reached an agreement with Serbia to take steps toward the formation of a common state. His goals did not coincide with those of the Serbs, however, and the agreement produced little of substance. In any case, Strossmayer soon retired from political life. After the moderate elements of the National Party supported the 1868 *Nagodba* (Compromise), which Strossmayer opposed, the National Party lost its preeminent place in Croat political life. Many Croats now began to embrace more radical ideas about how to achieve Croat national aims.

Ante Starčević was the first Croat leader to break with the idea of South Slav unity in the 1850's.[24] A one-time enthusiast of the Illyrian Movement, Starčević became increasingly disillusioned with the Serbs' lack of interest in South Slav unity, and the Croats' lack of progress in uniting Croatian lands into a viable political unit. After 1848, this son of a military frontiersman took up political cudgels to fight for an independent Croatian state. Carrying the idea of a Croatian state right to its extreme, he contemplated a greater Croatia, including Bosnia, and refused to recognize the existence of any other South Slav nations besides the Bulgarians. Starčević insisted that Croatia must be considered a fully sovereign nation. Together with Eugen Kvaternik, he established the

---

23. When the National Party dominated the Sabor in 1947 and 1948, it declared Croatian the official language and extended the authority of the Sabor. Baron Josip Jelačić, who was Ban of Croatia at this time, promoted the Illyrian idea and cooperated with the National Party. He instructed officers in the Military Frontier not to accept any orders except those issuing from Zagreb. After 1848, Jelačić became only a figurehead under Austrian administration.

24. For a discussion of Ante Starčević see Mario S. Spalatin, "The Croatian Nationalism of Ante Starčević, 1845-1871," *Journal of Croatian Studies,* 15 (1975): 19-146; G. Gerald Gilbert, "Pravaštvo and the Croatian National Issue," *East European Quarterly* 12 (1)(1978): 57-68.

Party of Croatian Rights which espoused an integral Croat nationalism
and vehemently opposed the Habsburgs.[25]

The most striking aspect of Starčević's ideology was its markedly anti-
Serb tone. In contrast to the South Slav unity promoted by the Illyrian
Movement and Strossmayer, Starčević emphasized the distinctive elements of Croatian culture and history.[26] Praising the "glorious" nature of
Croatia's history as the defender of Christiandom, he disparaged the
accomplishments of other Slavs, especially Serbs, whom he described as
"beggars" and "slaves." Well aware of the difficulty posed by the large
number of Serbs residing in historically Croatian territory, Starčević
attempted to deny the historical validity of the existence of the Serb
nation in Croatia. This coupling of a virulently anti-Serb stance with
support for an independent state became an unfortunate legacy of this
strand of the nineteenth century Croat national movement.

The third unitarist strand of Croat national ideologies arose at the
beginning of the twentieth century as a host of new political parties were
formed in Croatia.[27] Several of these parties were interested in fostering
cooperation between Serbs and Croats which had been absent in the previous two decades. In 1905, a group of Serbs and Croats met in the
Dalmatian coastal city of Rijeka and adopted a political platform calling
for the establishment of an independent South Slav state.[28] Several

---

25. Although the Party of Croatian Rights advocated the establishment of an
independent state, it more immediately supported a trialist solution within the
framework of the Habsburg Empire. The Party of Croatian Rights put forth a
political program in the 1860s, based on the principles of Croatian state right,
which called upon the Habsburg Monarchy to restore Croatian territorial
integrity along the lines of the medieval kingdom with all of its ancient rights of
self-government and the establishment of a third kingdom within the framework
of the Monarchy.

26. Although Strossmayer and Starčevič took fundamentally different
approaches to the question of Croatian statehood, practical political realities led
them both to endorse an independent political unit within the Habsburg
Monarchy. In 1892 these two men, who represented opposite poles in the Croat
national movement, met in an effort to effect a reconciliation. Although their parties retained separate identities, they adopted a common program. This program
called for the union of all Croatian territory, probably within Hungary, although
it left open the possibility of a trialist solution.

27. The main parties operating in the Croatian lands at this time were the
National Party, the Croat-Serb Coalition, the Party of Croatian Rights, the Serbian
Independent Party, and the Croat People's Peasant Party.

28. There was a history of greater political cooperation among Serbs and
Croats in Dalmatia. For example, the Party of Croatian Rights was founded in

months later, an alliance of both Serb and Croat political parties was
formed which endorsed this platform. The Croat-Serb Coalition was
comprised of the Party of Croatian Rights, the Croatian Progressive
Party, the Serbian Independent People's Party, the Serbian People's
Radical Party and the Social Democratic Party of Croatia and Slavonia.
Its goal was to achieve South Slav unity in the Habsburg Empire to be
followed by the union of all South Slavs.[29]

In contrast to the Yugoslavism of Strossmayer and the Illyrian
Movement, the enthusiasm for South Slav unification which swept Croat
politics before the First World War was of a more unitarist variety.
Enthusiasm for Serbia was high after the recognition of the independent
Serbian Kingdom and many Croats as well as Serbs envisioned Serbia as
the Piedmont of any larger South Slav state. Consequently, while some
members of the Serb-Croat Coalition continued to endorse the kind of
federal arrangement envisioned by Strossmayer, others began to advocate a more unitary state. This was especially true of Serbs in Croatia
who saw centralization as a way of strengthening their ties with Serbs in
Serbia. When Svetozar Pribićević, a Serb from Croatia, inherited the leadership of the Coalition in 1910, its emphasis became even more unitarist.[30]

Many youths were also attracted to a unitarist version of a South Slav
state based upon the expansion of the Serbian Kingdom. Students returning from studies in Prague under the influence of Tomas Masaryk began
to question the state right basis of Croat national ideology and to advocate unity with Serbia. They endorsed the idea of national oneness
(*narodno jedinstvo*), that Serbs, Croats and Slovenes were three tribes of
one Yugoslav nation, and believed all differences between them to be
nonorganic and therefore reversible.[31] This program of unification also

Dalmatia by Ante Trumbić and Frano Supilo, who were also founders of the
Croat-Serb Coalition.

29. The Croat-Serb Coalition held power briefly in 1906 and locally intermittently thereafter. Hungary opposed the Coalition and tried to break its power (in
the 1909 Zagreb Trial members of the Serb-Croat Coalition were accused of being
tools of the Serbian state) but it remained intact until 1918.

30. For a discussion of Svetozar Pribićević and his ideas and role in the Croat-
Serb Coalition, see Hrvoje Matković, *Svetozar Pribićević i samostalna demokratska
stranka do šestojanuarske diktature* (Zagreb, 1972).

31. For example, factions of the Young Croats and followers of Josip Frank
accepted the Yugoslav ideal, which they saw as a new stage in Starčević's teach-
ing. They drew together on a new platform which supported a unitarist version
of Yugoslav ideology. See Mirjana Gross, "On the Integration of the Croatian
Nation: A Case Study in Nation Building."

appealed to many of the "revolutionary" youths who embraced Socialist and anarchist ideals at this time.[32] When members of the Croat-Serb Coalition engaged in negotiations with Serbs during the First World War about establishing a common state, this unitarist sentiment obscured very fundamental differences of opinion among Croats about the shape of the new state.

Although pro-Yugoslav ideas caught fire in Croatia before the First World War and exerted great influence on the Croat national movement, they did not extinguish suspicions about Serb intentions, especially toward the large Serb population residing in Croatia's historical territory. The vehicle for articulating these suspicions was the Pure Party of Rights established by Josip Frank in 1898. The followers of Frank, called "Frankovci," continued to espouse the virulently anti-Serb views propagated by Ante Starčević. Although they recognized the existence of the Serb nation in Serbia, they refused to acknowledge the existence of Serbs in Croatia and Bosnia-Hercegovina. Nevertheless, while proclaiming Starčević as their leader, the Frankovci in fact reversed his policy of opposition to the Habsburgs and began to look to Vienna for protection from Hungary. They also renounced Starčević's aim of creating an independent Croatian state outside the monarchy. Frank argued that Croatia must support the Habsburgs against the Serbs and wait until the monarchy was consolidated as a great power; the Habsburgs would then grant Croatia autonomy and reorganize the Empire along trialist lines. After Frank's death in 1911, the Pure Party of Rights became increasingly clericalized. In addition to the doctrine of the national incompatibility of Serbs and Croats and the need to Croatize Serbs living in Croatia and Bosnia and Hercegovina, Frankovci now insisted that the Catholic and Orthodox faiths were completely incompatible. This religious opposition to Serbs became an important element of the Ustasha ideology which emerged in the interwar period.

While Croats struggled to define their nation and its political shape, Serbs faced less complex circumstances in forming their national movement. First, the population of Serbia was much more homogeneous and was united by a linguistically based nationalism. In contrast to Croats who spoke several dialects, practically all Serbs spoke the štokavian dialect. In the nineteenth century, the linguist Vuk Karadžić devised a standard orthography for the Serbian vernacular and reformed the Cyrillic alphabet. These efforts ensured the adoption of a common dialect and orthography by Serb peasants as well as intellectuals; it also ensured

---

32. For more on the "revolutionary youth" see Aleksa Djilas, *The Contested Country*, 35-37.

that Serbs would continue to use the Cyrillic alphabet while Croats mainly used the Roman script. Karadžić argued that anyone speaking the štokavian was a Serb, thus broadening the definition of the Serb nation to include štokavian-speaking Catholic Croats and Bosnian Muslims.[33]

Despite Karadžić's efforts to bring Catholic and Muslim štokavians into the Serb nation, the Serbs were primarily united by Eastern Orthodoxy. Not only were practically all Serbs of the Orthodox faith, the autocephalous Serbian Orthodox Church had a history of close links with the Serbian state. During the medieval Serbian Kingdom, an archbishop was established at Peć (by King Stefan who was the brother of the first archbishop, Saint Sava); in the mid-fourteenth century King Dušan declared himself Emperor and raised the Peć archbishop to the status of patriarchate.[34] During the long Turkish occupation which began shortly thereafter, the Serbian feudal system and the nobility were almost completely destroyed, strengthening the power of the church. Although the Serbian Orthodox hierarchy was nominally subject to the Ottoman Sultan, the church retained a great deal of independence, especially after the Patriarchate of Peć was restored in 1557. Consequently, it became a symbol of independent Serbian political authority and the repository of Serb national consciousness. Thus language and religion were the essential, though occasionally contradictory, elements of Serb national ideology; all Orthodox Slavs speaking štokavian were considered Serbs who should be united within Serbia's borders.

The formation of the Serbian state in the early part of the nineteenth century reinforced this national ideology. With the anti-Ottoman uprisings of 1804 and 1815, Serbs began to liberate themselves from Ottoman rule; they also began the process of creating a modern state. By the middle of the century, Serbia had a functioning Parliament (Skupština), a judicial system and a ruling Serbian dynasty. In 1878, Serbia (and Montenegro) was formally recognized as a sovereign state by the western powers; four years later, the Kingdom of Serbia was proclaimed. The existence of the Serbian state, and the fact that Serbs were not anxious to emphasize its existing borders with so many Serbs scattered in sections of Austria-Hungary, meant that state right arguments were not as central

---

33. See Banac, *The National Question in Yugoslavia*, 80-81.

34. The Serbian Kingdom, which reached its apex under Stefan Dušan (1346-1355), was centered in southwest Serbia, Montenegro, Kosovo and northern Macedonia. Although remnants of the state survived until the beginning of the fifteenth century, its political power was essentially destroyed after the battle of Kosovo in 1389.

to Serb national ideology (except when Serbs emphasized their claims
over Kosovo and Macedonia). Since they had their own state, Serbs were
also less receptive to the idea of South Slav unity. Primarily assimilation-
ist, they were concerned with retrieving their brethren across the border.

In 1844, Serbia's minister of the interior, Ilija Garašanin, prepared a
secret document (*Načertanije*) that articulated the goals of the Serb
national movement and Serbia's relations with other South Slavs. This
document, which "laid the foundations of the Great Serbian policy of
[South Slav] unification," was accepted by virtually all of Serbia's political elite.[35] Garašanin equated Serbia's interests with the interests of South
Slavs more generally. Though he occasionally had contacts with
Strossmayer and other proponents of South Slav unity, Garašanin was
not sympathetic to the Illyrian Movement. Rather, he believed that Serbs'
primary goal must be the strengthening and centralization of the Serbian
state; then, Serbia would expand to encompass other Serbs and possibly
all South Slavs.[36] Almost twenty years later when Garašanin was prime
minister, he attempted to execute this plan of expanding the Serbian state
by working toward the annexation of Bosnia. Garašanin hoped to foment
an anti-Ottoman uprising in Bosnia and Hercegovina, which would be
supported by the colonists in the Military Frontier. This uprising would
provide the pretext for Serbia's intervention in Bosnia and its ultimate
annexation to the Serbian state.

The Serbian political parties formed in the nineteenth century shared
similar views on Serbian national goals and relations with other South
Slavs. And, in contrast to Croat peasants who were still excluded from
political life, Serb peasants, brought into politics by the Radical Party,
supported these views. The National Radical Party, formed by Nikola
Pašić in the 1870s, believed that Serbia's primary task was to join Serbs
living outside Serbia to their homeland. Less interested in the South Slav
unity espoused by many Croats, the Radicals had few contacts with
Slovenes and Croats, and these were usually at the latter's initiative.[37]
When the Independent Radicals split off from the Radical Party in 1901,
they endorsed the same national aims, though with a slightly more pro-
Yugoslav tone. A group of youths and intellectuals who formed the
organization Slavic South (*Slovenski jug*) in 1903 attempted to promote
Serb-Croat cooperation and called for the establishment of an all-

---

35. Banac, *The National Question in Yugoslavia*, 83.

36. Djilas, *The Contested Country*, 29.

37. For a discussion of the Radical Party's contacts with Croats and Slovenes
during this period see Dragoslav Janković, *Srbija i jugoslovensko pitanje, 1914-1915*
(Belgrade, 1973), 172.

Yugoslav party. They never represented a dominant strand in Serb political life, however, and they were countered by such ultranationalist Serb
organizations as the Black Hand.[38] Though they sometimes supported
the movement for South Slav unity across the border, Serb political parties remained committed to creating a greater Serbian state that would
unite the entire Serb nation. This vision of the Serbian state was upper-
most in the minds of Serb politicians as they contemplated the formation
of a Yugoslav state during the First World War.

Wartime and Unification

When the First World War began, Serbs and Croats encountered new
circumstances in which to achieve their political aims. Initially, Serb
politicians appeared more receptive to the idea of South Slav unification.
In the fall of 1914, the Serbian government stated its war goals in the Niš
Declaration and endorsed the unification of Serbs and Croats in one
state. Prime Minister Nikola Pašić's support for a South Slav state was
due more to Allied pressure, however, than to a sincere change of heart
about the future shape and character of Serbia. Hoping to induce
Bulgaria to enter the war on their side, the Allies attempted to turn
Serbia's attention away from its territorial designs southward toward
Bulgaria and direct it northward toward Croatia and Slovenia. When the
Allies lost interest in this matter in the next year, Pašić's concern for a
South Slav state also declined. He returned to his earlier conviction that
Serbia could best realize its aims by expanding its borders to incorporate
all areas where Serbs constituted a majority or to which they had histori-
cal claims.[39]

As the war drew to a close and Wilson began to champion self-determination among the Slavs, Pašić once again displayed more interest in
South Slav unification. In July 1917, he met at Corfu with various members of the Yugoslav Committee, set up by Croat proponents of South
Slav unity such as Ante Trumbić and Frano Supilo (members of the
Croat-Serb Coalition), and endorsed the establishment of a new state
encompassing Serbs, Croats, and Slovenes. Nevertheless, Pašić made it
clear that he conceived of such a state essentially as an expansion of

---

38. *Ibid.*, 150-180.
39. *Ibid.*, 200-205.

Serbia, which would be based on a unitary political arrangement.[40] Since the negotiations at Corfu left several important questions about the future character of the state unresolved, it was agreed that Croatia's status in the new state would be decided by majority voting at the Constituent Assembly to be held after the founding of the new state.

Although members of the Yugoslav Committee championed unity with Serbia from the outset of the war, most Croat politicians initially rejected the Niš Declaration and advocated a "trialist" solution which would grant Croatia autonomy similar to Hungary within a Habsburg state.[41] Some Croat leaders (Starčevićists) advocated an independent Great Croatia which might later unite with Serbia; others like Stjepan Radić supported a Croat-Slovene state within Austria-Hungary. Pribićević and the Croat-Serb Coalition remained loyal to the Hungarian Crown until the end of the war.

When Austria-Hungary weakened at the end of the war, Croat leaders were forced to search for other solutions to Croatia's future. In October 1918, a group of delegates from the Sabor formed a National Council which called for a free Croat and Slovene state.[42] As Austro-Hungarian authority disintegrated over the next several weeks, this Council began to govern Croatia. Euphoric at their sudden rise to power, but also fearful of losing Dalmatia and of anarchy, Croat leaders looked to Serbia to bolster their position with the Allies and to provide military order in the countryside. These practical concerns and the genuine enthusiasm of many Croat leaders for the South Slav idea prompted them to endorse the immediate establishment of an independent South Slav state. At the end of the month, the National Council passed a motion, over the one dissenting vote of Stjepan Radić advocating unconditional unification with Serbia and Montenegro. On December 1, 1918, Council members met Prince-Regent Aleksandar in Belgrade, where he proclaimed the establishment of the Kingdom of Serbs, Croats, and Slovenes.

Given the hastiness of unification, it was not surprising that disagreements about the character of the new state soon arose. Serbs and

---

40. Trumbić's effort to have voting according to "tribal" blocs was defeated. See Dragoslav Janković, *Jugoslovensko pitanje i Krfska deklaracija 1917* (Belgrade, 1967), 230-250.

41. See Janković, *Srbija i jugoslovensko pitanje, 1914-1915,* 393; Bogdan Krizman, *Raspad Austro-Ugarske i stvaranje jugoslavenske države* (Zagreb, 1977).

42. These delegates met along with Slovene and Croat delegates from Austria who had formed their own People's Council (*Narodni svet*). For a discussion of Slovene activity during this period, see Janko Pleterski, *Prvo opredeljenje Slovenaca za Jugoslaviju* (Belgrade, 1976).

Croats had very different ideas about the new kingdom. Most Serbs believed they should hold a preeminent position in the new state, by virtue of their sacrifices in the war and their previous political experience.[43] Their national ideologies and political experience inclined them to support an expansion of the Serbian state on the basis of unitarism. Although most Croats did not generally share Serbs' enthusiasm for a unitary state, in the chaotic circumstances at the end of the war immediate unification with Serbia seemed the best way to achieve their national goals. Their national ideology and political experiences left them with conflicting approaches toward the new state, ranging from unitarism to secessionism. Divided by these different views, they were ill-equipped to respond to Serbian unitarist pressures.

In the months after the formation of the new kingdom, Serbs and Croats did little to resolve their differences about whether the state should be organized along federal or unitary lines. It is possible that some problems between Serbs and Croats might have been resolved differently if they had been tackled immediately after the war. Instead, during the long wait for a new constitution, Serbs simply assumed control of the new political institutions.[44] The Serbian Parliament was expanded to form the basis of the Provisional Assembly in 1918 and, despite the protests of Croat delegates, the Sabor was deprived of its authority.[45] At the same time, the Serbian bureaucracy and army spread into Croatia and alienated the local population by occasionally behaving like an occupying power. By the time elections to the Constituent Assembly were held in the fall of 1920, a unitary political arrangement had been virtually established, without the acquiescence of Croats.

Interestingly, the person who worked most tirelessly to achieve a unitary state order was Svetozar Pribićević who had been head of the Croat-Serb Coalition before the war. Pribićević, who was acknowledged to be the main leader of Serbs in Croatia, was a passionate proponent of centralization. As minister of the interior in the new state, Pribićević pursued a relentless campaign against Radić and the Croat Republican Peasant Party (CRPP) who opposed a unitary state order. Pribićević

---

43. Serbia's sacrifices during the war were truly staggering. The country lost about one fifth of its population and suffered tremendous physical destruction.

44. Elections for the Constituent Assembly were delayed until after the peace conference delineated the borders of the new state.

45. Branislav Gligorijević, *Parlament i političke stranke u Jugoslaviji, 1919-1920* (Belgrade, 1979). See Hrvoje Matković, *Svetozar Pribićević i samostalna demokratska stranka do šestojanuarske diktature.*

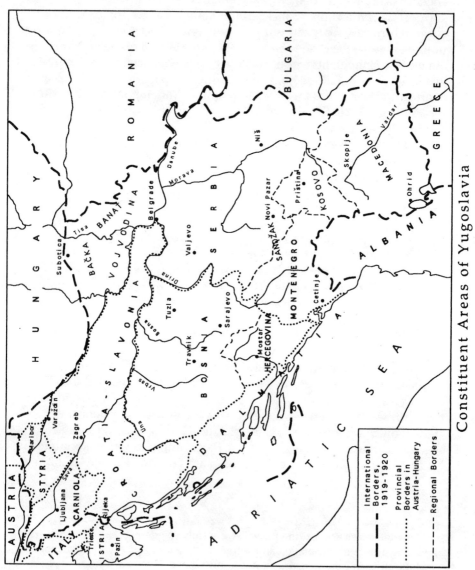

Constituent Areas of Yugoslavia

International
Borders,
1919-1920

Provincial
Borders in
Austria-Hungary

Regional Borders

joined forces with Ljubomir Davidović leader of the Independent Radical Party, to form the Democratic Party which endorsed a platform more Yugoslav and unitarist than the Radicals' political program.[46] When Davidović appeared prepared to consider negotiating with Radić and to introduce administrative decentralization, Pribićević left the Democratic Party to form the Independent Democratic Party in 1924. His support for centralization and his opposition to Radić allowed Prime Minister Pašić to claim that the fight over centralization was simply an internal Croat affair.

In November 28, 1920, the long-awaited elections to the Constituent Assembly were held under relatively free conditions. The results of the elections to the Constituent Assembly revealed Croats' deep resentment of the centralized arrangement of the Yugoslav state. Radić's Croat Republican Peasant Party which had campaigned on the platform of an independent Croatian republic, was the great victor in the elections in Croatia.[47] Despite its electoral strength, the CRPP did not participate in the formulation of the new constitution. Objecting to the oath of loyalty to the king required of participants in the Constituent Assembly, and to the government's refusal to consider the validity of the terms of Croatia's joining with Serbia in 1918, the CRPP refused to send its delegates to Belgrade. Instead, the fifty CRPP delegates held an alternative National Assembly in Zagreb, which called for the establishment of a Croatian republic. The CRPP also convinced the rest of the Croat delegates to withdraw from the Constituent Assembly, thereby ensuring Croat hostility to the new constitution.

In any case, the Serb leadership in the Constituent Assembly proved unwilling to endorse any federalist or decentralized state order. Instead, Pašić proposed a constitution that would be legislatively unitarist but administratively decentralized. This latter provision was effectively negated, however, by the already existing administrative centralization.[48] In 1920, with the majority of the delegates to the Constituent Assembly abstaining, Pašić's proposal was accepted and a unitary solution to

---

46. The Independent Radical Party was formed in 1901 from a progressive wing of the Radical Party.

47. Roughly half the delegates elected to the Constituent Assembly were members of parties advocating a unitary state arrangement: the National Radical Party, the Serbian Democratic Party, and the agrarian parties. Joseph Rothschild, *East Central Europe between the Two World Wars*, 214.

48. In April 1922, an administrative law was adopted which organized the country into thirty-three departments which were tightly controlled by the central government.

Yugoslavia's constitutional order was adopted.[49] From the start, it was an order that lacked legitimacy among the Croat populace. Henceforth, the most urgent question in the new kingdom became designing a constitutional order that would, if not ensure Croats' support, at least diminish their hostility to a manageable level.

Čaršija, King, and the New Yugoslav State, 1921-1928

With the adoption of the Vidovdan Constitution in 1921, Serb political leaders ensured their hegemonic position in the new state. They now faced the task of creating a bureaucratic and administrative system capable of governing effectively and unifying the conglomerate of nationalities included in the new state. Their inability to resolve the Croat question impeded their efforts to accomplish this task. Despite increasing Croat disaffection with the unitary political order, Serb leaders refused to reopen the constitutional question or to increase Croat political autonomy. Their failure to address the Croat question effectively undermined the viability of the democratic system and ultimately resulted in the imposition of an authoritarian political order.

Radical Party leader Nikola Pašić had expended considerable energy to get a unitary political order adopted in the Vidovdan Constitution, and he was determined to preserve that order by ensuring the Radicals' predominant political position. Adept at parliamentary maneuvering, he took advantage of the system of parliamentary seating which was skewed heavily in favor of the winning party. The Radicals quickly established their dominance in Parliament and adopted a strategy of divide and rule. Together with the Democratic Party and the Independent Democratic Party after its split, they attempted to keep Croats out of the political arena. The Yugoslav Muslim Organization developed a clientelist strategy and the Slovene People's Party a coalitionist strategy, both of which allowed them to reach an accommodation with the Serb ruling party, often at the expense of Croats. This alliance, combined with repressive measures resulting in the periodic imprisonment of CRPP officials, effectively reduced Croat participation in political affairs.

---

49. Over the next several months, numerous other delegates left the Constituent Assembly from the Peoples' Club (Party of Croatian Rights, Progressive Democratic Party, the Croat People's Union, and members of the Yugoslav Committee) as well as the Communists and the Slovene People's Party.

Serb dominance of political life did not, however, produce political stability. In the decade after the war, there was a new cabinet almost every six months. Several factors produced fissures in the Serb ruling elite, undermining its attempt to provide direction to Yugoslavia's turbulent political life. In addition to the difficulties of maintaining a stable government without the CRPP, and the splits in their own ranks between the Serb Radical Party and the Democratic Party, Serb politicians were divided by the king. King Aleksandar was very popular at this time due to his role as commander in chief of the armed forces in the First World War. Like several of his predecessors, he was also bent on undermining the power of the Serb political parties, and the Radical Party in particular. He skillfully played off one against another to the detriment of Parliament. Bickering between Serb leaders and the crown impeded the ability of both to create a strong and effective state.

Despite increasing disaffection in Croatia and the instability of the governing coalitions, the Radicals continued to keep the CRPP out of government and to oppose constitutional revision. Moreover, after their initial support for administrative decentralization, the Radicals passed an administrative law in the spring of 1922 which organized the country into thirty-three centrally controlled administrative units. The Radicals' unwillingness to consider administrative decentralization along the lines of "historical units" infuriated Croats and did little to create an effective administrative system. Although at times the Serbian bureaucracy poured into areas of Croatia, further antagonizing the local population, it did not become an effective tool of the Belgrade government. The new administrative bodies continued to be viewed as artificial creations and much of the administrative activity remained in the hands of local Peasant Party officials. Pašić briefly softened his attitude toward Radić and the CRPP in 1923, pledging to undo this administrative "parcelization" (*parcelizacija*) and to support constitutional revision. When his political position solidified several months later, however, Pašić resumed his previously hostile stance toward the CRPP.

Despite Serb efforts to exclude the CRPP from the parliamentary process, it became increasingly clear that no government could long survive without Croat representation. Pašić and the Radicals were unwilling to govern with the CRPP, but they were unable to govern without it. Finally, in 1925, frustrated by his inability to forge a stable coalition without the CRPP, and encouraged by Radić's conciliatory moves, Pašić invited Radić to form a government with him. Though this new coalition might have broken the stalemate over the Croat question, its accomplishments were meagre. True, there was less wrangling over the constitutional question after Radić abandoned his republican views and endorsed the Vidovdan Constitution and the Karadjordjević dynasty. But

Radić's new position was not translated into any sincere goodwill between the Serb and Croat ruling parties.

Distracted by a corruption scandal that led to his resignation from the government in 1926, Pašić failed to use Radić's participation in the government as an opportunity to address some larger questions about the constitutional order. Pašić's death shortly thereafter left the Radical Party splintered by factional struggles. These were encouraged by the king, who saw his chance to reduce his rivals' power by dividing them. Preoccupied with internal matters and fed up with Radić's policies, the Radicals demanded that Radić leave the cabinet. In the spring of that year, Radić departed from the government in Belgrade, along with several other CPP leaders. Acrimony between the Radicals and the Croat Peasant Party (CPP), as it was now called, quickly returned. During the next two years until the proclamation of royal dictatorship in 1929, the increasingly fractured and ineffectual Radicals made no further strides toward resolving the Croat question.

Although the Serb political elite managed to alienate Croats by its centralist political arrangements and hegemonic position, it failed to use this position to execute much-needed economic reform. The developmental needs of the interwar Yugoslav state were staggering. The newly formed state emerged from the war with a devastated agricultural sector and huge war loans. Industrial production was at a primitive level, particularly in the southern part of the country. Pointing to its past experience with state-sponsored industrial development, the government in Belgrade promised a vigorous policy of reconstruction and economic development. But its inability to develop an effective administrative apparatus, harnessed to a legislative plan of national priorities, and its political preoccupation with the Croat question, rendered this policy a largely empty promise.

The most pressing problems facing the government were in the agricultural sector, and in 1919 the state took a dramatic step toward resolving them with the promulgation of a major land reform bill. In those areas such as Slavonia and Vojvodina where large estates continued to prevail, a system of small landholdings resembling that existing in Serbia was established. This move, which increased productivity at least in the short term, combined with the favorable prices that agricultural products received abroad, resulted in a period of relative agricultural prosperity in the decade after the war. With the sudden drop in agricultural prices brought on by the Depression, however, the failure of the government's agricultural program became apparent.[50] After land reform brought the desired effect of reducing potential political tensions, further investment in this sector ceased. Nor was credit made available on reasonable terms to the peasant small landholders. With the exception of Slovenia, where the cooperative system continued to provide cheap credit and services to its members, cooperatives remained starved for funds and plagued by political corruption. Moreover, instead of using its funds to subsidize these already existing organizations, the central government set up equally capital-starved and ineffective rivals.

As agricultural overpopulation increased and peasant indebtedness climbed, the government was finally forced to take more drastic steps. From 1932 to 1936, it passed a series of laws intended to alleviate these problems. While this legislation resulted in a temporary easing of the pressure, the peasants remained as short of credit and the sector as starved for investment as ever. Only in the mid-thirties did the government reluctantly provide a way to ease the problems in this area; the trade agreements signed with Germany opened up a desperately needed market for Yugoslavia's agricultural goods. But as the German web tightened around its borders, it became clear that the Yugoslav government would pay an enormous price for its failure to address successfully the problems in this sector.

Governmental attempts to promote industrial development were not much more impressive, although this sector was declared to be top priority. The policy of import substitution and high customs tariffs pursued by the government proved ill-conceived. The country simply did not possess the necessary infrastructure, market and technical expertise to forego importing some "factors of production," and this strategy of protecting national markets resulted in an isolation which Yugoslavs could little afford.[51] Moreover, the government in Belgrade failed to devise a tax policy that would foster domestic capital accumulation and promote growth in high priority domestic industries. Not only did the tax structure antagonize Croatia where the rates were higher, it also had the effect of encouraging investment in urban construction, which contributed little or nothing to the nation's long-term development. An estimated fifty to sixty percent of the domestic capital formation went into housing; and

---

50. For a thorough discussion of the government's agricultural policies during the interwar years, see Jozo Tomasevich, *Peasants, Politics and Economic Change in Yugoslavia* (Stanford: Stanford University Press, 1955).

51. Ivan Berend and Gyorgy Ranki, *Economic Development in Eastern Europe in the Nineteenth and Twentieth Centuries* (New York and London: Columbia University Press, 1974), 208.

in a country where lack of capital was the chief obstacle to domestic economic development, this policy had obviously harmful effects.[52]

The government was forced to turn abroad for another source of capital, where it obtained loans at very high interest rates which were beyond its capacity to pay. Moreover, a good portion of the loans went to enlarging the state apparatus and pet projects of the political and business elite. Spectacular fortunes were made during these years as the Serb *čaršija* used its state connections to obtain favorable business deals. The ability of bureaucrats and administrators to use their official position to enhance their economic and social status hindered the emergence of any reforming zeal among this group. Although some progress was made in national development during these years, the Belgrade government had precious little to show for the promises of economic development it had made. At the end of the interwar period, Yugoslavia remained one of the poorest countries on the European continent, beset by social and economic problems and threatened by a national conflict of immense proportions.

Stjepan Radić and Croatian Statehood, 1918-1928

During the years of political democracy in the Kingdom of Serbs, Croats, and Slovenes, the CRPP became the leading political force in Croatia and its charismatic leader, Stjepan Radić, its most important political personality.[53] Radić, who was gifted with boundless energy, galvanized Croat peasants into political action on behalf of the Croat national cause. He adopted many positions on Croatia's national goals, making and breaking tactical alliances with dizzying speed, but his commitment to achieving greater political autonomy for Croatia remained constant. His political strategy can be broken into three phases: the first phase from 1918 to 1925 when the CRPP refused to recognize the new political order, the second phase beginning in 1925 when the CRPP entered the government in coalition with the Radicals, and the third phase in 1927 and 1928 when the CPP formed an oppositional coalition with the Independent Democrats.

In the years before and during the war, Radić had been an ardent proponent of achieving Croatian statehood by reorganizing the Habsburg

---

52. Tomasevich, *Peasants, Politics and Economic Change in Yugoslavia,* 686.

53. For more on Stjepan Radić see Bogdan Krizman, *Korespondencija Stjepana Radića* I-II (Zagreb, 1972-1973); and Zvonimir Kulundžić, *Stjepan Radić, Politički spisi (autobiografija, članci, govori, rasprave)* (Zagreb, 1971).

Monarchy. Though not opposed to the idea of South Slav unification, he looked mainly to the Slav nations within the Habsburg state to create a new federation of Slavs. The program adopted by the Croat People's Peasant Party (CPPP), founded by Anton and Stjepan Radić in 1903, endorsed a Danubian federation in which Croatia (including Dalmatia, and later, Bosnia-Hercegovina) would comprise one of five state units united under the Habsburg dynasty. When this program was made impossible by the collapse of Austria-Hungary at the end of the war, Radić remained skeptical of plans to unite with Serbia in a South Slav federation. Fearing that recognition of the Karadjordjević dynasty and failure to procure guarantees of Croatian political autonomy would result in Croatia's political subordination in the new state, Radić vehemently opposed the National Committee's endorsement of immediate and unconditional unification with Serbia and Montenegro in 1918.[54]

Radić's opposition to the new state carried over into the postwar period. In the two and one-half years before the adoption of the Vidovdan Constitution, he continued to fight against unification, calling for the establishment of a neutral Croatian republic within a broader South Slav federation.[55] At the CPPP's first congress in February 1919, the party changed its name to the Croat Republican Peasant Party (CRPP) in order to emphasize its opposition to the Serbian dynasty, and Radić landed in jail shortly thereafter for making speeches against the king. In 1921, after its very strong showing in the elections, the CRPP refused to send its delegates to Belgrade, and held an alternative meeting of the Sabor which denounced unification with Serbia and declared its support for an independent Croatian republic.

After the Vidovdan Constitution was passed, and it became clear that the Allies would not support major changes in Yugoslavia, Radić modified his approach and began to seek a solution to the question of Croatian statehood within the borders of Yugoslavia.[56] Calling for "a sovereign Croatia within the boundaries of the commonwealth of Serbs, Croats, and Slovenes," he continued to press for constitutional revisions to achieve a Croatian republic, and attempted to set up an extra parlia-

---

54. For more on Radić's activities during the war see Bogdan Krizman, "Stjepan Radić i Hrvatska pučka seljačka stranka u prvom svjetskom ratu," *Časopis za suvremenu povijest* 2 (1970).

55. For more on Radić's activities during this period see Banac, *The National Question in Yugoslavia*, 226-248.

56. Stjepan Gaži, "Stjepan Radić: His Life and Political Activities (1871-1928)," *Journal of Croatian Studies* 24-25 (1973-1974): 13-32.

mentary "federalist bloc" to press for these reforms.[57] At the same time, Radić engaged in direct talks with Pašić. In exchange for remaining outside the parliamentary process, he extracted promises that the government would discontinue the administrative division of Croatia, appoint a royal governor to govern there, and cease all political persecution of Croats and Slovenes. Disillusioned when these pledges were not honored, Radić launched a campaign to solicit support from abroad for Croat aims. He pleaded his case in France and Britain, and when this effort proved unsuccessful, appealed for Soviet help. After a trip to the western capitals, he arrived dramatically in the Soviet Union in 1924, where he joined the Krestintern, the peasant counterpart of the Comintern.[58]

The year 1925 marked a major turning point in Radić's approach to the question of Croatian statehood and the beginning of a new phase of his political strategy for gaining this goal. Frustrated by his inability to make any real headway outside the government and by his inability to procure support from abroad for a major reordering of the Yugoslav political system, Radić began to rethink his strategy. His imprisonment on charges of sedition in 1924 and the ban of the CRPP under the expanded *Obznana* increased his doubts about the Peasant Party's previous political strategy. Consequently, in an apparent about-face which startled many of his followers, Radić decided to recognize the current political order and become a full participant in the parliamentary process.[59] After the elections of 1925 he endorsed a new platform which stated that (1) the CRPP would no longer press for federalism but would support Croatian autonomy introduced by constitutional change; (2) the CRPP would support a modified monarchy; and (3) the CRPP would cut its ties with the Krestintern (Communist Peasant International). Radić further agreed to drop the word republican from the CRPP's name, which was changed to the Croat Peasant Party (CPP). In the spring of that year, Radić entered into the government with the Radicals.

The almost two years in which Radić governed with the Radicals were not a fruitful time for the Croat Peasant Party. Although Radić continued to push for constitutional reform, he made little headway in Parliament

---

57. *Ibid.*, 1.

58. See Mira Kolar-Dimitrijević, "Put Stjepana Radića u Moskvu i pristup Hrvatske republikanske seljačke stranke u seljačku internacionalu," *Časopis za suvremenu povijest* 3 (1972).

59. Various CPP leaders such as Trumbić and Lorković never forgave Radić for this abrupt shift in tactics and left the CPP in protest over his decision to recognize the current political order.

on this or other legislative matters, such as his proposals concerning communal self-government. Moreover, he antagonized his colleagues by his often abrasive tone in addressing Serb ministers and his inflammatory public statements. Frustrated by this lack of success, he cooperated with the king's efforts to bring down Pašić through a corruption scandal in 1926, only to find himself excluded from the government shortly thereafter. He now resumed his more familiar position as promoter of Croatian political autonomy in opposition to the government.

After his departure from the government at the beginning of 1927, Radić established an alliance with his old enemy Svetozar Pribićević, former minister of the interior and head of the Independent Democratic Party.[60] Though Pribićević had previously supported a unitary political order, the two men now found they had more in common, since both were opposed to the government. Moreover, given his political base among Serbs in Croatia, Pribićević was an attractive ally for Radić. Consequently, shortly before the elections in 1927, the CPP and Pribićević's Independent Democratic Party (IDP) established the Peasant-Democratic Coalition (PDC). Both parties agreed to work toward a "correct" execution of the Vidovdan Constitution while maintaining their separate party platforms.[61]

After they failed to put together a "concentration" government at the beginning of 1928, Pribićević and Radić began a vitriolic campaign against the government, calling for an end to Serbian hegemonism and corruption. Acrimony between the PDC and the governing coalition, especially the Radicals, reached the breaking point. During a particularly turbulent session of Parliament in June, a Radical Party delegate took out his pistol and shot Radić and several others. In the chaos that followed, the PDC called for the resignation of the government, the dissolution of the Parliament, and new elections. When the king refused, the PDC withdrew from Parliament and tried to convince Aleksandar to form a neutral government. A new government was formed under the Slovene Korošec, but the PDC refused to recognize it and went back on its earlier

---

60. For more on Radić's interactions with Pribićević see Hrvoje Matković, "Stjepan Radić i Svetozar Pribićević u jugoslavenskoj politici od ujedinjenja do šestojanuarske diktature," *Jugoslovenski istorijski časopis* 4 (1969).

61. The alliance between the CPP and the IDP began out of expediency since both groups were outside the government and looking for allies. It resulted, however, in Pribićević abandoning his support for unitarism. See Ljubo Boban, *Svetozar Pribićević u opoziciji, 1928-1936* (Zagreb, 1973) 1-13.

recognition of the Vidovdan Constitution.[62] Finally, in January 1929, the king took matters into his own hands, declared a royal dictatorship, dissolved the Parliament, and banned the political parties.

By the time Radić died of gunshot wounds in July 1928, he had transformed Croatian politics. Although Radić is frequently portrayed as an intransigent "obstructionist" who bears great responsibility for the deterioration of Yugoslav political life in the 1920's, a closer look at his activities during these years does not completely support this picture.[63] Radić began the decade as a republican, vehemently opposed to union with Serbia. He ended his political career having recognized the union with Serbia and the Karadjordjević dynasty. His public style may have been irritating and provocative, but his policies were undeniably flexible. Despite his multitude of tactics, Radić failed to accomplish his primary aim of achieving greater political autonomy for Croatia before his death. But he did succeed in building a national movement of massive proportions. The Croat Peasant Party brought Croat peasants into political life in much the same way that the Radical Party had mobilized Serbs a half century earlier, and secured for the CPP the right to speak in their name. After Radić, no Serb political leader could afford to ignore Croat political sentiments or the power of the CPP.

The CPP and King Aleksandar, 1929-1934

When King Aleksandar imposed a royal dictatorship in 1929, parliamentary life in Yugoslavia was at an all-time low. Due in part to his own interference in the parliamentary process, the party system was unstable and plagued by corruption. Most importantly, the Croat question continued to preoccupy political leaders and at times to paralyze the political system; a solution was nowhere in sight. Fed up with parliamentary wrangling over this question, the monarch was determined to impose his own solution on the country. He proved no more effective than his predecessors, however, in devising a more stable political order which could accommodate Croat national demands.

---

62. After Radić was shot, the PDC called for the resignation of the government. At the beginning of August, the PDC modified this position and instead began to attack the Vidovdan Constitution.

63. For example, see Joseph Rothschild, *East Central Europe between the Two World Wars* (Seattle and London: Washington University Press, 1974), 226. See also Alex N. Dragnich, *The First Yugoslavia* (Stanford, California: Hoover Institution Press, 1983).

Although Croats were initially optimistic that the king might improve the political situation in Croatia, their sanguine outlook was short lived. Aleksandar did take several steps in the first few months of the dictatorship to reduce the most obvious aspects of Serb political dominance. He diminished the preeminence of Serb cultural symbols and, for example, changed the country's name to the Kingdom of Yugoslavia. He also attempted to gain CPP support for the dictatorship by giving it more control over administrative appointments in Croatia. Whatever goodwill he might have earned by this move, however, was eroded by the administrative reform he undertook shortly thereafter. The country's thirty-three administrative units were reorganized into nine banovinas (governorships) which cut across Croatian territorial lines. With this move Aleksandar made it clear that he would not support any regional autonomy, let alone the introduction of a federal political system.

Aleksandar further engendered Croat hostility by banning all political parties. This ban not only made the CPP illegal, it failed to serve its ostensible purpose of reducing Serbian political dominance. The same Serb political leaders continued to dominate political life, especially after the king introduced limited political activity with the new constitution of 1931. Radical Party leaders simply formed a "neutral" government party, which continued to exclude CPP leaders and prevent their participation in the political arena. Moreover, the intermittent imprisonment of CPP leaders diminished the beneficial effect that the king's occasional overtures in their direction might have had.[64]

During the period of royal dictatorship, the CPP maintained its preeminent position in Croat political life. Though Radić's successor, Vladko Maček, did not possess Radić's charisma, he became a popular leader in his own right, and under his leadership the CPP continued to grow. Peasant populism and Croat nationalism still defined the party's creed, but the latter was now more strongly emphasized. The CPP, which resembled less a party than a movement, as CPP leaders were fond of calling it, had attracted a wide and diverse following. Its amorphous character was reinforced by the absence of formal institutional structures. Radić had run the party in a loose fashion. After Maček became president he too adopted this style, relying on only a few close personal advi-

---

64. This state-sponsored party had several names: in 1932 the Radical Peasant Democratic Party, in 1933 the Yugoslav National Party, and in 1936 the Yugoslav Radical Union.

sors.[65] This gave him a free hand in devising his strategy toward the Serb parties and dynasty.

Maček and other CPP leaders initially seemed receptive to the proclamation of royal dictatorship. Their hopes waned, however, when it became clear that the same politicians would govern now as before. In January 1929, Maček called for a reorganization of the state on the basis of six cultural-historical territories and for the formation of a "nonpolitical" government. After the 1931 constitution was introduced, the Peasant-Democratic Coalition attempted to rally support for constitutional revision. In 1932, it released a statement, the Zagreb Resolution (*Zagrebačke punktacije*), denouncing Serbian hegemony and calling for a federal system "established on an association of interests."[66] The king rejected any major constitutional revisions, though he initiated negotiations with Maček in 1931 and again when Maček was in prison in 1933.[67] Nevertheless, Maček remained convinced that Aleksandar could not govern long without him, and he decided to bide his time until the monarch offered him an acceptable deal.[68] It took King Aleksandar's death in October 1934 and changes in the external environment to end the political stalemate over the Croat question, but this strategy ultimately proved successful.

---

65. The CPP Main Committee, composed of six hundred members, which was supposed to choose the president, failed to meet on this occasion or thereafter. For a discussion of the CPP's organizational structure, see Fikreta Jelić-Butić, *Hrvatska seljačka stranka* (Zagreb, 1985), 1-30.

66. During his confinement, Pribićević changed his views. He now saw the king as the source of all troubles and endorsed republicanism and federalism. He disagreed with Maček's priorities, however, and argued that struggle against the dictatorship must take precedence over changing the state structure. For a discussion of Pribićević's views during this period see Boban, *Svetozar Pribićević u opoziciji, 1928-1936*.

67. In mid-1929, CPP leaders Juraj Krnjević and August Košutić went abroad to seek support for the CPP and a resolution to the Croat question. They initially embraced the idea of "the worse, the better," hoping that the king's dictatorship would force the world to take the Croat question more seriously. They also hoped to force Serb parties to concede to Croat demands.

68. Boban, *Svetozar Pribićević u opoziciji, 1928-1936*, 50-55. Pribićević and IDP leaders felt the PDC should oppose the regime more actively. Pribićević complained bitterly about Maček's "passivity" in his relations with the king and the Serb ruling parties during this period.

Prince Paul and the CPP, 1934-1939

When King Aleksandar was assassinated in 1934, the political situation in Yugoslavia did not initially improve. Ustasha involvement in the king's assassination had strained Serb-Croat relations, and the government remained unwilling to reopen the constitutional question. It did release Maček from prison as a gesture of good will, however, and several months later Prince Paul met with the Peasant Party leader. Maček had a good impression of the Regent, remarking that he did not see "a trace of Serbian chauvinism" in him.[69] At this meeting, Maček suggested solving the Croat question through the continuation of the dynastic dictatorship or the formation of a nonpolitical government which would organize new elections for a constituent assembly. Prince Paul, who doesn't seem to have had an equally high regard for Maček, rejected the CPP leader's proposals. He argued that a nonpolitical government would be weak in the foreign arena, and more importantly, that constitutional revision could not be considered until Prince Peter came of age in September 1941.[70] His second meeting with Maček a year later reached the same impasse. Still, small steps toward a resolution of the constitutional question were discernible. By 1936, both sides reportedly agreed in principle on the need to introduce a federal system, if not on the number or size of its units.[71]

While Maček and Prince Paul circled each other with greater interest, the United Opposition, comprised of several Serb parties, extended feelers to the Peasant-Democratic Coalition. In the fall of 1937, the PDC joined the United Opposition in a platform supporting a unified state with a Serbian dynasty, an end to the 1931 constitution, and new elections to a constituent assembly.[72] There was serious tension within this alliance between the Serb parties, which believed political democratization should be their first priority, and the CPP, which considered constitutional revision primary.[73] Nevertheless, the United Opposition did

---

69. Ljubo Boban, *Maček i politika HSS, 1928-1941* (Zagreb, 1972), vol. 1, 198.

70. *Ibid.*, 199.

71. *Ibid.*, 218-219. In a memorandum written by Robert Seton-Watson in 1936, he emphasized the points of agreement between the two sides. According to him, Maček had dropped any questions about the dynasty and both sides agreed in principle on a federation, although the number and size of its units remained to be worked out.

72. *Ibid.*, 291-293.

73. *Ibid.*, 295.

extremely well in the rigged 1937 elections, garnering 44% of the vote to the Yugoslav Radical Union's inflated 54%.

The prince and his government, who feared the size of this opposition, were now more inclined to look for a concrete solution to the Croat question. Paul replaced his powerful Serb prime minister Milan Stojadinović with Dragiša Cvetković, who began negotiations with the CPP. Maček considered including the United Opposition in these negotiations, but he was unwilling to jeopardize the possibility of agreement by taking into account the wishes of his Serb partners. Furthermore, the prince-regent was dead set against it.[74] So, Maček negotiated an agreement without his opposition partners, robbing the CPP of potential Serb support for the agreement once it took effect. In August 1939, after months of wrangling over the shape of the new state unit, the Cvetković-Maček Agreement (*Sporazum*) created a single Croatian "Banovina" and endowed it with considerable powers.[75] After almost two decades, an agreement was finally reached changing Croatia's status in the Yugoslav state.

The Croatian Banovina, 1939-1941: The CPP in Power

The *Sporazum* ushered in a new phase in resolving the Croat question and a new phase in the CPP's political activities. Previously, the Peasant Party had opposed the government, except for the brief period in 1926 and 1927. With the creation of the Croatian Banovina, the CPP assumed the responsibilities of the governing party and began to engage in the kind of state-building activities it had previously shunned. During the few years of the Banovina's existence, the CPP performed its new role with mixed success. Its attempts to institutionalize Croatia's autonomous political status were hindered by its failure to resolve some larger questions about the Yugoslav state order.

The *Sporazum*, based on a provision of the 1931 constitution which allowed the king "to take by decree all extraordinary and necessary measures" to defend the security of state, created a Croatian unit encompassing the prewar territory of Croatia, most of Slavonia, Dalmatia and parts

---

74. *Ibid.*, 295-305.

75. Cvetković and Maček reached an agreement in April 1939 but Prince Paul rejected it. He objected to the idea of carrying out a plebiscite in areas of Bosnia and the Vojvodina to determine whether they should be included in the Croatian Banovina. For a description of the negotiations see Ljubo Boban, *Sporazum Cvetković-Maček* (Zagreb, 1964), 139-190.

of Bosnia-Hercegovina.[76] The *Sporazum* stipulated that Croatia's definitive borders were to be fixed during a future reorganization of the state.
Meanwhile, Croat officials were granted authority over trade, agriculture, industry, forests, construction, mining, social questions, health, justice, physical education, and internal administration. In 1941, control
over the regional gendarmerie was added to this list.[77] National defense;
foreign affairs; the postal, telegraph, and telephone systems; and foreign
trade and commerce were left to the central government. A constitutional
court was to be established to adjudicate jurisdictional disputes between
the Banovina and the central government. When the *Sporazum* was
signed, a new cabinet consisting primarily of members of the Peasant-
Democratic Coalition and Croat Peasant Party was formed in Belgrade.
Parliament was dissolved and, pending new elections, the cabinet ruled
by decree. After the elections, Parliament was to ratify the Agreement
and devise a new constitution.

The new arrangement considerably strengthened the CPP, but also
subjected it to certain strains as it changed from an opposition to a governing party. During the previous several years, the CPP had greatly expanded its organizational network. After 1935, it founded in towns and
villages several landholders cooperatives (*gospodarska sloga*) for economic
issues and renewed the activity of the peasant cooperatives for cultural
and educational work among peasants.[78] In order to strengthen its position among workers of peasant origin, it renewed the Croat Workers
Union in 1935. All these groups received support from the new Croatian
government, which drew them into a corporatist network of political
organizations. Most importantly, the CPP's paramilitary force, the
Peasant Defense, now became the legal arm of the Banovina.

While these organizations strengthened the CPP and facilitated its
penetration of the population, other forces weakened the Peasant Party.
Many groups in the CPP rediscovered their differences now that they
were no longer working for the same clearly defined goal. Some objected
to the CPP's approach to various social and economic questions; others
opposed its "concessions" to Belgrade concerning Croatia's political
independence. There is little concrete evidence on the extent of "differentiation," the term used by Yugoslav historians, in the CPP at this time.[79] It

---

76. *Ibid.*, 194-199.

77. *Ibid.*, 209.

78. Jelić-Butić, *Hrvatska seljačka stranka*, 35-37.

79. For example, Ljubo Boban argues that the CPP was rapidly
"differentiating" during this period and that the Peasant Party entered the

is clear, however, that both Communists and Ustashas became more active during this period and influenced many CPP members.

The Ustashas posed a growing threat to the CPP's political position during these years, though Peasant Party leaders do not always appear to have perceived them as such. A fascist organization which embraced an integral Croat nationalism, the Ustasha dramatically increased its strength before the Second World War. Emerging from the Frankist variant of Croat national ideologies, it previously had been a relatively marginal force in Croat political life. Ustasha founder Ante Pavelić, a lawyer from Lika and formerly a leader of the Party of Croatian Rights, had vehemently opposed the Yugoslav state since its inception. After he went into exile in 1929, Pavelić began recruiting Croats living abroad and overseeing their political indoctrination and military training in a network of camps in Italy and Hungary.[80] In 1932, the Ustasha-Croat Revolutionary Organization was officially formed.[81] It pledged to use all means, including terrorism, to fight for an independent Croatian state, encompassing Bosnia and Hercegovina, which would grant political rights only to Croats. While Ustasha political activity was greatly restricted in Yugoslavia, Ustashas did manage to instigate an uprising in Lika in 1932 and to assassinate King Aleksandar in 1934.[82] Meanwhile, they waited for the most auspicious time, an Italian invasion of Yugoslavia, to return to their homeland and assume power.

The Italians had long seen the Ustashas as a useful tool in their efforts to expand militarily in the Balkans, though their support for the Ustasha organization fluctuated according to the dictates of Italian foreign policy. After public outcry over the assassination of King Aleksandar, the Italians decreased their support for the Ustashas and even briefly imprisoned Pavelić. When Nazi Germany began expanding militarily, however, the Ustashas returned to Italian favor. Mussolini considered

---

wartime period already in a greatly weakened state. See Boban, *Maček i politika HSS*, vol. 2, 150-165.

80. By the mid-1930s, the Ustashas were training approximately five hundred men in these camps.

81. See chapter two for a discussion of the Ustashas' relations with the Communists during this period.

82. In 1931, Ustashas in Yugoslavia instigated an uprising in the Velebit Range of Lika. A small group of Ustashas took over the local gendarmerie as a prelude to a Croat nationalist uprising. They were quickly overcome and the local population subjected to harsh repression. Though Pavelić was discouraged from initiating any more armed actions in Yugoslavia, the incident became a *cause celebre* among some left circles abroad. For a discussion of this uprising, see Bogdan Krizman, *Ante Pavelić i ustaše* (Zagreb, 1978).

Pavelić essential to realizing his expansionist aims in Yugoslavia, especially after Maček reached an agreement with Belgrade in 1939. Consequently, in January 1940, Pavelić was invited to meet with Italian foreign minister Count Ciano to discuss conditions for establishing an independent Croatian state, and he received assurances of Italian support for installing the Ustashas in power. Pavelić would have to wait a while longer for Mussolini to invade Yugoslavia; but it was clear that when he did, the Ustashas would play an important role.[83]

Ironically, Ustashas in Yugoslavia also received an important boost in morale and support from the thaw in Yugoslav-Italian relations in the spring of 1937. In an agreement between prime ministers Stojadinović and Ciano, both sides pledged to stop supporting terrorist groups hostile to the other. As a result, approximately two hundred and sixty Ustashas were returned to Yugoslavia, where Stojadinović believed he could keep a better eye on them.[84] He also wished to use them to weaken the CPP and consequently permitted many of them to resume political activity. Although formal Ustasha organizations did not exist in Yugoslavia at this time, Ustasha leaders established the cooperative *Uzdanica* (Hope) which gathered its followers into illegal paramilitary cells and founded the journal *Hrvatski narod* (Croat People) to spread the Ustasha message.

As Ustasha activity in Yugoslavia increased, its relations with the CPP deteriorated. In 1938, Ustasha leader Mile Budak met several times with Maček (who received him cordially) and criticized the Peasant Party leader for "going too far" toward an agreement with Belgrade. Although some Ustasha members advocated cooperation with the CPP in the 1938 elections, by 1939 all talk of cooperation between the two groups had ceased.[85] Pavelić vehemently denounced the *Sporazum* in 1939 and directed Ustasha organizations in the country to oppose the CPP. Maček and his Peasant Party now became a main target of Ustasha propaganda.

Despite this escalating anti-CPP propaganda, Maček was initially reluctant to move firmly against the Ustashas. The Peasant Party viewed the Communists as the main threat and directed their most repressive measures against the Communist Party of Croatia. Moreover, some of their organizations, especially the Peasant Defense units, had been infiltrated by Ustashas and could not be used against them. Finally, CPP leaders hesitated to damage Croat unity by attacking Croat nationalists.

---

83. *Ibid.*, 365-370. Though Mussolini discussed these plans for the Ustashas, Pavelić was unsure until the last moment that they would actually materialize.

84. For example, Mile Budak returned to Zagreb and became one of the main organizers of Ustasha activities in the country.

85. Krizman, *Ante Pavelić i ustaše*, 313.

After the outbreaks of Ustasha violence at the beginning of 1940, numerous Ustasha leaders were imprisoned. But the Croatian government remained preoccupied with other concerns and, for the most part, let this challenge to its authority go unchecked. This unwillingness to harness the Ustashas weakened the CPP's political position and further strained its already poor relations with the Serb political parties.

In addition to growing disunity within its own ranks, the CPP also faced serious economic and political problems in governing the Croatian Banovina. Shortly after its establishment, the new government became embroiled in a fierce struggle over finances. The Banovina's extensive powers of administrative competency were contingent upon reaching an agreement with Belgrade about finances. It was originally decided that since Croats comprised 29.5% of the population, 29.5% of federal revenue would be transferred to Croatia.[86] But the CPP objected to this arrangement, protesting that this revenue could not support poverty stricken areas such as Dalmatia. Finally in March 1940, a new regulation was signed granting Croatia certain tax raising powers previously under federal jurisdiction. While this effort to ensure fiscal autonomy ultimately proved successful and undoubtedly contributed to the government's popularity in Croatia, it diverted the Banovina's attention from other more pressing problems concerning the overall settlement of Yugoslavia's constitutional order.

The most serious problem the Peasant Party faced was growing opposition to the *Sporazum* from Serb political parties. Democrats and some Radicals began to demand a comprehensive solution to the state order instead of one that simply addressed the status of Croatia and to call for the establishment of a Serbian state unit with powers of jurisdiction similar to those granted Croatia.[87] Both parties attempted to incite opposition to the *Sporazum* among Serbs in Croatia, making significant inroads into support for the Independent Democratic Party. Though Maček wanted to hold elections first in order to solidify his position, the Radicals and Democrats insisted that the question of the state order be determined beforehand. Meanwhile, Serbs and Croats also began to argue over the status of Bosnia-Hercegovina, which they both claimed as their own territory. As relations between the opposition and governing parties worsened, Cvetković and Maček relied more on each other and avoided confronting these divisive issues. It became increasingly clear, however,

---

86. Boban, *Maček i politika HSS, 1928-1941*, vol. 2, 148.

87. Boban, *Sporazum Cvetković-Maček*, 303-316. Some Radicals refused to support establishing a separate unit for Serbia since that would mean endorsing federalism.

that there could be no solution to the Croat question independent of general constitutional reform and without the agreement of other political forces in the country. The CPP's attempts to avoid tackling this problem simply worsened its already strained relations with the Serb political parties and diminished its chances for negotiating a favorable settlement to the constitutional question in the future.

Less than two years after it was passed, the *Sporazum* was negated by the Axis invasion and occupation of Yugoslavia. Given its short existence, it is impossible to surmise whether the 1939 arrangement was a viable solution to the Croat question. Some Yugoslav historians have condemned Maček's attempts to establish the Banovina, charging that he was prepared to consider establishing an independent Croatia under Italian suzerainty if negotiations with Belgrade did not produce the desired result.[88] There is little concrete evidence to support this charge, or to view Maček's contacts with the Italians as anything more than efforts to strengthen his hand in negotiations with Belgrade.[89] It is true, however, that Ustasha elements advocating such a course had increasingly infiltrated CPP ranks. By introducing real, though partial, federalism, the *Sporazum* loosened the political deadlock over the Croat question. Nevertheless, it was only a first step. Final resolution of this problem required a new constitutional order. Whether the political consensus for major reform could have been created without the threat of war is questionable. The political experience of the Kingdom of Yugoslavia in the interwar years makes this outcome difficult to imagine.

88. For example, see V. Terzić, *Slom kraljevine Jugoslavije: uzroci i posledice poraza* (Belgrade, 1982); and Ferdo Čulinović, *Jugoslavija izmedju dva rata* (Zagreb, 1961), vols. 1 and 2.

89. In March 1939, Maček's associate, A. Carnelutti, met with Ciano in Italy. It is not clear whether Carnelutti had Maček's approval for this meeting; Maček claimed he did not. Carnelutti apparently suggested to Ciano that if negotiations with Belgrade failed, the CPP would support establishing an independent Croatia which would eventually be joined through a personal union with Italy. Boban argues that both the CPP and Italian leaders had good reasons to make contact at this point. According to him, the CPP was trying to overcome its international isolation, caused by Stojadinović's policies, and used this initiative to strengthen its hand in Belgrade. This policy was just one of several CPP initiatives at the time and should not be taken more seriously than Maček's overtures toward western countries. See Boban, *Maček i politika HSS*, vol. 1, 115-118.

Conclusion

In the first two decades of Yugoslavia's existence, the Croat question was the main preoccupation of all political groups and a major source of weakness in the Yugoslav state. During this period, Serbs and Croats occupied different political positions in the state order: Serbs controlled the political apparatus and were consequently most intimately involved in constructing the new state; Croats for the most part were in opposition to the government and bent on reforming the political order. The Croat question influenced the views of both groups toward the Yugoslav state and its constitutional order and determined their strategies for achieving their political goals. Ultimately, the elites of both groups failed to work out the relation between nation and state in a way that allowed them to build a viable South Slav state.

Although they dominated the apparatus of the Yugoslav state for most of the interwar period, Serb elites proved unwilling to adopt an effective strategy for balancing Croat national sentiments with their state-building goals. Their national ideology and political experience led them to envision a unitary state based on the expansion of Serbia. Looking largely to the experience of building the Serbian state in the past century, they were unable to comprehend that a centralized state was not necessarily a strong state. For them, responding to the national sentiments of Yugoslavia's national groups, especially Croats, meant unleashing destructive centrifugal tendencies. Consequently, in the first two years after the establishment of the new state, Serb leaders simply expanded the apparatus of the Serbian state to include the territories outside of Serbia. Moreover, in the Vidovdan Constitution of 1921, they rejected the adoption of a federal political order.

There is some possibility that even after Serbs rejected a federal state order they might have been able to mitigate Croat hostility toward the new state. However, they failed to introduce any meaningful form of political autonomy or the administrative decentralization that Pašić had promised. Nor did they attempt to procure Croat loyalty to the state by ensuring Croats a privileged position in the bureaucracy or army, a strategy that was occasionally employed toward other national groups in Yugoslavia. Although Pašić intermittently initiated negotiations with Radić, and later, King Aleksander and Prince Paul with Maček, they were unwilling to seek the kind of coalitional or consociational agreement that could have resulted in a stable political order.

Serbs' inability to address effectively the Croat question had two serious consequences. First, it hindered the government from introducing necessary social and economic reforms. The diversion of precious political resources into parliamentary squabbling over the Croat question hindered the government from undertaking a serious program of economic development. In 1939, Yugoslavia was plagued by economic and social problems of enormous proportions. Secondly, political stalemate over the Croat question undermined democratic institutions and ultimately allowed King Aleksandar to establish a dictatorship. As Serbs continued to dominate the state order in the next decade, the political atmosphere became increasingly polarized and violent. Although Aleksandar's successor, Prince-Regent Paul, was eventually forced to initiate a radically different approach to the Croat question and to accede to CPP demands for a federal order, the ensuing political reform could not entirely reverse the previous state-building failures of Serb political elites.

The Croat Peasant Party must also bear some responsibility for the state-building failures of the political elites in interwar Yugoslavia. Croats' national ideologies and political experience left them with conflicting sentiments toward the new South Slav state and how it should be organized. While they viewed the state as a necessary protection against powerful neighbors, they also possessed a strong desire for an independent political unit. The leadership of the Croat Peasant Party reflected this ambivalence toward the Yugoslav state by appearing at times to pursue a federal political arrangement and at other times to pursue the establishment of an independent Croatian state. This ambivalence created ill will among Serb leaders, who felt Croats were not always negotiating in good faith, and hindered Croats from seriously attempting to resolve difficult political and economic problems.

During the formative period of the Yugoslav state, when it might have been possible to reach an accommodation with Serbs about the state order, Radić refused to participate in the political process in Belgrade. Although he had the political courage to pursue negotiations with the Pašić government in 1925, Radić stopped short of earnestly seeking a coalition partner in the Serb political parties. Instead, in an attempt to weaken his opposition, he supported efforts by the king to divide the Radical Party by whatever means he could. In the 1930s, the Croat Peasant Party allowed itself to be increasingly infiltrated by separatist elements from the Ustashas and the Frankovci. Consequently, even as Maček was concluding the *Sporazum* establishing the Croatian Banovina, the CPP's commitment to the Yugoslav state was weakened. The failure of the CPP to tackle the pressing matter of constitutional reform once it assumed power in 1939, or to adopt a wider Yugoslav view, hindered its efforts to achieve an enduring solution to the Croat question within the Yugoslav state.

As the decade drew to a close in Yugoslavia, Serbs and Croats alike became increasingly preoccupied with the growing German threat on Yugoslavia's border. The Axis invasion of Yugoslavia would have resulted in the break-up of the state in any case; Yugoslav armed forces under the best of circumstances would have been helpless to prevent the occupation and dismemberment of their country. But the state-building failures of the interwar Serb and Croat elites, especially their inability to resolve the Croat question, undoubtedly weakened the Yugoslav state and contributed to the outbreak of civil violence in 1941.

2

The CPY and the Croat Question in the Interwar State

While the Croat question was the main preoccupation of the non-Communist political parties during the interwar years, it also monopolized the attention of the CPY. Communist goals in devising an effective approach to the Croat question were different, of course, from those of the non-Communist political parties. Rather than resolving it (which for most Serbs meant minimizing Croat opposition to a centralized political order and for most Croats meant instituting some kind of federal system through constitutional reform), Communists sought to exploit it to increase their own popular support and, ultimately, to further their revolutionary goals. However, Yugoslav Communists proved incapable of transforming national discontent, especially among Croats, into support for themselves. Indeed, the party was so divided by the Croat question that at one point it was in danger of sharing the fate of its Polish counterpart and being disbanded by the Comintern. Some scholars have attributed the CPY's failure to devise a sensible and credible approach to the national question to inept Comintern meddling.[1] While this perspective correctly highlights the damage caused by Comintern policy, it minimizes the genuine disagreement among Yugoslav Communist leaders about the character of national conflict in their country. The Croat question was at the heart of this disagreement and bitterly divided the party during the first two decades of its existence.

The Unification Period

Although the Croat question became extremely divisive to the CPY in later years, it figured little in party struggles during the unification

---

1. For example, see Ivan Avakumović, *History of the Communist Party of Yugoslavia* (Aberdeen, Scotland: Aberdeen University Press, 1964).

period.[2] The several Social Democratic Parties in the territory comprising the new Kingdom of Serbs, Croats, and Slovenes had different heritages and they disagreed on a number of questions; their unification into one party was a difficult task.[3] They did initially agree, however, on the best approach to the national question in the new state. Social Democrats from both areas held that Serbs, Croats, and Slovenes were three tribes of one nation and advocated a unitary political order. Unmindful of growing discontent with this order in Croatia, they expected the Croat populace to support the new Yugoslav state.

The three main Social Democratic parties in the South Slav lands of Austria-Hungary before the war took similar approaches to the question of Croatian statehood. Originally, these parties endorsed the Austro-Marxist position on the national question and advocated Croat cultural autonomy within Austria-Hungary. This approach was modified before the war when Croat and Slovene Social Democrats embraced South Slav political unity at the Ljubljana Conference in 1910. During the war, three different approaches to the Croat question emerged: some Social Democrats supported unification with Serbia, others continued to support South Slav unification within Austria-Hungary, and "leftists," concerned foremost with world proletarian revolution, neither supported nor opposed the establishment of a Yugoslav state. By the end of the war, these last two groups advocated unity with Serbia in a centralized political order. They had different ideas, however, about how to unite the numerous Social Democratic parties on Yugoslav territory and about the role of social democracy in the new state.

The Serbian Social Democratic Party (SSDP) had been historically less concerned with the national question and South Slav unity than Social Democrats in the South Slav lands of Austria-Hungary.[4] The SSDP was a

---

2. For a discussion of the Social Democratic position on the national question before and during the unification of Yugoslavia, see Ivo Banac, "The Communist Party of Yugoslavia during the Period of Legality, 1919-1921" in *War and Society in East Central Europe*, Ivo Banac (ed.) (Brooklyn, New York: Atlantic Studies, 1983); Aleksa Djilas, *The Contested Country*, 37-65; Gordana Vlajčić, *Jugoslavenska revolucija i nacionalno pitanje, 1919-1927* (Zagreb, 1974); Dušan Lukač, *Radnički pokret u Jugoslaviji i nacionalno pitanje 1918-1941* (Belgrade, 1972).

3. The four main Social Democratic parties were the Social Democratic Party of Croatia and Slavonia, the Yugoslav Social Democratic Party, operating primarily in Slovenia and including the Social Democratic Party of Dalmatia, the Social Democratic Party of Bosnia, and the Serbian Social Democratic Party.

4. The SSDP adamantly opposed federalism. In November 1918, Serb Social Democrats firmly rejected a demand by the Serbian Young Socialists in Paris to

more theoretically oriented party and was less inclined to engage in trade union work or to organize peasants, who were firmly under the sway of the Radicals. Consequently, it followed the doctrinaire line that the bourgeoisie was responsible for national unification. The SSDP's approach to the national question also reflected Serb national ideology, which was less interested in South Slav unity. By the beginning of the First World War, however, Serb Social Democrats adopted a position closer to that of the Social Democratic parties in Croatia and Slovenia and began to advocate the formation of a new South Slav state.[5]

During the first year of Yugoslavia's existence in 1919, disagreements among Social Democrats centered around the question of whether they should enter the new government. Numerous Croat and Slovene Social Democrats argued that the time was not ripe for revolution and that Social Democrats could best achieve their purpose by working for reform within the government. The left wing of the Social Democratic Party of Croatia and Slavonia and the majority of Serb Social Democrats opposed this so-called "ministerialist" strategy. Conflict between leftists and ministerialists peaked before the Unification Conference in January 1919. Croat Social Democrats were excluded from the Congress, and the new Socialist Worker's Party of Yugoslavia (Communist) (SWPYC) adopted the SSDP's general orientation toward the national question.[6] According the national question little importance, the Congress resolution simply stated that SWPYC favored a single nation state with self-governing regional and local units.[7]

---

establish the new Yugoslav state on a federal basis. See Gordana Vlajčić, *Osma konferencija zagrebačkih komunista* (Zagreb, 1976), 13.

5. The SSDP embraced this policy shortly after the Niš Declaration. See Janković, *Srbija i jugoslovensko pitanje, 1914-1915,* 280-310.

6. The fight over "ministerialism" began with the formation of the new state. It came to a head at the Social Domocratic Party of Croatia and Slavonia (SDPCS) Conference in January 1919. The Croat Social Democratic Minister Korać and his supporters passed a resolution denouncing bolshevism. Leftists, however, gained control of the trade unions in Croatia. After the conference they held a secret meeting and elected a leadership which gained the support of Zagreb Social Democrats, and they expelled the ministerialist leaders from the SDPCS in March 1919. They then directed the Serbian Social Democratic Party to hold a conference of all Socialist parties (Unification Congress) from which the SDPCS was excluded. See Banac, "The Communist Party of Yugoslavia during the Period of Legality, 1919-1921," 194-196; and Vlajčić, *Osma konferencija zagrebačkih komunista,* 15-18.

7. Many Social Democrats returning from the Soviet Union had endorsed the Bolshevik position of encouraging the rights of self-determination and federal-

Despite evidence of growing dissatisfaction over the unitary political order, especially in Croatia, Communists continued to ignore the national question. But the party was troubled by an incipient national struggle in its own ranks which reflected conflict between Serbs and Croats over centralization in the larger political arena. Conflict between centrists and leftists erupted soon after SWPYC was formed. Centrists objected to the radical revolutionary orientation of the party and the centralization of party organizations, though it was mostly Croats and Slovenes who contested the latter. In August 1919, Croat centrists demanded that the party be federalized on the basis of the old regional units and that it remain separate from union organizations. Meanwhile, despite SWPYC electoral gains, other centrists became uneasy with the revolutionary orientation of the party after several Communist leaders were arrested in the fall. These concerns prompted centrists to convene the Second Party Congress in 1920 in order to modify the party program.

The CPY founding congress (Vukovar Congress) in June 1920 dispelled the hopes of those centrists who wished to retain regional autonomy within the party. Party leftists gained control of the party leadership at the Congress and replaced the existing regional leaderships with secretariats whose members were appointed by the CPY Central Party Council.[8] Centrists in Croatia opposed this decision and in some instances refused to yield control of party newspapers and treasuries. They also resisted CPY efforts to centralize the unions and bind them to party organizations. Leftists succeeded in establishing their control over the unions shortly thereafter and expelled several Croat centrists from the CPY; but they were unable to establish unity within the party.[9]

---

ism. These Communists initially objected to the SSDP's orientation to the national question in Yugoslavia. By the spring of 1919, however, they had adopted the SSDP's position and endorsed the Congress resolution. For a discussion of these "Pelagićists" see Lukač, *Radnički pokret u Jugoslaviji i nacionalno pitanje, 1918-1941*, 20-22.

8. The Unification Congress had implicitly recognized the autonomy of regional party leaders by establishing executive committees in Belgrade, Zagreb, Ljubljana, Sarajevo, Novi Sad and Split.

9. Centrists from Serbia and Bosnia had stood aloof from this battle over centralization. But they entered the fray shortly thereafter when the Comintern published its twenty-one conditions for joining the international Communist movement. Objecting to these conditions, and the ultrarevolutionary emphasis of the Vukovar Congress, the centrists published a "Manifesto of the Opposition in the CPY" in November 1920. The Manifesto was written by Živko Topalović and signed by over one hundred Socialists from Serbia, Bosnia and Croatia. Many of these centrists were expelled from the party one month later. In June 1921, they

Elections to the Constituent Assembly in the fall of 1920 revealed that CPY insensitivity to Croat national sentiments had hurt its standing there. Though Communists did well in the elections, ranking fourth in total votes, they did relatively poorly in Croatia where they garnered only seven percent of the vote.[10] Until this time, Communists had refused to cooperate with Radić, viewing him, in the words of one Communist, "as a tool in bourgeois tribal competition and a hindrance to class struggle."[11] During the elections to the Constituent Assembly, the CPY denounced indiscriminantly the CRPP, "clericalists," and Frankovci.[12] After the election, in response to overwhelming popular support for the CRPP, the CPY began to court the Peasant Party. CPY Secretary Sima Marković contacted Radić directly and attempted to convince him of Communist support for a Croat peasant republic.[13] He also expressed sympathy for Croats in the Constituent Assembly and acknowledged that many Croats viewed themselves as a separate nation, though he did not agree with this view. Still, the CPY's opposition to federalism (let alone a Croatian republic) remained fundamentally unchanged and, not surprisingly, its overtures toward the CRPP produced no concrete cooperation.

By 1921, CPY leaders began to reexamine their attitude toward the CRPP and the Croat national movement. The *Obznana* (Pronouncement) of December 1920, in which the government decreed the dissolution of Communist organizations, and the Law for the Protection of the State passed nine months later outlawing communism greatly weakened the party.[14] As a result, Communist leaders began to question their nationalities policy, and their policy toward Croatia in particular. Moreover, the Comintern, which had denounced the Yugoslav state as a creation of Serbian chauvinism, increasingly criticized Communists' support for the Yugoslav state and their failure to champion Croat national aspirations. The growing popularity of Radić and the CRPP, and the support they received even from Moscow, forced the CPY to rethink its attitude toward the Croat national movement. During the next several years,

---

combined with Korać to form the Socialist Party of Yugoslavia. For a discussion of this struggle, see Vlajčić, *Osma konferencija zagrebačkih komunista*, 15-18; Lukač, *Radnički pokret u Jugoslaviji i nacionalno pitanje, 1918-1941*, 44-53.

10. Avakumović, *History of the Communist Party of Yugoslavia*, 45.

11. Lukač, *Radnički pokret u Jugoslaviji i nacionalno pitanje, 1918-1941*, 41.

12. *Ibid.*, 61.

13. Vlajčić, *Osma konferencija zagrebačkih komunista*, 19.

14. Mass arrests of Communists followed the passage of these two laws, almost bringing CPY activities, even in the trade unions, to a halt. By the end of 1923, the CPY had less than 1,000 active members.

Yugoslav Communists debated and fought over the best approach to the Croat question; this conflict ultimately left them divided and debilitated.

Conflict between Left and Right, 1921-1928

After the *Obznana,* two groups of leaders with different approaches to the Croat question emerged in the CPY. In May 1921, some Communist members of the Constituent Assembly formed a Central Party Council which, fearing the imminent arrest of party leaders, appointed an illegal party leadership in the country. The new leadership, consisting of several future "leftists," was charged with strengthening the illegal organization of the party. While this group adopted a more revolutionary orientation during the next several months, it also emphasized the importance of the national question. Meanwhile, a second center of CPY leaders was formed in Vienna in September of that year, consisting largely of Communists from Belgrade loyal to Sima Marković. This group of "rightists" took a more moderate stance on the question of revolution and at the same time minimized the importance of the national question.[15] These two centers issued contradictory instructions to Communist organizations in the country and refused to cooperate with each other. Both factions fought for control at the first party conference called a year later in Vienna.

At the First Party Conference in July 1922, in contrast to previous party congresses, the national question was a main topic of discussion.[16] At this conference, the left-wing and the right-wing elucidated their views on the Croat question for the first time. Rightists argued that

---

15. The terms left and right, when applied to the question of constitutional reform during this period, can be hopelessly confusing. The two terms generally describe the group's position toward revolution. Rightists took a more moderate stance toward the revolution. They emphasized the importance of reform and of concentrating on trade union work; for them the revolution was a more distant prospect. They also deemphasized the importance of the national question in Yugoslavia. Leftists were more revolutionary. They viewed the national question as more significant and wished to exploit its revolutionary potential.

16. The Conference refused to discuss this topic separately as requested by Novaković and other leftists. Most Yugoslav historians assert that the national question was not discussed explicitly until 1923. For example, see Janko Pleterski, *KPJ i nacionalno pitanje, 1919-1941* (Belgrade, 1971). Lukač argues that it became an important subject of discussion in 1922. See Lukač, *Radnički pokret u Jugoslaviji i nacionalno pitanje, 1918-1941,* 79-80.

nationalism was not strong among Croats but had recently been stirred up by the Croat bourgeoisie for its own purposes. They insisted that Croats could not be considered an oppressed people just because they were neglected by the Serb bourgeoisie. Rightists urged the CPY to support the "resolution of all national and tribal differences on the principle of self-determination," but they failed to elaborate this vague formula.[17] They also advocated cooperation with the Croat Bloc (a coalition of opposition parties), a position they repudiated several months later.

The Serb Kosta Novaković articulated the left's view at the conference. Although Novaković emphasized the importance of the national question to the Croat peasant, he opposed CPY cooperation with the Croat opposition and urged Communists to divide the Peasant Party's ranks. However, most of his fellow leftists from Croatia did not share his position toward the Peasant Party. Novaković also endorsed the "centrist" position that unions retain some autonomous powers at the regional (*oblasti*) level. Rightists prevailed at the conference and elected a new leadership with the rightist Mihailo Todorović as secretary general. They adopted a platform downplaying the importance of the national question. However, leftists refused to accept this outcome and took their grievances to the Comintern.[18]

The Comintern had already turned its attention to the CPY's nationalities policy on a number of occasions. As the factional struggles in the CPY leadership grew in 1922, the Comintern established a special Yugoslav Commission to consider this problem. In response to leftist complaints about rightist control of the first conference, the Comintern instructed leftists to accept the conference resolutions but changed the composition of the new leadership to include a leading leftist spokesman, Triša Kaclerović. At the Fourth Comintern Congress in 1922, both left and right factions presented their cases. They accused each other of opportunism and legalistic tendencies which, they claimed, had resulted in the party's failures in 1921. Rightists defended themselves from leftist charges that they acted prematurely and too harshly against the "centrists" in the CPY. They demanded that leftists adopt the resolutions of the first conference and pledge their loyalty to the current party leadership. Comintern leaders attempted to reach a compromise by making light of these disagreements and instructing Yugoslav Communists to overcome their "personal differences" by paying greater attention to organizational matters.

---

17. Vlajčić, *Jugoslavenska revolucija i nacionalno pitanje, 1919-1927*.
18. *Ibid.*, 63-87.

Despite Comintern efforts to quell the conflict between leftists and rightists in the CPY, hostility between the two groups appeared to have grown by the CPY's second conference in Vienna in May 1923.[19] At the conference, Kosta Novaković again presented the leftist position. He objected to Sima Marković's view that the national question was a bourgeois concern, arguing instead that it lay at the heart of the revolutionary movement in Yugoslavia.[20] Nevertheless, leftists did not go so far as to endorse the Comintern position that Serbs, Croats, and Slovenes were three nations. Rather, they believed the "tribal differences" between them could be overcome in the Yugoslav state. Although they would modify this position in the ensuing debate over the Croat question, at this point they were also skeptical of federalism, which they viewed as an exploitative tool of the Croat bourgeoisie.[21] The second conference adopted a leftist platform that stressed the importance of the national question and the right of self-determination.[22] It also advocated cooperation with other "organizations fighting for national justice" (the Croat Republican Peasant Party) and urged the CPY to develop its own autonomist program.[23] To this end, a discussion of the national question was launched.

Discussion about the national question occurred under the auspices of the People's Workers Party of Yugoslavia (PWPY), the legal political front of the CPY. The Belgrade journal *Radnik-Delavec* and the Zagreb journal *Borba* printed various polemical articles by CPY leaders. In May 1923, the editorial board of *Radnik-Delavec* outlined the questions the discussion should address and invited articles on the subject. The two most important questions were (1) the character of the "tribal" fight between the Serb bourgeoisie and the Croat and Slovene bourgeoisies and (2) given the character of this conflict, whether the best state would be federal, centralist, or one based on the principle of autonomy.[24] The ensuing discussion focused mainly on the character of the Croat national movement and Croat political demands.

The first person to respond to this invitation was the Serb Communist Pavle Pavlović in his two-part article in *Radnik-Delavec* at the end of June.

---

19. At this conference, in which the leftists were in a minority, the national question elicited a separate discussion.

20. Leopold Kobsa, "O gledištima KPJ na nacionalno pitanje u Jugoslaviji u razdoblju izmedju dva svjetska rata," *Naše teme* (July 1969).

21. Lukač, *Radnički pokret u Jugoslaviji i nacionalno pitanje, 1918-1941*, 120.

22. Vlajčić, *Osma konferencija zagrebačkih komunista*, 46-47.

23. Janko Pleterski, *KPJ i nacionalno pitanje, 1919-1941*. See also Lukač, *Radnički pokret u Jugoslaviji i nacionalno pitanje, 1918-1941*, 120.

24. Novica Vojinović, "Diskusija o nacionalnom pitanju u KPJ od 1918 do 1926 g.," *Prilozi za istoriju socijalizma* 8 (1971): 48-67.

This article represented a compromise between the views of the left and the right. Like other rightists, Pavlović derogated the importance of the national question, calling it a "mirage." Nevertheless, he sought to explain why the bourgeoisie had failed to accomplish its historical task of national unification. According to him, the Serb bourgeoisie had "forced" national unification during the war. In response, the Croat and Slovene bourgeoisies, especially the CRPP, had emphasized the "false national differences" of Yugoslavs.[25] Since they perceived themselves as culturally superior, Croat and Slovene leaders believed they should have a bigger say in running the state. Their pretensions, combined with Serbs' political avarice, had caused Serb and Croat bourgeoisies to compete with one another. Pavlović believed that CPY support for autonomy would be harmful in the present circumstances of national competition. The CPY should support self-determination, including the right to secession; but it must explain to the populace that these rights could be realized only by revolution and revolutionary methods, not by creating "tribal" blocs and movements.[26]

The Serb leftist Triša Kaclerović also supported the obligatory Leninist formula of self-determination in a draft resolution he prepared for the upcoming PWPY conference.[27] But he had a very different understanding of the roots of the Serb-Croat conflict and the manner in which it should be addressed. In contrast to Pavlović, Kaclerović placed the blame for this conflict squarely on the Serb bourgeoisie. Since the Slovene and Croat bourgeoisies were culturally and economically more developed, the Serb bourgeoisie felt compelled to suppress them. Serb repressive measures caused Croats to rally to the Croat bourgeoisie. Communists had failed to counter this development because they had no clear nationalities policy. According to Kaclerović, the CPY should support self-determination, including the right to secession, though only the CPY and the international proletariat could interpret this right.[28] However, he was reluctant to cooperate with the CRPP and denounced the "traitorous and confusing policies" of Radić.[29]

When Croat Communists entered this discussion at the end of August 1923, it took a more radical turn. In his articles published in August, the leftist Ante Ciliga offered a different solution to the national problem in

25. Lukač, *Radnički pokret u Jugoslaviji i nacionalno pitanje, 1918-1941,* 131.

26. *Ibid.,* 130-131.

27. *Borba,* 7/27/23; *Radnik-Delavec,* 7/8/23, cited in Lukač, *Radnički pokret u Jugoslaviji i nacionalno pitanje, 1918-1941,* 133-134.

28. Lukač, *Radnički pokret u Jugoslaviji i nacionalno pitanje, 1918-1941,* 133-134.

29. Vojinović, "Diskusija o nacionalnom pitanju u KPJ od 1918 do 1926 g.," 60.

Yugoslavia.[30] Ciliga objected to Serb Communists' tendency to understand the national question as a solely bourgeois concern. He argued that
such an understanding caused the CPY to underestimate the revolutionary power of national liberation movements. Like Kaclerović and
Pavlović Ciliga did not question the ultimately progressive goal of
"weaving together" Serb, Croat, and Slovene tribes. For this reason, he
saw Yugoslavia as a "necessary evil."[31] But, according to Ciliga, the Serb
bourgeoisie had caused Croat and Slovene separatism and was incapable
of furthering national unification. The CPY must therefore facilitate unification by supporting some form of political autonomy. Ciliga did not
clarify what he meant by autonomy, which he used interchangeably with
federalism, but he did call upon the CPY to develop a more precise definition of this term.

Another Croat intellectual, August Cesarec, took this support for federalism even further.[32] Although Cesarec, along with other prominent
Croat intellectuals, had been a member of the pro-Yugoslav revolutionary youth before the war, he did not advocate CPY support for a unitary
state under the present circumstances. Cesarec challenged the idea that
the new Yugoslav state was primarily a product of the war. Many other
factors had contributed to unification, he said, though the process was
subsequently hindered by different cultural and economic heritages.[33]
Like Kaclerović, Cesarec attributed Serbian hegemonism to the weakness
of the Serb bougeoisie. He argued that federalism was the best way to
reduce this hegemony. Federalism was the most appropriate political
system for a multinational society in transition from a national to a proletarian revolution. It allowed the populace to "outgrow" nationalism and
ultimately to support democratic centralism. But, even though he
believed federalism the best form of the state, Cesarec urged the CPY to
support confederation or even seccession if the Croat Republican Peasant
Party endorsed this goal.[34] Eventually the Croat bourgeoisie, which he
believed was represented by the CRPP, would compromise itself and the

30. *Borba*, 8/28,29,30/23; cited in Novica Vojinović, "Federalizam u koncepcijama KPJ u periodu 1919-1928," in *Medjunarodni radnički pokret* (Belgrade, 1972),
238.
31. Vojinović, "Diskusija o nacionalnom pitanju u KPJ od 1918 do 1926 g.," 48.
32. *Borba*, 8/16,23,30/23 and 9/6/23, cited in Lukač, *Radnički pokret u Jugoslaviji i nacionalno pitanje, 1918-1941*, 144-150.
33. Dušan Lukač, "Učesnici iz Hrvatske u diskusiji o nacionalnom pitanju u
NPRJ 1923g.," *Časopis za suvremenu povijest*, 35.
34. Lukač, *Radnički pokret u Jugoslaviji i nacionalno pitanje, 1918-1941*, 145.

CPY would attract Peasant Party supporters. Meanwhile, the party must support the goals of the Croat national movement, whatever their form.

These articles by Ciliga and Cesarec made even many leftists uneasy. In a draft resolution on the national question prepared for the PWPY conference and published at the end of September 1923, the leftist Djuro Cvijić took a more moderate position.[35] Cvijić argued that even though the Kingdom of Serbs, Croats, and Slovenes had been brought about by the war, it had established the conditions for creating one nation from three related (*srodni*) peoples. However, economic differences between the three national bourgeoisies had caused them to diverge after unification. At present, the kingdom was not a national but a multinational state in which the Serbs ruled over everyone else. The CPY must, Cvijić argued, help complete the first stage of bourgeois and national revolution in Croatia and Slovenia. This revolution would create the conditions for eventually forming a worker-peasant republic in the Balkans.[36] Communists should support the right of self-determination, including secession, though they must not advocate the latter. Cvijić believed there was little support for secession in Croatia, but he emphasized that in any case the right of self-determination would diminish Croat secessionist sentiment.[37]

Differences between rightists and leftists crystallized after CPY Secretary Sima Marković published his book, *The National Question in the Light of Marxism*, at the end of September 1923. Though he endorsed many leftist views on the causes of national conflict in Yugoslavia, Marković came to different conclusions. According to him, Yugoslavia was formed by the disintegration of the Big Powers at the end of the war and the machinations of the South Slav bourgeoisies. Marković argued that when Yugoslavia was formed, Serbs, Croats, and Slovenes were already three separate peoples. The theory of one people, three names (which Marković himself had supported until recently) did not, he now stated, have any scientific basis. Rather, it was devised by the Serb bourgeoisie in order to dominate the Croat and Slovene bourgeoisies.[38] Despite Serbian domination, Marković saw no evidence that Croats or Slovenes supported secession; rather, they sought self-determination in a common state with Serbs. Therefore, he argued, the national question was due to competition among the Yugoslav bourgeoisies; it was a constitutional question which could be resolved by legislative means. There

---

35. *Radnik-Delavec*, 9/23/23; *Borba*, 10/4/23, cited in *ibid.*, 151-156.
36. Lukač, *Radnički pokret u Jugoslaviji i nacionalno pitanje, 1918-1941*, 152.
37. Vojinović, "Diskusija o nacionalnom pitanju u KPJ od 1918 do 1926 g.," 51.
38. Lukač, *Radnički pokret u Jugoslaviji i nacionalno pitanje, 1918-1941*, 158-159.

were three possible solutions to internal relations in the kingdom: the centralist solution, supported until now by the Serb bourgeoisie; the federalist solution, the ideal of the Croat petty bourgeoisie; and the autonomist solution, supported by Muslims, Slovenes and some Croats. According to Marković, the Serb bourgeoisie was now prepared to concede autonomy to Croats and Slovenes. Therefore, the best solution to the national question would be "regional autonomy on the basis of the widest democracy."[39]

The publication of Marković's book had a profound impact on discussion of the national question in the CPY. For the first time, a major spokesman of the right-wing appeared to accept the leftist position that Serbs and Croats were separate nations and that supporting a unitarist political order was not in the CPY's best interest. Moreover, his emphasis on the national question as a constitutional concern forced CPY leaders on the left and right to articulate their views on the Yugoslav political order. Articles on the national question published during the next several months, though largely critical of Marković, focused on the relationship among communism, nationalism and federal institutions.

Rajko Jovanović, a Serb leftist, was the first to respond to Marković in an article published in *Borba* on October 3. Though Jovanović recognized Marković's book as an important attempt to address the national question, he faulted Marković for failing to criticize the unitaristic orientation of the CPY.[40] More importantly, he criticized Marković for reducing the national question in Yugoslavia to a constitutional question which, he said, would unwisely separate class and revolutionary struggle from national struggle.[41] A constitutional deal concerning the national question would create a unified bourgeoisie that would harm the workers movement. Nevertheless, though Jovanović believed the national question could not be solved by revising the constitution, he did not object to such revision.[42] Triša Kaclerović and other leftists similarly disagreed

---

39. *Ibid.*, 160.

40. This same criticism was made by Moša Pijade in his article "A Short Party History on the National Question," published in *Radnik-Delavec* on November 11, 1923. Pijade pointed out that the party's approach to this question up until now had been out of line with Comintern views on the subject. He also criticized Marković for failing to respond to attempts that he and Rajko Jovanović had made as early as February 1921 to prepare a separate resolution on this subject.

41. Lukač, *Radnički pokret u Jugoslaviji i nacionalno pitanje, 1918-1941*, 161.

42. *Radnik-Delavec*, 11/4/23, 11/8/23, cited in *ibid.*, 172-174.

with Marković's emphasis on constitutional reform but agreed that constitutional revision was desirable.[43]

Ante Ciliga was more critical of Marković. In an article published in *Borba* on October 11, he accused Marković (and Kaclerović) of exaggerating the backwardness of the Serb bourgeoisie in order to justify Serbian repression. According to Ciliga, Serbs and Croats clashed because they were two separate nations with two separate capitalist classes.[44] Since all Croats supported federalism, it was foolish of Marković to argue for Croatian political autonomy, which might soften Serbian hegemony but would not remove it. In an article published several days later that was highly critical of Cvijić, Ciliga elaborated his own concept of federalism.[45] Both Cvijić and Marković, he emphasized, thought that the fusion of Croats, Slovenes and Serbs would come too easily. While Ciliga praised Cvijić's support of federalism, he argued that it did not go far enough; the CPY should demand that the army be organized along national lines allowing Croats to perform their military service in Croatia.[46] He also disagreed with Cvijić's wariness toward the CRPP and urged the PWPY to write immediately to Radić and request his help in forming a peasant-worker republic.

Djuro Cvijić responded to these criticisms in several articles published in *Borba* in November and December 1923. He accused Ciliga of conducting an "unfruitful and disloyal" criticism of the Communist Party.[47] Objecting to Ciliga's assertion that the CPY's mistaken nationalities policy had weakened the Yugoslav workers movement, he argued that

---

43. Sima Marković responded to Jovanović's criticisms in *Radnik-Delavec* on November 11. He also published a short book, *The Constitutional Question and the Working Class of Yugoslavia*. In these works he argued that the national question could be transformed into a constitutional question only in certain special circumstances which, it so happened, existed in Yugoslavia. He defended the CPY policy of supporting "national oneness" during unification since the bourgeoisie had not yet placed the national question on the political agenda. He also elaborated his concept of autonomy which, he said, was not very different from federalism and would eventually evolve into the latter.

44. Vojinović, "Federalizam u koncepcijama KPJ u periodu 1919-1928," 241.

45. *Borba*, 10/18/23, cited in Lukač, *Radnički pokret u Jugoslaviji i nacionalno pitanje, 1918-1941*, 164-166. Rejecting Cvijić's stance that Croats were prevented in 1918 from completing their national revolution, Ciliga emphasized that the majority of Croats did not favor the Yugoslav state. Therefore, he argued, their grievances with the Yugoslav state and the roots of the Croat question lay much deeper than competition among the bourgeoisie.

46. Lukač, *Radnički pokret u Jugoslaviji i nacionalno pitanje, 1918-1941*, 165.

47. *Ibid.*, 170.

many other factors had hindered the CPY's work. Furthermore, he charged that some of Ciliga's positions were close to those advocated by the ultranationalist Frankovci.[48] Though he supported Ciliga's criticism of Marković, he disagreed with Ciliga's concept of federalism and, in particular, his support for virtually separate Croat, Serb, and Slovene armies which would serve on their own territories. Cvijić endorsed the formation of federal units and extensive local autonomy. But he viewed CPY support for revision of the Vidovdan Constitution, along federal or autonomist lines, as Austro-Marxist and retrograde.[49]

Though Marković received his harshest criticism from leftists, he did not escape censure from the right. In a series of articles published in *Radnik-Delavec* during November and December, the Serb rightist Života Milojković sought support for an increasingly discredited position toward the national question.[50] Milojković argued that the importance of the national question had been exaggerated in the recent discussion. Rejecting the idea that Serbs, Croats, and Slovenes were three separate nations, he accused Marković of inconsistency on this point.[51] He also disagreed with Cvijić's position on federalism and criticized the idea of a "worker-peasant government" as too abstract. According to Milojković, the national movement in Croatia was not progressive. Therefore, the CPY should not cooperate with the CRPP or encourage peasants to support nationalist ideology. Rather, the Communist Party should lead the struggle against nationalism and focus on economic and class issues. Communists should unify Yugoslavs into one working class movement, which would be easiest, Milojković thought, in a unified political system with local self-administration.[52]

By the end of the year, the polemic between Ciliga, Cvijić, and Marković had become increasingly rancorous. Nevertheless, a consensus emerged that the CPY should support some change in the constitutional system. While rightists such as Marković and Filip Filipović supported constitutional revision which would grant greater political autonomy to

---

48. Lukač, "Učesnici iz Hrvatske u diskusiji o nacionalnom pitanju u NPRJ 1923 g.," 40.

49. Vojinović, "Diskusija o nacionalnom pitanju u KPJ od 1918 do 1926 g.'" 51.

50. *Radnik-Delavec*, 11/15/23, 11/18/23, 11/25/23, 12/2/23, 12/23/23, 12/30/23; cited in Lukač, *Radnički pokret u Jugoslaviji i nacionalno pitanje, 1918-1941*, 178-181.

51. *Ibid.*, 179-180. Marković claimed that they were three separate nations but then advocated autonomy. If they really were, countered Milojković, then federalism would be the best system, though he admitted that Marković's notion of autonomy was virtually indistinguishable from federalism.

52. *Ibid.*, 180-181.

Croatia and Slovenia, leftists generally supported a federal system with some differences of opinion about its features. Moreover, most leftists believed constitutional reform to be only the first step toward a complete restructuring of Serb-Croat relations. Leftists, most of whom were Croats from Zagreb, knew the strength of the Croat national movement and the political power of the CRPP. Their primary concern was to devise a nationalities policy that would allow them to take advantage of Croat political discontent and to diminish Croat support for the CRPP. While rightists remained suspicious of cooperating with the Peasant Party, leftists generally urged such cooperation, though some, like Cvijić, warned against the threat of cooptation. During the next several months, as Radić improved his ties with Moscow, cooperation with the CRPP became the most important and divisive problem for the CPY.

At the CPY Third Land Conference in Belgrade in early 1924, the left-wing emerged victorious from the debate about the Croat question.[53] The conference adopted a position on the Croat question that modified slightly Cvijić's earlier draft. The resolution rejected Marković's idea of simply revising the Vidovdan Constitution and pledged to fight for a completely new federalist constitution.[54] It also advocated cooperation with the CRPP.[55] In the interests of encouraging unity, the resolution was put to a referendum in the PWPY, but it failed to pass in Belgrade and several other towns in Serbia. Since many rightists refused to accept the referendum, few provisions of the resolution were put into effect.[56]

In the months after the Third Land Conference, debate was renewed in party journals about cooperation with the CRPP. After Radić traveled to Moscow in June 1924 and joined the Krestintern, the Comintern pressured Yugoslav Communists to cooperate with the CRPP.[57] But rightists continued to oppose leftist attempts to forge an agreement with Peasant Party leaders. Viewing the CRPP as "an ordinary bourgeois party," rightists charged that the PWPY's (which was dominated by leftists) uncritical stance toward the CRPP jeopardized "the independent

---

53. Milojković tried to have discussion on the Croat question removed from the agenda, but he was overruled.

54. Ciliga advocated the establishment of regional armies but was overruled.

55. Lukač, *Radnički pokret u Jugoslaviji i nacionalno pitanje, 1918-1941*, 190.

56. There was resistance from regional (*oblasti*) secretaries in the PWPY. Several prominent Slovene Communists also rejected the resolution and accused the PWPY and the CPY of centralism.

57. For a discussion of the Fifth Comintern Congress, see Vlajčić, *Jugoslavenska revolucija i nacionalno pitanje, 1919-1927*, 133-150.

character of the CPY."[58] Leftists replied that the rightist position "masked Great-Serbian imperialism."[59]

In the fall of 1924, a commission was formed to work out an agreement between the two factions.[60] Serb rightists such as Political Secretary Marković and Filip Filipović were coopted into the PWPY leadership, but factional conflict continued. At the end of November, the commission criticized the rightist position and accused the CPY Executive Committee (a rightist stronghold) of failing to support self-determination, including secession, and an independent Croatian republic. The commission emphasized the revolutionary character of the current situation in Yugoslavia and the revolutionary potential of peasants. It also praised the CRPP and sent a letter to CRPP leaders asking them to cooperate in the upcoming elections.[61] By this time, however, Radić's relations with Moscow had begun to cool. Since he never had any intention of cooperating with Communists within Yugoslavia anyway, Radić decisively rejected PWPY overtures. This rejection weakened the leftist policy of cooperating with the CRPP; the policy of cooperation received a fatal blow when Radić entered the government the next summer.

Radić's decision to enter the government prompted the participants in the Third CPY Congress held in Vienna in May 1926 to reexamine CPY policy toward the CRPP and the Croat national movement. Although some leftists admitted that the right-wing had correctly evaluated the CRPP, others still believed that a coalition with the Peasant Party was possible.[62] The Congress, which again elected Sima Marković as secretary, adopted a resolution that represented a compromise position. Describing Radić's step as "the most crucial event in the political life of

---

58. Rightists made this same charge to the Comintern. Comintern policy was ambivalent during this period and criticized both rightists and leftists. On the one hand, it criticized the Zagreb party organization for its overly independent approach to the CRPP. On the other hand, it dismissed Milojković's stance toward the CRPP as "ignorant." See Lukač, *Radnički pokret u Jugosalviji i nacionalno pitanje, 1918-1941*, 213.

59. *Ibid.*, 208. Leftists argued that they never thought the CRPP was a revolutionary party and only intended to cooperate with it as long as it supported the goals of the revolutionary workers' movement.

60. *Ibid.*, 214. Discussion at commission meetings was extremely heated. In one instance, Ciliga attacked the Belgrade party organization and described CPY nationalities policy as "Serbian social-patriotic." Emphasizing the revolutionary potential of the CRPP, he defended the Zagreb party organization's cooperation with CRPP leaders.

61. *Ibid.*, 219.

62. *Ibid.*, 229.

Yugoslavia from its origin until today," it attacked him for "capitulating" and expressed confidence that peasants would reject his agreement with Pašić. According to the resolution, Radić's agreement with Belgrade would increase national antagonisms in Yugoslavia and the national question would be raised again in "a sharper form than before."[63] Meanwhile, CPY members were instructed to strengthen Communist circles in the Peasant Party and to champion the old platform of the CRPP—noncooperation with the government and support for a peasant republic.[64] Repeating its support for the right of self-determination, including secession, the CPY pledged to fight against national oppression and to establish a federation of worker-peasant republics in the Balkans.[65] Although the left and right factions continued to squabble during the next two years, this position on the Croat question remained essentially unchanged.

The Militant Years, 1928-1934

In 1928, the CPY fundamentally modified its position on the Croat question and began to endorse a separatist solution to the problem of Croatian statehood. The Sixth Comintern Congress held in the summer of 1928 adopted a more confrontationalist line concerning cooperation with bourgeois forces. Insisting that Yugoslavia could not be reformed in its existing form, it called for the break-up of the Yugoslav state and a revolutionary assault upon the existing political regime. The Fourth CPY Congress in Dresden in October 1928 followed suit. It now advocated unequivocally Croatia's secession from Yugoslavia (though Communists did not specifically discuss the borders of a new Croatian state) and denounced all cooperation with the CPP. The Congress resolution pledged Communist support for secession "without any conditions or reserve" and the CPY subsequently issued several directives calling for armed insurrection against Serb hegemonists.[66]

While the timing of the CPY's shift in policy toward the Croat question was a result of the Comintern's new line, the adoption of a separatist position was also related to indigenous political factors. Radić's assassination and Aleksandar's personal rule created a more militant atmo-

---

63. *Ibid.*, 229.

64. Vlajčić, *Osma konferencija zagrebačkih komunista*, 64.

65. Lukač, *Radnički pokret u Jugoslaviji i nacionalno pitanje, 1918-1941*, 234.

66. *Ibid.*, 245.

sphere in Croatia which encouraged Communists to adopt insurrec-
tionary tactics.[67] CPY leaders believed that the new conditions would
create a revolutionary situation, especially in Croatia where opposition
to Aleksandar was strong. Moreover, some leftists saw this ultrasepa-
ratist policy as a potentially more effective way of reponding to the
national movement in Croatia by outflanking the CPP.[68] Since their
intermittent support for Radić and a federal political arrangement had
failed to generate much approval from Croats, they hoped that opposition to the Yugoslav state would improve the CPY's standing. Finally, in
the months prior to the Fourth Congress a new "militant" group in the
CPY, which received Comintern support, attempted to stop factional
fighting in the Communist Party by denouncing both the left and right
wings.[69] Led by Josip Broz Tito and future Communist Party of Croatia
Secretary Andrija Hebrang, the "militants" focused primarily on economic questions and called for a strengthening of Communist agitation
among workers.[70] Advocating a more activist approach, they adopted
the new Comintern line on greater confrontation with the authorities.

---

67. In the weeks after Radić was shot, Tito and the Zagreb Party Committee
attempted to channel spontaneous outbursts into more militant protests. These
demonstrations became violent, and several people were killed and many
Communists arrested. See Ivan Jelić, *Komunistička partija Hrvatske, 1937-1945*
(Zagreb, 1981), vol. 1, 51.

68. Lukač, *Radnički pokret u Jugoslaviji i nacionalno pitanje, 1918-1941*, 253. Some
Zagreb Communists like Cvijić objected to the new emphasis on breaking up the
state and continued to support the idea of a worker-peasant republic.

69. At the Eighth Party Conference of the Zagreb Party Committee in February
1928, the "militants" challenged the leftist leadership, which had its stronghold in
this organization. Organizational Secretary Josip Broz Tito, aided by Zagreb
Party Committee (ZPC) member Andrija Hebrang, objected to Political Secretary
Dušan Grković's assertion that the CPY's biggest danger was from the right. Tito
charged the ZPC with failing to follow the decisions of the Comintern and the
CPY Third Congress and with engaging in factionalist activities. Tito and
Hebrang passed a resolution that omitted charges against the rightists and called
for the ideological strengthening of party members; Tito was elected political secretary. In April, the Comintern drafted an open letter, which was rejected by
rightists in Belgrade, praising the new Zagreb group. As a consequence, the
Regional Committee for Serbia was dismissed in June and the Comintern
appointed a temporary leadership until the Fourth Party Congress could be
called in October of that year. At this Congress, Marković finally endorsed the
open letter and called upon all recalcitrant party organizations to follow his
example. See Vlajčić, *Osma konferencija zagrebačkih komunista.*

70. *Ibid.,* 124-127.

The more militant Comintern line adopted by the Communists, however, soon proved disastrous for the CPY. Aleksandar's regime responded in an effectively brutal manner to the CPY's increased attacks on the authorities, and Communist ranks were soon depleted by arrests and shootings. Most of its leaders, such as the former political secretary Djuro Djoković, were either killed or received long prison sentences; the rest were forced to flee abroad where they provided ineffective leadership to party cadres in the country. During the next few years, CPY membership dropped still further and the Communist Party moved to the fringes of political life. Moreover, though Communists had hoped that a separatist policy would increase their support among CPP sympathizers, they failed to make any headway against the firmly entrenched Peasant Party. Radić's death and the king's dictatorship had simply increased the numbers and the intensity of the Peasant Party's support.

With the new policy toward the Croat question, support for the CPP was also abandoned. In the weeks after Radić was shot, CPY leaders both praised and denounced him.[71] But they were almost unanimous in their criticism of his successor. Maček was attacked for squelching the revolutionary tendencies of the Croat national movement and reacting passively to Aleksandar's personal rule.[72] Communists were instructed to stop participating in CPP organizations.[73] The Fourth Congress resolution warned against workers' "opportunism" in Dalmatia, where CPY members had "overestimated the role of the bourgeoisie of the repressed nation," and had tried to enter as a "faction" into the CPP. When the CPP (with the IDP) adopted the Zagreb Resolution in 1932, the CPY dismissed it for failing to take a clear position on self-determination.[74]

As part of its attempt to draw support away from the CPP, the CPY also established its own political organization for Croats. In 1932, the Croat National Revolutionary Movement (CNRM) was founded in order to extend Communist influence among Croat peasants. The CNRM program endorsed self-determination, including secession, and denounced all "agreements, compromises or interventions" to solve the Croat question.[75] It also attacked the Croat Peasant Party for soliciting help from

---

71. *Ibid.*, 245. Communist leaders displayed a variety of attitudes toward Radić. Some called him leader of the "Croat liberation movement"; others judged him ineffective and unconcerned with social reform.

72. Jelić, *Komunistička partija Hrvatske, 1937-1941*, vol. 1, 53.

73. *Ibid.*, 52. Immediately after Radić was shot, the CPY enjoined all political parties to challenge the regime.

74. *Ibid.*, 330.

75. *Ibid.*, 31.

other countries. The CNRM turned out numerous publications from abroad, but it never developed into more than a propaganda tool. Unable to compete effectively with the CPP or Ustashas, it was abandoned when the Popular Front strategy was adopted in 1935.[76]

In addition to establishing the CNRM, the CPY also attempted to increase its contacts with the Ustashas, or the "Croat national revolutionaries," as the Comintern called them. Communist cooperation with the Ustashas did not come about quickly, despite their similar positions on Croat separatism. In 1929, for example, the CPY denounced Pavelić's agreement with Macedonian separatists.[77] But as Comintern pressure on the CPY to cooperate with the Ustashas escalated, interaction between them increased, especially abroad.[78] In 1932, the CPY praised the Ustashas' Velebit uprising in Lika and called upon Croats to "support with all their force the struggle of the Ustashas."[79] Yugoslav Communists saw the Ustasha as a movement of several tendencies, however, and denounced the terrorist methods of "Croat fascist elements" such as Pavelić.[80] In August 1933, the CPY resolved to devote greater attention to national-revolutionary organizations, but little concrete cooperation resulted.[81] Perhaps the most extensive interaction between Communists and Ustashas occurred in prison, where they frequently joined forces in confronting prison authorities.[82] Nevertheless, Ustasha adherents seldom embraced the Communist cause; though Communists may have endorsed a separate Croatian state, they did not share the Ustashas' passionately held anti-Serb views. As the Ustashas became increasingly anti-Communist in the mid-thirties, relations between these two groups worsened. In 1935, when the Popular Front policy was endorsed, the CPY ceased all formal cooperation with Ustashas in Yugoslavia and abroad.

---

76. *Ibid.*, 31-32.

77. *Ibid.*, 30.

78. This subject is treated scantily in the Yugoslav literature on the interwar period. For a description of CPY relations with the Ustasha during this period, see Djilas, *The Contested Country*, 108-116. See also Avakumović, *History of the Communist Party of Yugoslavia*, 108-111.

79. Lukač, *Radnički pokret u Jugoslaviji i nacionalno pitanje, 1918-1941*, 256.

80. *Proleter*, #28, 12/32.

81. Lukač, *Radnički pokret u Jugoslaviji i nacionalno pitanje, 1918-1941*, 260.

82. Milovan Djilas, *Memoirs of a Revolutionary* (New York: Harcourt Brace Jovanovich, 1973), 132.

The Popular Front in Croatia, 1935-1939

When the Comintern adopted the Popular Front line in 1935, and called upon Communists to cooperate with bourgeois parties in the fight against fascism, several important changes were made in CPY policy toward the Croat question. Although the CPY continued to support the right of self-determination, it no longer advocated the break-up of the Yugoslav state and Croatia's immediate secession.[83] This policy was spelled out in a resolution adopted at the Split plenum in June 1936 which stated: "Though the CPY struggles for the right to self-determination of the oppressed nations, it does not insist on the break-up of Yugoslavia at any cost; rather, every nation has the right to determine with whom and how it will establish its state unit."[84] Calling for free parliamentary elections for all Yugoslav nations (including Bosnia-Hercegovina, Macedonia, Vojvodina, Slovenia and Montenegro), the CPY emphasized the particular need to reinstate the Croatian Sabor. Although the term federalism was not yet used, the CPY began to advocate a federal program based on the autonomy of various national units. Party organizations which failed to adopt the new, more positive tone toward the Yugoslav state were instructed to diminish their emphasis on Croatian secession. For example, at the beginning of 1935, the CPY Central Committee criticized the Regional Committee of Croatia-Slavonia for acting as if Croatia's secession were "an end rather than simply a means to the liberation of Croats and all other people."[85]

The Popular Front policy involved both establishing a popular front from above, by attempting to forge alliances with CPP leaders, and creating a Popular Front from below, by infiltrating CPP organizations and coopting its members. Consequently, the CPY renewed attempts to cooperate with Maček and the CPP.[86] It was decided that agitation within CPP organizations would replace the CNRM's previously unsuccessful attempts to attract CPP members. Attacks on the Peasant Party in previous years had damaged the CPY's political position in Croatia and had

---

83. Lukač, *Radnički pokret u Jugoslaviji i nacionalno pitanje, 1918-1941*, 292.

84. Jelić, *Komunisticka partija Hrvatske, 1937-1945*, vol. 1, 43.

85. *Ibid.*, 270.

86. At the Fourth Land Conference in December 1934, the CPY was still critical of the CPP. It charged that the CPP's "passivity" hindered the national revolutionary struggle and described the CPP as an enemy of Communists. But it also admitted that in previous years it had underestimated the "peasant national liberation movement." In any case, this policy was modified by the Split plenum shortly thereafter. See Jelić, *Komunistička partija Hrvatske, 1937-1945*, vol. 1, 43.

demoralized its cadres. Communists in Croatia now hoped to improve their position by cooperating with the CPP and coopting its members. Consequently, they once again praised the CPP's revolutionary qualities and chastised Communists skeptical of the Peasant Party. Communists were instructed to join the Peasant Party and to work from within "to transform the CPP into a true national-revolutionary movement."[87]

In order to draw support away from the CPP and to counter its charges that the internationalist CPY was not interested in the Croat question, the CPY founded a separate Communist Party of Croatia (CPC).[88] At its first meeting on August 1, 1937, attended by sixteen delegates from most parts of Croatia, the CPC pledged that its primary task was "to fight for the national liberation of the Croat people."[89] It also called for elections to a constituent assembly in which relations among Yugoslavia's national groups would be reworked. The new party endorsed a three-pronged Popular Front strategy in Croatia: (1) to establish formal cooperation with the CPP leadership (the United Opposition) through the Communists' legal arm, the United Workers Party (UWP); (2) to infiltrate CPP unions and peasant cooperatives and create left-wing groups sympathetic to Communist goals; and (3) to create a broad front with Croat left intellectuals.

CPY leaders cautioned, however, that establishing the CPC did not signify federalization of the party and that separate party platforms would not be tolerated.[90] There was a great deal of confusion at this time about why a separate Communist Party of Serbia was not established. Some Croat delegates at the conference expressed concern that since Serbs were a majority in the CPY Central Committee, they would continue to rule the affairs of the Communist Party. CPY leaders insisted that they were not forming a separate Communist Party of Serbia because there was simply no demand for it; since Serbs were the domi-

---

87. See Lukač, *Radnički pokret u Jugoslaviji i nacionalno pitanje, 1918-1941*, 280.

88. The idea of establishing a separate party was first mentioned by Comintern instructor G. Alihanov in mid-1934. Massive arrests of Communists in late 1935 and 1936 delayed the foundation of the CPC until 1937, when it was constituted during one of Tito's trips to the country. See Jelić, *Komunistička partija Hrvatske, 1937-1941*, vol. 1, 57.

89. The new CPC leadership consisted of Central Committee Secretary D. Špoljarić, Pavle Gregorić, Andrija Žaja, Josip Kraš, B. Adžija, Anka Butorac, I. Dujmić, D. Petrović, V. Janić, Vicko Jelaška, L. Kurir.

90. See Jelić *Komunistička partija Hrvatske, 1937-1945*, vol. 1, 58-70.

nant nation in Yugoslavia, class struggle and national struggle were not intertwined in this area of the country.[91]

The CPY pursued formal cooperation with the Peasant-Democratic Coalition (of which the Croat Peasant Party was a member) beginning in the mid-thirties. After the Peasant Party entered the Bloc of Popular Agreement (United Opposition) in 1937, Communists asked repeatedly to join the Bloc. The CPY revived the United Workers' Party in the fall of 1937 to facilitate its cooperation with the United Opposition; in 1938 the United Workers' Party's name was changed to the Workers' Party.[92] But the CPP (and all other political parties except the Socialists) consistently rejected cooperation with the Communists. Although Maček was intermittently friendly to private overtures from individual Communists and occasionally adopted a position favorable to the CPY, he always publicly denounced communism and frequently charged the United Workers' Party with attempting to disrupt Croat unity.[93] After such persistent rebuffs, the CPY was forced to extend its influence by approaching the CPP rank and file.[94]

At the Fourth Land Conference in the fall of 1934, the CPY leadership charged that organizational work among peasants had been harmfully neglected and instructed party members to extend their influence in CPP rural organizations. As Peasant Party cooperatives became more active in the late 1930s, Communists increased their participation in these groups.[95] In 1937, the Communist Party of Croatia established a Peasant Commission to oversee Communist agitation in the villages.[96]

---

91. CC CPY member Parović wrote an article in the July-August issue of *Proleter* in 1935, explaining why there was no demand for a separate Communist Party in Serbia.

92. In the fall of 1937, the Main Initiative Committee of the Yugoslav Workers' Party (YWP) was established in Zagreb. YWP committees were also established elsewhere in the country. At a YWP conference in 1938, which was attended by delegates from all over the country, the YWP's name was changed to the Workers' Party. For more on this party, see Jelić *Komunistička partija Hrvatske, 1937-1945, vol. 1,* 47.

93. *Ibid.,* 81.

94. *Ibid.,* 198. The CPC resorted to harsher criticism of the CPP and some CPC members began to question the Popular Front policy.

95. Communists were also more active in the *Seljačko Kolo* set up by the Independent Democratic Party among Serbs in Croatia.

96. The Peasant Commission was comprised of Nikola Rubičić, Šime Balen, and Martin Franekić. Jakov Blažević, a Partisan leader in Lika and later public prosecuter in Croatia defended the Commission from accusations that it was cut

Communist sympathizers in trade unions were ordered to establish contact with the peasant cooperatives. The CPC also launched a propaganda
campaign which emphasized the similarity of Communists' and Radić's
ideals.[97] This effort to increase the Communists' presence in CPP peasant
organizations was relatively successful, except in Dalmatia where fierce
resistance by Peasant Party members forced the CPC to establish
separate, mainly cultural, peasant organizations.

The CPC had less success in infiltrating CPP trade union organizations, though Croat Communists greatly expanded their union activities
during this period. Indeed, organizing trade unions preoccupied the
CPC. Most CPC leaders were trade union activists and the party's rank
and file was recruited through union membership.[98] There were two
rival networks of trade unions in the Kingdom of Yugoslavia at this time;
the CPP supported the Croat Workers Syndicate (CWS) and the largely
Socialist United Workers' Socialist Syndicate (UWSS). Finding themselves shut out of the CWS, Communists concentrated their attention on
the UWSS.[99] Croat Communists had the most success in penetrating the
UWSS and, despite strong Socialist resistance, by the mid-thirties they
established their predominance in the UWSS for Croatia and Slavonia.[100]
Socialists in the UWSS had previously been extremely critical of the
CWS. Communists now tried to curb this criticism, with mixed success
even in their own ranks, and called for an alliance with the CWS. The

---

off from party organizations and too independent of the CPC. *Povijest i falsifikat*,
39.

97. For more on this aspect of CPC policy see Mladen Iveković, *Hrvatska lijeva
inteligencija, 1918-1945*,(Zagreb, 1970), vol. 1, 288-318.

98. Jelić, *Komunistička partija Hrvatske, 1937-1945*, vol. 1.

99. *Ibid.*, 123. In 1932, the CPY called on Communists in Yugoslavia to
strengthen their position in the UWSS. The Fourth Land Conference and the CPY
resolution of March 1935 called for Communists to engage in legal activity in the
unions. In Croatia, Communist penetration of the UWSS had already begun in
1929.

100. After Communists had established their predominance at the UWSS Regional Conference for Croatia and Slavonia, they began to publish the journal
Radnik which argued that the UWSS for Croatia and Slavonia should operate
independently of UWSS headquarters in Belgrade. This position contradicted the
CPY call for working class (and union) unity but made more sense in Croatia
where Socialist criticism of the CWS made cooperation between the two unions
impossible.

CWS refused to cooperate, however, and the two unions continued to compete fiercely for the loyalty of Croat workers.[101]

Another important aspect of the CPC's Popular Front strategy was its attempt to establish better relations with the Croat left intelligentsia. In contrast to the party organization in Serbia, which concentrated on illegal organizational work, the CPC focused on establishing links with the populace and operated more through the legal WPP. Many Croat intellectuals greeted the CPC's Popular Front strategy with enthusiasm and debated with Communist leaders about a variety of topics, ranging from the merits of dialectical materialism to the best form of cooperation with the CPP.[102] The discussion reached its height with the publication of the journal *Pečat*, edited by Miroslav Krežla, a towering figure of the left intellectual scene in Zagreb. The Popular Front's success in generating support among students and intellectuals, however, soon aggravated those who believed it undermined Leninist precepts and, before long, relations between CPC leaders and Croat left intellectuals deteriorated.

Conflict between CPY and CPC, 1938-1940

By the late 1930s divergent approaches to the Croat question once again appeared within Communist ranks. Although the CPY had established the Communist Party of Croatia in an effort to turn Croat discontent into support for itself, the CPC soon manifested different ideas about how to accomplish this task. CPC and CPY leaders agreed on the main aspect of Communist policy toward the Croat question—support for a unified Yugoslav state based on a federal political order. They increasingly disagreed, however, on other aspects of CPY policy toward the Croat question, particularly relations with the Croat Peasant Party.

After Tito became effective head of the CPY in 1937, it underwent several changes which strengthened and expanded it. Tito was determined to build a strong, highly unified party and to put a halt to conflicts between Communists in exile and those who had remained in the country. When many Yugoslav Communists abroad disappeared in Stalin's purges, Tito began to build a new leadership from relatively young and less fractious leaders. Many more old cadres were purged in the next few months. Concerned foremost with unifying and strengthening the CPY,

---

101. Jelić, *Komunistička partija Hrvatske, 1939-1941*, vol. 1, 142. The UWSS Communist delegates did extremely well in the elections of 1937 and 1938, often better than the CWS delegates.

102. Stanko Lasić, *Sukob na književnoj ljevici* (Zagreb, 1970), 153-224.

Tito advocated concentrating on the CPY's capacity to engage in underground struggle. While he implemented the Popular Front line, he did not want it to divert Communists from the task of creating an illegal apparatus or subject them to nationalist pressures that had been the cause of factional struggle in the past.

As the CPC expanded its participation in various trade union and peasant organizations, Tito and other Communist leaders worried that the Popular Front in Croatia had gone too far. Tito feared that CPC Communists were too engaged in legal work and therefore vulnerable to pressures from the Croat Peasant Party. He also objected to the CPC's tendency to take a more moderate political line in order to facilitate cooperation with its bourgeois allies. According to Ivo Lola Ribar, head of the Communist Youth of Yugoslavia, many Communists saw "liberal deviation" in Zagreb as the biggest danger facing the party.[103] During this year and the next, CPC leaders adopted several positions at odds with the CPY line. These disagreements finally caused Tito to intervene in order to ensure that the CPC remained more independent of other political forces in Croatia.

The CPC first deviated from the CPY line when the CPY attempted to forge a political alliance with groups perceived in Croatia as opposing Croat national interests. After the *Anschluss* in March 1938, the CPY called for joining forces with the Yugoslav National Party and the Yugoslav Workers' Party, which were excluded from the United Opposition but opposed to the Stojadinović government. CPC leaders refused to collaborate with the Socialists, however, since they feared that Socialist sympathies for a unitary state order would jeopardize their support among the Croat populace.[104] This breach of discipline must have infuriated Tito, who was determined to unify the fractious Yugoslav party.

The CPC's refusal to offer separate candidates in the fall elections was even more troublesome. Communist leaders in Croatia had initially agreed with the CPY decision to enter the December 1938 elections independently and had prepared their own list of candidates. Worried that separate Communist candidates would divide the opposition and expose Communist cadres to arrest, however, they reversed this decision in

---

103. When Ribar made this comment, Ivan Supek defended himself by saying that since 1935 Croat Communists had simply been trying to establish a Popular Front. "Exactly," remarked Ribar, "but with Communist leadership; however, you enter into Maček's bloc as inferiors, without even being named as partners." Ivan Supek, *Krivovjernik na ljevici* (Bristol, England: BC Review, 1980), 69.

104. Jelić, *Komunistička partija Hrvatske, 1937-1945*, vol. 1, 225.

November and supported Peasant Party candidates instead.[105] A CPY investigation into this incident in December accused the CPC of committing a "grave error" by withdrawing the Communist slate of candidates and concluded that in Croatia the Party of the Working People (PWP) was too sensitive to pressure from left intellectuals. CPC trade union and peasant committees were also characterized as excessively independent of party control. Tito also appears to have decided at this time that a thorough reorganization of the CPC was needed in the future to correct these problems.[106] Meanwhile, several CPC leaders were reassigned to new functions.

At the same time that Tito was at odds with the CPC, he became alarmed by the behavior of Communists in Dalmatia. The tendency in Croatia to concentrate on legal work was strongest in Dalmatia. The most influential Communist leader in Dalmatia, Vicko Jelaska, head of the PWP, generally avoided illegal activities and, for this reason, refused to lead the illegal CPC Regional Committee for Dalmatia. In order to revitalize party work in Dalmatia, a new Regional Committee was established in the summer 1938. But its leader, an ally of Jelaska, was equally uninterested in increasing CPC activity. Consequently, the Regional Committee was dissolved several months later and three prominent Dalmatians, including Jelaska, were expelled from the party. Jelaska retained his leadership of the PWP, however, and party work languished until Tito reorganized the entire CPC a year later.[107]

Tensions between CPC and CPY leaders increased when the Croatian Banovina was established in August 1939. While both the CPY and CPC initially reacted positively to the *Sporazum*, the CPY soon denounced the Croat Peasant Party for not allowing Communists to function more freely in the Banovina. Cognizant of the Peasant Party's immense support in Croatia, the CPC was noticeably less critical of the CPP.[108] The CPC was also reluctant to criticize the *Sporazum*, which it had previous praised, for fear of alienating its growing support among Peasant Party sympathizers. As CPY criticism of the *Sporazum* intensified during the next several months, the CPC's divergent views on this question became increasingly apparent.

---

105. *Ibid.*, 218-222. Former Social Democrats, Božidar Adžija and Mladen Iveković, the most visible Communists in the PWP, apparently had misgivings about entering the election independently, as did Josip Kraš and Andrija Žaja in the CPC.

106. See Jelić, *Komunistička partija Hrvatske, 1937-1945*, vol. 1, 223-231.

107. *Ibid.*, 230.

108. *Ibid.*, 254.

Tito finally moved to reorganize the CPC when its leaders supported the government's military mobilization in the fall of 1939. In line with the Comintern's opposition to the "imperialist war" after the Hitler-Stalin Pact, the CPY opposed this mobilization. Concerned about the threat of Italian encroachments on Croatian territory, the CPC did not. Angered by this failure to support the CPY line, Tito moved against CPC leaders in the next several weeks, replacing General Secretary Josip Kraš with the Serb Rade Končar and removing Žaja and Špoljarić from the CPC Central Committee.[109] The Dalmatian party leadership was also reorganized and a new Regional Committee formed, with the Croat Vicko Krstulović in charge.[110] After this reorganization, the CPC fell in step with the CPY's line and became more critical of the CPP.[111] Though the party still encouraged Communists to infiltrate Peasant Party organizations, it warned repeatedly against "tailism," the tendency to become coopted by the Peasant Party. Moreover, as the Banovina increased it repression of Communists, the CPC was forced into an illegal posture more in line with party organizations elsewhere in the country.

Once the CPY had asserted control over CPC leaders, it moved to reign in "revisionist" intellectuals and students. The publication of Krežla's journal *Pečat* in 1939, which featured a lively discussion of philosophical issues and of various controversial political concerns, had stirred up intellectual debates brewing in Croatia for the last decade. This discussion appeared to some Communist leaders to undermine the very foundations of communism. Communists in Croatia such as Ognjen Prica and Otokar Keršovani objected to the publication in *Pečat* of articles by several "revisionists," especially the influential writer Zvonimir Richtmann.[112] Krežla attempted to defend these contributions to his

---

109. M. Bukovec and Ivan-Stevo Krajačić were coopted into the CPC leadership at this time. Končar appears to have been virtual head of the CPC since the beginning of 1939, though he was not officially appointed until March 1940. The new CPC leadership confirmed in the fall of 1940 consisted of Rade Končar, Ivan-Stevo Krajačić, M. Bukovec, Pavle Gregorić, Anka Butorac, D. Saili, M. Oreškovič, Karlo Mrazović, Vladimir Bakarić, Leo Mates and M. Franekić.

110. Jelić, *Komunistička partije Hrvatske, 1937-1945*, vol. 1, 284. In October, Edvard Kardelj came to Split to organize meetings of those Communists who were opposed to Jelaška. The Executive Committee of the PWP was reorganized and Jelaška lost his position.

111. *Ibid.*, 284.

112. Richtmann challenged the supremacy of dialectical materialism, arguing that while it may accurately describe social processes it cannot be depicted as the law of all nature. Prica, who had carried on a polemic with Richtmann since

journal and was himself attacked as a "pessimist" who lacked conviction in proletarian victory.[113] Although CPC leaders attempted to provide more stringent guidelines to intellectual discussion, their efforts to control this debate had little effect. Consequently, in the spring of 1940, Tito stepped in. Though he tempered his criticism of Krežla, he launched a harsh campaign against the "Trotskyist" *Pečat* and the Zagreb revisionists.[114] This campaign reached its height in the summer of 1940 when the CPY published its *Literary Notebooks*, a collection of articles attacking Zagreb revisionism.[115] The Slovene Edvard Kardelj's criticism was typical when he charged revisionists with "ideologically destroying the workers' movement at a time when its compete intellectual (*idejno*) unity [was] a precondition for it to realize its historical task."[116] Finally, in the fall, several revisionists were expelled from the CPC and *Pečat* ceased publication. Zagreb left intellectuals ceased to be a critical voice in the party until 1944.[117]

The First CPC Conference and the Fifth CPY Land Conference in the fall of 1940 criticized the Popular Front in Croatia and articulated a notably harsher line toward the Peasant Party than in the past several years. The CPC resolution stated that class struggle had increased since the outbreak of the "imperialist" war, making cooperation with the Croat Peasant Party impossible. In his address to the Fifth Land Conference, Tito admitted that the CPY had mistakenly ignored peasant support for the CPP in the past. But he warned that the CPC had ventured too far in the other direction in its Popular Front policy.[118] It had allowed itself to

---

Prica's release from prison in 1937, accused Richtmann of attempting to establish a United Front in the ideological realm.

113. Prica attacked Krleža in his November article in *Proleter*. Krleža answered with *Dialectical Antibarbarus* in *Pečat* in December.

114. In an article in *Proleter* in April/May 1940, Tito charged that Zagreb revisionists were working directly against the party line. Lasić, *Sukob na književnoj ljevici*, 224.

115. These articles were by Djilas, Kardelj, Prica, Koča Popović, and Todor Pavlov. See *Književne sveske* 1 (Zagreb, 1940): 1-311.

116. Lasić, *Sukob na književnoj ljevici*, 232.

117. For more information about the "conflict on the left," as it is known in Yugoslav historiography, see Jelić, *Komunistička partija Hrvatske, 1937-1945*, vol. 1, 380-386; Supek, *Krivovjernik na ljevici*, 55-96; Iveković, *Hrvatska lijeva inteligencia, 1918-1945*, vol. 1, 232-241; Lasić, *Sukob na književnoj ljevici*, 145-245.

118. *Peta zemaljska konferencija KPJ* (Belgrade, 1980), 17. In his address, Tito listed the reasons for removing the CPC leadership: (1) it ignored organizational work, (2) it wrongly informed the Politburo of the party's stand in Croatia, (3) it adopted a divergent policy toward the 1938 elections, (4) it resisted the CPY

be "swallowed up" by CPP organizations and it was plagued by "liberalism."[119] According to Tito, the political situation in Croatia had changed since the *Sporazum*; the CPP was losing popularity and Communists stood to gain support from disillusioned peasants. Indeed, the *Sporazum* had exacerbated the national question by bringing the Kingdom of Yugoslavia closer to the Axis Powers, which were encouraging national conflict. Tito, and Milovan Djilas in his address on the national question, emphasized that the CPP was incapable of solving the national problem.[120] Therefore, Communists in Croatia were to stop cooperating with the Croat Peasant Party and to demonstrate its "bankruptcy" to the populace.[121]

In the fall of 1940, despite its success in attracting popular support, CPY leaders declared the Popular Front a failure in Croatia. The shift away from cooperation with the Croat Peasant Party was just one more tactic in the constant search for a strategy that would allow Communists to diminish the power of the CPP in Croatia without relinquishing their separate identity. In 1940, the CPC was instructed to concentrate on party work and preserve its own identity. But CPC leaders knew this meant that Communists would be isolated in Croatia. Like the Serb Radicals, Communists in Croatia discovered they could not live with the Croat Peasant Party and they could not live without it. When war broke out and Communists attempted to elicit support for the resistance movement, relations with the CPP would become the most important tactical question in Croatia.

Conclusion

During the interwar period Yugoslav political life was wracked by conflict over how to resolve the Croat question. Croats and Serbs struggled over how to define the relation between nation and state and whether they should establish a federal or unitary political system. The CPY also contended with these questions. Occupying the fringes of polit-

---

Central Committee directive on the defense of the country after the *Anschluss*, (5) it resisted the CC CPY position on the outbreak of the war, sticking more closely to Maček's position. Tito stressed the "opportunism" of this approach and especially criticized CPC "opportunists" in Dalmatia. See *Peta zemaljska konferencija KPJ*, 22-25.

119. *Peta zemaljska konferencija KPJ*, 17.
120. This report was written by Pijade and corrected by Djilas.
121. *Peta zemaljska konferencija KPJ*, 22-25.

ical life, except during the brief period from 1918 to 1920, the CPY was not involved directly in building the Yugoslav state. Rather, it sought to turn Croat discontent into support for itself in order to further its own revolutionary goals. Bitterly divided over the significance of Croat national aspirations, however, Communists were unable to exploit them to their own purpose. Leftists and rightists in the mid 1920s and CPC and CPY leaders in the late 1930s adopted fundamentally different positions on the overall organization of the Yugoslav state, the character of the Croat national movement, and the best approach to the Croat Peasant Party. Although Comintern shifts in policy, which bore little relation to political realities in the country, hurt the CPY's political effectiveness, the major source of disunity and weakness within the party must be attributed to conflict over these issues.

Shortly after the formation of the new Yugoslav state, the CPY leadership launched a debate about the character of the conflict between Serbs and Croats and whether Communists should advocate a federal or unitary state order. Although Communists expressed a range of views which shifted over time, Communists in Serbia generally downplayed the importance of nationalism in Croatia and advocated a more centralized state order; they were also reluctant to cooperate with bourgeois political parties like the CPP. In contrast, Communists in Croatia argued that national sentiment in Croatia must be taken into account, and that Communists should support a federal state; they also advocated cooperation with the Croat Peasant Party. This difference in views led to serious factional conflict and prompted Comintern intervention on numerous occasions.

In 1928, the Comintern shifted its policy and began to call for the break-up of the Yugoslav state and a militant struggle against the existing political order. Although the CPY fell into line, factional struggle over the Croat question did not completely subside, and there was more enthusiasm for this policy, at least initially, in Zagreb. Nevertheless, despite Communist attempts to outflank the CPP by adopting a more radical position on the Croat question, the CPY did not succeed in breaking the hold of the Croat Peasant Party over the population, or in turning Croat discontent into support for itself. Sporadic attempts to cooperate with the Ustashas in Yugoslavia and abroad also proved ineffective and they were soon abandoned with the initiation of the Popular Front policy in 1935.

By the time the Popular Front policy was introduced in Yugoslavia, debate within the Communist Party over the organization of the Yugoslav state had subsided; Communists now began to endorse a federal political order, though what this federal program meant was not elucidated. Despite Tito's attempts to unify the Communist Party, divergences in Communists' approach toward the Croat question persisted. The newly established Communist Party of Croatia began to adopt different positions than the CPY leadership on various political questions affecting Croat national interests. The CPC supported Peasant Party candidates in the elections of 1938 and took a more favorable position toward the establishment of the Croatian Banovina. Communists in Croatia understood that they must respond to the national sentiments of the population in order to elicit popular support and achieve their revolutionary aims. Operating in Croatia, the CPC adapted its tactics and strategy to the overwhelming political reality to the power of the Croat national movement and the Croat Peasant Party. This orientation, and the difficulties it sometimes caused within the Yugoslav Communist Party, carried over into the Second World War. It provided the essential backdrop to the CPY's approach to the Croat question during this period and the impetus for the formulation of the federalist state-building strategy.

3

Mobilizing Popular Support in Croatia, 1941-1942

When war erupted in Yugoslavia in April 1941, the Communist Party of Yugoslavia found itself in radically altered circumstances in which to achieve its political goals. With leaders of the other major parties in exile or politically inactive, the CPY now began to organize and lead a resistance movement to the occupying powers. At the same time, it sought to build organizational and institutional structures from which it could launch itself to power after the war. During the first two years of the war, the party focused on eliciting popular support for the Partisan resistance by mobilizing the populace into military and political organizations.

The key to the Communists' success in achieving their political goals during the war, not only in Croatia but in the entire country, was generating Croat support for the Communist-led Partisan movement. However, during this crucial phase of mobilization, the situation in Croatia posed numerous difficulties. First, Communists faced the enormous problem of wooing Croats away from the Croat Peasant Party, which opposed the CPY strategy of military resistance to the occupying forces. Moreover, in order to attract Croat support, the Communists had to convince Croats they could fulfill their national aims, a difficult task given their support for a Yugoslav state. Finally, the large number of Serbs in Croatia, who joined the Partisans in the early stages of the war, made attracting Croats more difficult.

Invasion and Partition

The circumstances of Germany's strike against Yugoslavia are well known. Hitler was angered by the March 27 coup, which removed Prince Paul's government after it signed the Tripartite Pact, and replaced it with one initially less friendly to the Germans.[1] The new government quickly attempted to placate him, but on April 6, German forces invaded Yugoslavia, aided by Italian, Bulgarian and Hungarian troops.[2] Eleven days later, with the king and members of the government already in exile, Yugoslav military authorities signed an unconditional surrender with the Germans.[3] The war in Yugoslavia was officially over; the occupation had begun.

All the participants in the invasion now received a piece of Yugoslavia. The country was partitioned beyond recognition: (1) Under the authority of Ante Pavelić and his Ustasha movement, the Independent State of Croatia (NDH) was created, encompassing the previous territory of the Croatian Banovina, including the whole of Bosnia and Hercegovina but excluding large parts of the Croatian Littoral, the Dalmatian coast, and the islands, which were annexed by Italy; and Medjumurje, which was annexed by Hungary. (2) Slovenia was annexed and divided among Germany, Italy, and Hungary. (3) Germany occupied Serbia and the Banat and in August 1941 established a collaborationist regime under Milan Nedić, a former minister of defense and general of the Royal Yugoslav Army.[4] (4) Macedonia was divided between Bulgaria and the Italian satellite Albania (which also annexed the Kosovo-Metohija region and the salients of eastern Montenegro). (5) Italy

----

1. The coup was carried out by a group of mostly Serb military officers, General Simović, General Bora Mirković, Major Živan Knežević and others. After the coup, the Regent was forced to abdicate and Prince Peter was pronounced king. A government was formed which Maček, after much hesitation, joined on April 4.

2. On April 6, 1941, twenty-four divisions of the German Army crossed the borders of Yugoslavia from the south and east. German planes launched an air attack on Belgrade while motorized troops headed toward the capital. Two days later, they were joined by Bulgarian forces in their offensive. On April 11, Italian and Hungarian forces entered the fray; the former headed up the coast from Albania and the latter occupied Vojvodina.

3. By April 13, as German troops were reportedly closing in on the Supreme Headquarters located in Sarajevo, Prime Minister Simović transferred his authority as chief of staff to General Danilo Kalifatović, the chief of the Supreme Command in the Rear, and instructed him to ask the enemy for an armistice. The next day, along with King Peter and the other members of the cabinet, he flew to Athens, from there to Palestine, and finally on to Cairo and London. On April 17, General Janković, deputy chief of staff of the Supreme Command, signed an unconditional surrender with the German department chief of staff and instructed units of the Yugoslav Army to turn over their arms and men to the local German commanders.

4. The Banat was administered by the local German minority.

occupied Montenegro and planned to create a separate kingdom attached to Italy as a vassal state. (6) Hungary occupied Medjumurje, Prekomurje, Baranja, and Bačka. With the occupation, Yugoslavia ceased to exist as a state.

Shortly after the invasion, a Yugoslav government in exile was formed in London. It was the same as the government before the war, excluding the ministers of the Yugoslav Muslim Organization who had withdrawn in April.[5] After arriving with great fanfare in England, the government immediately began to squander its political capital.[6] Squabbling broke out among cabinet ministers, particularly between members of the Croat Peasant Party and the Serbian parties. In the first few months after the invasion, Prime Minister Simović and King Peter appeared to blame Croats for Yugoslavia's rapid capitulation, suggesting that "events in Croatia" had prevented the Yugoslav army from performing well.[7] As news of massacres of Serbs in the Independent State of Croatia trickled in during the summer, strains within the government in exile grew. In October, a letter from the Serbian Orthodox Patriarch smuggled to the west claimed that Ustashas had killed 180,000 Serbs in the first four months of the war.[8] This claim provoked acrimonious disputes between Serb and Croat ministers, which were taken up in more strident tones by the emigre community in the United States. Vice Premier Juraj Krnjević, who was Maček's representative in the government in exile and CPP secretary general, defended Croats against what he felt were unfair accusations, and insisted in a series of speeches and articles in the fall that Croats were not responsible for Ustasha actions.[9]

---

5. Croat Peasant Party members of the government were Juraj Krnjević, Ivan Šubašić, Juraj Šutej, Ilija Jukić, and Rudolf Bićanić.

6. Ilija Jukić, who was assistant foreign minister in the government in exile, describes how well the Yugoslav government was treated because of the pro-Allied March 27 coup. According to him, this special treatment "culminated in a splendid ceremony at St. Paul's Cathedral on September 12 to celebrate King Peter's coming of age." Ilija Jukić, *The Fall of Yugoslavia* (New York and London: Harcourt Brace Jovanovitch, 1974), 90.

7. Slobodan Nešović and Branko Petranović, *AVNOJ i revolucija* (Belgrade, 1983), 55.

8. Bogdan Krizman, *Jugoslavenske vlade u izbjeglištvu 1941-1943: Dokumenti* (Zagreb, 1981), 133.

9. Nešović and Petranović, *AVNOJ i revolucija*, 62. See also Krizman, *Jugoslavenske vlade u izbjeglištvu 1941-1943*, 133.

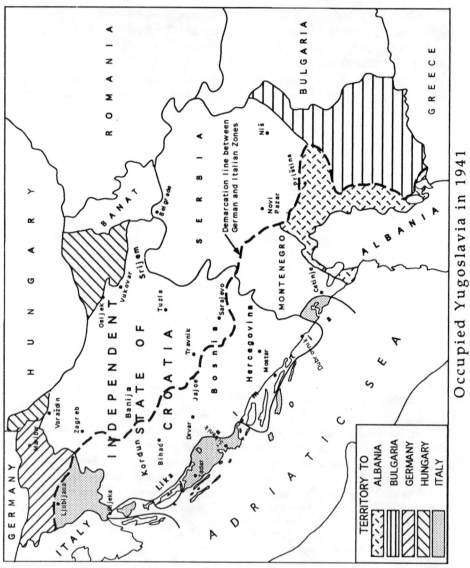

Occupied Yugoslavia in 1941

Ministers of the Yugoslav exile government also began to argue over the shape of the postwar state. Reluctant from the start to endorse the 1939 *Sporazum*, which Croats considered the basis of any discussion, several Serb ministers became increasingly hostile to this agreement. In turn, Croat Peasant Party ministers moved away from Krnjević's relatively mild tone in the summer and his assurances about a Serb-Croat consortium. In November, Krnjević and two other Croat ministers produced a document many Serbs thought gave only lukewarm support to the Yugoslav state. The Bićanić memorandum, named after one of its authors, Rudolf Bićanić, acknowledged that since "Croatia [desired] to live in security from attack by her neighbors," she "was prepared to strengthen her ties with Serbs and Slovenes and to live in community with them within the borders of Yugoslavia."[10] The document emphasized, however, Croats' desire to govern their own affairs "in accordance with centuries-old ideas about the Croatian state." As in the interwar period, the political implications of this desire were disputed by Serb and Croat ministers.

By the end of 1941, the Yugoslav government in exile was paralyzed. Simović was distrusted by many Serb politicians for his ostensibly conciliatory stance toward Croats, though he had not earned any popularity with the latter for it. Despite British support, he was removed from power in January 1942 and replaced by Slobodan Jovanović, Serbia's greatest historian. The crisis in the government subsided momentarily, but the new cabinet proved no more capable of resolving its debilitating internal conflicts.

The government in exile, particularly its Serb ministers, looked to the Chetnik resistance movement in Yugoslavia to bolster its fortunes. The Chetniks were formed by a small group of Serb officers in northern Bosnia, led by General Staff Colonel Dragoljub (Draža) Mihailović who fled to the hills after the defeat of the Yugoslav army. Like the previous Chetnik fighting bands in Serbia, the Chetniks under Draža Mihailović began to organize for guerrilla resistance against the occupying powers.[11] In May, Mihailović and his men moved south and established their

---

10. Krizman, *Jugoslavenske vlade u izbjeglištvu 1941-1943*, 110.

11. Draža Mihailović's Chetniks had only a loose connection with the several Chetnik associations in interwar Yugoslavia. The head of the main prewar Chetnik association, Kosta Pećanac, formed his own detachments in southern Serbia. In August he began to cooperate with the Germans in their campaign against the Partisan forces.

headquarters at Ravna Gora in central Serbia.[12] From there, they intended to build a resistance force, harass the enemy, and wait for Allied assistance to launch a general uprising.

Mihailović was initially reluctant to contact the government in exile, which he blamed for Yugoslavia's humiliating defeat. However, when the British and the Yugoslav government in London recognized Mihailović as the only legitimate commander of the resistance forces in the fall of 1941, Mihailović began to communicate with them regularly. The Chetniks received a tremendous boost of morale from their recognition as the Yugoslav Army of the Homeland, but this recognition did not enhance their resistance to the occupying forces. Although Chetniks cooperated with Communists during the uprising against Axis forces in the summer, German reprisals were fierce and Communist successes threatening; the Chetniks soon became reluctant to engage in anti-Axis military actions. By the end of 1941, most Chetnik commanders began to cooperate with Germans and Italians in actions against the Communists.

Cooperation with the occupying forces ultimately undermined Chetnik support at home and abroad. Moreover, Chetniks' inattention to building political structures and their inability to elicit support from non-Serbs put them at a disadvantage with Communists in the struggle for political power during the war. Based on the erroneous assumption that they were indispensible to the Allies, Chetniks made few efforts to build a solid base of support in the country outside their natural Serb proponents. Chetnik political goals, such as the return of King Peter and the establishment of a Great Serbian unit within Yugoslavia after the war, had a Serbian flavor that did not appeal to Yugoslavia's other national groups.[13] By the time the Chetniks adopted a more complete program of social and political reform at the beginning of 1944, they could not compete with the political and military organizations Communists had established during the previous four years.

Chetniks were concentrated in Serbia and Montenegro, but they also had significant forces in Croatia and Bosnia. These forces, which were

---

12. Tomasevich puts their strength at five to ten thousand. Jozo Tomasevich, *The Chetniks, War and Revolution in Yugoslavia 1941-1945* (Stanford, California: Stanford University Press, 1975), 141.

13. Although the Chetniks characterized themselves as a purely military force, they also had political goals. These were often differently defined by local commanders in the first few years of the war, but they generally included the return of King Peter and the establishment of a Great Serbian unit within Yugoslavia. Chetniks planned to establish a military government after the war until a new civilian government could be formed.

strongest in the area of Croatia where Lika, Dalmatia, and Bosnia meet, recognized Mihailović as their leader, though they operated mostly independently of him. Groups of Chetniks in Croatia were initially formed by Serbs who had fled from Ustasha massacres into Italian occupied Dalmatia, especially Split and its hinterland.[14] Since their primary aim was to protect Serbs from Ustasha massacres, differences arose almost immediately between Communists and Chetniks in Croatia about whether to fight the Italians and Ustashas, or just the latter.[15] After their break in November 1941, Communist-led Partisans engaged in a deadly battle with Chetniks, not only for their physical survival but for the hearts and minds of Serbs in Croatia.

The Independent State of Croatia

The Independent State of Croatia was founded on April 10, 1941, several days before the Yugoslav army officially surrendered.[16] Slavko Kvaternik, who headed the armed forces in the new state, proclaimed in the name of Ante Pavelić: "according to God's favor, the good will of our Allies, and the long suffering, centuries-old struggle of the Croat people" the "resurrection of our independent state of Croatia."[17] Five days later,

---

14. The first Chetnik activity began when Serbs in Split organized aid for Serb refugees from the Independent State of Croatia. Fikreta Jelić-Butić argues that Chetnik activity was directed from the start by Italians. She describes how Serb "nationalists" like Niko Novaković, Dobroslav Jevdjević-Longo and Boško Desnica were approached by the Italians in July and requested to return to their home regions. There, they were to organize Chetnik units which would siphon off support from the Communists. See Fikreta Jelić-Butić, *Četnici u Hrvatskoj, 1941-1945* (Zagreb, 1986), 35-41.

15. *Ibid.*, 44. In August, CPC leaders objected to Chetnik contacts with the Italians in Lika. On August 25, 26, at the height of Ustasha massacres of Serbs, Chetnik leaders Novaković, Radjenović, and Djujić met with Italian officers and urged them to reoccupy the second and third occupation zones.

16. For a complete treatment of the Ustasha regime see Fikreta Jelić-Butić, *Ustaše i Nezavisna Država Hrvatska,* 1941-1945 (Zagreb, 1977); and Bogdan Krizman, *Pavelić izmedju Hitlera i Mussolinija* (Zagreb, 1980). Nazi leaders initially opposed the Italian plan to install Pavelić as the head of the Indepedent State of Croatia. But after Maček refused to discuss their plans to install him as head of a German backed Croatian government, the Germans turned their attention seriously to Pavelić and the Ustashas. Jelić-Butić, *Ustaše i Nezavisna Država Hrvatska,* 64-65.

17. Krizman, *Jugoslavenske vlade u izbjeglištvu 1941-1943,* 30. Kvaternik's proclamation was a purely German affair; the Italian government and Pavelić

Pavelić made his way to Zagreb from Italy, accompanied by a few hundred Ustasha supporters.[18] During the next several weeks, he decreed the new laws of the Ustasha state, which were based on Ustasha ideology formulated during the previous decade.

The two main aspects of the Ustasha's political program were establishing a Croatian state and building a new social order. Ustashas viewed the Independent State of Croatia as purely Croat, a bulwark of western civilization against the Serb.[19] Ustashas stressed the supposed continuity between their beliefs and Starčević's ideals, referring to him as the father of their state and the inspiration of their cause. Arguing that Croats possessed special state-building capabilities, they intended to build a racially pure Croatia. As Kvaternik explained soon after he came to power: one third of the Serbs in Croatia would be forced to convert to Catholicism, one third to leave, and the remainder would be exterminated.[20] In April, Pavelić declared that all Serbs residing within the Independent State of Croatia had forfeited rights to protection and citizenship. In June, racial laws were passed prohibiting Serbs (and Jews and Gypsies) from employment in state service and outlawing interracial

---

abroad had little part in it. On April 4, Wesenmayer and other German representatives had Ustasha leaders Mile Budak, Slavko Kvaternik, and Mladen Lorković draw up a resolution stating that Yugoslavia had ceased to exist. They proclaimed an independent Croatian state and called upon Germany to support it. Jelić-Butić, *Ustaše i Nezavisna Država Hrvatska, 1941-1945,* 67.

18. There was a great deal of tension in those first few weeks between the local Ustashas and Ustashas who had returned to Zagreb with Pavelić. For more on this see Krizman, *Pavelić izmedju Hitlera i Mussolinija,* 52-55.

19. For a discussion of how Ustashas interpreted Starčević's views see Jelić-Butić, *Ustaše i Nezavisna Država Hrvatska, 1941-1945,* 142.

20. The Ustasha regime reached an agreement in June with Germany that Germany would expel a certain number of Slovenes to Croatia and Croatia would then expel an equal number of Serbs to Serbia. The expulsions were to occur in three phases. In the first phase, 5,000 Slovene intellectuals and "undesirables" would be expelled directly to Serbia, except Catholic clergy who would be sent to Croatia. In the second phase, from July 18 to August 30, 25,000 Slovenes would be sent to Croatia, which would expel an equal number of Serbs to Serbia. In the third phase from September 15 to October 31, 65,000 Slovenes would go to Croatia and an equal number of Serbs from Srijem would be expelled to Serbia, plus another 30,000 Serbs whom Ustasha authorities wanted to deport. This agreement did not work well in practice and before long Germans in Serbia refused to take Serbs from Croatia, claiming they did not have room for them. Krizman, *Pavelić izmedju Hitlera i Mussolinija,* 126.

marriages. New laws regulated Orthodox conversions.[21] Before long, bands of Ustashas began rampaging through Serb villages and killing those Serbs who did not have the good fortune to flee or convert.[22] These policies created chaos and the Ustasha's allies soon criticized them for failing to maintain order.[23]

The new Ustasha state was organized according to fascist precepts, delineated in the founding documents and constitution of the Ustasha movement in 1932 and 1933.[24] The *Poglavnik*, or Chief as Pavelić styled himself, was bolstered by a leadership cult and constituted the sole source of authority. All political parties were disbanded and, though the Sabor met several times in 1942, its function was to express the *Poglavnik's* will, not to legislate. Ustasha leaders attempted to staff a new administration, but there were not enough loyal Ustasha supporters to accomplish this task and most civil servants retained their posts.[25] Ustasha attempts to channel the population into various corporate groups met with equally little success.[26] The Ustashas paid most attention to the armed forces, organizing them into three main branches: the Home Guard, which functioned as the regular army, the Ustasha Army, which constituted the Ustasha's shock troops, and the gendarmerie.[27]

---

21. Members of the Serbian Orthodox church were now required to obtain permission from local authorities before converting to Catholicism. Krizman, *Pavelić izmedju Hitlera i Mussolinija*, 117-119.

22. There was a difference in views between German officers in Croatia like Glaise von Horstenau, who deplored Ustasha massacres of Serbs, and Kasche, who condoned them. In a meeting with Pavelić in June 1941, Hitler urged him to take a harsh stance toward the minority (Serb) problem in Croatia, and suggested that Pavelić carry out "nationally intolerant" policies for fifty years. Krizman, *Pavelić izmedju Hitlera i Mussolinija*, 49.

23. Ustasha apologists argue that if the government had not adopted extremist policies toward the Serbs, which overburdened its capacities, it would have been a viable political entity. For example, see Jare Jareb, *Pola stoljeća hrvatske politike* (Buenos Aires, Argentina, 1960).

24. For a description of these documents, see Bogdan Krizman, *Ante Pavelić i ustaše* (Zagreb, 1978), 86-90.

25. Jelić-Butić, *Ustaše i Nezavisna Država Hrvatska, 1941-1945*, 99-110.

26. *Ibid.*, 151-155. In August 1942, Ustashas presented in greater detail their social goals. They denounced the idea of class conflict and attempted to join the several groups and professions they claimed comprised the Croat nation into a "main union."

27. *Ibid.*, 114-123.

Though the number of troops grew over the next several months, these forces were unable to keep order in the new Croatian state.[28]

The most difficult task facing Ustasha leaders was to reconcile their rhetoric on Croatian independence with German and Italian demands. From the heady pronouncements issued in Zagreb at this time, the more harsh realities of Croatia's situation could scarcely be gleaned. Though an officially sovereign state, the Independent State of Croatia was divided into two zones of occupation: the Italian zone covering the southern half of Croatia's territory, running along a line approximately fifty miles west of Zagreb and Sarajevo; and the German zone to the north, including northern Bosnia, Slavonia, and the Karlovac region. The Italian area was further divided into three zones: zone one, along the annexed coastal region, and zones two and three, from the annexed zone to the demarcation line.[29] The regular Croatian army, or the Home Guard, was responsible for keeping order in the entire state, but it was subject to the command of the occupying authorities.

Germany considered Croatia part of the Italian sphere of influence. Nevertheless, it had considerable economic interests in Croatia. A May 16 economic agreement guaranteed the Reich unlimited use of Croatia's industrial base and natural resources.[30] These extractions and the export of Croat manpower to Germany were obvious signs of Croatia's subordination to the German war machine, and they were unpopular with the Croat populace. Moreover, though Germany originally intended to withdraw its troops quickly from Croatia, Partisan resistance made this impossible. Some German officials tried to convince Hitler of the advantages Germany would derive from playing a more active role in Croatia. For example, Glaise von Horstenau, the representative of the German armed forces in Zagreb, disputed Hitler's and Ribbentrop's view that Croatia was in the Italian sphere, and urged them to take advantage of Croats' allegedly strong pro-German sentiments.[31] During the first two years of the war, however, Nazi leaders continued to instruct that German occupying forces play only a limited role in Croatia.

---

28. *Ibid.*, 122. By the end of 1941, Ustasha forces numbered: Home Guards—70,000, Ustasha Army—15,000, gendarmerie—8,000. In the summer of 1941, Pavelić volunteered Croat units for the front, but even Kvaternik thought this idea ludicrous since these troops were performing so poorly at home.

29. These three zones were agreed upon before the invasion and a specific agreement confirming them was signed on April 23, 1941.

30. Germans were interested in Croatia's aluminum, copper, and coal. According to Jelić-Butić, they also imported about 55,000 workers from Croatia to Germany. Jelić-Butić, *Ustaše i Nezavisna Država Hrvatska, 1941-1945*, 123.

31. Krizman, *Pavelić izmedju Hitlera i Mussolinija*, 11-19.

Italian demands were much more troublesome for the Ustashas. In conversations with Mussolini and Italian Foreign Minister Ciano before he came to power, Pavelić promised to satisfy Italian claims to the Adriatic coast.[32] When Ciano and Pavelić met in Ljubljana on April 25 to discuss their bilateral relations, Pavelić was forced to keep this promise. The Rome Protocols, signed on May 18, called for Italian annexation of large portions of Dalmatia, including all but three Adriatic islands, parts of the Croatian Littoral, and the Bay of Kotor.[33] The northern portion of this territory was annexed directly to Italy; the remainder constituted the Governorship of Dalmatia with the Governor directly responsible to Mussolini. A member of the Italian royal family was declared King Tomislav II of the Independent State of Croatia, though he never set foot inside his domain.[34]

Pavelić tried to present these blows to Croatia's sovereignty in the best light. In a speech to an Ustasha gathering on May 21, he thanked the "great leaders of the two Axis powers" for helping Croatia to establish her independent borders. Assuring the populace that it possessed a truly Croatian monarch, he promised the new king would be "only a Croatian king and no one else's."[35] He also emphasized the importance of Bosnia-Hercegovina to the new state in an effort to justify the loss of Dalmatia, and insisted that the Muslims residing there were the most racially pure Croats. Ustasha leaders considered Bosnia-Hercegovina an essential part of their new state and, in the summer of 1941, they dispatched the Ustasha's best troops there in order to secure their rule. But the regime was unable to solidify its hold over large areas of Bosnia and especially Hercegovina. Despite these efforts to demonstrate his autonomy, Pavelić appeared dependent on Italian and German support and extremely vulnerable to their demands. As a result, his credibility as self-proclaimed protector of Croatia's interests was greatly diminished.

32. When Pavelić met with Ciano on January 23, 1940, they agreed on the future borders of the Independent State of Croatia. Ciano first argued that the Ustashas would have to assume power by their own efforts, but Pavelić convinced him that this strategy was too difficult and unlikely to succeed. Krizman, *Ante Pavelić i ustaše*, 326-328.
33. For the text of the Rome Protocols, see Nešović and Petranović, *AVNOJ i revolucija*, 23-24.
34. Relieved that he was not forced to accept a customs union with Italy, Pavelić was apparently satisfied with the agreement, and according to Glaise von Horstenau, was more self-confident upon his return from Rome. Krizman, *Pavelić izmedju Hitlera i Mussolinija*, 34.
35. *Ibid.*, 49.

It is difficult to measure precisely Croats' initial support for Pavelić.[36] The Ustasha organization was a relatively minor, underground group before the war and had a much smaller following than its fascist counterparts in Italy and Germany. The vast majority of Croats supported the Croat Peasant Party, not the Ustasha movement. Many Croats were undoubtedly sympathetic, however, to Pavelić's demands for an independent Croatian state. Judging from the crowds that turned out to greet him in April, some may have hoped to find in him the first modern leader of such a state.[37] Archbishop Stepinac was certainly not alone when he proclaimed the new state "the hand of God in action."[38] The Independent State of Croatia was far from independent, though, and this realization dampened what measure of enthusiasm Pavelić initally evoked. In order to broaden its popular base, the Ustasha regime was forced to look to the other major political force in Croatia, the Croat Peasant Party.

The Croat Peasant Party

When Pavelić assumed power in April 1941, the Ustashas, and especially the Germans, believed it essential to ensure CPP compliance to the new regime.[39] However, their efforts in this direction met with only mixed success. Maček refrained from denouncing Pavelić outright, but he refused to endorse him or to sanction the participation of several pro-Ustasha CPP leaders in the new government.[40] Nevertheless, on April 10, by German request, Maček issued a statement calling upon the "entire Croat people, to obey the new government" and for "all members of the CPP who are in administrative postions...to remain in [their] places and

---

36. For a social profile of Ustasha support, see Jelić-Butić, *Ustaše i Nezavisna Država Hrvatska, 1941-1945,* 72-73.

37. Maček describes the enthusiasm with which many Croats greeted the Germans. See Vladko Maček, *In the Struggle for Freedom* (New York: Robert Speller and Sons, Inc., 1957), 230-231.

38. Nešović and Petranović, *AVNOJ i revolucija,* 18.

39. Krizman, *Pavelić izmedju Hitlera i Mussolinija,* 59. Slavko Kvaternik advocated granting the CPP three or four ministries in the new government but Pavelić was apparently uninterested in this proposal.

40. Several CPP members such as Janko Tort ić, Lovro Šušić, Zvonko Kovačević, Josip Berković, and Stjepan Hefer joined the government, but their participation was not sanctioned by Maček.

to cooperate sincerely with the new government."[41] As a result of this statement, military units of the Peasant Defense controlled by the CPP laid down their arms peacefully and were mostly absorbed into the Home Guard.[42] A similarly orderly transfer of civil authority occurred. Since the Ustashas did not have enough members to take over civil administration, they usually retained those CPP officials who did not actively oppose them.

During the next several months, Ustasha leaders alternately wooed and suppressed Peasant Party members. They initially pressured CPP functionaries to declare themselves in favor of the new regime, threatening them with prison if they refused to comply. After the CPP was declared illegal, numerous Peasant Party officials were arrested. Many were released a few months later, however, when the Ustashas launched a campaign to gain CPP support. In August, a gathering of former CPP members was organized in the hopes of attracting Peasant Party leaders to the Ustasha movement.[43] When this effort failed, Pavelić lost interest in seeking CPP support. But his weak position and Axis pressure prompted him to renew the search for CPP allies before the end of the year.

During the weeks after the invasion, Maček met with his advisers to map out CPP strategy. Though the CPP was outlawed, Maček remained at liberty until his arrest at his home in Kupinec in August. In the meantime, the Peasant Party adopted a strategy similiar to those of pro-Allied political parties elsewhere in occupied Europe. Convinced that the ultimate outcome of the war and the fate of their own country would be decided by the "big powers," CPP leaders sought to maintain their organizational structure and bide their time until victory and Allied troops were near; only then would military resistance begin.[44] The CPP pursued a seemingly sensible strategy of relying on its overwhelming strength in Croatia and "sitting tight" for the duration of the war; but its strength was slowly drained by the circumstances in which it found itself.

---

41. Nešović and Petranović, *AVNOJ i revolucija*, 18. For Maček's account of how the Germans elicited this statement from him, see Maček, *In the Struggle for Freedom*, 229.

42. Jelić-Butić lists numerous incidents in which the Peasant Defense cooperated in raids against Serbs and participated in disarming units of the Yugoslav Army. Fikreta Jelić-Butić, *Hrvatska seljačka stranka* (Zagreb, 1983), 45-62.

43. Jelić-Butić, *Ustaše i Nezavisna Država Hrvatska, 1941-1945*, 194.

44 For Maček's account of this strategy see Maček, *In the Struggle for Freedom*, 227.

The Croat Peasant Party entered the war with a great deal of political clout and popular support. Both the Ustashas and the Communists perceived it as their main rival and obstacle to achieving their goals. Several characteristics of the Peasant Party undermined its strength during the war, however, ultimately permitting the Communists to gain political control in Croatia. First, the CPP did not possess the resources or inclination to wage an underground military struggle, preferring instead to rely on the Allies to resolve the military situation and support its political goals; nor did the Allies expect it to engage in immediate military actions. Moreover, without any experience in illegal work, the CPP was vulnerable to Ustasha arrests and harassment. The Peasant Party was especially hurt by Maček's arrest in August 1941 and his confinement throughout the war. Before the Axis invasion, almost all decisions had been made by Maček and a few trusted political advisors.[45] Though he became a powerful symbol around which to rally CPP members, his confinement virtually paralyzed the party. Furthermore, wartime pressures increased the fissures in an already fragmented party. Peasant Party members had diverse political interests; some supported the Ustashas, some had Communist sympathies, and the moderate majority grouped around Maček. As a portion of its membership sided openly with the Ustashas or the Communists, the party was fractured and drained. Finally, the CPP's position in the government in exile hurt the party's standing in the country. Croat ministers had poor relations with the British, who were convinced of their separatist sympathies and attempted to bypass them in their dealings with the Yugoslav government.[46] The CPP's failure to develop a Croat resistance force equivalent to the Serb Chetniks further diminished its standing with the Allies. Most importantly, it left a vacuum in the resistance movement in Croatia which the Communists ultimately succeeded in filling.

The CPY's Response to the Invasion

When war erupted in Yugoslavia in April 1941, CPY leaders quickly adapted to the dramatic change. The party possessed several characteristics which suited it for organizing a resistance movement: organizational

45. Jelić-Butić, *Hrvatska seljačka stranka*, 28-37.

46. For a discussion of British relations with the government in exile, see Mark Wheeler, *Britain and the War for Yugoslavia* (New York: Columbia University Press, 1980); Vojmir Klajković, "Jugoslavenska vlada u emigraciji i saveznici prema pitanju Hrvatske, 1941-1944," part 1, *Časopis za suvremenu povijest* 1 (1973).

unity, a countrywide base of operations, clandestine networks, a cadre with tremendous élan accustomed to operating underground—and it attempted to use these to its advantage. The CPY leadership survived the invasion and occupation intact. During the first few weeks of the war, it met frequently in Zagreb to evaluate the new situation and devise a wartime strategy.

The CPY's strategy was two-pronged: to resist the occupying powers and to press for fundamental social and political change. Communist leaders did not call for an armed uprising against the occupying powers until Germany invaded the Soviet Union in June. Meanwhile, they instructed Communists to gather arms, to expand and strengthen the party's organizational network, and to establish military detachments.[47] In several appeals released during the next few weeks, the CPY exhorted the population to resist the occupying powers and their collaborators with strikes, boycotts, and more overt forms of sabotage where possible. CPY leaders could not have predicted the enormous political success they experienced during the war, but they perceived the revolutionary potential of the new situation. In his speech outlining CPY strategy at the May Consultation, attended by Communist delegates from most of the country, Tito emphasized the dimensions of this revolutionary opportunity. The old machinery of the state, he asserted, would be either defunct or compromised by the end of the war; the CPY's task was to take control of it.[48] In order to do so, the party would have to create a mass movement.

The CPY used a combination of class and national appeals to draw the population into the Partisan resistance movement. In the first three months of the war, the population was urged to resist economic exploitation by the Ustasha government and the Axis powers who, as one flyer put it, "talk against captialism but then forbid strikes and the tariff movement."[49] Party cadres were instructed to discuss the problems of inflation, labor conditions, and food shortages in their appeals to the population. Communists organized protests against low wages, price increases and the export of labor to Germany. After June 22, Yugoslav

47. Ivan Jelić, "Tito i NOB u Hrvatskoj 1941 g.," *Časopis za suvremenu povijest* (1984): 112.
48. "Zaključci Aprilskog savetovanje KPJ održanog u Zagrebu 1941 g.," in *Zbornik dokumenata i podataka o narodnooslobodilackom ratu jugoslovenskih naroda (Zbornik dokumenata NORa)*, II/2/7.
49. Marijan Rastić, *Izbor iz arhivske gradje Komunističke partije Jugoslavije i Komunističke partije Hrvatske za povijest 1941 g. u Hrvatskoj, Arhivski Vjesnik*, XIV (Zagreb, 1971) 27.

Communists called for an uprising against the occupying forces and a fundamental change in the old political order. Despite Stalin's frequent exhortations to Yugoslav Communists to subdue their revolutionary rhetoric, social and political revolution was an essential part of the CPY's appeals to the population throughout the war.

As has been frequently noted, Tito's wartime strategy was at odds with Stalin's on a number of points.[50] During the first two months of the war, until the Soviet Union was invaded on June 22, the CPY adopted a hostile stance toward the fascist regimes, even though the Molotov-Ribbentrop Pact was still in effect. As the war progressed, CPY emphasis on revolutionary change diverged noticeably from Stalin's more moderate stance. Anxious to avoid antagonizing their western allies, the Soviets instructed Communist parties to concentrate on building a popular front with other political groups and on resisting the enemy, not on achieving Communist political goals. For this reason, they opposed Tito's attempts to establish new political institutions during the war. Nevertheless, despite Stalin's opposition, state-building remained a major part of the CPY's wartime strategy and was an essential component of its success in gaining power after the war.

In addition to its emphasis on social transformation, the CPY used national sentiments to mobilize the population in two ways. First, it aroused hatred toward the occupying powers and generated a patriotic fervor. During the spring and summer of 1941, numerous appeals were made to the population to unite and "drive all foreign powers from the land." "Brotherhood and unity in the struggle against the invader" became the slogan heard everywhere in Partisan camps. Images of past heroic struggles against occupying enemies were evoked and numerous references made to the common struggle of all Slavs. The CPY also portrayed itself as the champion of narrower national interests. The struggle against the invader, Tito stressed, was also a struggle against the old repressive order based on Serbian hegemony. By joining the CPY Partisan movement, Yugoslavia's national groups could ensure the demise of the old repressive system and achieve their national aims. The CPY avoided identifying itself with Yugoslav unitarism. In its appeals to the public, the term Yugoslav was rarely used; separate sections in CPY propaganda addressed each national group and emphasized different concerns.

Although the CPY promised to fight for national justice, it did not specify how this would be achieved within the framework of a Yugoslav

---

50. For example, see Paul Shoup, *Communism and the Yugoslav National Question* (New York and London: Columbia University Press, 1968), 60-101.

state. Party propaganda simply declared that after repulsing the Axis forces, "the people of Yugoslavia [would] on the basis of equality decide on their mutual relations"; more concrete discussion of this complicated problem was avoided. The CPY attempted to use national sentiments to elicit support and at the same time to remain committed to a unified state. But for a large proportion of Croats, the fulfillment of the former precluded the latter. When Communists began to shape a new political order during the last two years of the war, these two aspects of their strategy began to conflict. This problem was most acute in Croatia where CPC emphasis on Croatia's autonomy hindered CPY efforts to construct a centralized state.[51]

Communists faced enormous obstacles in eliciting Croat support for the Partisan movement. Their awareness of this fact is evident from the disproportionate amount of attention Croatia received in party directives and discussions during the spring of 1941. Since the Peasant Party refused to advocate military resistance to the occupying forces and the Ustashas, most Croats were reluctant to join Partisan units. CPY leaders also knew that support for Pavelić, however attenuated, was due in part to Croat desires for independence. Simply appealing to anti-German or anti-Italian sentiments would not easily rouse a population whose loyalty was to the Croat national movement, not to the Yugoslav state, especially since it appeared to some Croats that German and Italian support might be the only way to achieve their national aims. Finally, Communists found it difficult to appeal to Serbs and Croats simultaneously in Croatia and to organize them into the same resistance movement. Antagonism between these two groups, heightened by Ustasha

---

51. Various observers have remarked on the similarity between the CPY and the Communist Party of China (CCP) in their use of nationalism to mobilize the population. (For example, see Chalmers Johnson, *Peasant Nationalism and Communist Power*, Stanford: Stanford University Press, 1962.) In both cases, the Communist Party was able to generate popular support by drawing on the nationalist impulses of the population and by fighting against enemy forces. There are important dissimilarities between the two cases, however, and the dynamics of using nationalism to mobilize the population in Yugoslavia raised more complex problems for the CPY. In China, the Han Chinese, among whom the CCP concentrated its attention, comprised the vast majority of the population. Though the CCP did attempt to capitalize on the national discontent of the non-Han minorities when it was in those parts of the country, it did not, for the most part, have to address the more particular national concerns of other national groups in China since these were insignificant. By contrast, the CPY could not afford to ignore the national sentiments of Yugoslavia's constituent nationalities since Serbs comprised less than fifty percent of the population.

massacres of Serbs, meant that recognition of one was often perceived as a declaration of enmity by the other. Convincing Serbs and Croats in Croatia to fight side by side in the same detachments was a monumental task.

In the first two months of the war, CPC propaganda attempted to discredit both the Ustashas and the Croat Peasant Party. The CPC launched an attack on Pavelić aimed at dispelling the notion that the "comedy of the Independent State of Croatia" could fullfill Croats' desire for their own state. CPC flyers labeled Pavelić a stooge of the Germans and Italians, and the Ustashas as fascist marauders who made a mockery of Croat national aspirations. The fact that Pavelić had sold a huge portion of Croatian territory to the Italians and proclaimed an Italian King of Croatia proved he was unfit to defend Croatian statehood. His capitulation to the Italians could never be justified as a "sacrifice of national liberation" as he claimed.[52] CPC appeals reminded Croats that Germans and Italians had coveted Croatian lands for centuries. Croats could achieve their national aims only by expelling these traditional enemies and repossessing the annexed Dalmatian and Istrian territory.[53] As Pavelić's dependence on the occupying powers became more obvious, this propaganda became more effective.

The best approach toward the Croat Peasant Party proved more complicated to devise. Though Maček refused to condemn the Independent State of Croatia, he could hardly be denounced as a stooge of the Germans. His western sympathies were well known and he had rebuffed German overtures. The CPC faced a familiar dilemma in its relations with the Peasant Party; it could either attempt to elicit the cooperation of CPP leaders, which had not proved successful thus far, or denounce them and risk alienating CPP supporters. Communist policy toward the CPP during the next few years vacillated between these two approaches, neither of which produced satisfactory results. While the CPC did not pursue the all-out attack on Maček that it did on Pavelić in the spring of 1941, it criticized CPP leaders harshly. Maček and other bourgeois leaders were held responsible for the fall of Yugoslavia and accused of "paving the way" for Pavelić. As one CPC flyer put it, Pavelić was simply continuing the "deceptive and traitorous" policies of the Croat Peasant Party.[54] In their instructions to party organizations, CPC leaders emphasized that Croats were disheartened by CPP cooperation with

---

52. *Ibid.*, 33-35, CC CPC Report #1.
53. Arhiv Instituta za historiju radničkog pokreta Hrvatske (AIHRPH) KP-3/2.
54. Jelić-Butić, *Hrvatska seljačka stranka*, 129.

Pavelić; the Communists' task was to rouse these disillusioned Peasant Party followers to their cause.[55]

An equally important theme of CPC propaganda was the CPY's essential role in achieving Serb and Croat national aims. CPC flyers stressed that Communists were the only political force capable of ensuring national liberation. In appeals to Croats, the CPC vowed it would never permit a return of the "Versailles order" and of Serbian hegemony. Serbs in Croatia were also reassured that Communists had their interests at heart. As one flyer put it, Communists would achieve "not only the national liberation of Croatia...[but] ensure the national equality of Serbs in Croatia."[56] Party leaders knew that the success of the resistance movement hinged on Serb-Croat cooperation. Hence, they constantly warned that the occupying powers were encouraging national animosity in order to divide and rule and urged Serbs and Croats to join forces in resisting this strategy.

CPY Unity and the Case of Vazduh

The first serious challenge that Croat national sentiment posed to Tito and other Communist leaders in their efforts to build new political and military organizations concerned the question of party unity. Given the strong support in Croatia for the establishment of an independent state (though not necessarily in its current form) and the actual physical dismemberment of the country, some Communists in Croatia appear to have believed that conditions dictated the formation of an independent Communist Party of Croatia. This position had enormous implications not only for the shape of the resistance movement but for the shape of the state the Communists hoped to build by the end of the war. At the very least, some party members felt that Tito's revolutionary line, adopted after the June 22nd invasion of the Soviet Union, was not appropriate to the conditions in Croatia. The attempt by a Comintern functionary to establish a parallel Communist leadership in Croatia con-

---

55. On at least one occasion, Tito revealed quite a different opinion of Croats' views of CPP leaders. He wrote: "If the Ustasha gentlemen are counting on the fact that the Croat people have become disappointed in the leadership of the CPP because of its policies, then they should go to Croat villages and hear from whom the Croat peasants are rightfully expecting their salvation." Tito, *Sabrana djela*, vol. 7, 32-33.

56. Rastić, *Izbor dokumenata KPJ i KPH*, 26-30.

vinced Tito that he must intervene in Croatia to ensure party unity in the entire territory of Yugoslavia.

Shortly after the invasion and partition of Yugoslavia in the spring of 1941, Tito became concerned that some Communists in Croatia believed that since Croatia was now a separate state, the CPC should become a separate party. In an article written in May, entitled "Why We Are Still in the CPY," he chastised Communists in Croatia for their confusion about this matter and enumerated the reasons why the CPC had been established within the CPY.[57] The CPY had joined all national forces under its auspices during the interwar period, he wrote, not because it supported the previous Kingdom of Yugoslavia, but to oppose better its political foes. Similarly, all Communists in Yugoslavia should now join forces, Tito stated, and once victorious, "we will arrange our fraternal relations among ourselves in the best manner for ourselves and our peoples."[58] Tito was careful to mention that support for a unified Communist Party did not necessarily mean the CPY advocated a unified Yugoslavia. Nevertheless, despite his remarkably circumspect tone, his conclusion was unequivocal: the CPC would remain within the organizational confines of the CPY and continue to take its orders from Tito and the Politburo.[59]

Shortly after the May Consultation, Tito moved his headquarters to Belgrade and then again to western Serbia at the end of September. From there, he attempted to keep a close watch on events in Croatia. CPC leaders were expected to report biweekly to Tito and to consult with him on all important matters. In May, Tito dispatched CPY Central Committee member Vladimir Popović a Montenegrin Communist who had fought in the Spanish Civil war, to Croatia, where he served as Tito's mouthpiece and observer. Shortly thereafter, Popović was incorporated into the leadership of the CPC. Popović, Andrija Hebrang, Rade Končar (who was captured by the Italians in November 1941), and Vladimir Bakarić composed the inner core of leaders in the Communist-led Partisan movement in Croatia. Tito also sent Politburo member Edvard Kardelj and CC CPY member Ivo Lola Ribar to Croatia regularly during the war.[60]

---

57. Tito, *Sabrana djela*, vol. 7, 16-19. This article, "Zašto smo u sastavu KPJ" appeared in *Srp i čekić* #3-4-5, 6/41.

58 *Ibid.*

59. Tito, *Sabrana djela*, vol. 7, 16-17. This article appeared in *Srp i čekić* #3-4-5, 6/41.

60. Kardelj spent much of the summer of 1941 in Croatia and he and Ivo Lola Ribar were put in charge of the Commissariat for Nonliberated Territories, estab-

Despite Tito's attempts to supervise closely events in Croatia, Croat leaders were often left to their own devices during this period of the war. Communication between Croatia and the Supreme Staff was frequently interrupted for long intervals, leaving CPC leaders to respond independently to the situation in their own regions.[61] Occasionally these parochial concerns pulled CPC leaders in directions different from those envisioned by Tito, who had the interests of the entire movement in mind. Though he tolerated some differences of opinion by regional leaders, especially at the beginning of the war, Tito did not hesitate to set them "on course" when necessary.

After the German invasion of the Soviet Union on June 22, 1941, Tito became alarmed at an attempt by a Comintern functionary, Josip Kopinič (often referred to as Vazduh), to take over the Zagreb party organization and set up a parallel CPC leadership.[62] Shortly after the invasion began, the Comintern instructed Yugoslav Communists to organize all domestic political forces for immediate military action against Axis powers. In response, at a July 4 Politburo meeting in Belgrade, the CPY called for an armed insurrection. Communists in Croatia now faced the more difficult task of launching an uprising against Italians, Germans, and Ustashas. As the CPC reacted to the new situation, Kopinič moved to establish an independent party organization in Croatia.

Kopinič, who functioned as the radio liaison between CPY leaders in Belgrade and the Comintern, believed Communists in Croatia were delaying military resistance, despite Stalin's clear instructions to the contrary.[63] He became convinced that CPC recalcitrance could only be

---

lished in Zagreb in the spring of 1942. Although Ivo Lola Ribar was not one of the most important members of Tito's entourage during this period, his extensive reports to the CPY leadership indicate his vocal and active participation in events in Croatia.

61. According to Vladimir Bakarić, from January to June 1942 there was almost no contact between the Main Staff of Croatia and the Supreme Staff. Vladimir Bakarić, *To su bila čudesna vremena, dani herojstva* (Zagreb, 1971).

62. Vazduh was not Kopinič's real conspiratorial name. It was Bakarić who first refered to him as "Vazduh" (which means air in Serbo-Croatian)—a man out of air, or without firm footing. This nickname was also an allusion to Kopinič's radio link with Moscow.

63. Josip Kopinič is an enigmatic and controversial figure in Yugoslav Communist history. Of Slovenian descent, Kopinič was a Comintern and probably a Soviet secret police (NKVD) functionary. He spent most of his years before the war working in Moscow until he was sent to Zagreb in 1939.

explained by enemy penetration at the highest levels.[64] He was joined in his campaign against the CPC leadership by Pavle Pap, a member of the CPC Central Committee and a radio operator in Zagreb.[65] In a cable sent to Tito on July 1, Kopinič accused Popović, Končar, and Srebrnjak (Antonov), an agent of the Soviet military counterintelligence, of being spies. Tito responded to Kopinič on July 6, and though acknowledging that CPC leaders had made certain mistakes, chastised Kopinič for making charges against "the entire family," that is, the whole party. Failing to receive the response he sought from Tito, Kopinič repeated his charges to the Comintern that the CPC had been penetrated and requested permission to "remedy" the situation.[66] In response, the Comintern entrusted Kopinič "to create another center which will carry out the line ordered by us."[67] Kopinič used this apparent endorsement from the Comintern to convince Zagreb Party Secretary Anton Rob to undertake a major operation—rescuing Communists held in the Kerestinec prison—independently of the CPC leadership.[68]

Rescuing Communists in Kerestinec became top priority for CPC leaders when the execution of several CPC prisoners on July 9 highlighted the precarious situation of other Communists held there.[69] This notoriously brutal Ustasha prison contained Communists incarcerated by the Banovina government who were transferred to Ustasha authority in

---

64. Ivan Jelić, *Tragedija Kerestinca* (Zagreb, 1987), 38-43, 182-183. According to Kopinič, he asked CPC leaders several times about their plans for military action against the Nazis, but they appeared to him reluctant to act. Zagreb Party Secretary Anton Rob reportedly told Kopinič that Hebrang, Končar, and Popović had threatened to expel from the party anyone who began armed actions against the Germans. Kopinič claimed that when he met with Popović and Pap on June 22, Popović insisted that it made no sense to blow up bridges since the Russians would be in Yugoslavia within a few weeks, and he called Kopinič a "coward" for thinking otherwise. In a later report to the CPY investigatory commission, Končar denied ever having promised to blow up a local railway line.

65. Pap also wrote a letter to Tito on July 1 in which he complained that "certain comrades in the Military Committee" were "objectively and perhaps not only objectively" sabotaging resistance activity. See Cenčić, *Enigma Kopinič*, vol. 2, 200. See also Jelić, *Tragedija Kerestinca*, 178-179.

66. *Ibid.*, 226.

67. Kopinič says he cabled back that only the CPY had the authority to remove the CC CPC, but such a document, if it exists, is in Soviet archives. Cenčić, *Enigma Kopinič*, vol. 2, 226.

68. Kopinič also asked Bakarić to help establish a new CPC leadership, but he refused.

69. Among those executed were Adžija, Keršovani, Richtmann, and Prica.

April, and numerous others who had been arrested since that time. On July 10, CPC leaders Končar, Popović, Mrazović, and Hebrang met and decided to mount a rescue attempt on July 14.[70] Unknown to CPC leaders, the Zagreb party organization, at Kopinič's instigation, devised its own rescue plan for Saturday night, July 13.[71] When CPC leaders discovered this plan the day it was to go into effect, they vehemently criticized the Zagreb party organization for its risky and poorly conceived arrangement and for failing to consult with them; they also decided that at this point they had no choice but to support the plan. Not surprisingly, the rescue attempt was a complete failure as in the confusion various groups of Communists failed to arrive at the appointed time or place; of the approximately ninety prisoners who fled the prison, only eight survived.[72]

As a result of the bungled prison escape, Tito formed a commission to investigate the activities of Kopinič and his CPC rivals.[73] He dispatched Serb party leader Blagoje Nešković to Zagreb where he was joined by Popović and Kardelj. Several days later, Tito decided to remove the entire Zagreb party organization and to give other members of the CPC Central Committee (CC) the "strongest reprimand." While he objected to Kopinič's machinations, and asked the Comintern to have him removed,

---

70. Mrazović devised a plan. On the night of July 14, groups of Communists from the surrounding areas would make their way into Kerestinec and aid prisoners in breaking out of the prison. Trucks driven from Zagreb earlier that evening would wait outside and convey the prisoners to their destination, for some, Zagreb, and for the majority, the liberated territory of Kordun and Banija.

71. At a given signal, Communists inside Kerestinec would overpower the guards and make their way to a particular exit. They would be met there by Communists who would provide logistical support as the prisoners charged through the prison gates. *Ibid.*, 85-88. See also Vladimir Dedijer, *Novi prilozi za biografiju Josipa Broza Tita* (Rijeka and Zagreb, 1982), vol. 2, 437-470.

72. Given the riskiness of attempting to overpower prison guards from the inside, the operation proceeded remarkably smoothly. In less than half an hour, the ninety or so Communist prisoners managed to tie up their guards, without raising a general alarm, and to make their way to the designated exit. At this point, the escape went awry, since no one was there to meet them. The fleeing prisoners failed to notice the truck waiting outside and they took to the woods on foot. There, they were hunted by Ustasha troops. Most were killed in shootouts and those who were captured were executed shortly after their return to Kerestinec.

73. The unsuccessful prison-break was discussed the next day at a rancorous meeting of CPC leaders in Zagreb and at a July 16 Politburo meeting in Belgrade. Dedijer, *Novi prilozi za biografiju Josipa Broza Tita,* vol. 2, 469; Jelić, *Tragedija Kerestinca,* 123-128.

he also believed CPC shortcomings responsible for the fiasco at Kerestinec. In a letter to the CPC Central Committee on July 17, he charged it with failing to comprehend the situation in Croatia after June 22.[74] Instead of engaging in military action, he wrote, CPC leaders had wasted time discussing the competency of the "military line." Tito compared Croatia unfavorably to other areas of the country where he believed the resistance movement was making greater strides. "We are sorry," he wrote, "that once again things had to come to such a stand, particularly in the Croatian CC."[75] Communists in Croatia were instructed to rectify their mistakes and to organize resistance activities as quickly as possible.

The "case of Vazduh" remains a controversial event in Yugoslav historiography. Was it an attempt by Croat Communists, as some have charged, to establish a separate Communist Party in Croatia? Were CPC leaders deliberately ignoring CPY and Comintern instructions? Did the Comintern try to create a separate CPC or use the Zagreb party organization to aim a blow at Tito? Or was Kopinič's personal ambition largely responsible for the July fiasco? What was the significance of this affair for CPY efforts to mobilize Croats and Serbs into the Partisan movement?

It is possible that the Comintern believed a separate CPC would be more effective after Yugoslavia was partitioned. It is even conceivable, though there is no concrete evidence to suggest this, that the Comintern initiated Kopinič's actions regarding the Zagreb party organization. In any case, the Soviets were clearly concerned, indeed frantic, to initiate anti-Axis resistance abroad to slow down the German military advance. Their communications with Yugoslav Communists and Kopinič repeatedly stressed this point. They were undoubtedly worried by Kopinič's reports on Croatia, hence their instructions that he take action to hasten armed resistance against the Germans.

What about accusations that some Communists were attempting to establish a separate party? Again, there is insufficient evidence to support this conclusion. The participants in these events all denied this intent. Rob himself appears to have been a reluctant and unfortunate pawn of Kopinič. True, there was enough confusion about whether a separate CPC was warranted in the new conditions that Tito had felt compelled to caution against it the previous May, and some participants in the July events may have wished for such an outcome. But CPC leaders Hebrang, Popović, and Končar do not appear to have been confused about this matter.

---

74. Jelić, *Tragedija Kerestinca*, 186-188.
75. *Ibid.*, 186-188; Cenčić, *Enigma Kopinič*, vol. 2, 273.

Some Communist leaders at the time attributed the Kerestinec fiasco to the fact that the CPC was "once again" out of step with the rest of the party. CPC leader Pavle Pap in his report to the investigatory commission charged that the "old sickness of 1939" had reappeared in the party leadership in the spring of 1941, suggesting that the CPC was influenced unduly by such "liberal" forces as the CPP.[76] Tito implied the same in his letter of July 17.[77] CPC leaders evidently disagreed among themselves about the tactics of armed resistance, with some of them taking a more moderate line. Though there are no minutes from CPC meetings in the spring and summer of 1941, later accounts indicate that some leaders felt it premature to organize widespread military activities.[78] In Croatia, where the party was less conspiratorial and acutely aware of the national aspirations of the populace, massive insurrection against the new Croatian state must have seemed a less appealing tactic. Ustasha power was at its height at this time, and taking on the Germans, Italians, and Ustashas was a formidable task indeed. Moreover, CPP support in the countryside was overwhelming and it was difficult for the CPY to organize there. As Vladimir Bakarić described in his account of this period, CPC members preferred to conduct military diversions in the cities where they were stronger.[79] Finally, CPC members had less experience with illegal work and many of them hesitated to go underground with the party when the Ustashas took power.

Whether CPC leaders had difficulty launching the uprising because of these obstacles, or because several of them consciously delayed military resistance, cannot be fully ascertained. In any case, it is important not to exaggerate differences between CPC and CPY actions at this time. The CPC did not call for an armed uprising in the days immediately following the invasion of the Soviet Union, but neither did the CPY.[80] During the investigation of events at Kerestinec, CPC leaders mollified Tito by explaining that they had attempted to initiate armed resistance as soon as

---

76. Cenčić, *Enigma Kopinič* vol. 2, 200.

77. Jelić, *Tragedija Kerestinca,* 186-188.

78. Pavle Pap charged that Hebrang and Popović were reluctant to initiate military resistance to the occupying powers. Cenčić, *Enigma Kopinič,* vol. 2, 200; see also Vladimir Bakarić, *To su bila čudesna vremena, dani herojstva* (Zagreb, 1976), 15.

79. Bakarić, *To su bila čudesna vremena, dani herojstva,* 15.

80. Several days after the invasion, a CPC circular directed party members to move gradually from passive resistance and sabotage to strikes and demonstrations and finally to armed struggle. Some areas could only offer passive resistance; areas such as Dalmatia, Lika, and Slavonia were instructed to establish guerrilla bands. Jelić, *Tragedija Kerestinca,* 160-163.

it became clear that this was the CPY line. Moreover, CPC leaders were not the only Communists who had difficulty adjusting to the new situation after June 22. Serb party leader Blagoje Nešković was also reprimanded by Tito for failing to initiate actions quickly enough in Serbia.[81]

Kopinič must be held in large part responsible for the bungled prison escape and for the actions of the Zagreb party organization. He appeared to several Communists at the time, as Popović put it, "sick with ambition." Kardelj suggested that Kopinič "perhaps unconsciously intended to strike at [Tito] and the entire leadership."[82] Tito also thought Kopinič at fault, though he was powerless to have him removed against Comintern wishes. Whether Kopinič simply wanted to accelerate military resistance or had more ominous motives remains the subject of debate.[83] His actions clearly created confusion among CPC leaders and hindered military resistance in Croatia in the days following the invasion of the Soviet Union. In the end, the failed prison escape robbed the CPC of numerous cadres and valuable leaders. It also had the effect, however, of hastening the CPC's transformation into a conspiratorial party capable of organizing widespread military resistance and a popular uprising against the occupying powers.

Ultimately, the most important outcome of the incident of Vazduh was that it excluded the possibility of establishing an independent Communist Party in Croatia. Tito and other party leaders, including those in Croatia, understood the important political implications of establishing a separate party organization, and they appear to have been firmly opposed to this strategy. Henceforth, though attempts would be made in Croatia to carve out the largest sphere of decision-making authority, all efforts to construct the new state would be within the framework of a unified Yugoslavia.

The Uprising and the Problem of Serbs in the Movement

The uprising against the occupying powers began in Croatia at the end of July. Armed resistance broke out in much of Yugoslavia at this time; portions of western Serbia were under Partisan control and almost

---

81. Dedijer, *Novi prilozi za biografiju Josipa Broza Tita*, vol. 2, 357.
82. *Zbornik dokumenata NORa*, II/2/28.
83. For Kopinič's version of events, see Cenčić, *Enigma Kopinič*. See also Dedijer, *Novi prilozi za biografiju Josipa Broza Tita*, vol. 2, 470-477. For a more incriminating view of Kopinič's motivations for setting up a separate CPC leadership, see Milenko Doder, *Kopinič bez enigme* (Zagreb, 1986).

all of Montenegro was in revolt. In many regions resistance began spontaneously. In others, it was organized by Communists, sometimes in cooperation with Chetniks. In Croatia, the uprising began in the southern and western part of the country: Lika, Kordun, and Banija, where large numbers of Serbs took to the hills to escape Ustasha massacres.[84]

The influx of Serb recruits to Partisan ranks during the uprising offered the Partisans certain advantages; it also caused them many problems. Threatened by Ustasha massacres, Serbs in Croatia had nothing to lose in fighting an obviously superior enemy. They were dedicated and desperate fighters. But as the Partisans became predominantly Serb, attracting Croats became more difficult. Croats began to perceive the Partisans as a Serb or Chetnik force, and the Ustashas did all they could to reinforce this image, referring to Partisans as "Serb Communists" or "Communist Chetniks" in an effort to discredit them. In the atmosphere of hatred generated by Ustasha massacres and Chetnik reprisals, it was extremely difficult to unite Serbs and Croats in the same resistance movement. This difficulty was exacerbated by Serb Partisans' tendency during the first two years of the war to behave as if they were members of an exclusively Serb organization.[85]

Communist leaders worried about the preponderance of Serbs among Partisans in Croatia from the first days of the uprising. Vladimir Popović complained about this problem to Tito in August 1941, and party leaders continued to discuss it in their communications during the winter and spring of 1942.[86] In the fall of 1941, Tito repeatedly urged CPC leaders to recruit more Croats since the Partisans could not become a significant force in Croatia without them. "The weakness of the Partisan movement in Croatia," Tito wrote in October, "is that it includes the Serb population in Kordun and Lika etc., but a very small number of Croat peasants...

---

84. Croatia can be divided into three areas of resistance activity: (1) regions in southern and western Croatia in which liberated territory was established, (2) areas such as Dalmatia and the Croatian Littoral in which Partisan detachments were active militarily, and (3) areas north of the Sava and Kupa rivers where there was little or no resistance activity. For a detailed description of the uprising see Dušan Bilandžić et al, *Komunistički pokret i socijalistička revolucija u Hrvatskoj* (Zagreb, 1969), 209-215.

85. Croat exclusivity was also a concern of CPC leaders, and some Partisan units displayed hostility toward Serbs. For example, CPC leaders objected to a leaflet issued in Bjelovar in the summer of 1941 that did not mention "the terror being perpetrated against Serbs" and did not invite Serbs to join with Croats in a common struggle. *Zbornik dokumenata NORa*, II/V/ 143-153, CPC Circular #3.

86. For example, see *Zbornik dokumenata NORa*, V/3/126; *Zbornik dokumenata NORa*, V/3/137; AIHRPH KP-6/159, Bakarić to CC CPC, 12/27/41.

Everything depends on the Croat people."[87] The movement in Croatia will never succeed, he wrote again the following spring, until Croats compose the majority in Partisan units.[88] CPC leaders knew that, in order to avoid becoming entangled in communal violence, they must resist national exclusivity and encourage Serbs and Croats to fight together in Partisan detatchments. But accomplishing this task became increasingly difficult as mutual distrust between these two nations grew.

Some Partisans began to display worrisome attitudes of Serb exclusivity in the fall of 1941. Partisan forces in Croatia received their initial burst of support from Serbs seeking to protect their lives and homes from Ustasha destruction. These Serbs fought furiously to fortify their own villages against Ustasha incursions but balked when asked to liberate Croat villages. As one Partisan commander complained: "They [Serb recruits] expect us to defend their interests, and if we don't, they refuse to support us."[89] The most glaring example of this behavior was in the heavily Serb populated territory of Kordun, where Partisans established a "little republic" encompassing mostly Serb villages.[90] According to Vladimir Bakarić, Partisans in Kordun fought only to expand or defend the borders of their republic, which they memorialized in Partisan songs; otherwise they "slept."[91] Kordun Partisans showed little interest in contacting neighboring Croat villages or in recruiting Croats into their detachments. Indeed, the surrounding Croat villages knew nothing of what occurred inside Kordun liberated territory and many believed the Partisans there to be Chetniks.[92]

Communist leaders viewed Partisans' tendency to establish liberated territory primarily in Serb-populated areas of Croatia as particularly dangerous to the movement. Yugoslav Communists had adopted a strategy of establishing large liberated territories where they could build political institutions and influence, even though this strategy hindered the mobility required by guerrilla tactics. Failing to build these political institutions in Croat areas would prevent Communists from establishing a viable power base there.

Partisans in Croatia were also frequently hostile toward Croats in their midst. Croats sympathetic to the uprising were sometimes suspected of

---

87. Tito, *Sabrana djela*, vol. 7, 137. See also Tito, *Sabrana djela*, vol. 7, 193.

88. Tito, *Sabrana djela*, vol. 9, 205, Tito to the Main Staff of Croatia, 4/7/41. See also AIHRPH KP-7/79.

89. AIHRPH KP-8/119.

90. *Zbornik dokumenata NORa*, V/3/126, Bakarić to the Supreme Staff, 3/28/42.

91. *Zbornik dokumenata NORa*, V/3/133.

92. *Zbornik dokumenata NORa*, V/3/126.

being spies, and instead of being greeted warmly upon their arrival in liberated territory, were interrogated with suspicion.[93] Bakarić described this attitude toward Croats, which was expressed in a question put to him by a detachment commander. How could Bakarić be one of theirs, the commander asked, if he was a Croat?[94] As a Partisan from Banija put it, "Serbs have fought and liberated themselves. Why should they now fight for Croats? Let [Croats] do that themselves."[95] Partisan commanders warned repeatedly of the "chauvinism" these attitudes engendered, but they were often helpless to temper it during the first two years of the war.[96]

Partisan commanders were forced to walk the difficult line of protecting Serbs from Ustasha massacres and refusing to participate in communal violence. Hostility toward Croats occasionally resulted in reprisals against them, and Partisan commanders were sometimes unable to prevent raids by Partisan forces upon Croat villages in retaliation for earlier pillages of Serb villages. Moreover, distinguishing Ustashas from the Croat civilian population was frequently a difficult task, even when Partisans were inclined to try. Partisan detachments sometimes took measures against entire Croat villages suspected of Ustasha sympathies, and those Croats who weren't killed or imprisoned as Ustasha symphathizers were often subjected to harsh restrictions.[97] Feeling like they were in hostile territory in Croat villages, Partisans often did little to make themselves more palatable to the Croat population.[98] Usually they

---

93. Bakarić described the unfriendly treatment accorded Croats in a letter to the CC CPC in January, 1942. *Zbornik dokumenata NORa,* V/3/22-25.

94. *Zbornik dokumenata NORa,* V/2/118.

95. AIHRPH KP-12/317.

96. AIHRPH KP-10/234.

97. A commander from Banija described the difficulty of winning over Croats in villages where Partisans were forced to kill many Ustashas: "That is a consequence of our breakthrough into such bloody villages (and they are the majority in Banija) where there are few who haven't gotten blood on their hands and where we had to kill many Ustashas. Besides that, those Ustashas who didn't have blood on their hands were often killed." AIHRPH KP-10/243.

98. In a letter to the CPY Central Committee on April 1, 1942, Popović described some mistakes the Partisans had made in the first year of the war: "In addition to this organizational weakness, our leaders and some party organizations committed impermissible mistakes from a propaganda point of view in carrying out the party line of a unified front. In some places more, in some places less, and particularly at the beginning, they 'Serbed it up,' and that was reflected in Partisan actions conducted in Croat villages." AIHRPH KP-8/98.

would pacify these villages quickly and then depart for more receptive Serb ground.[99]

Serb Partisans were especially hesitant to recruit Croat members into their detachments, fearing they would be unreliable fighters.[100] CPC leaders emphasized the importance of attracting Croats from the Home Guard to Partisan ranks. But Partisans often avoided recruiting captured Home Guards or shunned them when they expressed a desire to join.[101] Croats were also frequently excluded from the administrative bodies established in liberated territory.[102] CPC leaders complained that these bodies were often used to promote exclusively Serb interests, instead of providing a means of attracting Croat support.[103] They instructed Partisan units to concentrate on organizing Croats, especially CPP members, into national liberation committees.[104] As a CPC directive in May explained: "It must be made clear to every party member and every Partisan that we won't accomplish our task, we won't mobilize Croat villages into the struggle, if we go into Croat villages with the intention of disarming them, hold some meeting, and then pull out, but only if we remain there, organize a government and defend that village in case of enemy attack."[105]

Realizing their survival depended upon it, CPC leaders attempted to curb Partisan hostility toward Croats. CPC leaders decided a Croat, Vladimir Bakarić, should be appointed political commissar of the Main Staff of Croatia.[106] Croats, who due to their party pedigree were also generally appointed as political commissars in Partisan detachments, were instructed to impress upon Partisans the importance of "brotherhood and unity" and the need to recruit Croat fighters. A party circular released in December 1941 emphasized that commissars should avoid

---

99. AIHRPH KP-8/185.

100. *Zbornik dokumenata NORa*, V/3/35.

101. *Zbornik dokumenata NORa*, V/3/30.

102. AIHRPH KP-10/243. Banija party leaders gave figures for Serb and Croat party membership in the summer of 1942. Although Croats were about one half as numerous as Serbs among the general population in the area (48,700 to 91,300), they comprised less than one third of the party membership (63 to 337).

103. *Zbornik dokumenata NORa*, II/2/93. See also Tito, *Sabrana djela*, vol. 8, 63, Letter to the CC CPC, 1/1/42

104. AIHRPH KP-11/245.

105. AIHRPH KP-8/185.

106. Orešković was originally appointed political commissar, but he was killed before he could take this position. Partisan leaders then debated whether Vladimir Bakarić or Andrija Hebrang should have the job, and it went to the former. Bakarić, *To su bila čudesna vremena, dani herojstva*, 22.

esoteric topics of Marxism-Leninism and concentrate on practical questions like relations between Serbs and Croats, "the mobilization of the Croat citizenry," and increasing Croat participation in the national liberation committees.[107] Despite these efforts, however, political commissars were often ignored by the rank and file, and circumvented by Partisan commanders, who resented commissars' interference in what they believed to be their own sphere of authority.[108]

Vladimir Bakarić engaged in a particularly fierce battle with Kordun Partisans to curb their tendency toward "Serbing it up" (*srbovanje*) and their hostility toward Croats. At the beginning of January 1942, Bakarić sent a sharply critical letter to Kordun Partisans, instructing them to improve relations with nearby Croats and to obey orders from the Main Staff.[109] He complained repeatedly to CPC leaders about the attitude of Kordun Partisans toward Croats and, charging that they were trying to set up "some kind of court," threatened to settle accounts with them.[110] Bakarić was particularly upset that Kordun Partisans had failed to solicit support from captured Home Guards, and he instructed Kordun Communists that henceforth all Home Guards were to be induced to join Partisan ranks.[111] In one instance, he objected, Kordun Partisans had taken four hundred Home Guards prisoner and had failed to recruit a single one![112] Refusing to accept Croat recruits because they might not be reliable, he wrote, was akin to "a nonswimmer who won't go into the water until he has learned to swim."[113] Croats would learn to trust the Partisans, and the Partisans learn to trust Croats, only if they fought together in the same Partisan detachments.

After sharp prodding by Bakarić at a meeting of the Main Staff attended by Kordun Partisans at the end of January, Kordun Partisans admitted their mistakes and promised to change their behavior toward Croats. Shortly thereafter, the political commissar of the Kordun Partisan detachments sent out a directive concerning relations with Croats.[114] The directive attempted to diminish Serb resentment of Croats by explaining

---

107. *Zbornik dokumenata NORa,* V/2/93.

108. During the first year of the war there was much discussion about how to delineate the spheres of authority between political commissars and Partisan commanders. For example, see AIHRPH KP-1/9, CC CPY to political commissars in Croatia, 1/29/42.

109. *Zbornik dokumenata NORa,* V/2/118.

110. *Zbornik dokumenata NORa,* V/3/23.

111. *Zbornik dokumenata NORa,* V/3/35.

112. *Zbornik dokumenata NORa,* V/3/30.

113. *Zbornik dokumenata NORa,* V/3/35.

114. *Zbornik dokumenata NORa,* V/3/32.

why many Croats had failed to join the Partisan movement. Croats had been left to Ustasha propaganda, the directive stated, which every day bombarded them with claims that victory for the Partisans would mean defeat for them. Only greater Partisan attention to Croats' fears would cure them of this false notion. Recruiting Croats and establishing good relations with them was top priority for all Partisans since, the political commissar wrote, "without the participation of Croats we cannot attain our final goal." Despite this directive, and continual reminders from CPC leaders, some Partisans continued to shun Croat recruits.[115] Serb chauvinism among Partisans remained an extremely worrisome problem for CPC leaders, particularly since Peasant Party hostility toward the Partisans made attracting Croat support difficult.

The Popular Front

As part of their effort to elicit Croat support, Communists in Croatia attempted to form a Popular Front with the Croat Peasant Party in the summer of 1941. When the Soviet Union was invaded on June 22, the Comintern instructed the CPY to initiate formal cooperation with the major political parties and to establish an "anti-fascist front." Consequently, Communists approached political and military groups all over the country. In Slovenia, they established a Liberation Front with Christian Socialists, Sokol (a gymnastic organization) members, and various cultural groups. Though Communists did not reach formal agreements with political parties in other parts of the country, in some places they cooperated informally during the uprising in the summer. In Croatia, where the Popular Front was deemed most necessary, however, it proved the biggest disappointment.

CPC leaders introduced the National Liberation Front in Croatia in July. At the beginning of August, a CPC directive outlined the goals of the Popular Front policy, which were repeated the next day in the first issue of *Vjesnik*, the mouthpiece of the National Liberation Front. *Vjesnik* called upon "all patriots, members of the Croat Peasant Party, and the Independent Democratic Party" to join the National Liberation Front and "to drive out the occupying forces, depose the collaborationist regimes and enable the people themselves to chose their government and politi-

---

115. CPC leaders complained of this attitude in numerous letters to Tito and the Supreme Staff. For example, see Main Staff in Croatia to the Supreme Staff, 3/28/42, *Zbornik dokumenata NORa*, V/3/126. See also *Zbornik dokumenata NORa*, V/3/137.

cal order according to the free will of the majority."[116] The tone of the newspaper was conciliatory and stressed the common interests of the Communists and the CPP. It pointed out that only a small number of Croats in the Peasant Defense had cooperated with the authorities or participated in Ustasha massacres of Serbs, and urged Croats opposed to Pavelić, especially soldiers in the Home Guard, to join the uprising to build a "free, independent, and progressive Croatia."[117]

Eliciting cooperation from Maček and other CPP leaders was crucial to the Popular Front policy in Croatia, so the Communists' previous criticism of Maček ceased. In June and July, intermediaries approached Maček and other Croat leaders in Zagreb and asked them to join the National Liberation Front. Although he expressed disapproval of Pavelić and his policies, Maček emphatically rejected any cooperation with the CPY, retorting that he would have "nothing to do with the Communists."[118] According to one CPP member, who later became a Communist sympathizer, when he approached Maček about the possibility of cooperation with the Partisans in 1943, he received the reply: "Whoever deals with them, shall not deal with me." On this point, Maček never wavered.

Despite Maček's rejection of their offer to cooperate, CPC leaders continued to search for allies in the Peasant Party. Prisons had been a traditional place of interaction between members of the two groups; however, the harsher conditions of Ustasha camps made such contact difficult. Consequently, Tito instructed the CPC to intensify its search for Peasant Party leaders who remained at liberty and were willing to go underground with the resistance movement.[119] In fact, the CPC had little success finding CPP collaborators anywhere in Croatia, inside prison or out. Vladimir Popović described to Tito the difficulty of attracting CPP leaders who "bow toward the Ustashas, occupy important places in state service, arm themselves, and wait while the Communists come to blows with the occupiers and the Ustashas."[120] Still, Tito persisted. "We have heard nothing from you about the National Liberation Front," he complained at the end of August. "The question of a joint front of all demo-

---

116. *Dokumenti historije Komunističke partije Hrvatske: Vjesnik 1941-1943* (Zagreb, 1955), 9.

117. Rastić, *Izbor iz arhivske gradje KPJ i KPH*, 199/51-53.

118. Jelić-Butić, *Hrvatska seljačka stranka*, 132

119. Tito, *Sabrana djela*, vol. 7, 110, Tito to CC CPC, 9/5/41.

120. Cited in Jelić-Butić, *Hrvatska seljačka stranka*, 136.

cratic and patriotic elements in Croatia...is the most important task which stands before all progressive fighters."[121]

Tito raised the idea in mid-August of establishing a National Committee as the mouthpiece of the Popular Front, and instructed the CPC to find Peasant Party leaders willing to join it.[122] It is doubtful that this attempt would have succeeded, given the reluctance of other political groups to participate in such a body. In any case, Tito was discouraged from pursuing it by Soviet leaders, who did not wish to disturb their relations with the government in exile.[123] Though Soviet opposition to Tito's plans to establish a central political body during the next two years was a continual source of frustration to him, it may have been a blessing in disguise. The CPY could not have controlled a central political body in 1941 as it did later in the war. Furthermore, it forced the party into a mobilizing strategy based on building political structures from below that ultimately proved advantageous to it.

As part of their effort to build support from below, Communists established administrative bodies or national liberation committees in the localities.[124] The Popular Front policy had initially called for establishing committees of the National Liberation Front, which would "serve as the executive arm of the coalition of political forces."[125] Since no real political cooperation with the CPP materialized, these bodies did not in fact exist. Instead, local bodies appeared over the summer in liberated areas, spontaneously at first, and then under the direction of Partisan units. When they moved into an area, Partisans removed local political officials and replaced them with national liberation committees which conducted civil administration and assisted in gathering military supplies. These local political bodies gave the Partisans a great advantage over the Chetniks, who paid little attention to political organization. They also allowed the CPC to control more directly Peasant Party members who joined the Partisans.

By the end of the summer of 1941, the Popular Front had received virtually no support from CPP leaders, all of whom held firm to Maček's line. As a result, the CPC began to appeal more directly to CPP rank and

---

121. Tito, *Sabrana djela*, vol. 7, 8, Tito to CC CPC, 8/17/41.

122. *Zbornik dokumenata NORa*, V/1/8, Tito to Končar and Popović, 8/41.

123. Janko Pleterski, "Perspektiva federativnog ujedinjenja u novoj Jugoslaviji kao faktor NOBa," *Časopis za suvremenu povijest* 3 (1973): 5.

124. For more on these political organizations, see Branko Petranović and Vojislav Simović, *Istorija narodne vlasti* (Belgrade, 1979), 179-181.

125. For a discussion of the committees of the National Liberation Front, see Dušan Živković, *Narodni front Jugoslavije, 1935-1945* (Belgrade, 1978), 130-144.

file.[126] At the beginning of September, the CPC published an appeal to Peasant Party members and soldiers in the Home Guard filled with references to Croat national aspirations. It exhorted CPP members to "remember your illustrious tradition, the spirit of the great Matija Gubec, the struggle of Radić and the struggles of many other fighters and martyrs for the freedom of the Croat people and go bravely into battle, the battle for the liberation of the Croat people and all the peoples of Yugoslavia."[127] In the next CPC circular in December, party members were criticized for relying too heavily on CPP leaders "who [had] shown hostility to the movement," and were instructed to concentrate their efforts on ordinary CPP members. By associating the Communist-led resistance with the Croat national movement, the CPC hoped to overcome the reluctance of these CPP members to join the Partisan ranks.

Enemies on All Sides

The unsuccessful attempt to establish a Popular Front with the CPP ended abruptly at the end of 1941 when open hostilities with Chetniks erupted in Serbia, and Yugoslav Communists abandoned their efforts to forge a political coalition with "bourgeois" political leaders. A period began, known as the period of "left deviationism" in Yugoslav historiography, in which Communists emphasized class confrontation and the imminence of proletarian revolution. CPC leaders initially hoped this new emphasis would help attract Croats to the movement, but instead they found their popularity in Croatia seriously eroded.

Communist cooperation with Chetniks during the uprising in Serbia and elsewhere in the country had been tenuous from the start. The Chetniks had objected to initiating an uprising, and they had joined it mainly to preserve their influence among Serbs. Though the two groups carried out parallel actions, they did not combine operations, for their goals, organizations, and tactics were very different. Tito and Mihailović met several times in October to formalize their cooperation, but neither man was prepared to relinquish control of the resistance movement, and

---

126. *Zbornik dokumenata NORa*, II/2/53.

127. *Zbornik dokumenata NORa*, V/1/62-65. Matija Gubec was a Croat peasant leader who led a peasant rebellion in 1573 against the feudal lords in Croatia. The rising was put down and its leaders arrested, leaving the legacy of Gubec as a folk-hero.

they failed to reach an agreement.[128] Chetniks became convinced that the Partisan strategy of confrontation with the occupying forces demanded too high a price in reprisals against the Serb population, and they were alarmed at the future political implications of allowing Communists to play a significant role in the resistance movement. Even as they negotiated with Tito, they decided that opposing the Communists must be their first priority.

On November 1, Chetniks attacked Partisan headquarters at Užice. The Partisans counterattacked at Ravna Gora several days later, but they were unwilling to destroy Mihailović for fear of angering Moscow. Within a few days, their uneasy alliance was transformed into an implacable and relentless enmity. In mid-November, Chetniks began combined operations with the Germans against the main Partisan forces in Užice. Caught off guard and quickly overwhelmed by the superior forces surrounding them, Partisans suffered serious losses and were forced to retreat to the regions of northern Montenegro and the Sandžak. Serbia became a Chetnik stronghold for the next three years and CPY fortunes declined precipitously in Montenegro. Many insurgents who had participated in the July uprising now switched sides and became vehement opponents of the Communists.

Military attack from the Chetniks, whose leader was appointed Supreme Commander of the Yugoslav Army in the Homeland, left the Communists feeling besieged on all sides. Partisan forces now had to fight simultaneously the occupying powers and the Communists' domestic political foes. CPY leaders characterized the new situation as a menacing onslaught of capitalist forces against them and, in December, Tito announced that henceforth the struggle against bourgeois forces, foreign and domestic, would become preeminent.[129] "Do not forget," he warned Kardelj and Ribar, "that all the forces of reaction, both Croat and Serb, are united against us today on the basis of class interest."[130] Party members were instructed to move from the "first stage" of political struggle for a bourgeois political order to the "second stage" of greater

---

128. Tomasevich argues that the Chetniks were not negotiating in good faith since they had already contacted the Germans to discuss operations against the Partisans. Tomasevich, *The Chetniks, War and Revolution in Yugoslavia, 1941-1945,* 148.

129. *Dokumenti centralnih organa KPJ, NOR i revolucija,* 2/62/206-212, Tito to Ranković, 12/14/41. See also Nešović and Petranović, *A VNOJ i revolucija,* 163, CC CPY to CC CPS 1/1/41.

130. Tito, *Sabrana djela,* vol. 9, 34.

class confrontation and proletarian revolution.[131] In this phase, Communists would rely more exclusively upon the workers and poor peasants to resist the occupying forces and prepare for the new proletarian state.

This emphasis at the beginning of 1942 on opposition to domestic bourgeois forces meant greater confrontation with Peasant Party leaders. In a series of directives in January and February, Tito instructed CPC leaders to denounce Maček in the harshest terms. "The time has passed," he wrote, "to be considerate toward Maček and his company."[132] Maček "is not simply harmful but traitorous," more dangerous than the government in exile, which though it opposes us, is "helpless to influence the development of events in our country."[133] Therefore, "it is more important to attack [the government in exile's] followers here in the country, like Maček and other democratic elements which openly collaborate with the occupying forces."[134] Communists in Croatia were also told to begin a campaign against "kulaks," who were viewed as class enemies and as supporters of the Communists' main political rival in Croatia. The CPC was instructed to appeal to the class interests of poor peasants and to isolate CPP followers in the countryside. As Tito wrote: "Winning the peasants must proceed along the line of differentiation in the village...dividing the poor and middle peasants from the kulaks, who comprise the focal point of the reactionary leadership with Maček at its head."[135] Though "kulaks" who cooperated with the Partisans were suspected of being CPP infiltrators and were to be purged from Partisan ranks, Tito also cautioned that Communists should not slacken their efforts to attract sympathetic CPP members.[136]

CPC leaders approved of this new line, especially its greater criticism of Chetniks. Ivo Lola Ribar informed Tito that Popović and Hebrang had endorsed enthusiastically the new approach which they believed would allow Communists "to take advantage of the crisis." "In particular, our

---

131. There was some disagreement among CPY leaders about this new tactic. At a meeting of the CPY Regional Committee for Bosnia-Hercegovina at Ivančić on January 7 and 8, Tito and other top leaders discussed this matter heatedly. Some Communists like the Bosnian Avdo Humo argued that this new line would lead to a harmful sectarianism. For more on left deviationism, see Branko Petranović, "O levim skretanjima KPJ krajem 1941 i u prvoj polovini 1942," *Zbornik za istoriju* 4 (1971).

132. Tito, *Sabrana djela*, vol. 8, 63.

133. *Ibid.*, vol. 9, 35.

134. *Ibid.*

135. *Zbornik dokumenata NORa*, I/1/201.

136. Tito, *Sabrana djela*, vol. 9, 34.

sharpening of attitude toward the Chetniks, [and] the danger of a return of greater Serbian hegemony...," Ribar wrote, "will be a bridge over which many elements will cross to us."[137] Hebrang agreed, predicting that the new line would "resound among the Croat masses and [would] greatly facilitate their activization."[138]

In January, CPC leaders directed party organizations to follow the new line of "unmasking" Maček and denouncing Chetnik treachery. Anti-Chetnik rhetoric increased noticeably, as did criticism of Maček and the government in exile.[139] Dalmatian Communists were instructed to break all contacts with CPP leaders, even though, as one Dalmatian leader objected, these negotiations had recently begun to progress.[140] A campaign was launched, vigorously in places, to clear "kulaks" from the national liberation committees.[141] Still, CPC leaders were reluctant to attack Maček too strongly and criticism of him was not nearly as harsh as it would be at other points in the war. [142]

Although the CPC ordered negotiations with CPP leaders halted in Dalmatia, it did not stop looking for Peasant Party leaders willing to cooperate. In February, CPC leaders contacted several "pro-Russian" members of the CPP. After several meetings, they agreed that, while retaining its separate party structure, the CPP would establish a National Committee with CPC representatives and join the national liberation committees at the local level.[143] Tito endorsed this development enthusiastically, but Peasant Party leaders were unable to procure Maček's approval and the entire proceeding came to a halt.[144] Ribar initiated contacts with other CPP leaders and communicated through an intermediary with August Košutić Radić's son-in-law and one of Maček's closest associates. Košutić insisted that cooperation would be possible only if the CPP were given authority over peasants in the resistance movement and retained a separate military command. Ribar

---

137. Ivo Lola Ribar, *Ratna pisma* (Belgrade, 1978), 51-53; *Zbornik dokumenata NORa*, II/2/103.

138. AIHRPH KP-7/186, Hebrang to CC CPY, 2/13/42.

139. AIHRPH KP-7/75, "CPC Announcement to the Croat People," 1/15/42.

140. AIHRPH KP-7/72.

141. AIHRPH KP-9/158. Anka Berus described an extensive campaign against kulaks in the Croatian Littoral.

142. *Vjesnik*, for example, remained virtually silent about him during this entire period.

143. Ribar, *Ratna pisma*, 54-58.

144. Jelić-Butić, *Hrvatska seljačka stranka*, 130-147.

reportedly dismissed these "stupidities" out of hand, and agreement with CPP leaders remained as elusive as ever.[145]

Communists were not the only ones struggling to attract support from CPP members at this time. In January 1942, Ustasha leaders also renewed their efforts to gain CPP cooperation by announcing that they would reconvene the Croatian Sabor. All delegates from the 1915 Sabor and the 1939 Skupština who did not oppose the Ustasha regime were invited; sixty of the ninety-three eligible CPP members attended.[146] The CPP delegates used the first Sabor meeting as an opportunity to raise the issue of Maček's imprisonment, however, and circulated a petition calling for his immediate release. Finding himself unable to control the Sabor, Pavelić was forced to disband it by the end of the year. Although the Peasant Party appeared to be drifting, CPP leaders retained a sense of cohesiveness and a loyalty to Maček that made it difficult for either the Ustashas or the Communists to use the party for their own purposes. In spite of its inactivity, most Croats remained loyal to the Peasant Party and were convinced that it would play a crucial role in the postwar political settlement.

By March 1942, CPC leaders' hopes had faded that the more radical anti-Chetnik, anti-Maček line adopted in January would enhance Communist popularity. The benefits the CPC had derived from attacking Chetniks appeared to have been outweighed by the drawbacks of attacking Maček. CPC leaders reported to Tito in February and March that, despite their hostility toward the Ustasha regime and its spring mobilization drive, Croats were still reluctant to join the Partisans.[147] Ivo Lolo Ribar cautioned that Communist Party influence was still weak in the villages and that unless Communists improved their performance there the CPP would soon use Croat peasants against them. "I emphasize," he wrote, "that in spite of the stirrings in Croatia, the situation [here] still lags behind and is weaker than that in any other area of Yugoslavia. We must concentrate all of our party's attention here or we will pay for it tomorrow."[148] The CPC may have succeeded in deepening "differentiation" among CPP members, as Ribar reported, but it had not expanded Croat support for the Partisan movement.

CPC emphasis on class conflict also had the effect of increasing hostility toward Croats in Partisan ranks. The fine distinction between denouncing Maček and other CPP leaders as bourgeois traitors and wel-

---

145. *Ibid.*, 147.

146. For more on the Sabor meetings in 1942, see *ibid.*, 64-66.

147. Ribar, *Ratna pisma*, 54-58.

148. *Ibid.*, 66-67, Ivo Lola Ribar to Tito, 2/23/42.

coming CPP rank and file into their units was too confusing for many Partisans. CPP supporters were often viewed with hostility, as "kulaks" to be removed from their midst. This was particularly true in liberated areas such as Kordun, where the predominantly Serb Partisans were extremely hostile to local Croats. Moreover, the radical rhetoric of social transformation appears to have scared off many of the peasants needed to create a mass movement in Croatia.[149] As in most other areas of the country, the period of "left deviationism" resulted in an increase in the already existing antagonisms, the most important of which were along national lines. Given the predominance of Serbs among Partisan rank and file in Croatia, this increase threatened to have very negative consequences.

By April, the CPY became alarmed that its emphasis on immediate revolution was diminishing its support, and Communist leaders began to rethink their tactics. Moreover, Soviet pressure to abandon this line increased. In March, Stalin castigated CPY leaders for stressing class warfare and called upon them to "give serious thought to your tactics in general" in order to achieve a "true Popular Front of all enemies of Hitler and Mussolini in Yugoslavia."[150] In a March speech modeled after Stalin's "dizzy with success" counterpart, Tito warned against militant excesses and called for a more prudent application of the national liberation line.[151] In several speeches and articles in April, he spoke particularly of the perils of "sectarianism" in Croatia. "It would be a mistake," Tito wrote, "to accuse the entire Croat Peasant Party and its lower level leaders of the wrongdoings of Maček and some CPP leaders."[152] The CPC was instructed to differentiate more carefully between CPP leaders and CPP followers, and to elicit more effectively the latter's support. The "main task of all Communists," Tito ordered, was to establish the National Liberation Front, "especially in Croatia where the least has been done in this regard."

In response, CPC leaders took steps to tone down their class rhetoric. In a letter to Tito in April 1942, Vladimir Popović admitted that the CPC had failed to create a Popular Front in Croatia and that its "sectarianism"

149. See Ribar, *Ratna pisma*, 110-114.

150. Stephen Clissold, *Yugoslavia and the Soviet Union, 1939-1973: A Documentary Survey* (Oxford: Oxford University Press, 1975), 146.

151. Milovan Djilas, who had been removed from Montenego the previous fall for his "leftist errors," was reprimanded, along with Moša Pijade who was with him in Montenegro, for his conduct at the time.

152. Petranović, "O levim skretanjima KPJ krajem 1941 i u prvoj polovini 1942 g.," 209.

had "greatly hindered the struggle for mobilizing the Croat masses."[153] The CPC instructed party organizations to criticize the Croat Peasant Party for betraying Croats' national interests, not their class interests, and warned them against "putting all CPP members into the same basket."[154] A directive issued shortly thereafter explained that Stalin had called for a bourgeois-democratic, not a Communist, revolution.[155] Despite these warnings, however, hostility toward CPP members as "kulaks" and class enemies was never far from the surface among Communist cadres and some CPC leaders.

The Struggle for Survival

While Communists in Croatia struggled with the problems of sectarianism, their support among Serbs began to erode as a result of Chetnik successes. In the spring of 1942, Chetnik strength increased markedly in most parts of Yugoslavia for a number of reasons. First, recognition by the government in exile strengthened the Chetniks' popular standing among Serbs and attracted a number of new recruits. Secondly, Chetnik cooperation with the occupying forces in campaigns against the Partisans gave them a source of arms and supplies, and a reprieve in most areas from direct harassment by Axis forces. Finally, Chetniks were able to take advantage of the "red terror" of this period, especially in Montenegro and Bosnia, to increase their support.[156]

As a result of these factors, numerous Partisan supporters in Croatia switched their allegiance to the Chetniks in the spring and summer of 1942. Reports poured in from the countryside that the Chetniks had, as one Partisan put it, "sprouted a root among the people," and that many villagers previously friendly to the Partisans had fled or closed their doors to them.[157] One Partisan described the harmful effect of Chetnik propaganda which denounced the Communists as an Ustasha force as

---

153. AIHRPH KP-8/98.

154. AIHRPH KP-9/179. See also AIHRPH KP-9/153.

155. AIHRPH KP-8/104.

156. Terror perpetrated by CPY members increased dramatically during this period and reached critical proportions in Montenegro and Hercegovina. Although the extent of and responsibility for this terror are still disputed, it is clear that the dramatically increased terror of "left deviationism" had negative effects on the CPY's standing with the population in these areas.

157. *Zbornik dokumenata NORa*, V/5/62/247. In a May 15 letter to the CPY Central Committee, CPC leaders reported troubles caused by increasing Chetnik influence. *Zbornik dokumenata NORa*, V/4/173.

follows: "The arrival of our troops made the people run away as if the Ustashas were coming, which means that Chetniks have succeeded in showing that we are associates of the Ustasha and opposed to the Serb people."[158] Chetniks also successfully subverted Partisan units, and numerous detachments, including commanders, went over to their camp.[159] Commanders struggled to regain control of vacillating units but it was often difficult to induce Partisan detachments to take actions against Chetniks.[160] CPC leaders did not exaggerate when they wrote of the Chetnik "menace" to the Supreme Staff in May.[161]

Chetniks in Croatia were also bolstered by cooperation with the occupying authorities and the Ustashas. The Germans were reluctant to use Chetniks in actions against Communists and opposed the Italian policy of arming them for this purpose. But practical concerns often prevailed when all available forces were needed to defeat the Partisans and, despite German objections, the Chetniks participated in the spring campaign against Partisans in eastern Bosnia.[162] The Italians began to organize the Chetnik forces in their areas into the Voluntary Anti-Communist Militia (MVAC), which they supplied and controlled.[163] When the Italians withdrew from occupational zones II and III in June 1942, the Ustashas agreed to permit MVAC forces to continue operating in these areas. Ustasha authorities also attempted to conclude limited agreements with Chetniks and, in June, they released instructions for

---

158. *Zbornik dokumenata NORa,* V/5/62. See also report from the Croatian Main Staff to the Supreme Staff on 5/25. *Zbornik dokumenata NORa,* V/4/84/323.

159. Between February and June 1942, Chetniks carried out putsches in five of the six detachments in eastern Bosnia. The special volunteer army units that Tito had established in the spring to attract Chetnik recruits were especially susceptible to Chetnik subversion. Tomasevich, *The Chetniks, War and Revolution in Yugoslavia, 1941-1945,* 161.

160. *Zbornik dokumenata NORa,* V/5/42/136. Partisan headquarters in the fourth zone complained about this difficulty in a report to the Main Staff of Croatia on June 19.

161. *Zbornik dokumenata NORa,* V/4/84

162. Paul N. Hehn describes the tension between German commanders in the field who wished to use Chetnik troops against the Partisans, and the German High Command, which never approved of this policy. Paul N. Hehn, *The German Struggle against Yugoslavia—Guerrillas in World War Two* (New York: Columbia University Press, 1979).

163. This force, which contained 29,627 Chetnik soldiers, was commanded by Trifunović-Birčanin until he died in February 1943, and then by Mladen Žujović-Aćinović.

negotiating with Chetnik commanders in the field.[164] Both Ustashas and Chetniks were wary of these agreements. Ustashas worried about the long-term effects of arming Chetniks, especially since Chetnik forces engaged in actions against them and occasionally massacred Croats. Chetnik commanders worried about how agreements with Ustashas would affect their popular support, especially since the fact that the MVAC received payment from the Ustashas made MVAC soldiers look like mercenaries. Nevertheless, their desire to defeat the Partisans overcame their mutual suspicions, and they cooperated on several occasions.[165]

Ustasha cooperation with Chetnik commanders reflected a shift in their policy toward Serbs in the spring of 1942. Due to German prompting and the Partisan threat, Ustasha leaders began to back away from their most radical racial solutions and large-scale massacres of Serbs.[166] Realizing that killing or forcing all Orthodox Serbs in Croatia to convert was an unrealistic task, Ustasha authorities extended citizenship to Orthodox believers who joined the new Croatian Orthodox Church.[167] The decision to create the new church was announced in February 1942, and it was established under the authority of Bishop Hermogan, a Russian, in June of that year. By softening their policies toward Serbs, Ustasha leaders, and especially German authorities in Zagreb, hoped to lessen Serb support for the Partisan movement in Croatia.

Hurt by the increase in Chetnik strength caused by these Italian and Ustasha policies, the CPC attempted to use Chetnik cooperation with the occupying and Ustasha forces to discredit them. Partisan propaganda denounced Chetnik deals with the Ustasha authorities and Chetnik contacts with the Italians and Germans. *Vjesnik* warned that "the Chetnik band has now replaced the Ustasha as the main tool of the occupiers

---

164. Jelić-Butić, *Četnici u Hrvatskoj*, 114.

165. *Ibid.*, 114-122.

166. Already in the summer of 1941, some German officers in Croatia argued for a more "constructive" solution to the Serb problem, including considering members of the Serbian Orthodox Church to be members of the Croat nation. Krizman, *Pavelić izmedju Hitlera i Mussolinija*, 130.

167. A very few Orthodox priests who remained in the Independent State of Croatia (it has been estimated that in 1941, 334 priests out of 577 were killed or deported) cooperated with the new church "in an effort to protect their parishioners." About 200,000 to 300,000 Orthodox Serbs were forcibly converted during the war or asked to be received into the Catholic Church. For more on the treatment of members of the Serbian Orthodox Church during this period, see Stella Alexander, *Church and State in Yugoslavia since 1945* (Cambridge, England; New York: Columbia University Press, 1979).

against our people."[168] Communists also attempted to play on Croat fears of Chetniks, claiming that a Chetnik victory would result in reprisals against Croats.[169] Tito instructed CPC leaders to emphasize in their appeals to Croats that Chetniks were fighting against Croat national aims, and to explain carefully the differences between Chetniks and Partisans.[170]

These attacks on the Chetniks' increasingly collaborationist posture, and the Partisans' return to an appeal based primarily on national concerns, resulted in a gradual lessening of the Chetnik threat over the next several months. But Chetnik successes indicated just how susceptible Serbs in Croatia were to the Chetnik message. In addition to the Chetniks' espousal of anti-Croat views, the ideal of a greater Serbian state encompassing those areas of Croatia with a large Serb population must have appealed to many Serbs in Croatia in the circumstances created by the NDH. Central party leaders believed they must be sensitive to these concerns if they were to keep the loyalty of the Serb population which had contributed so much to the military efforts thus far in the war.

Despite continued troubles with the Chetniks, Communist fortunes began to improve slowly in mid-1942. In June, Chetnik and Axis offensives forced the main Partisan troops out of Serbia and Montenegro and they began their "long march" northward to western Bosnia. With the bulk of their forces stationed in Bosnia and western Croatia, the Partisans now planned to fight primarily in this area of the country. Their presence there strengthened Partisans in Croatia who continued to hold large areas of liberated territory, despite combined Italian, German, and Chetnik attacks during the spring offensive. Tito was particularly sanguine about the Partisan movement in Croatia where, he wrote in a telegram to the Comintern at the beginning of July, "the situation...is extremely favorable for us."[171] The CPC had survived the chaos and destruction of the first few months of war and had built new political and military organizations. Nevertheless, though Communists were relieved to have lived through their first winter, Tito's optimism was premature. The CPC still had not won the sympathy of the vast majority of Croats, whose support was crucial to their success. "One thing is certain," CPC leader in Slavonia Dušan Čalić insisted, "the CPP has the

168. *Vjesnik*, 11/42.
169. Tito, *Sabrana djela*, vol. 9, 209.
170. Ribar, *Ratna pisma*, 85-86, Tito and Ivo Lola Ribar to the CC CPC, 4/8/42.
171. Tito, *Sabrana djela*, vol. 11, 97. See also *Zbornik dokumenata NORa*, II/1/167.

masses and those who haven't gone over to the Ustasha. These people are watching [CPP leaders'] houses and waiting."[172]

Watching and Waiting: In Search of Support

In the fall of 1942, after nearly a year and a half of resistance, the Communist-led Partisans still had not made any real headway in gaining support from members of the Croat Peasant Party. Cognizant of the Peasant Party's continuing grip on the political loyalties of the Croat population, Communists in Croatia tried a variety of strategies to elicit support, if not from Maček himself, then from other less well-known leaders. As liberated territory expanded, Communists' contacts with CPP functionaries increased. Both sides initiated negotiations aimed at increasing cooperation between the two groups, but they almost always broke down because of disagreements over the role of CPP members in the Partisan movement. While some Peasant Party leaders were content to be absorbed into Partisan ranks, most desired organizational and operational autonomy. Communist leaders objected to their demands, for they feared that allowing CPP leaders to operate freely in liberated territory would undermine their political position. Indeed, they were convinced that many Peasant Party members had already "infiltrated" Communist ranks and had "seized a position from which they could agitate in the interests of the reactionary bourgeoisie." In several instances, CPC leaders sent specific instructions to cadres in the field to beware of Peasant Party leaders who had crossed into liberated territory and were agitating for the renewal of the CPP. "These people pose a very serious threat," warned a CPC letter to the District Committee of Pokuplje at the beginning of December, "and they must be prevented from gaining a foothold in the Partisan movement."[173]

CPC leaders also attempted to maintain control over contacts with CPP functionaries in the field, and they admonished local party leaders several times during the summer of 1942 for failing to inform them of these contacts. In June 1942, Zagreb party leaders established contact with a group of Peasant Party members who expressed interest in cooperating with them. Negotiations with them continued under Ivo Marinković, who came to Zagreb as secretary of the CPC Regional Secretariat in September. During the next several weeks, two documents were drawn up outlining possible future cooperation. As in previous

---

171. AIHRPH KP-10/234.
173. Jelić-Butić, *Hrvatska seljačka stranka*, 163.

cases, the negotiations produced no concrete results.[174] Nevertheless, CPC leaders felt they had not been included in a process they regarded as highly important, and they reprimanded Marinković and Saili, the head of the Zagreb party committee, for failing to keep them sufficiently informed.[175] They also accused Saili and Marinković of being "immature" and "insufficiently on guard" in their approach to the CPP.[176] Indeed, in a letter to the CC CPY in November, CPC leaders questioned whether such cooperation with the Peasant Party would simply strengthen it and they advocated a more cautious approach.[177]

While contacts between CPP and CPC leaders increased in the country, Peasant Party leaders abroad stepped up their criticism of the Communists. Shortly after the Bićanić memorandum was released in November 1941, Krnjević withdrew from the government in exile and seemed to be leaning toward a separatist resolution of the Croat question.[178] However, as the threat from the Communist movement in Croatia grew, Krnjević modified his tactics. Although reports he received from CPP leaders in Yugoslavia derogated the importance of the Partisan movement, the scope of its activities was becoming clearer. CPP ministers shared with their Serb counterparts a desire to prevent Communists from gaining power in Yugoslavia, or more immediately, to prevent Communists from gaining recognition for their resistance activities that could contribute to their strength. Consequently, Krnjević began to join with other ministers in the government in minimizing Communists' role in the resistance. Insisting that CPP sympathizers were fighting the Nazis, Krnjević attempted to convince the Allies that a resistance force separate from the Partisans existed in Croatia (something of which the British remained erroneously convinced until 1943). This switch in tactics

---

174. The CPP agreed to participate in the National Liberation Front and the national liberation committees, to denounce those CPP members supporting Pavelić and Mihailović, and to instruct CPP members to join Partisan units. (AIHRPH KP-13/413.) CPP interlocutors informed their leaders in prison of these negotiations and sent a copy of the documents to Maček. Marinković also solicited the response of CPC leaders. (AIHRPH KP-13/365).

175. AIHRPH KP-3/XI/42.

176. AIHRPH KP-14/480.

177. AIHRPH KP-14/480. This letter to CPY leaders reflects the tone of Andrija Hebrang, who was released from Ustasha custody several weeks earlier, and began acting as head of the CPC at about this time. Hebrang adopted a sharper stance toward CPP leaders in November and December, which will be discussed in more detail in the next chapter.

178. Vojmir Klajković, "Jugoslavenska vlada u emigraciji i saveznici prema pitanju Hrvatske, 1941-1944," part 1, *Časopis za suvremenu povijest* 1 (1973): 118.

may have delayed Allied discovery of Partisan strength in Croatia, but it probably did the CPP more harm than good. British (and American) impressions of Croat members of the goverment did not improve, and Communists were now able to charge CPP collusion with Chetnik forces, though such cooperation never occurred.

As CPP criticism of Communists increased abroad, the CPC intensified its denunciations of Maček in the Partisan press. In the summer of 1942, *Vjesnik* launched a virulent attack on him, charging that his cooperation with the Chetniks would result in "a Great Serbian government which would destroy the Croat people." As before, however, harsh criticism of Maček did not produce the intended effect of turning CPP members against him. Attempting to elicit Maček's cooperation did not work, but neither, it seems, did denouncing him. After several weeks of attacks on Maček, Ivo Lola Ribar expressed concern about the lack of CPP "defections" to the Partisans. In a letter to Tito in August 1942, he suggested a more "elastic" approach toward the Peasant Party leader; harsh criticism of Maček had damaged CPC relations with CPP members, he argued, and it would be better to criticize those CPP leaders who were cooperating directly with the Ustashas.[179] Kardelj was also frustrated by the difficulty of eliciting support from Croats and, placing part of the blame for this problem on the persistance of "sectarianism" in Croatia, he urged CPC leaders to establish a Popular Front in Croatia similar to the Liberation Front in Slovenia.[180] As Communists contemplated the postwar political arrangement, relations with Maček and the CPP became an increasing source of contention among them.

Bihać

In the fall of 1942, the question of the postwar political order was raised in earnest. In a letter to Tito at the end of August, Ivo Lola Ribar urged that since this question "was on everyone's lips," the CPY should present its position on the future political arrangement clearly to the Croat population. Communist leaders in Croatia knew that in order to attract CPP members they needed to convince them that Communists would protect Croat national interests. It was one thing to "unmask" Maček, but as long as the Communist Party was perceived as unable to achieve Croat national goals, it would fail to elicit widespread Croat

---

179. *Zbornik dokumenata NORa*, II/5/52, Ivo Lola Ribar to Kardelj; *Zbornik dokumenata NORa*, II/5/69, Ivo Lola Ribar to Tito.
180. *Zbornik dokumenata NORa*, II/5/103.

support. Moreover, since the CPY was preparing to convene a central political body, discussion of the postwar order could no longer be avoided. In the previous weeks, region-wide national liberation committees had been established in Croatia and most other areas of the country, drawing the network of district and local organizations into a hierarchical structure of permanent political bodies.[181] The stage was now set for the formation of a wider federal body to coordinate these committees and draw them into a central governmental apparatus.[182]

The first meeting of this body, the Antifascist Council of the People's Liberation of Yugoslavia (AVNOJ), was held in the Bosnian town of Bihać on November 26 and 27, 1942. This assembly of fifty-four representatives of the Partisan movement from most of the country (except Macedonia and Slovenia) declared itself the supreme political body of the National Liberation Front. Tito had intended to make this Council an interim government but at the last minute Stalin prevented him from doing so. Nevertheless, the Council assumed the character of a *de facto* government, and announced that henceforth no political authority in the country would be recognized except that of the national liberation committees.

Documents released during and after AVNOJ did not specify the form of the postwar state, but they did suggest some of its features. Since the beginning of the war, the CPY had not altered significantly its nationalities policy. Yugoslavia's national groups were urged to fight together to achieve their national goals within Yugoslavia. The CPY confirmed its commitment to a unified state within the approximate borders of interwar Yugoslavia at the first session of AVNOJ. The Assembly statement called upon the peoples of Yugoslavia to "rise up in arms in the great People's Liberation War against the occupiers, and for the freedom and fraternal unity of Serbia, Montenegro, Croatia, Slovenia, Bosnia-Hercegovina, and Macedonia."[183] Although federalism was not specifically mentioned, it was suggested in the following promise to the Slovenes: "In the new Yugoslavia, Slovenia will be free and united. From Trieste to Špilja, from the Kupa River to Celovec [Klagenfurt], she will enter [into this union] with all those rights which will make it possible

---

181. The regulations concerning the national liberation committees passed in Bosanska Krajina in September 1942 declared that these political bodies were permanent. For more on these regulations, see Petranović and Simović, *Istorija narodne vlasti*, 113.

182. AIHRPH KP-10/228.

183. Nešović and Petranović, *AVNOJ i revolucija*, 89.

for her to rule over the Slovene people herself on her own soil."[184] In an article published several days later, Tito also reaffirmed the CPY's support for the right of self-determination, including secession, though he cautioned that this right would be denied to "enemies of the people" like the Ustashas.[185]

After the November meeting, AVNOJ took several steps to erect the new governmental structure. It elected an executive committee, consisting of one president and three vice-presidents, which established administrative departments in the areas of the economy and finance, health, internal affairs, social questions, foreign relations, and propaganda. These bodies began to coordinate their respective spheres of authority in liberated territory, though it was over a year before their activity became significant. CPY leaders also decided to duplicate the structure of AVNOJ at the regional level. These regional antifascist councils would be responsible for guiding and coordinating the activities of the national liberation committees and constructing regional administration along departmental lines.

At the AVNOJ meeting, Tito urged CPC leaders to establish a regional body in Croatia as quickly as possible. Andrija Hebrang, who attended the meeting as acting secretary of the CPC, enthusiastically described the decision to establish federal political bodies as "enormously significant" for the Partisan movement at home and abroad.[186] According to him, the Land Antifascist Council for the People's Liberation of Croatia (ZAVNOH) would be "representative of the people" and therefore include individuals from the previous political parties who "support the national liberation struggle."[187] Hebrang instructed CPC organizations to find suitable candidates for ZAVNOH, including CPP members sympathetic to the Partisans, in time for the upcoming founding session of ZAVNOH.[188]

In spite of delays, organizing ZAVNOH proceeded relatively smoothly. But its jurisdiction and relations with AVNOJ were more troubling. First, what was the nature of the relationship between AVNOJ and ZAVNOH? Was the Croatian Council intended only to carry out decisions adopted by AVNOJ or did it have some authority to make policies

---

184. Slobodan Nešović, *Stvaranje nove Jugoslavije 1941-1945* (Belgrade, 1981), 84.

185. Tito, *Sabrana djela*, vol. 13, 95-102.

186. AIHRPH KP-15/557. Andrija Hebrang to Vladimir Popović, 11/30/42.

187. *Ibid.*

188. *Zemaljsko antifašističko vijeće narodnog oslobodjenja Hrvatske (ZAVNOH)*, *Zbornik dokumenata 1943* (Zagreb, 1975), 115. See also AIHRPH KP-17/617.

on its own? Second, who would have authority over areas with mixed populations like Bosnia-Hercegovina and Vojvodina, which were claimed by both Serbia and Croatia? Would these areas establish their own councils and, if not, how would they be divided? It was clear that the process of establishing council jurisdiction would bear importantly on the future shape of the state and the resolution of the Croat question. As the process of defining and establishing these institutions got underway in 1943, conflict arose over the extent of CPC and ZAVNOH authority to determine policy in Croatia and the resolution of the Croat question in the postwar state.

Conclusion

In 1941, Yugoslavia was invaded and partitioned by the Axis powers. Already weakened by conflict over the Croat question in the interwar period, the Yugoslav state was now broken into a number of political units. With the establishment of the Independent State of Croatia, the Croat fascist organization, Ustasha, claimed to have resolved the Croat question. However, conflict over this question simply increased in the circumstances wrought by the war. As Ustashas began to exterminate and deport the Serb population living within the borders of the NDH (this was part of the Ustasha "solution" to the Croat question), Serbs, Croats, and Muslims were engulfed in a brutal civil war. And, Yugoslavia's interwar political elites were helpless to stop the violence. While the government-in-exile in London engaged in bitter and barren disputes over the failures of the interwar state, CPP leader Vladko Maček, who in any case was imprisoned by Ustasha authorities, pursued a largely passive policy toward the occupying and Ustasha authorities.

In the midst of this disintegration of the Yugoslav state and violent conflict among its national groups, the CPY attempted to build a countrywide resistance movement. Its organizational unity, countrywide base of operations, and clandestine networks gave it several advantages in creating Partisan units. From the outset, the CPY pursued political as well as military objectives. Party leaders began to build party organizations and political institutions at the local level that would mobilize the populace to the Partisan cause and ultimately provide the framework of a new political order. This attention to state-building objectives gave the CPY a crucial advantage over its rivals, who paid little attention to building political structures during the war.

Nationalism was an essential part of the CPY's mobilizing strategy from the beginning of the war. The CPY knew it must address the national sentiments of the population in order to elicit support, especially in Croatia where there was considerable national discontent. Consequently, Communists used appeals based on nationalism, both against the occupying powers and in support of the particular national goals of Yugoslavia's several nations, in their efforts to mobilize the population. The Communist Party's federal program, which had been adopted before the war, was presented as the best means of achieving these particular national aspirations, though Communists avoided specific discussion of their federal model. The CPY's Yugoslav orientation was reinforced by the leadership's decisive resistance to the establishment of an independent Communist Party of Croatia in the first few months of the war.

The CPY's attempt to use nationalism to mobilize the population was only partially successful in Croatia during the first two years of the war. While Serbs joined the Partisan movement in large numbers, Croats did not. The CPY's support for a unified Yugoslav state was viewed with suspicion by many Croats whose loyalty to the interwar state was not strong. The CPY's federal program was also viewed with suspicion given the highly unified and centralized character of the Communist Party. Moreover, Communist attempts to appeal to anti-invader sentiment were less effective among Croats who felt they might need Axis support to achieve their national aims. The preponderance of Serbs in the movement also made attracting Croats difficult as Croats perceived the Partisans to be a mainly Serb organization. And, the behavior of these Serb Partisans in the first two years of the war often reinforced this image. Although they sometimes joined the Partisan movement, Croats continued to look mainly to the Croat Peasant Party to achieve their national goals.

This difficulty in mobilizing Croat support had important consequences for the Communists' state-building activities during the war. Communists in Croatia became convinced that the CPC would never succeed there unless it appealed more directly to the national sentiments of Croats. When Hebrang became head of the CPC at the end of 1942, he adopted a policy more responsive to Croat national aims. As the construction of political institutions at the federal level got underway in 1943, Hebrang attempted to create a decentralized political order which would give Croatia a wide measure of autonomy. This federalist strategy was essential, he believed, to overcoming the difficulties of mobilizing the Croat population into the Communist-led resistance movement, and ultimately, to building a unified Communist state. The origins and shape of the federalist strategy, and the way in which it responded to the national sentiments of Croats, is the story of the next chapter.

4

Hebrang and the Federalist Alternative, 1943-1944

The beginning of 1943 signaled a new phase in the CPY's state-building activities as it began to institutionalize its political gains at the regional and federal level. During this crucial period of the CPY's state-building efforts, Andrija Hebrang was secretary of the CPC and his views had a major impact on this process. Hebrang was an extremely powerful leader in Croatia during his almost two-year tenure as secretary of the CPC.[1] Many of the other young and relatively inexperienced CPY Politburo members had been picked by Tito when he revived the party in the several years before the war. Very much Tito's juniors, they readily deferred to him on important matters. In contrast, Hebrang was a man of Tito's generation, a long-time Communist who had joined the party in 1919 at the age of twenty. A young clerk of peasant origins, he was one of the many youths recently settled in Zagreb who joined the Communist Party at that time. By the outbreak of the war, Hebrang had achieved a certain stature in the party by virtue of his long imprisonment from 1928 to 1941 and his old friendship with Tito, which was solidified when Hebrang offered Tito crucial support against Zagreb party leaders in 1928.[2] Given his relatively secure position among Communist leaders, Hebrang was inclined to act independently in matters important to him, and less likely to be challenged by other party leaders who respected his friendship with Tito.[3]

---

1. It is not clear exactly when Hebrang was appointed secretary of the CPC Central Committee, but shortly after his release from Ustasha custody in September 1942 he began to function as head of the CPC.

2. See chapter 2, 46-47.

3. For example, Djilas claims that the reason Hebrang was not subject to a party investigation after his release from prison in 1942, as was the common pro-

Hebrang's personal qualities also made him a natural, if highly controversial leader. Strong-willed, sometimes arrogant and patronizing, he could also be extremely charming and often prompted great loyalty among his followers. Like Tito, he had the ability, in the midst of a guerrilla war, to surround himself with the trappings of power, which commanded respect among peasant recruits, though it irritated some Communists.[4] As a result of his inclination to act autonomously in matters important to him and his ability to build a regional base of support, Hebrang was able to pursue an independent policy toward the Croat question. If his efforts had succeeded, a very different party-state would have resulted than the one that ultimately emerged at the end of the war.

Hebrang was determined to carve out the largest possible sphere of authority for ZAVNOH and the Communist Party of Croatia. Communist leaders knew that attracting Croat support for the Partisan movement was essential to the outcome of their struggle not only against the occupying forces, but against their domestic political foes. Hebrang was convinced the CPC must respond more fully to Croat national aspirations in order to gain this support and to loosen the Peasant Party's grip over the Croat population. While dedicated to establishing Communist political dominance, Hebrang resolved to procure some real measure of autonomy for ZAVNOH and the CPC; only in this way, he believed, would it be possible to build a mass movement in Croatia.

The CPY did not intend to create a decentralized federal state, however, but to introduce a highly centralized political order on the Leninist model, and Tito objected to Hebrang's attempts to increase the autonomy of Croatian political institutions. In 1943, Tito began to centralize the Partisan movement, both in the military and the political sphere, and to reduce the autonomy regional party leaders had acquired in the first two years of the war. Hebrang's attempts to stress the autonomous powers of ZAVNOH and to respond foremost to Croat concerns threatened this centralization of the party and the state it sought to create. The struggle between Tito and Hebrang that occurred during this period was not merely between two domineering and powerful Communist leaders, or even over differences in their tactics. Rather, it was a struggle over the

---

cedure, was due to his friendship with Tito. See Milovan Djilas, *Wartime* (New York and London: Harcourt Brace and Jovanovich, 1977), 209.

4. These characteristics offer a clue to the personal element of the struggle between these two men. Given their ability and desire to command the situations and people in their purview, it is not surprising that they clashed over policy in Croatia. Nevertheless, there appears to have been little personal acrimony between Tito and Hebrang at this point in the war.

distribution of power between the central and regional party organizations, between two different visions of how to build a new party-state.

Croatia and the Allies: The CPP Stirs

At the beginning of 1943, the Allies, the government in exile and the Communists all began to look with greater interest toward Croatia. During the first two years of the war, Croatia had been less significant than Serbia in Allied calculations concerning Yugoslavia. Memories of Serb military valor for the Allied cause in the First World War, and the publicity given Chetnik resistance in Serbia focused Allied attention on this part of the country. By 1943, however, as the prospect of Hitler's defeat became more likely, Croatia began to assume greater significance in Allied military plans. After German withdrawals in Africa, the Allies turned their attention to the Axis' southern flank and prepared for an invasion of Italy or a landing on the Adriatic coast. Since much of the Adriatic coast was in NDH territory, the Allies were extremely interested in the conditions their troops would encounter in the event they landed there. Consequently, it was essential for them to form a clearer picture of the military and political situation in Croatia.

The British knew very little about conditions in Croatia during the first two years of the war. Most of their operatives had landed in the southern areas of Yugoslavia, where they were instructed to attach themselves to Draža Mihailović's staff, and they had scanty knowledge of the political situation elsewhere in the country.[5] Officials in London relied for information upon Croat ministers in the government in exile, whose reports emphasized the existence of a substantial resistance force in Croatia operating independently of the Communists.[6] Suspecting that this information was not entirely accurate, the British decided to send observers to Croatia to ascertain the character of the "green cadres," as the non-Communist forces were called, and the Communist guerrillas active in this area. At the beginning of 1943, they dispatched two inves-

---

5. The British and the Yugoslavs did send a Yugoslav, Reserve Infantry Lieutenant Stanislav Rapotec, into Croatia in January 1942 on an intelligence gathering mission. However, when he returned from his mission in July, they appeared uninterested in his report that the CPP had mounted little active resistance. See Stevan Pavlowitch, *Unconventional Perceptions of Yugoslavia, 1940-1944* (New York: Columbia University Press, 1985), 67-105.

6. Vojmir Klajković, "Jugoslavenska vlada u emigraciji i saveznici prema pitanju Hrvatske, 1941-1944," part one, *Časopis za suvremenu povijest* 2-3 (1971).

tigative missions consisting of Canadians of Yugoslav origin, followed
by a three-man British party, to the Main Staff of Croatia. These missions
provided a very different picture from the one the British had been get-
ting.[7] Some of their members were highly impressed with Partisan military activity and had little regard for the military or political strength of
the CPP. Before long, their reports convinced British ministers that the
Communist-led Partisans, whom they believed to be primarily Croat,
were the most effective military force in this part of the country.[8]
Although the British continued to believe erroneously that some non-
Communist guerrillas were operating in Croatia, they became less and
less interested in these forces.

There were various ideas circulating at this time about Croatia's place
in the postwar order. While George Rendel, the British ambassador to the
Yugoslav government, believed that Yugoslavia could not be renewed
after the war, Foreign Secretary Eden believed Yugoslavia should be
reconstructed along federal lines. Roosevelt argued that Serbia should be
established as an independent state and Croatia placed under trustee-
ship. Another idea discussed on both sides of the ocean, which had the
support of many Croat ministers in the government in exile, was to create a Danubian federation under Habsburg rule that would include
Croatia. Whatever their views on Croatian statehood, these men all
agreed that the Croat Peasant Party would be essential to counter
Communist influence in the postwar political order.[9]

As the British received information about the dimensions of
Communist activity in Croatia, however, they became convinced that
CPP leaders were not doing enough to encourage military resistance to
the Axis forces. Consequently, although they continued to support the

---

7. For an account by one of the two British officers sent to the Main Staff of
Croatia, see Major William Jones, *Twelve Months with Tito's Partisans* (Bedford,
England: Bedford Books, 1946).

8. There were several proposals circulating during 1943 and 1944 to persuade
the Partisans in Croatia and the Chetniks in Montenegro and Serbia to join forces
in resisting the Axis powers and to agree on a demarcation line between their
two forces. Colonel Bailey, who was with Mihailović's forces in Montenegro, first
proposed that the British divide Yugoslavia into two separate Partisan and
Chetnik zones for the purposes of administering military aid, but this proposal
was vetoed by the Foreign Office. In mid-May, the British command in the
Middle East issued orders to Mihailović that would have divided Yugoslavia into
two separate zones, but Mihailović refused to obey these orders and they were
soon rescinded.

9. Vojmir Klajković, "Jugoslavenska vlada u emigraciji i saveznici prema
pitanju Hrvatske 1941-1944," part two, *Časopis za suvremenu povijest* 1 (1973).

Croat Peasant Party as an essential political force in Croatia, they began to pressure Krnjević and CPP ministers to initiate resistance activities in cooperation with the Communists. As the short-term goals of assisting the most active military force in Yugoslavia became more important, long-term political objectives concerning postwar arrangements assumed a secondary place in British calculations. Their relations with all political groups in Yugoslavia, Chetniks, Communists, and the Croat Peasant Party, were shaped increasingly by the overriding goal of inflicting maximum damage on the enemy; the political consequences of supporting the most effective resistance fighters would be faced at a later date.

Due to British overtures toward the Communists in the spring of 1943 and pressure from the cabinet to begin more active military resistance, CPP ministers began to reevaluate their strategy. It was clear to them that they must act or risk losing the support of their own rank and file and of the western Allies, upon whom they relied to place them in power after the war.[10] In order to improve relations with Serb ministers in the government in exile, CPP leader and government minister Krnjević took a tougher stance toward the Ustasha regime and expressed support for a united Yugoslavia. Nevertheless, despite a British inspired reorganization of the cabinet at the beginning of January, and the exclusion of the Serb nationalist Momčilo Ninčić, relations between Serb and Croat ministers continued to deteriorate.

In an effort to improve their image with the Allies, Croat ministers also began to present their case in the press. In a series of interviews and articles in the first months of 1943, they emphasized the pro-western sentiment of Croats and insisted that a substantial force of CPP sympathizers was actively fighting the enemy.[11] Rudolf Bićanić argued particularly energetically that the Partisans in Yugoslavia were primarily Croat

---

10. Ilija Jukić argues that CPP ministers' belief that the Allies would intervene on their behalf prevented them from taking any concrete action toward creating a resistance force. Croat ministers believed that the British and Americans would establish a federation in the Danubian basin and that Croats would then be able to decide at their leisure whether to break away from the Serbs and join the league of Catholic states. According to Jukić, Krnjević was so dependent on the Allies that he often engineered clashes in the cabinet in the hope that they would intervene and impose their own solution. See Ilija Jukić, *The Fall of Yugoslavia* (New York: Harcourt Brace Jovanovich, 1974), 148.

11. In the United States there was an effort to publicize the "Green Army" in Croatia reputedly operating under Maček's leadership and consisting of 40,000 to 70,000 men.

and that they were being directed by CPP leaders in the country.[12] Most importantly, although CPP ministers in the government in exile did not yet follow British urging to cooperate with the Communists, they did instruct CPP leaders in the country to prepare for more active resistance against the Axis forces.[13] As Krnjević put it to CPP leaders in Zagreb, they must create some kind of Draža Mihailović in Croatia or risk losing the battle for Allied support.[14]

As a result of these communications from Croat ministers in London, and the rapid growth of the Communist-led resistance, CPP leaders in Croatia also began to reexamine their political and military strategy. Many of them had grown increasingly restive and uneasy with the CPP policy of "waiting," and they cast about in search of a more effective response to the events that had engulfed them. In the spring of 1943, numerous Peasant Party organizations, which had been inactive until now, held meetings to discuss the current situation. However, it quickly became apparent that the last two years of war had only deepened divisions among them about how to respond to the Ustasha regime and the Communist resistance.

Among CPP members who were not cooperating with the regime, three distinct approaches could be discerned. Some left-leaning organizations like "the old Radićists" in Dalmatia began to call for cooperation with the Partisans, though they remained loyal to Maček.[15] Many more organizations put out flyers urging CPP members not to join the Partisans and to maintain their Peasant Party loyalties. A group of CPP members in the Croatian Littoral started a new journal, *Politički Vjesnik*, aimed at convincing Croats to keep their distance from the Partisans and to prepare to resist the occupying powers more actively. How this resistance was to be mounted, however, was never spelled out.[16] A third group of CPP members, while looking more carefully toward the post-

---

12. Klajković, "Jugoslavenska vlada u emigraciji i saveznici prema pitanju Hrvatske, 1941-1944," part two, 20.

13. Šepić, *Vlada Ivana Šubašića*, 99.

14. Klajković, "Jugoslavenska vlada u emigraciji i saveznici prema pitanju Hrvatske, 1941-1944," part two, 22.

15. Mile Konjević, "Formiranje i rad IO H(R)SS na oslobodjenom teritoriju 1943-1945," *Zbornik—Historijski Institut Slavonije* 7 (1975): 27-28. For a discussion of the increase in CPP activity at this time see Milica Bodrožić, "O nekim pitanjima politike Hrvatske seljačke stranke prema NOP u Hrvatskoj 1943 g.," *Časopis za suvremenu povijest* 1 (1973): 33-50.

16. Bodrožić, "O nekim pitanjima politike Hrvatske seljačke stranke prema NOP u Hrvatskoj 1943 g.," 33-50.

war political settlement, was not prepared to endorse cooperation with Partisans or any greater resistance effort of their own.

An analysis of Croatia's political future that appeared in the CPP newspaper *Veritas* at the beginning of 1943 reflected the prevailing mood of this last and largest group within the Peasant Party. Its authors considered three main questions. Who would win the war? In whose sphere of interest would Croatia fall after the war? What, if anything, should Croats do while the war was being fought? Their analysis emphasized the importance of Croatia to British, American, German, and Soviet plans for the postwar arrangement. It presented various scenarios for Croatia's political future depending on who won the war and how much influence the Soviet Union gained in the event the Allies emerged victorious. These CPP members anticipated that regardless of the war's outcome, Croatia's fate would be determined at a future peace conference where the CPP would advocate an independent Croatia, or if need be, decide about relations with other members of a multinational state. Concluding with the familiar exhortation for Croats to "save themselves biologically," they instructed that when Maček gave the signal, Croats should defend their territory and establish a Croatian state under his leadership.[17]

Allied interest in Croatia, and the stirrings among some CPP members it prompted, greatly concerned the CPC leadership in Croatia. Communist leaders feared the Allies might use the opportunity of opening a second front to land troops in Croatia and determine Croatia's political future in favor of the CPP.[18] Edvard Kardelj expressed this concern in a letter to Tito in mid-January 1943, and warned that, though the Allies might support the Partisans militarily, they might also intervene to bring other political groups to power.[19] Hebrang was especially alarmed by Allied policy toward Croatia, which he believed was ultimately aimed at ensuring CPP dominance at the war's end.[20] Hebrang feared that, with Allied support, the Peasant Party would reassert its traditional hold over political life in Croatia and prevent the Communists from achieving their political goals. Consequently, despite

---

17. Arhiv Instituta za historiju radničkog pokreta Hrvatske (AIHRPH) HSS-21/131.

18. In a letter to Dimitrov in October 1943, Tito told him that the Partisans would defend the country militarily if the Allies landed on the Adriatic coast. Tito, *Sabrana djela*, vol. 17, 54.

19. Ivan Jelić, *Komunistička partija Hrvatske, 1937-1945* (Zagreb, 1981), vol. 2, 241-242.

20. AIHRPH KP-19/829. In this directive to district committees in February 1943, Hebrang revealed his deep concern about the CPP's future political plans. See also AIHRPH KP-16/6011, CPC Circular, 12/42.

Britain's greater receptivity to the Partisan movement in Croatia in the spring of 1943, Hebrang took a very harsh stance toward the Allies.[21]

At the same time Hebrang denounced Allied support for CPP objectives, he adopted a three pronged strategy to diminish popular support for the Peasant Party. First, he attempted to discredit and isolate Maček by denouncing him harshly in the Partisan press. Second, he attempted to woo CPP members to the Partisan movement by encouraging ZAVNOH to endorse Peasant Party goals. And third, Hebrang created a separate organization of CPP leaders in ZAVNOH to oversee all aspects of CPP participation in the Partisan movement. Hebrang knew the CPC would never succeed in Croatia unless it attracted the majority of Croat peasants to its cause. He also knew these peasants would not join the Partisan movement unless it appeared to satisfy their national aspirations. The Partisans therefore had to offer a political program that could champion the Croat national cause and steal some fire from the CPP; ZAVNOH was essential to this task.

Founding ZAVNOH

The Communist Party of Croatia used ZAVNOH to elicit Croat support in several ways. First, ZAVNOH was intended to minimize Communist visibility in the movement and to dispel the belief that the Partisans were a purely "red" affair. Communist leaders emphasized that all political groups could participate in ZAVNOH and made special efforts to recruit Peasant Party members as ZAVNOH delegates. Second, by stressing the particularly Croat character of ZAVNOH, the CPC hoped to convince Croats that it could fulfill their national aspirations; ZAVNOH was said to embody the ideals of the Croat national movement and the realization of its political aims. Finally, the CPC attempted to identify itself with the social and economic program of the Croat Peasant Party and to reduce fears that the Partisans would establish Communism in Croatia. ZAVNOH announced that it would not eradicate private property or introduce major social and economic changes after the war.

---

21. The CPC press complained bitterly about "western imperialists" and their support for Maček. For example, in an article written in *Naprijed*, CPC leader Pavle Gregorić accused the Allies of disregarding the right to self-determination guaranteed by the Atlantic Charter and warned that the Partisans would not relinquish this right if the Allies attempted to "lean on" Maček when the Axis forces were defeated. *Naprijed*, #18, 8/18/43, 1.

The speeches and documents adopted at the ZAVNOH founding conference in June 1943 emphasized that the new institution would dedicate itself to achieving the aims of the Croat national movement. At the founding conference and in the weeks after, the CPC strongly emphasized Croatian autonomy and sovereignty. Though the Communists never imitated the heavy peasant idiom of most Peasant Party leaders, the descriptions of ZAVNOH in speeches at the Congress drew heavily upon the traditions and language of the Croat national movement.[22] Kardelj and Hebrang described the foundation of ZAVNOH as the culmination of a centuries-long struggle for a Croatian representative body, and this description was echoed in the conference resolution.[23] CC CPC member Karlo Mrazović in his speech similarly portrayed the CPC as the only organization capable of achieving the goals of the Croat national movement in the tradition of Croat leaders such as Josip Juraj Strossmayer.[24]

CPC leaders also took great pains to emphasize that ZAVNOH was not composed exclusively of Communists. Croat Peasant Party leaders who participated in the first session were given ample opportunity to express their support for ZAVNOH and the Partisan movement. In their widely publicized speeches and in a series of articles published shortly thereafter, they echoed CPC leaders' glowing descriptions of ZAVNOH. They also denounced the head of the Croat Peasant Party, Vladko Maček, for his poor leadership during the last decade and praised the CPC as an organization more capable of achieving Peasant Party goals. According to them, the Partisan movement truly expressed the ideals of the Peasant Party's founder, Stjepan Radić, which had been perverted by Maček in the years before the outbreak of war.[25] In his speech to the Council, CPP leader Filip Lakuš argued that if Radić were alive today he would favor the kind of revolution the Communists had launched.[26]

Croatia's future social and economic order was also discussed in ZAVNOH documents. ZAVNOH leaders assured the population that they had no intention of introducing major social and political reforms during or after the war. Denying that the national liberation movement was promoting any radical change, a ZAVNOH document released at the end of May stated that the movement recognized "the inviolability of private property and the widest possible opportunity for demonstrating

22. *ZAVNOH, Zbornik dokumenata* (Zagreb, 1964-1975), vol. 1, 178-220.

23. *Ibid.*, 171-174, 175-179.

24. *Ibid.*, 179-181.

25. For example, see *Vjesnik*, #6, 5/22/43, 1.

26. *ZAVNOH, Zbornik dokumenata*, vol. 1, 196-197.

initiative in industry and other economic activities."[27] These assurances were repeated at the second session of ZAVNOH in October 1944, when Hebrang further outlined ZAVNOH's social and political program. Pledging that ZAVNOH would take measures to ensure a more equitable distribution of agricultural holdings in Croatia, he also promised that the country's capital investment would be "harnessed" to contribute to the widest possible social good.[28]

As part of its effort to decrease Communist visibility and increase Croat participation in the Partisan movement, the CPC also emphasized that henceforth ZAVNOH would be the main Partisan political organization in Croatia. As one directive put it, ZAVNOH would now assume ninety percent of the political tasks of the movement.[29] Party organizations were instructed to play a less visible political role and were criticized for the previously "dictatorial fashion" in which they had run the national liberation committees, since this mode of operation made the Partisans vulnerable to accusations that they had introduced a Communist dictatorship.[30] In other words, while appealing to the national aspirations of the Croat population, party organizations were to learn how to play an important role behind the scenes.

In the weeks following the founding session of ZAVNOH, it became clear that the CPC intended to give the widest possible interpretation to ZAVNOH's powers to include all major decisions affecting Croatia. ZAVNOH and its officials were accorded a more prominent place than AVNOJ and its officials in the Partisan press.[31] Similarly, CPC and ZAVNOH publications sometimes lauded the National Liberation Army of Croatia without mentioning the National Liberation Army of Yugoslavia or the Supreme Staff. This emphasis on Croatian sovereignty was clearly expressed in a ZAVNOH appeal to soldiers in the Home Guard, released shortly after the founding congress, which stated: "Join us immediately without hesitation and you will be fighters for the complete freedom and independence of Croatia, in which Croats will be their own masters and themselves arrange their homeland."[32]

Hebrang's emphasis on the autonomy of Croatian political and military institutions, however, soon aroused the ire of other Communist

---

27. *Ibid.*, 132-133.

28. *Ibid.*, 459.

29. AIHRPH KP-26/1522, CC CPC to Anka Berus, 8/8/43.

30. AIHRPH KP-26/1522.

31. AIHRPH KP-2/28, CPC to CPC Regional Committee for Dalmatia, 5/25/43.

32. ZAVNOH, *Zbornik dokumenata*, vol. 1, 277.

leaders. In the spring of 1943, Communist leaders Vladimir Popović and Ivo Lola Ribar warned Hebrang that he had incorrectly elevated ZAVNOH to the same status as AVNOJ.[33] Ivo Lola Ribar complained again to Tito several months later that CPC propaganda erroneously minimized the role of AVNOJ. Protesting against CPC instructions to party organizations to popularize Croatian political institutions more than Yugoslav ones, he wrote: "I think this question in general ought not to be posed in this way. Our institutions in Croatia should be popularized as an expression of our stance [in favor of] national self-determination, while our common institutions (VŠ [Supreme Staff], AVNOJ) should be popularized as an expression of the interconnectedness of the nations of Yugoslavia in the struggle for freedom. Thus the popularization of one or the other has its place and should not be talked about in first or second order."[34] Milovan Djilas also objected to Hebrang's strong emphasis on Croat interests, which he feared was causing tension with Serb cadres. During a trip to CPC headquarters in mid-August 1943, he complained to Sreten Žujović and Edvard Kardelj that Hebrang's approach was contrary to the CPY policy of nonpreferential treatment of particular national groups.[35]

Tension between Hebrang and CPY leaders over the delineation of authority between AVNOJ and ZAVNOH increased after the Croatian Council made a series of decisions in anticipation of the second session of AVNOJ in the fall of 1943. In September, ZAVNOH released a statement declaring Istria, the Croatian Littoral and Dalmatia to be part of Croatia and guaranteeing autonomy to the Italian minority in these areas.[36] Tito objected to this wide interpretation of ZAVNOH's power. In a sharp reprimand to the CPC shortly thereafter, he instructed that henceforth all such decisions would be made by AVNOJ and issued in its name. "Otherwise," he wrote, [these decisions] will not have significance for external powers and they will signify separatism which all the Allies oppose."[37] Tito's reprimand indicated that ZAVNOH would not be permitted to make unilateral decisions in matters concerning Croatia's borders, its relations with other republics or its policy toward national

---

33. AIHRPH KP-21/1015.

34. AIHRPH KP-2/28.

35. Milovan Djilas, *Wartime* (New York and London: Harcourt Brace Jovanovich, Inc., 1977), 312-317.

36. *ZAVNOH, Zbornik dokumenata*, vol. 1, 397.

37. Tito, *Sabrana djela* (Belgrade, 1977-1980); vol. 17, 3, Tito to Main Staff of Croatia, 10/1/43. Tito also told CPC leaders that they should have specified that ZAVNOH offered cultural not political autonomy to the Italian minority.

minorities. Nor were certain boundaries to be exceeded in publicizing ZAVNOH decisions; all significant decisions were to refer to AVNOJ as a higher authority. Most importantly, Tito made it clear that party discipline must be maintained and that all important questions, even those pertaining exclusively to Croatia, were to be decided by the central party leadership, not by the head of the CPC.

The CPC took Tito's admonition somewhat to heart and, at the second meeting of ZAVNOH held two weeks later, refrained from mentioning certain matters pertaining to Yugoslavia as a whole in its final declaration. The CPC understood, Hebrang wrote to Tito, that such matters properly belonged to AVNOJ's purview.[38] Nevertheless, the second meeting of ZAVNOH reached decisions on a wide range of social and political questions, from the organization of the Yugoslav federal political system to various social and economic reforms.[39] Not only did these decisions anticipate AVNOJ discussion of these matters, the CPC made it clear that it understood ZAVNOH's role as providing the basis for such discussions and, as such, the source of AVNOJ's authority.[40]

ZAVNOH and the CPP Executive Committee

Shortly after the founding conference of ZAVNOH, Hebrang took a further step toward fostering Croat participation by creating a separate organization of Peasant Party members who were sympathetic to the Partisan cause but who were unwilling to completely endorse Partisan aims and Communist authority. Undermining the entrenched political loyalty of Croat peasants to Maček and the Peasant Party was Hebrang's highest priority. By creating a new Peasant Party organization, he hoped to draw CPP members into what they believed to be a legitimate offshoot of the Croat Peasant Party, but one which the Communists could control. As with other aspects of Hebrang's political strategy, several CPY leaders had reservations about his attempt to create a new CPP organization. Some of their objections were based on minor tactical concerns. But the real source of conflict was whether the CPC or the central party leadership should determine this important aspect of state-building in Croatia. Relations with the Peasant Party had put the CPC at odds with CPY leaders repeatedly during the interwar period. As Hebrang attempted to

---

38. *ZAVNOH, Zbornik dokumenata,* vol. 1, 501.
39. *Ibid.,* 459.
40. *Ibid.,* 501.

forge his own policy toward the Peasant Party, these tensions surfaced once again.

Hebrang first had the idea of forming a separate organization of CPP members sympathetic to the Partisans in the spring of 1943, but he had difficulty finding anyone he considered suitable to lead this organization.[41] By the time ZAVNOH was founded in June, the CPC had found a Peasant Party leader whom it could cast as head of a new CPP organization. Božidar Magovac, former editor of the pre-war CPP newspaper *Slobodni dom*, fit the CPC's purposes in a number of ways. First, he was the best-known Peasant Party leader who had agreed to cooperate with the Partisans. As the editor of *Slobodni dom*, Magovac was widely recognized among CPP members as an important figure in the party.[42] His previous editorship also put him in an excellent position to be a major spokesman and propagandist for the Partisan cause without posing the political threat that one of the most important CPP leaders like Košutić might. Moreover, Magovac had done nothing more politically objectionable since the beginning of the war than having refused to cooperate with the Partisans on previous occasions.[43] Finally, Magovac was extremely accommodating toward Hebrang personally and appears to have struck the Communist leader as a man who could be easily influenced.[44]

The upsurge in CPP members joining the Partisans and Magovac's appearance in liberated territory created a great deal of interest among Communist leaders about relations with the Peasant Party. There was a sense among central party leaders that many tactical questions about the CPP needed to be answered at this criticial point in building new political institutions in Croatia. During the summer of 1943, Tito dispatched Ivo Lola Ribar, Sreten Žujović, and Milovan Djilas to observe the situation in Croatia and to evaluate CPC relations with the Peasant Party.[45] During the next several weeks, Communist leaders considered major aspects of strategy and tactics toward the CPP. Although they agreed

---

41. Vladimir Bakarić, "Black Notebook," *Vjesnik*, 12/14/84, 3-7.

42. For more on Magovac's prewar activities see Dinko Šuljak, "Božidar Magovac—u vrtlogu podvale, spletke, i izdaje," *Hrvatska revija*, 119 (September 1980): 416-430.

43. Konjević, "Formiranje i rad IO H(R)SS na oslobodjenom teritoriju 1943-1945," 30. Magovac reportedly rejected CPC requests for cooperation with the comment that the Communists "would need them" before too long. For Communists' impressions of Magovac see AIHRPH KP-23/1167.

44. See letter from Belinić to Hebrang, 6/3/43, AIHRPH KP-23/1167.

45. Tito, *Sabrana djela*, vol. 16, 106. Tito to the CC CPC and the Main Staff of Croatia 8/14/43.

they should seek to divide CPP members from their leaders, the best way to accomplish this task was not entirely clear. How, for example, should cooperation with Magovac take shape? Should the CPP Executive Committee form local organizations which would function in coalition with the national liberation committees? What should be CPC policy toward Maček? Should Communists appeal to Radić's heritage and stress the compatibility between his views and those of the Communist Party? While not always agreeing among themselves, CPY leaders found fault with Hebrang's approach to a number of these questions.

The most pressing problem facing Communist leaders was how to organize the CPP Executive Committee. Shortly after Magovac crossed into liberated territory in June, Kardelj wrote Tito that he thought cooperation with Magovac through some sort of "main committee" was a good idea.[46] As Magovac began issuing instructions about organizing *Slobodni dom* representatives and choosing members of the Executive Committee, Tito became alarmed that revitalizing CPP organizations would endanger Communist control over Peasant Party participants in the movement. Consequently, in mid-August he instructed Hebrang and Kardelj that no separate CPP organizations should be established or revived in the localities. "It would be a mistake," he wrote, "to establish some sort of new CPP as a basis for cooperation. Creating a new CPP is a purely internal affair of those who wish it."[47] Hebrang was also anxious to prevent the renewal of autonomous CPP organizations and he informed Magovac that no local Peasant Party organizations should be established. In order to maintain Magovac's goodwill, however, CPC leaders continued to hold out the promise that such autonomous organizations would be permitted in the future.[48] Meanwhile, CPC leaders encouraged Magovac to organize representatives of *Slobodni dom*, though they assured Tito that they would control these representatives through their own people in the field.[49]

Although Tito opposed establishing separate CPP organizations, he was prepared to give CPP members in the National Liberation Army a measure of autonomy. In August, he instructed the Main Staff of Croatia to form a "Radić Brothers" detachment from a unit of five hundred Home Guards who had expressed interest in cooperating with the Partisans. This unit would be permitted to retain separate CPP political commissars, in addition to the Partisan commissars, which would spread "the

46. *Zbornik dokumenata NORa*, II/10/206-207.
47. Tito, *Sabrana djela*, vol. 16, 106.
48. AIHRPH KP-27/1711.
49. Tito, *Sabrana djela*, vol. 16, 281, Kardelj to Tito, 8/14/43.

ideology of Radić" in the unit.[50] The CPC balked at the idea of allowing separate CPP political commissars, however, and the Main Staff of Croatia issued orders that there would be no "double" political commissars in the "nonparty" National Liberation Army.[51] Tito persisted. In a letter to the Main Staff several days later he wrote: "You do not have the right to reject the conditions of the Radićists for...their own commissars in the units under our command...Not double but equivalent, according to the agreement with them, so that they will have trust in us."[52]

Despite CPC assurances to Tito that Magovac would not be permitted to establish separate organizations, some Communists thought CPC policies were strengthening the Peasant Party. For example, Ivo Lola Ribar objected that the publication of *Slobodni dom* was "breathing life into the left circle of the CPP."[53] Enabling Magovac to publish simply diverted attention from the task of convincing CPP members to join the national liberation movement. Furthermore, Ribar criticized CPC attempts to encourage Peasant Party members to denounce Maček for betraying Radić's program. Although he did not object to CPP members praising Radić of their own accord, Ribar warned that Communists should not get involved "in defending the wisdom and goodness of this man....This position [is] not only dangerous," Ribar wrote, "but contrary to the line which was confirmed in our last meeting with Old Man [Tito] before our departure."[54]

Edvard Kardelj, in contrast, agreed with the CPC's attempt to discredit Maček by stressing his divergence from Radić's aims; but he was uneasy about the way in which Maček was being attacked in the CPC press. In a series of articles in *Naprijed* in August and September discussing relations with the CPP, Kardelj praised the historically "progressive role" of the peasant movement and argued that Maček had nothing in common with the CPP's peasant roots. According to Kardelj, the Peasant Party had become increasingly divided as many CPP members realized the potentially catastrophic effects of Maček's policies. He believed that Communists should not remain aloof from this struggle within the CPP, since Croat participation in the movement and, ultimately, the outcome of the movement itself was at stake.[55] Rather, they must make clear to

---

50. Tito, *Sabrana djela*, vol. 16, 287, Tito to the Main Staff of Croatia, 8/27/43.

51. Tito, *Sabrana djela*, vol. 16, 287, Main Staff of Croatia to the Headquarters of the Second Corpus.

52. Tito, *Sabrana djela*, vol. 16, 157.

53. AIHRPH KP-2/28.

54. *Ibid.*

55. *Naprijed*, #18, 8/18/43, 1.

Croat peasants and CPP members the "direct connection" between the creed of the Radić brothers, on the one hand, and the goals of the national liberation movement, on the other.[56] Nevertheless, though Kardelj criticized Maček in this and other articles, he warned that the CPC was endangering its politicial support by conducting various "unmasking" campaigns which the Croat public was not ready to support.[57] Voicing these concerns to Tito in mid-August, Kardelj argued that Croats were unwilling to accept accusations about Maček's treachery and that they should be convinced instead of the "folly" of his policies.[58] Anti-Maček harangues by CPC and ZAVNOH leaders would only alienate CPP members from the Partisan movement.[59]

Kardelj also discussed the status of the Executive Committee in his analysis of relations with the Peasant Party. According to him, CPP members cooperating with ZAVNOH should be permitted to retain their Peasant Party loyalties and a range of political views. Previously he had praised the CPC's campaign against "red sloganeering" in Croatia for successfully "raising the population to the leadership of the CC [CPC] and ZAVNOH."[60] However, Kardelj also pointed out in his articles in *Naprijed* that vacillating CPP members were often treated as if they were Ustashas instead of being evaluated in terms of their willingness to participate in military resistance.[61] Kardelj objected to the excessively rigid standards applied to CPP members cooperating with the Partisans. Indeed, Kardelj argued that cooperation with some CPP members might take the form of a coalition in which their goals would be negotiated jointly. "The National Liberation Front," he wrote, "would not be a fighting force if it were exclusively a coalition of parties. It is natural, how-

---

56. *Naprijed*, #17, 8/11/43, 1.

57. *Naprijed*, #19, 8/25/43, 1.

58. Tito, *Sabrana djela*, vol. 16, 281.

59. As a result of the concerns expressed by Kardelj and other Politburo members, the Communist party in Croatia began to back away from its harsh criticism of Maček. Whether this was due to any real change of heart by Hebrang is difficult to say for certain. He was inclined to take an aggressive stance toward Maček, which suggests that he probably bowed to pressure from Tito and other CPY leaders to moderate his policy toward Maček. There are no documents indicating that Tito instructed Hebrang to halt CPC attacks on Maček, but according to one Yugoslav scholar, Tito delivered such instructions verbally to Kardelj, who conveyed them to Hebrang. Conversation with Ivan Jelić, 5/87.

60. *Zbornik dokumenata NORa*, II/9/281.

61. *Naprijed*, #19, 8/25/43, 1.

ever, that in a movement like the national liberation front elements of such a coalition exist for a time."[62]

In an article in *Naprijed* in September, Milovan Djilas endorsed a different notion of ZAVNOH than the temporary coalitional arrangement described by Kardelj. According to Djilas, CPP members who insisted upon looking at things "through their party glasses" should not be tolerated. Like Ribar, Djilas rejected the idea of conferring special status on CPP members in ZAVNOH; rather, all Croats should join the Partisan movement as individuals and their party membership should be ignored. Many CPP members simply have not grasped the fact that their policies help the enemy, he wrote, and that their purely party concerns are an impediment to Croat unity in the national liberation movement. "People who present things in a narrow party light appear to be taken in by the stories of reactionaries about the danger of the CPP drowning in a Communist sea, and they won't or don't want to see that, in this way, they in fact break up the fighting unity that has already been established."[63] Djilas concluded that Peasant Party members must be prevented from taking advantage of ZAVNOH and that maintaining unity within the Croatian Council should be the CPC's highest priority.

Hebrang also contributed several articles to *Naprijed* in which he discussed relations with the CPP and attempted to defend his policies toward the Peasant Party from the criticism of other Communists. Although he and Kardelj agreed on several points, they differed in their stress on certain problems and dangers in cooperating with the CPP. In an article in *Naprijed* in September titled "Break the Resistance of Sectarianism," Hebrang admonished Communists who refused to cooperate with Peasant Party members sympathetic to the movement. Certain "stubborn comrades" were fearful of cooperating with CPP members, he wrote, because they worried too much about its political implications. Dismissing such fears as unfounded, Hebrang argued that the CPC and CPP would be drawn closer together through their joint struggle in the national liberation movement. He also criticized those Communists who feared that *Slobodni dom* was not attacking Maček harshly enough, and insisted that CPP members should not be judged according to Communist criteria.[64]

Despite his dismissal of these fears about cooperating with CPP members, Hebrang was extremely concerned about the possible negative consequences of CPP participation in ZAVNOH. He worried that along with

---

62. *Naprijed*, #20, 1/9/43, 1.
63. *Naprijed*, #23, 9/22/43, 3.
64. *Naprijed*, #21, 9/8/43, 2. See also *Naprijed*, #22, 9/15/43, 2.

the wave of new members, a number of "doubtful elements" had infiltrated the Partisan movement. The CPC leader expressed this concern
strongly in an article published in *Naprijed* two weeks later. Although he
repeated that Communists must be receptive to CPP members, he
warned against the threat of CPP "speculators" joining the Partisan
movement and damaging it from within. Urging Communists to be on
the lookout for saboteurs, he wrote: "The question of strengthening and
consolidating the National Liberation Army and all Partisan organizations and institutions is inextricably bound with purging from the fighting ranks, and especially from positions of leadership, all doubtful and
hostile elements."[65]

The dual messages of these two articles conveyed Hebrang's strong,
sometimes contradictory views. On the one hand, party organizations
were instructed to encourage CPP members to join the Partisans without
renouncing their Peasant Party loyalties. On the other hand, Communists
were told to denounce Maček vigorously and to be vigilant against CPP
infiltrators. In the past, Communist views toward the CPP had been
fraught with tensions and contradictions as party leaders balanced elements of confrontation, cooptation, and cooperation in their relations
with the Croat Peasant Party. Hebrang's own strategy in the summer of
1943 included all three elements. Presented in his characteristically
uncompromising fashion, the result was a policy that often appeared to
call upon contradictory impulses. Hebrang stressed opposition to CPP
leaders and urged Communists to confront them aggressively outside of
Partisan ranks and within. He also fashioned a strategy of cooptation,
based on creating an alternative CPP leadership in liberated territory.
Finally, he championed cooperation with CPP members and was impa-
tient with those Partisans who judged CPP members "according to
Communist criteria." But rank and file Communists often found it difficult to weave together the various parts of this policy. At least some local
leaders appear to have been uncertain whether they should attack or
conciliate CPP members, since Hebrang's approach sometimes seemed to
recommend both. The very complexity of his approach reflected the
dimensions of this extremely difficult problem for Communists in
Croatia.

After several weeks of intense debate among Communist leaders in
the late summer of 1943, discussions began in earnest with Magovac
about founding the CPP Executive Committee. While Magovac continued to extol the benefits of mutual cooperation in these discussions, he
also began to hint that he would interpret the powers of the Executive

---

65. *Naprijed*, #24, 9/29/43, 2.

Committee more widely than the CPC wished.[66] In an article in *Slobodni dom* in mid-September, he criticized the national liberation committees for failing to express the will of the people. It was "as clear as the sun," he wrote, that CPP members should constitute a majority in the national liberation committees in those areas where they predominated.[67] Although Magovac was forced to retract this suggestion several days later, claiming that "certain people" had misunderstood his meaning, he continued to push for a wide interpretation of the Executive Committee's powers.[68] At a meeting of a local national liberation committee shortly thereafter, he suggested that once the CPP Executive Committee was established, ZAVNOH should change its personnel and its name to become a more representative body.[69]

The meeting of Communist and Peasant Party leaders in which the final conditions for establishing the Executive Committee were hammered out was very turbulent. The meeting began on October 12, the day immediately preceding the second ZAVNOH conference, and it dragged through the night and the following day. Tempers flared as Magovac and his supporters squared off against CPC leaders and "Radićists" (the name given to the more pro-Partisan CPP leaders) such as Škare, Lakuš and Frol.[70] Magovac wanted to ensure some autonomy for the CPP Executive Committee, and he objected to a CPC proposal that the Committee resolution be issued in ZAVNOH's name. He was also reluctant to endorse all of ZAVNOH's previous decisions.[71] According to AVNOJ President Ivan Ribar who attended the meeting, Magovac was unhappy with his election as secretary of ZAVNOH and sought a position that would reflect more of a coalitional relationship between the Executive Committee and ZAVNOH.[72] Finally, after a great deal of squabbling over its composition, the Executive Committee adopted a resolution which was presented at the second ZAVNOH conference. Pledging support for the first ZAVNOH resolution, the Committee declared itself in favor of cooperation between Croats and Serbs in Croatia, the "brotherhood" of Slovenes, Croats, Serbs, and Bulgars, popu-

---

66. *Slobodni dom*, #8, 9/12/43.

67. *Ibid.*

68. *Slobodni dom*, #9, 9/19/43.

69. Jelić-Butić, *Hrvatska seljačka stranka*, 219.

70. For a description of the meeting see Konjević, "Formiranje i rad IO H(R)SS na oslobodjenom teritoriju 1943-1945," 40. See also Šuljak, "Božidar Magovac—u vrtlogu podvale, spletke, i izdaje," 419-421; and Jelić-Butić, *Hrvatska seljačka stranka*, 226.

71. Šuljak, "Božidar Magovac—u vrtlogu podvale, spletke i izdaje," 419-421.

72. Ivan Ribar, *Uspomene iz NORa* (Belgrade, 1961), 142-143.

lar sovereignty and the right of self-determination. It also endorsed the
right of the majority, the "family equality of women," and freedom of
association, speech and religious beliefs.[73]

Despite some setbacks at the second session of ZAVNOH, Magovac
remained determined to carve out maximum autonomy for himself and
the Executive Committee. Consequently, at the second meeting of
AVNOJ several days later, he sought support from Tito which he could
use to strengthen his hand with Hebrang and the CPC. As disagreements
among party leaders about relations between AVNOJ and ZAVNOH
increased over the next several months, Magovac attempted to exploit
these to his own advantage.

AVNOJ and the Limits of Croat Autonomy

The decisions passed at the second meeting of AVNOJ at the end of
November 1943 delineated for the first time the contours of the federal
system and were a major step in the Communists' state-building efforts.
At this meeting, the federal basis of the new state was officially pro-
claimed; the AVNOJ resolution affirmed that Yugoslavia would ensure
the equality of Serbs, Croats, Slovenes, Macedonians, and
Montenegrins.[74] AVNOJ also recognized the explicitly governmental
nature of the political bodies established since its first meeting a year
earlier, including "the National Committee for Serbia, ZAVNOH, the
National Committee for Slovenia, the Anti-fascist Council of National
Liberation of Bosnia-Hercegovina, the AVNO for Montenegro and the
Bay of Kotor, AVNO for the Sandžak and the initiative committee of
ASNO Macedonia."[75] The question of whether Yugoslavia would be a
republic was left until the end of the war; meanwhile, AVNOJ declared
that the king would not be permitted to return until a plebiscite had
determined the popular will.[76]

AVNOJ did not establish the basis for organizing the federal units
until April 1945, and many questions about the borders of the republics
were postponed until the last year of the war. But it did address the
question of how to divide power between the federal government and
the federal units. AVNOJ specified that the laws of federal units, which
would have the character of states, must be in accordance with AVNOJ

73. AIHRPH IO HSS #64.
74. Slobodan Nešović, *Stvaranje nove Jugoslavije* (Belgrade, 1981), 219.
75. *Ibid.*, 228.
76. Branko Petranović, *Revolucija i kontrarevolucija* (Belgrade, 1983), 148.

legislation. The federal units would assume reponsibility for all administrative competencies not specifically assigned to the National Committee
(the government set up by the Partisans) but in the case of disagreements, federal laws would prevail.[77] Similarly, while both federal and
republic officials would be represented in the National Committee, the
Presidency retained the right to control the National Committee and the
governments of the federal units.[78]

One of the most important questions for Serb-Croat relations and the
character of the federal system in Yugoslavia was the status of Bosnia-
Hercegovina. The decision to establish a separate Antifascist Council for
Bosnia-Hercegovina several days before the AVNOJ meeting was of fundamental importance for the character of the federal system. This area
had long been a sore spot in relations between Serbia and Croatia, both
of which claimed it for their own. Because of its multiethnic composition,
it could not be considered a national homeland like Yugoslavia's other
five regions. Consequently, before the war the CPY had supported some
kind of autonomous status for this area.[79] By 1943, however, CPY leaders
began to reevaluate this approach. In mid-November, the Regional
Committee of Bosnia-Hercegovina brought a proposal before an AVNOJ
committee, composed of Djilas, Žujović and Pijade to establish Bosnia-
Hercegovina as a separate republic.[80] Although Bosnia-Hercegovina was
not a nationally homogeneous area, the Regional Committee argued that
its unique and very complicated problems could be worked out best in
its capacity as a separate unit.[81]

A powerful impetus for establishing Bosnia-Hercegovina as a separate
republic appears to have come from the CPY's desire to resolve this
question in a way that would ease Serb-Croat tensions. As long as both

77. At the meeting, AVNOJ established ministries for national defense, foreign
affairs, information, internal affairs, culture, economy, finance, transportation,
health, economic renewal, social politics, justice, supplies, mining, and construction and forestry.

78. Petranović, *Revolucija i kontrarevolucija*, 148-149.

79. Nešovic, *Stvaranje nove Jugoslavije*, 228. The first hint that its approach to
this question might have changed and that Bosnia-Hercegovina might be given
the status of a federal republic came in the statement of the National Committee
which declared: "Sincere and brotherly cooperation is necessary to you all,
Croats, Muslims, and Serbs, so that Bosnia-Hercegovina, as a unit in our brotherly community, can move foward to the satisfaction of all." But over the next
several months no regional council was established for this area, apparently due
to the opposition of several Politburo members.

80. *Ibid.*, 228.

81. *Ibid.*, 229.

Croatia and Serbia had competing claims to the area, there was little hope that a resolution to the Croat question could be achieved within the framework of a federal Yugoslav state. When Djilas, Žujović and Pijade sat down to discuss the status of this area, it immediately became clear that the region could not be attached to either Serbia or Croatia without raising serious problems between them. Consequently, the Committee decided to establish Bosnia-Hercegovina as an autonomous region with direct links to the central government.[82] However, this solution was subsequently overruled by Kardelj and Tito, who were sympathetic to the Regional Committee's arguments. Instead, they decided to grant Bosnia-Hercegovina the status of a separate republic. [83]

Although Tito emphasized the importance of the new federal system outlined at the second session of AVNOJ, he did not intend for this federal system to decentralize power.[84] Federalism was intended to reassure Yugoslavia's national groups, especially Croats, that they would be accorded equal status in the new state. But, in fact, power would remain in the hands of the Communist Party, which Tito, like Lenin, had no intention of federalizing. Party organizations were instructed to maintain tight control over the various regional councils, and they were reminded on numerous occasions that the CPY would emulate the Bolshevik model of federalism.[85] Indeed, although it adopted a new federal state structure, the second meeting of AVNOJ inaugurated a period of centralization within the Partisan movement. Wartime conditions had previously prevented the central party leadership from closely controlling the activities of regional party leaders and Partisan commanders. As the military situation improved in the spring of 1943, however, Tito took steps to reassert control within the party and the army. This move to centralize the movement, which coincided with Hebrang's attempt to carve out maximum political autonomy for ZAVNOH and the CPC, brought the two Communist leaders increasingly into conflict.

The Soviet type of federal system adopted by AVNOJ was intended to centralize power through a unitary one-party system. But in the actual division of power that evolved over the next several months, ZAVNOH and the CPC possessed a great deal more power than that envisioned under the Soviet model. Located in relatively stable liberated territory, ZAVNOH expanded rapidly. By the end of 1943, ZAVNOH ministries

---

82. *Ibid.* 229-230. This account of events was given by Rodoljub Čolaković, a member of the Regional Committee who participated in this meeting.

83. *Ibid.*, 230.

84 *Nova Jugoslavija*, 3/44.

85 For example, see AIHRPH NOV-2/162.

were turning out a stream of directives on all aspects of social and political life in Croatia.[86] Its administrative departments were well staffed and had established effective lines of communication with liberation committees in the localities. Regulations were debated and legislation passed concerning peasant debt and landholdings, currency, banking, health care and education. In most of these areas AVNOJ had not yet begun to function efficiently, so ZAVNOH referred to no higher political authority. Communist leaders were struck by the contrast between the rough and ready atmosphere of CPY headquarters where AVNOJ was located and the well-established headquarters of the CPC and ZAVNOH.[87] Djilas described his impression of ZAVNOH from his visit there in the fall of 1943 as follows:

> Nowhere was the power structure as conspicuous and real as on this liberated territory. It was evident not only in the better dress and food of the staffs and agencies, but also in the official, bureaucratic mode of operation. ZAVNOH, the Antifascist Council of National Liberation of Croatia, was headed by my former prisonmate Pavle Gregorić, a long time Communist; it had every appearance of an assembly and a government, though Gregorić was as accommodating and informed as one could wish. All kinds of schools were operating; agencies exchanged reports and circulars.[88]

The political structure of ZAVNOH was further expanded at its third session in May 1944 at which it was proclaimed the Croatian Sabor, the highest legislative and executive body in Croatia.

In a series of speeches and articles in the spring of 1944, Hebrang elaborated his ideas about ZAVNOH and the Sabor's place in the new federal system. According to Hebrang, as the true expression of Croatian sovereignty, the Sabor was responsible for making decisions on all matters pertaining to the Croatian republic. "And this means," he wrote, "that Croats alone, through their Sabor as the vessel of sovereignty, independently decide their fate. In other words, this means that only the Croatian Sabor as an expression of the democratic will of Croats and Serbs in Croatia can make authoritative decisions about the internal order of Croatia and about her relations with other peoples and states."[89]

---

86. See *ZAVNOH, Zbornik dokumenata*, vols. 1, 2.

87. AIHRPH KP-15/507, Hebrang to Popović,11/20/42.

88. Djilas, *Wartime*, 314. For a similar description of CPC headquarters see Jones, *Twelve Months with Tito's Partisans*, 4-5.

89. *Vjesnik*, #14, 7/25/44, 1.

Hebrang distinguished the new federal system from the 1939 *Sporazum* established by Maček, which had left Croatia "under the domination of the Serb clique from Belgrade." In contrast, the new Republic of Croatia was truly autonomous and expressed the sovereign will of its citizens. The Sabor, which had sole power to decide upon a union with other South Slavic nations, had legitimized Croatia's inclusion in the new federal Yugoslavia by endorsing the decisions made by AVNOJ. This union of South Slavs, provided it respected Croatia's sovereignty, would best protect Croatian statehood, since historical experience had shown that Croats, like other small peoples of the Slavic South, must band together to ensure their territorial integrity.[90] Indeed, Hebrang emphasized that the idea for the Yugoslav state had been born in the ideals of the nineteenth-century Croat national movement, and that these ideals would be realized in the postwar political order. As he stated at the third session of ZAVNOH:

> We fellow members of ZAVNOH are not realizing today the aspirations of only the current generation; we are realizing the aspirations of the best Croat sons and the best ideas of the Croat past. I remind you that the idea about the joint state of South Slavs, the idea of Yugoslavism, arose in no other place than Croatia. It was born in the Croat Revival before 1848. The Illyrianists gave birth to the idea of *jugoslavenstvo*, the idea of a state of South Slavs. From then until now, this idea has been preached; the best sons and the best minds of our people have fought for its realization. It is sufficient for me to mention the illustrious Strossmayer and Rački, democrat and fighter Supilo, and the republican and federalist Radić. They all carried in their hearts that which we are accomplishing here today.[91]

These views on the independent authority of Croatian political institutions proved increasingly out of step with the ideas Tito and most Politburo members held about the new federal system. At a meeting shortly after the second session of AVNOJ attended by Tito, Djilas, Ranković, Žujović, and Bakarić, ZAVNOH's "mistaken line" and its failure to emphasize AVNOJ sufficiently were criticized.[92] As ZAVNOH expanded its functions, it made decisions in areas Tito believed should fall under the authority of AVNOJ, although in many cases AVNOJ simply did not possess the capacity to handle these matters. In March, Tito warned the ZAVNOH Executive Committee that until a decision was given by AVNOJ, ZAVNOH was forbidden to establish a system of

---

90. *Ibid.*

91. *ZAVNOH, Zbornik dokumenata, 1944* (Zagreb, 1970), vol. 2, 604 .

92. Dedijer, *Novi prilozi za biografiju Josipa Broza Tita*, vol. 2, 1155, Bakarić diary.

"people's courts" as it had announced the previous month.[93] When several weeks later a CPC publication failed to mention Yugoslavia in the obligatory slogans included at the end of most articles, Tito ordered Hebrang to modify his emphasis on Croatian autonomy. "Correct immediately this slogan in your paper *Žena u borbi*: 'Long live free and united Croatia in a fraternal federal community with free Serbia and free Slovenia,'" he wrote. "It is unbelievable that you could fail to pay attention to the remaining peoples [in Yugoslavia] and leave out the word Yugoslavia. According to our deep conviction, this is not accidental but is in accord with your line which may have catastrophic consequences if it is not corrected in its most important aspects."[94]

Perhaps even more disturbing to Tito than this emphasis on the autonomy of Croatian political institutions was Hebrang's tendency to forget the dictates of democratic centralism within the Communist Party. Hebrang acted at times like the leader of an independent organization, with interests distinct from the movement as a whole. Convinced that this behavior threatened the unity of the party and the state it was building, Tito attempted to regulate closely Hebrang's activities and to curb any displays of excessive independence. Tito cautioned Hebrang several times not to take initiatives in foreign policy and in relations with the Allies without specific instructions from the central party leadership.[95] He also chastised Hebrang for failing to maintain proper relations with higher party authorities. In the spring of 1944, when Hebrang complained about Tito's harsh criticism of the CPC for its failure to communicate regularly with the CPY, Tito reminded him that it was "the right and duty of the CC CPY as the highest party forum" to oversee and correct the work of the regional party organizations.[96] He further admonished Hebrang for the "tone" of his letter which he insisted was not appropriate for communications with higher party organs.[97]

Hebrang, for his part, appears to have felt that Croats were not always treated fairly, even within the party. On several occasions he reacted sensitively to what he perceived were negative attitudes toward Croat contributions to the Partisan movement. In a letter to Ranković at the beginning of 1943, Hebrang defended the CPC from such criticism by fellow Communists: "Comrade Anka [Berus] has arrived at our place. She has told me that in Bosnia very bad stories are being spread about us. For

93. *Ibid.*, 1062.
94. Tito, *Sabrana djela*, vol. 19, 214; *Zbornik dokumenata NORa*, II/12/460.
95. Dedijer, *Novi prilozi za biografiju Josipa Broza Tita*, vol. 2, 1039.
96. Tito, *Sabrana djela*, vol. 19, 115.
97. *Ibid.*, vol. 19, 280.

example, even responsible functionaries say things like: 'Croats betrayed us without [firing] one bullet,' 'they betrayed us on April 6' etc. These stories are either the result of a lack of understanding about the true nature of things here or the result of enemy propaganda. I maintain that this [storytelling] is not only very unpleasant and harmful, but untruthful and that it is necessary to curtail it."[98]

Tension between Hebrang and the central party leadership was also evident in the military sphere during this period as Tito attempted to tighten control over the military forces in various regions of the country. Due to difficulties in communications, military command in the Partisan movement during the first two years of the war had been fairly decentralized. By 1943, however, conditions were ripe for a greater centralization of the military structure. In Croatia, Tito created two main corpuses whose commanders were responsible to the Supreme Staff. Moreover, in the summer of 1943 he removed the stubbornly independent Croat commander of the Main Staff, Ivan Rukavina.[99] Rukavina had angered Tito by refusing to send Croat forces to the Supreme Staff during the fourth offensive in the spring of 1943. Although it appears that the Supreme Staff may have realized later that the disposition of forces in Croatia made this task difficult, it refused to let this challenge to its authority go unpunished.[100]

During the next several months, Tito attempted to rein in the Main Staff of Croatia and on several occasions ordered it not to act before consulting him. In the spring of 1944, worrying that CPC leaders were gaining too much control over the disposition of Home Guard officers who had deserted to the Partisans, Tito instructed the Main Staff not to distribute any of these Home Guards among military units in Croatia without his knowledge and permission.[101] Warning against the "local patriotism" of certain military commanders and units, he insisted that such regional concerns were to be subordinated to the more general military interests of the Partisans as a whole.[102]

---

98. AIHRPH KP-19/843.

99. Tito, *Sabrana djela*, vol. 16, 53.

100. Milovan Djilas, *Wartime*, 313. In his account of this period Bakarić states that he supported Rukavina's decision not to send forces from Croatia to the Supreme Staff during the fourth offensive. According to Bakarić, Tito did not understand the disposition of forces in Croatia or he would never have given this order. See Vladimir Bakarić, *To su bila čudesna vremena, dani herojstva*, (Zagreb, 1971), 12.

101. Dedijer, *Novi prilozi za biografiju Josipa Broza Tita*, vol. 2, 1068.

102. Tito, *Sabrana djela*, vol. 14, 289, Tito article in *Bilten* #23-27, 4/44.

At the same time that Tito was centralizing military command in Yugoslavia, Hebrang was attempting to subordinate the Main Staff of Croatia to greater CPC control.[103] The process of centralization occurring in the Partisan movement as a whole in 1943 was also occurring in Croatia. During the first two years of the war, the CPC leadership had been scattered and decimated; with CPC leaders in Zagreb and the Main Staff in the countryside, communication between them was difficult. Consequently, though the political commissar of the Main Staff Vladimir Bakarić played an active role in accommodating military strategy to political goals, the Main Staff of Croatia often worked in isolation from CPC supervision. Hebrang was determinined to change this arrange-ment, and he clashed repeatedly with Bakarić and Rukavina who objected to his closer supervision of the Main Staff.[104] On several occa-sions, Hebrang reprimanded Rukavina for his failure to comply with party discipline and sought Tito's support in his struggle against the Partisan commander.[105] Viewing himself as an advocate for the military needs of Partisan forces in Croatia, Hebrang also complained to Tito that he should support Hebrang's efforts on behalf of these forces more fully, especially since Tito was not familiar with the situation in Croatia.[106] This complaint must have irritated Tito, who understood the direction of support to be entirely reversed. Though Hebrang was more of a political than military leader, his attempt to dominate the Main Staff and his understanding of its relationship with the Supreme Staff must have added to the growing tension in his relations with Tito and the central party leadership.

The CPC and Dalmatia

Another source of disagreement between Hebrang and other CPY leaders concerning the character of federal relations in the new state was the status of Dalmatia. Dalmatia had posed special problems for CPC leaders during the first two years of the war. This region historically had been independent of the Regional Committee for Croatia. Recognizing its separate status in the pre-1918 political arrangement, the CPY had estab-

---

103. AIHRPH KP-33/2205, minutes from CC CPC meeting, 3/24/44. At this meeting, Bakarić complained about the extent to which the Main Staff of Croatia was being subordinated to CPC control.

104. AIHRPH KP-33/2205.

105. AIHRPH 15/507, Hebrang to Popović, 11/20/42.

106. *Ibid.*

lished a regional committee for Dalmatia which reported directly to the central party leadership. When the Communist Party of Croatia was created in 1937, Dalmatian Communists were subordinated to the CPC Central Committee in Zagreb. Nevertheless, they retained their regional committee status and a tendency to operate independently of Zagreb party leaders. Though Communists were relatively strong in Dalmatia, especially the Communist youth organization in Split, they operated largely through the CPC's legal political arm. Even after a series of purges in 1938 and 1939, many party organizations remained loyal to previous leader Vicko Jelaska, who was stubbornly independent in his tactics and his relations with CPC leaders.[107]

CPC leaders believed there was strong popular support for the uprising in Dalmatia, especially in northern Dalmatia, which local Communist leaders were failing to exploit. Consequently, in August, CPC Central Committee members Pavle Pap and Marko Kovačević were dispatched to Dalmatia to prod Dalmatian leaders into action.[108] Although Dalmatian party leader Vicko Krstulović argued that conditions in Dalmatia were not ripe for an uprising, the Regional Committee agreed to form several military units and to activate them within three days.[109] When the newly formed units were decimated by enemy troops, however, the Regional Committee refused to conduct further military activities.[110] Končar reprimanded the Regional Committee for its military failures and subsequent inactivity, charging it with "adventurism," "impetuousness" and, not altogether consistently, with "unsatisfactory political independence."[111] But the Regional Committee continued to insist that the political situation was different in Dalmatia where Serb Orthodox elements were lacking.[112] Conflict between the Regional Committee and the CPC Central Committee subsided after Končar was captured by the Italians in mid-November, and their contact became more erratic. But tensions over the extent of Dalmatian autonomy remained.

---

107. See chapter 2, 67-68.

108. At a fractious Regional Committee meeting on August 7, Pap and Kovačević criticized Dalmatian Communists "for focusing on strikes and diversionary activity instead of initiating armed struggle." Drago Gizdić, *Dalmacija 1941* (Zagreb, 1958), 240-243.

109. Jelić, *Komunistička partija Hrvatske, 1937-1945*, vol.2, 93. Krstulović made this argument at a CC CPC meeting on July 8 and recommended that the CPC organize the uprising in Kordun and Lika instead.

110. Gizdić, *Dalmacija 1941*, 240-243, 292-294.

111. *Zbornik dokumenata NORa*, II/16/41.

112. *Zbornik Dokumenata NORa*, V/30/40; Gizdić, *Dalmacija 1941*, 446.

By the beginning of 1943, communications between the CPC leadership and the Regional Committee of Dalmatia were so sporadic that the Regional Committee was temporarily placed under the competency of the CPY. While this change probably pleased many Dalmatian Communists, it soon became intolerable to Hebrang and the CPC. Hebrang saw the CPY's authority over the Regional Committee as an unacceptable intrusion into the CPC's purview, and he believed it encouraged separatist sentiment in Dalmatia. Dalmatia's direct subordination to the CPY also had disturbing implications for Croatia's shape in the new federal system. Hebrang was convinced that ZAVNOH's popularity in Croatia was contingent on maintaining its control over areas under Italian rule. Consequently, he was determined to reassert CPC control over Dalmatian Communists and to increase their participation in ZAVNOH.

In his struggle with Dalmatian party leaders, Hebrang felt that Tito was not doing all he might to ensure CPC authority over the Regional Committee for Dalmatia.[113] In December, he complained twice about the wording of Tito's speech at the second meeting of AVNOJ, which referred separately to Dalmatia and Croatia. Hebrang argued that distinguishing between Croatia and Dalmatia in this manner made it sound as if Dalmatia were not part of Croatia. Tito dismissed this complaint, and warned Hebrang he was mistaken in suggesting that the CPY was encouraging Dalmatian separatism.[114] Nevertheless, the CC CPY sent a sharply critical letter to the Regional Committee for Dalmatia shortly thereafter, cautioning against "outbursts of local patriotism and youthful vanguardism."[115] The Regional Committee was instructed to work energetically "toward uprooting local patriotism as an unhealthy and damaging phenomenon, alien to Communism and the people's soldiers."[116]

Despite Tito's warning to the Dalmatian Regional Committee, the problem of CPC jurisdiction over Dalmatia worsened because of disagreement in the spring about where the Regional Committee should be located. After Tito moved to Vis, the Regional Committee also trans-

---

113. Strained relations between Dalmatian party leaders and the CC CPC were heightened by the personal antipathy between Regional Committee Secretary Vicko Krstulović and Hebrang.

114. Tito, *Sabrana djela*, vol. 18, 95; Dedijer, *Novi prilozi za biografiju Josipa Broza Tita*, vol. 2, 1050.

115. Tito, *Sabrana djela*, vol. 19, 246; Gizdić, *Dalmacija 1944-1945* (Zagreb, 1964), 91.

116. Gizdić, *Dalmacija 1944-1945*, 91.

ferred its headquarters to the island and requested permission to remain there indefinitely.[117] Hebrang ordered the Regional Committee to return to the mainland, but the Committee received permission from Tito to stay on Vis until the situation "cleared up," and it ignored the CPC's instructions.[118] Incensed at what he perceived to be another display of Dalmatian intransigence, Hebrang dispatched CPC leaders Jakov Blažević and Dušan Brkić to Dalmatia to investigate the situation there.[119] Brkić's report on the Regional Committee's behavior was very critical, reiterating the familiar charge that the Regional Committee displayed separatist tendencies.[120]

The CPY stepped in to mediate this feud, criticizing both the CPC and the Regional Committee. In a letter at the beginning of September 1944, Ranković insisted that "the Regional Committee must extirpate all unhealthy tendencies of autonomism" or "loose relations with ZAVNOH."[121] His criticism of the Communist Party of Croatia was even less forgiving. Ranković and Kardelj both characterized Hebrang's treatment of the Regional Committee as "too sharp" and "overly sensitive." Indeed, Kardelj described Hebrang's attitude toward the Regional Committee as "paranoid" and prompted by nationalist sentiments.[122] During the spring and summer of 1944, Hebrang's harsh line toward the Regional Committee met with increasing disapprobation from Tito and other top Communist leaders, and their mutual suspicions over this matter grew.

Hebrang and the Serbs

Hebrang also found himself at odds with Tito and other CPY leaders concerning the potentially damaging effects of his emphasis on Croatian autonomy on the Serb population in Croatia, and especially on Serb cadres in the movement. Hebrang's approach was aimed at modifying the image of a Serb-dominated Partisan movement that had developed in Croatia during the first two years of the war. However, his attempts to

---

117. *Ibid.*, 105.

118. Tito, *Sabrana djela,* vol. 19, 152. See also Jelić, *Komunistička partija Hrvatske* (Zagreb, 1981), vol. 2, 330; and Gizdić, *Dalmacija 1944-1945,* 192-193.

119. Gizdić, *Dalmacija 1944-1945,* 234.

120. AIHRPH KP-39/2549, Ranković to CC CPC 9/2/44.

121. *Ibid.*

122. AIHRPH KP-39/2549, Ranković to the CC CPC 9/2/44; Kardelj to Tito, 9/30/44, cited in *Naša reč* XXXIII 313 (1980): 10-12.

increase Croat visibility in the movement appear to have made many Serbs uneasy. As the CPC constructed a Croatian government based on ZAVNOH, Serbs in Croatia began to question their place in the postwar state. Would they be guaranteed the social and political equality the Partisan movement promised them? What kinds of provisions would be made for the maintenance of their cultural life? Some Serb Partisans, who had suffered at the hands of the Ustashas and had done much of the fighting in Croatia so far, may have felt the CPC's increasing emphasis on Croat interests galling and even threatening.[123]

Like other Communist leaders, Hebrang appears to have been sensitive to the need to reassure Serbs in Croatia that they would have full equality in Croatia after the war. While he did not emphasize Serb rights and equality in his speech to the first session of ZAVNOH as much as some leaders like Kardelj, he was careful to pay homage to the disproportionate military burden the Serbs had carried thus far.[124] In his speeches to later ZAVNOH sessions and in numerous articles in the Partisan press, Hebrang spoke at greater length about ZAVNOH's commitment to supporting the cultural and political equality of Serbs in Croatia. For example, at the second session of ZAVNOH in October 1943 Hebrang stated: "Serbs in Croatia, who have spilt their blood and suffered huge sacrifices, have demonstrated their enormous love toward their Croatian homeland. It would be a disservice to the Serb people, to the enormous sacrifices they have borne, even to think of denying [them] the same rights that Croats will have. Serbs deserve to be completely free and equal with Croats."[125]

As part of its effort to reassure Serbs about their equal status in ZAVNOH, the CPC established a newspaper for Serbs in the summer of 1943. The new newspaper, *Srpska riječ* (Serb Word) was intended to be a kind of parallel publication to *Slobodni dom*, the newspaper of the CPP Executive Committee. Though also dominated by its editor Rade Pribićević, a former member of the Independent Democratic Party, it never became as much his personal property as *Slobodni dom* did Magovac's. Articles by various Serb Communist leaders stressed the importance of cooperation between Serbs and Croats in Croatia.[126]

---

123. Djilas, *Wartime*, 315. Djilas reported after his trip to CPC headquarters in the summer of 1943 that many Serbs in Croatia appeared dissatisfied and apprehensive about CPC policies.

124. *ZAVNOH, Zbornik dokumenata*, vol. 1, 171-173.

125. *Ibid.*, 459.

126. For example, see the article by Stanko Opačić-Ćanica,"Život i put Srba u Hrvatskoj," *Srpska riječ*, 9/10/44, 2.

The CPC took a step further in its efforts to repond more vigorously to Serbs in Croatia with its decision to create a Serb Club in the fall of 1943. Formed by Serb delegates to ZAVNOH in January 1944, the Serb Club was intended to represent the interests of Serbs cooperating with the Partisan movement and to articulate their concerns to the Croatian Council. Rade Pribićević was chosen as president and an executive council formed of mostly Communist Party members. The Serb Club was also expected to act as an advocate of Serb cultural and political rights by explaining to Serbs their right to use the Cyrillic alphabet, to fly the Serbian flag, and to promote Serb culture through *Srpska riječ* and other means.[127] Most importantly, club members were charged with the task of countering Ustasha propaganda that the Partisan movement in Croatia was pro-Croat and would persecute Serbs if victorious.[128]

Despite these measures to assuage the fears of Serbs in Croatia, by the spring of 1944 it was evident that some Serb participants in the movement, particularly in the Kordun region, were extremely unhappy about CPC emphasis on Croat concerns. A long-standing feud between the all-Croat Agitprop Committee of the District Committee of Karlovac and the primarily Serb propaganda department of the National Liberation Committee for Kordun reached the boiling point in February when the Agitprop Committee was dismissed for failing to pay enough attention to the difficult economic and social conditions of Serbs in Kordun.[129] A more serious incident occurred in May, when several Partisan detachments of Serb recruits deserted to the Germans.[130] A commission formed to investigate this incident discovered widespread dissatisfaction among Kordun Partisans with what was perceived to be "sectarian" propaganda depicting Serbs as internationalist, Communist, and anti-religious. Disgruntled Serb Partisans complained that the CPC had refused to permit the use of Cyrillic in Partisan publications and had forbidden discussion about the massacres of Serbs during the first two years of the war. They also complained about the lack of Serb representatives in

---

127. *Ibid.*

128. *Srpska riječ*, #5, 11/21/43, 1.

129. Djuro Zatezalo, *Četvrta konferencija Komunističke partije za okrug Karlovca, 1945* (Karlovac, 1985), 49-51.

130. *Ibid.* 53-55. On April 26, 1944, the Partisan commander of the Kordun region, Joco Eremić, deserted to the Germans, taking several hundred soldiers with him. On May 15, his associate, Stevo Kosanović Jabučar, assistant commissar of a group of Partisan detachments, led about ninety Partisans over to the Germans. The Regional Committee reacted swiftly and offered them amnesty if they returned, which most of them did.

ZAVNOH and the CPC Central Committee.[131] According to them, the CPC had failed to give Serbs sufficient guarantees of their equal rights in the new state.

Alarmed by the dimensions of this discontent, the CPC moved quickly to punish the offenders from the Kordun detachments and to contain future incidents of this sort. More than a dozen well-known Partisans involved in the desertion were arrested and brought to trial in mid-July. Despite a popular show of support on their behalf by Partisan sympathizers from Kordun, CPC leaders presiding over the trial dispensed harsh punishments. Five Partisans were put to death and the rest received long prison sentences. Moreover, the CPC initiated a thorough investigation and purge of party organizations in Kordun. All party members from this area were required to appear before a commission of high party officials, and many were expelled from the party or transferred to other positions.[132] As morale plunged in these areas, several members of the CPY Politburo became increasingly concerned at the effect of Hebrang's policies on Serb support for the Partisan movement in Croatia, a concern which persisted.

The Struggle with Magovac

While Hebrang was struggling to contain the damage his policy might have had on Serb morale in Croatia, he found himself embroiled in an increasingly bitter conflict with Magovac for control of the CPP Executive Committee. Fearing that Magovac was attempting to increase his authority over the Committee by soliciting support directly from Tito, Hebrang took harsh steps against him and other CPP leaders. This put him on a collision course with Tito, who was anxious to preserve the appearance of amiable relations with the CPP Executive Committee in order to procure Allied political support.

Relations between the CPY and the Allies reached a turning point in the fall of 1943 and had a crucial impact on the Communist Party's state-building efforts. Allied military support for the Partisans had been increasing during the past year, and in the fall of 1943 for the first time the balance favored the Partisans over the Chetniks. Although the Americans continued to veto British plans for a landing in the Adriatic, the Moscow Foreign Ministers Conference in mid-October 1943 and the Teheran Conference a month later, confirmed the importance of military

---

131. *Ibid.*, 55.
132. Zatezalo, *Četvrta konferencija KPH za okrug Karlovca 1945*, 59.

aid to the Partisans and pledged to step up "commando operations" in the Adriatic.[133] By the end of the year, the British were delivering quantities of supplies on a regular basis and had several military missions stationed with the Partisans.

Tito was not satisfied, however, with the purely military recognititon he had received from the Allies. He also wanted Allied support for Partisan political objectives and achievements. If the Partisans were to succeed in remaking the Yugoslav state and establishing the political institutions outlined at the first meeting of AVNOJ, they needed at least limited recognition from the Allies. With this in mind, Tito hurriedly convened the second session of AVNOJ at the end of November to coincide with the Teheran Conference. By declaring AVNOJ's intention to establish a new federal government while the Allies were meeting in Teheran, the CPY leader hoped to induce them to endorse the party's more explicitly political goals.

This strategy soon produced the desired results. At the beginning of December, the British responded favorably to the decisions taken by AVNOJ and during the next several weeks Churchill wrote warmly to Tito about postwar political arrangements.[134] Churchill's growing enthusiasm for Tito and the Partisans was apparent in his speech to Parliament on February 22, 1944, in which he described Tito as "an outstanding leader, glorious in the fight for freedom."[135] In a series of letters in December and January, Churchill informed Tito that, though the British would continue to support King Peter, they had no desire to dic-

---

133. At the Teheran Conference, the Americans and the British disagreed about policy toward Yugoslavia. The British (supported by Eisenhower) favored greater support of Partisans as part of a possible plan to move troops north through the Ljubljana Gap once Allied objectives in Italy had been achieved. Roosevelt and Marshall wished to concentrate on the invasion of France without any diversionary commitments. They were supported in this plan by the Soviets who otherwise had very little to say about the situation in Yugoslavia. For a discussion of Allied policy toward Yugoslavia at this time see Roberts, *Tito, Mihailović and the Allies*, 187-296.

134. The Americans did not respond as favorably as the British to the second session of AVNOJ, and they were unwilling to acknowledge, as were the British, that the Partisans were offering more military resistance than the Chetniks. Moscow's reaction to the second session of AVNOJ was also very hostile at first and the Soviets forbade Radio Free Yugoslavia from broadcasting the declaration until they observed the British government's favorable reaction.

135. Cited in Roberts, *Tito, Mihailović and the Allies*, 196.

tate the future government of Yugoslavia. He also assured Tito that they would give no further military or political support to Mihailović.[136]

Tito was determined to do everything in his power to secure maximum political support from the Allies and, in a major shift of strategy during the next several months, he adopted a more moderate political stance. As Tito increasingly assumed the role of a statesman, not just a Communist general secretary, he presented himself as a moderate politician willing to deal with all "uncompromised" political forces; Communist and revolutionary rhetoric subsided in the Partisan press. In his correspondence with Churchill, Tito took great pains to reassure him that the National Committee and AVNOJ would include political groups of all persuasions in its ranks.[137] And he must have been gratified to hear Churchill state in Parliament that, though the Communists had begun the Partisan movement, "a modifying and unifying process [had] taken place and national conceptions [had] superceded."[138] In interviews with Western correspondents, the CPY leader similarly described the national liberation movement as comprised primarily of peasants with non-Communist political loyalties.[139]

Croatia was essential to Tito's efforts to elicit support from the Allies and to convince them of his moderate political intentions. Since the British continued to perceive the Partisans as a primarily Croat force, they looked to this area of the country to see how the Communists would behave politically. Tito was therefore concerned that the CPC do nothing to damage Churchill's increasingly favorable opinion of the Partisans. He wanted to create the impression that various political groups in Croatia were cooperating harmoniously in support of a moderate political program. Above all, the appearance of unity between the Communists and members of the CPP must be maintained.

At the second session of AVNOJ, Tito cautioned the Croat delegates that they must avoid all "sectarian" reference to revolutionary or Communist goals.[140] CPC leaders were told to avoid unnecessary criticism of Maček, since this would create an unfavorable impression on the Allies.[141] Tito was also at pains to secure Magovac's cooperation at the

---

136. *Ibid.*, 191-196, Churchill to Tito 1/8/44.

137. *Ibid.*, 191-196, Tito to Churchill, 2/9/44.

138. *Ibid.*, 195.

139. For example, see Tito's interview with English and American journalists. Tito, *Sabrana djela*, vol. 20, 60.

140. *Ibid.*, vol. 17, 301.

141. Dedijer, *Novi prilozi za biografiju Josipa Broza Tita*, vol. 2, 1150.

second session of AVNOJ.[142] Magovac was appointed vice-president of
the government, and CPP members of ZAVNOH, Frol and Škare, were
included as secretaries of the National Committee. In a conversation with
Magovac lasting several hours, Tito expressed appreciation "for the value
of the CPP Executive Committee and its efforts up until now."[143] The
CPY leader assured Magovac that the Communists had no intention of
launching a revolution in Yugoslavia and that they sincerely desired to
cooperate with all political groups, especially the Croat Peasant Party.

In the weeks following the AVNOJ meeting, Magovac attempted to
use the attention he received from Tito to increase his own popular support and to redefine his relationship with the CPC. In an article titled
"Our Tito" published in *Slobodni dom*, Magovac compared Tito to the
revered peasant leader Matija Gubec and suggested that Tito was so
much like Radić in his outlook that he even expressed himself in Radić's
words.[144] Portraying Tito as "a great and reasonable leader" with whom
the CPP could agree, Magovac emphasized that Tito had given the
Executive Committee and Magovac his fullest support.[145] In a letter to
Hebrang on December 20, he stated that in light of his recent conversation with Tito, relations between the Executive Committee and the CPC
should be placed "on a stronger and more sincere footing." Protesting
that recent CPC behavior toward the Executive Committee was incorrect
and contrary to the basis of his conversation with Tito, Magovac threatened to hold up publication of *Slobodni dom* unless relations between the
two groups improved.[146]

Hebrang became increasingly alarmed at Magovac's attempts to use
Tito to strengthen his position. He complained rancorously to Tito that
Magovac's "head had swelled" after AVNOJ, and that while he used to
think the CPC important, "now it was just 'Tito this' and 'Tito that.'"[147]
While Tito saw Magovac as a useful tool in his effort to gain political
recognition from the Allies, Hebrang was most interested in using him to
undermine the CPP's political position in Croatia. Ever mindful of Allied
support for the Peasant Party and its potential threat to the CPC's political gains, Hebrang's first priority was to diminish Maček's popularity
and prevent the Allies from orchestrating his return to power after the

---

142. Tito, *Sabrana djela*, vol. 20, 60.

143. *Slobodni dom*, #14, 12/25/43, 1.

144. *Slobodni dom*, #14, 12/25/43, 1.

145. Dedijer, *Novi prilozi za biografiju Josipa Broza Tita*, vol. 2, 1155, Bakarić
diary, 1/15/44.

146. AIHRPH KP-30/1940, Magovac to Hebrang, 12/20/43.

147. AIHRPH KP-32/2098.

war. In order to use Magovac and the Executive Committee to weaken the Peasant Party, it was essential that they be subordinated to Communist control.

Hebrang was convinced that Magovac was using the Executive Committee to preserve the CPP's political position and even to bolster Maček's popularity.[148] He may also have worried, as did other CPC leaders like Bakarić, that Magovac intended to bypass ZAVNOH and establish a coalitional arrangement directly with Tito.[149] After Maček, who was carefully guarded, was moved by the Ustashas from his country house at Kupinec to Zagreb in December 1943, Hebrang's fears grew that Magovac would collude with Maček to win back CPP members sympathetic to the Partisans. At the beginning of February, Hebrang warned Tito that Magovac was in contact with Maček and other CPP leaders, who were attempting to convince the Executive Committee to represent their own interests in the Partisan movement.[150]

Hebrang responded to this threat from Magovac by renewing his harsh attacks on Maček, suspended since the previous fall, and by denouncing Allied support for the CPP.[151] He also pressured Magovac to break contact with CPP leaders loyal to Maček and to criticize Maček publicly.[152] Numerous articles by Hebrang and other CPC leaders warned against Maček's "spies" in the national liberation movement and denounced Allied support for the government in exile and the Croat Peasant Party.[153] A CPC directive in January warned that "reactionary forces" in England and America, which had reacted "hysterically" to the recent AVNOJ decisions, were attempting to ensure that Maček retained his political postion after the war.

Hebrang also took steps to circumscribe Magovac's activities and bring him under tighter CPC control. He now required Magovac to submit all *Slobodni dom* materials to him before publication and objected strenuously when Magovac altered material after it had been reviewed.[154] Moreover, the CPC began to harass and intimidate

---

148. AIHRPH KPJ box 2, Hebrang to Tito, 12/18/43.

149. Bakarić, "Black Notebook."

150. AIHRPH KP-32/2098, Hebrang to CC CPY 2/2/44.

151. Reversing its decision of the previous fall, in mid-February ZAVNOH instructed its organizations to criticize Maček more directly, *ZAVNOH, Zbornik dokumenata*. vol. 2, 146. For Maček's description of this harsher policy toward the CPP see Maček, *In the Struggle for Freedom*, 249.

152. AIHRPH KPJ box 2.

153. For example, see the article by Hebrang in *Naprijed*, #35-36, 1/6/44, 2. See also *Naprijed*, #38-39, 2/3/44, 1; and *Vjesnik*, #4, 2/26/44, 1.

154. AIHRPH KP-33/2219, AIHRPH KP-34/2237.

Magovac's supporters. Various Executive Committee members loyal to Magovac were denied permission to operate freely in liberated territory and were occasionally physically harmed.[155] Tension between Hebrang and Magovac increased when Hebrang ordered a CPP leader whom Magovac had guaranteed safe passage arrested in Magovac's apartment. Infuriated by this incident, Magovac complained bitterly to CPC leaders that they could not be trusted to keep their word.[156] Hebrang refused to relent and insisted that Magovac expel individuals from the Executive Committee who, as he put it, "were sitting on two chairs."[157] Magovac, who usually maintained a conciliatory tone with Hebrang, backed down; but relations between the two men continued to deteriorate.[158]

As the CPC's campaign against the Peasant Party and the Allies escalated, Tito became increasingly dissatisfied with Hebrang's policies. He feared that Hebrang's harsh denunciations of Maček, and increasingly of Magovac, were having a negative effect on Allied opinion. He was particularly angered by the anti-Allied tone of several CPC publications which he felt had talked about Allied commanders in "an insulting and misleading way."[159] In a sharply worded letter to Hebrang at the end of January, Tito instructed him to correct his position toward the Allies immediately. "The writing in your press," he wrote, "is creating big difficulties for us and is causing great harm to the impression the Allies have of our national liberation struggle. It is mostly inexact, sectarian and often provocative. It becomes an argument in the hands of our enemies against recognizing the NKOJ [National Committee] and creates the impression that there is a Communist revolution going on here."[160]

Tito was also upset that Hebrang appeared to place parochial concerns above the welfare of the entire Partisan movement and the Yugoslav state as a whole. "You must comprehend the serious fact," he wrote, "that we represent a state [and that these] various attacks may cause serious difficulties to its position."[161] Some Politburo members like Djilas apparently also felt that CPC attacks on the Allies for their role in creat-

155. Dinko Šuljak, "Božidar Magovac—U vrtlogu podvale, spletke, i izdaje," *Hrvatska revija* 119 (September 1980): 422. Šuljak, who was a representative for *Slobodni dom* at this time, describes the extreme hostility many Executive Committee members encountered from Communists in the field.

156. AIHRPH KP-33/2219, Hebrang to Magovac 3/29/44.

157. *Ibid.*

158. AIHRPH KP-34/2237.

159. AIHRPH NOV-2/166; AIHRPH NOV-2/114; AIHRPH NOV-2/118; AIHRPH NOV-119; AIHRPH NOV-2/120.

160. AIHRPH NOV-2/166.

161. AIHRPH NOV-2/118.

ing the "Versailles" state of Yugoslavia displayed insufficient loyalty to the Yugoslav state "at the very time blood was being spent to preserve it."[162]

In retrospect, it appears that both Hebrang's and Tito's fears about the Allies were unfounded. The British had a very poor opinion of the CPP at this point in the war, and they were unwilling to take any steps to support the Peasant Party that might alienate the Partisans. Reports and memoranda from British observers in Croatia presented uniformly negative assessments of the role and prospects of the CPP. For example, a memorandum written by Stephen Clissold in February 1944 vigorously denied that the CPP had been involved in any serious resistance effort. "Since 1941 the CPP has shown no sign of constructive activity," he wrote, "nor has it developed any effective resistance movement of its own. 'Progressive circles' within the party (Jančiković and his group) have done nothing to indicate that they might form a nucleus for any resistance group which might receive Allied backing as an alternative to supporting the Partisans...In any case, it can be said with certainty that the days of the reign of CPP as the dominant political force in Croatia are over and it is unlikely that they will return."[163]

A second memorandum written shortly thereafter by the British mission to the Main Staff of Croatia was equally blunt. "Maček has committed suicide through his continued passivity," the memorandum stated, and "the CPP has ceased to exist as an expression of the peasant mind."[164] It concluded with an favorable assessment of the CPP Executive Committee which it described as "the nucleus of a new CPP."[165] That the British had no hopes Maček and Tito would reach any kind of agreement was indicated by their refusal to grant Šubašić's request in January 1944 that he be permitted to travel to Yugoslavia to help reconcile the two men.[166] With the prospect of an agreement between Maček and Tito unlikely, the British began to throw their support almost entirely behind the Partisans.

The extent to which the British were committed to supporting the Partisans in Croatia can be seen by their negative reaction to several CPP and Home Guard envoys who attempted to contact them at this time. After the capitulation of Italy in September 1943, CPP ministers from the

---

162. Djilas, *Wartime*, 372.
163. Stephen Clissold, "Britain, Croatia and the Croat Peasant Party, 1939-1945," unpublished article, 1979, 20.
164. *Ibid.*, 21.
165. *Ibid.*, 21.
166. Šepić, *Vlada Ivana Šubašića*, 136-150.

government in exile urged Peasant Party leaders in Yugoslavia to reach an agreement with the Partisans. When CPP leader Tomašić requested permission from the British to come to Istanbul to discuss this matter, he was rebuffed firmly. CPP leader Tomo Jančiković, who succeeded in reaching Italy at about this time, informed the British he wished to travel to London for discussions with Krnjević, but the British held him in Italy instead.[167] The British reacted with even greater suspicion to the overtures of Home Guard Colonel Ivan Babić at the beginning of 1944, and in response to Partisan complaints that Babić was a war criminal and should be handed over to them, they interned him. In short, they were unwilling to jeopardize their relations with the Partisans for CPP emissaries whose promises to raise forces against the Germans they had little hope would be realized and whose past conduct often appeared questionable. Nor were they willing to rock the boat with the Partisans by interfering in their relations with CPP leaders in Croatia. Indeed, the British worried that their contacts with Babić might have caused the Partisans to renew their criticism of Maček![168]

Tito found a mouthpiece for his dissatisfaction with Hebrang's attitude toward the Allies and various Peasant Party leaders in CPC leader Vladimir Bakarić, who was currently on Vis working for AVNOJ. In the spring of 1944, Bakarić emerged as a staunch opponent of Hebrang's tactics, which he criticized to Tito and Kardelj on several occasions. In an analysis of relations with the CPP written in April 1944, Bakarić argued that CPC criticism of Maček and its campaign against "speculators" and "vacillators" had created panic in the party.[169] Instead of using the Executive Committee to attract CPP members, the CPC had polarized the Committee's leadership and polemicized its supporters. Attempting to completely dominate Magovac, Hebrang had refused to see that a temporary coalition between the CPC and the Executive Committee might be necessary during this period. Moreover, by attacking Magovac, Hebrang had denigrated the new government established by AVNOJ, of which Magovac was a vice-president.

Apparently with Tito's blessing, Bakarić presented these criticisms to Hebrang at a meeting of the CC CPC on March 24th. Bakarić faulted Hebrang for his failure to promote unity in the movement and warned that CPC preoccupation with controlling the Executive Committee had

---

167. Clissold, "Britain, Croatia and the Croat Peasant Party," 18-20; and Šepić, *Vlada Ivana Šubašića*, 136-150.

168. Jelić-Butić, *Hrvatska seljačka stranka*, 255.

169. Bakarić, "Black Notebook."

hindered ZAVNOH from doing its job.[170] Although Kardelj, who was present at the meeting, had encouraged Bakarić to have his say, Bakarić must have been disappointed with Kardelj's lukewarm support in his confrontation with Hebrang. Although Kardelj agreed after the meeting that Hebrang was "hard" and that Bakarić had taken the correct measures against him, during the meeting he maintained that it was difficult to criticize CPC policies since they had achieved such success.[171] In any case, Hebrang refused to accept Bakarić's criticism either of his approach toward Maček or his attempts to restrain Magovac. Although he admitted he might have employed harsh methods, he insisted they had been necessary to curb the harmful activities of Magovac and other CPP leaders.[172]

By the spring of 1944, Tito felt that Hebrang's emphasis on Croat concerns had become a serious problem for the Partisan movement. In mid-April, he instructed Hebrang to come to Drvar where the Supreme Staff was located. At a meeting attended by Kardelj, Ranković, Milutinović, Djilas, and Bakarić, he sharply criticized CPC policies. Tito charged that Hebrang had displayed Croat "nationalist deviations" which were extremely dangerous to the unity of the party. He also accused Hebrang of misapplying the federal system adopted at AVNOJ by failing to link Croatia with Yugoslavia strongly enough in CPC propaganda. Moreover, Tito objected to the fact that the CPC had "underplayed" the role of the Communist Party of Yugoslavia in Croatia, focusing instead on the Communist Party of Croatia. Finally, Tito faulted Hebrang for overestimating the strength of the Peasant Party and for pursuing unnecessarily harsh tactics toward Maček and the Executive Committee.[173] Impressing upon Hebrang the extent to which his approach had deviated from the CPY line, Tito instructed him to correct his mistakes when he returned.[174] Nevertheless, though Tito believed it necessary to reassert control over the Communist Party in Croatia, he stopped short of severely disciplining the CPC. Like Kardelj, he may have felt that no harsher

---

170. AIHRPH KP-33/2205, minutes from the CC CPC meeting, 3/24/44. See also Bakarić, *To su bila čudesna vremena, dani herojstva* (Zagreb, 1971), 52-57.

171. AIHRPH KP-33/2205.

172. Dedijer, *Novi prilozi za biografiju Josipa Broza Tita*, vol. 2, 1157, Bakarić diary.

173. Marko Belinić, *Put kroz život* (Zagreb, 1985), 130; Tito, *Sabrana djela*, vol. 19, 335.

174. For an account of this meeting see Belinić, *Put kroz život*, 130-133. See also Tito, *Sabrana djela*, vol. 19, 335.

measures against Hebrang were warranted at the moment since his policies were producing successful results.

Hebrang took Tito's instructions with him when he returned to Croatia, but he was unwilling to admit mistakes in his own work to other CPC leaders. At a CPC meeting several days later, Hebrang conveyed Tito's message that "we must emphasize *jugoslavenstvo* in order to build more successfully a new Yugoslavia and to strengthen the brotherhood and unity of the peoples of Yugoslavia."[175] However, he did not specifically criticize CPC emphasis on the autonomy of ZAVNOH and other Partisan political organizations. Nor did he explicitly reject direct attacks on Maček, though he did tell Communist cadres to restrict their "frontal struggle against the CPP."[176] Communists need not fear vacillating and uncertain elements among the Partisans, he reminded them, because they were sufficiently strong to "cook" CPP members who did not behave. [177] As on previous occasions, the CPC leader appears to have been chastised but not converted.

Although Hebrang was forced to curb his campaign against Peasant Party leaders, he was determined to settle accounts with Magovac and to break his power in the Executive Committee. This was especially important since the CPC was preparing to establish the National Liberation Front for Croatia in May. Kardelj had urged Tito several months earlier to permit the establishment of the Front in Croatia, which would operate as a loose coalition of political groups in support of the Partisan movement. Hebrang also believed that creating a Popular Front for Croatia would be an effective way "to tie the hands of the CPP."[178] He thought it essential, however, to assert full control over the Executive Committee first.[179] The question of how the CPP was to be organized within the

175. AIHRPH KP-34/2272.

176. AIHRPH KP-43/2272. The Partisans in Croatia would never achieve their goal to "realize a free Croatia in a federal Yugoslavia," he wrote, unless they engendered widespread support for a common cause. AIHRPH KP-42-XI/3880. See also AIHRPH KP-42-XI/3881.

177. AIHRPH KP-42-XI/3880.

178. *Zbornik dokumenata NORa*, II/12/15. See also Petranović and Nešović, *AVNOJ i revolucija*, 712.

179. Some Yugoslav historians and participants in these events have argued that Hebrang intended the Popular Front to be a real coalition of parties and they point to the fact that in the first declaration of the National Liberation Front for Croatia in March the participating groups signed separately, creating the impression of separate political parties. For example, see Bakarić's speech at the CPC Congress in 1948, *Drugi kongres KPH* (Zagreb, 1949), 71-72. It seems clear, however, that while Hebrang thought that creating the impression of a genuine coali-

Liberation Front provided the occasion for the final showdown with Magovac.

In mid-April, Hebrang informed the CPP Executive Committee that the CPC was preparing to hold a conference to pick the leaders of the National Liberation Front of Croatia, after which liberation front organizations would be established in the localities. Although he still did not rule out the possibility of establishing separate CPP committees in the villages, he urged the Executive Committee to refrain from doing so until the National Liberation Front was firmly established in the field.[180] Organizing national liberation front committees first would obviously increase the CPC's ability to control local Peasant Party organizations. Pro-CPC members of the Executive Committee accepted this plan, Magovac did not, and it was decided to settle this matter at an Executive Committee meeting at the end of April. CPC leaders went to some lengths to pack this meeting to ensure that their point of view would prevail.[181] With only two members of the Executive Committee supporting him, Magovac was thoroughly outgunned.[182] The resolution adopted at the meeting clearly reflected the tone of the majority of pro-CPC members and the Executive Committee accepted the CPC proposal on organizing the National Liberation Front. The editor of *Slobodni dom* was effectively curbed. Although he retained his position as vice-president of the National Committee, his power in the Executive Committee and *Slobodni dom* declined steadily.

With Magovac's power checked, Hebrang prepared to incorporate the CPP Executive Committee into the new Partisan political institutions in Croatia. The Communist Party of Croatia appeared well on its way to undermining the Peasant Party and contesting its position as leader of the Croat national movement. Hebrang had been forced by Tito to adjust his approach to the Croat question, but the next few months would reveal that he had not fundamentally revised it. Indeed, he continued to emphasize the autonomy and sovereignty of Croat political institutions and to pursue his policy toward the CPP with great vigor and

---

tion was useful for generating support, he had no intention of relinquishing control over the CPP Executive Committee and thereby jeopardizing the CPC's predominance in the Front.

180. AIHRPH KP-34/2215.

181. AIHRPH KP-42-XI-3874. Party and ZAVNOH organizations were instructed to send pro-CPC Executive Committee members to the meeting.

182. For a description of the meeting see AIHRPH KP-42-XI/3879, Hebrang to Tito, 5/3/44. See also AIHRPH IO HSS #74; *Naprijed* #51, 4/29/44; and *Slobodni dom*, #4, 5/3/44.

determination. The CPC leader found himself increasingly frustrated, however, as Tito began to assert greater control over the process of state-building in Croatia and to reach important decisions concerning Croatia's political future without including the CPC or the Executive Committee.

The CPC and the Tito-Šubašić Agreement

The Tito-Šubašić Agreement in June 1944 opened a new phase in the CPY's state-building efforts and its approach to the Croat question. Previously, Communists had concentrated on building new political structures at the local or regional level; now, Tito negotiated an agreement to preserve these gains with the Allies and Yugoslav politicians from abroad. Consequently, major decisions about relations with the CPP and the character of federalism were taken out of Hebrang's hands; the CPC and ZAVNOH were superseded by the central party leadership and AVNOJ in negotiations over Croatia's future. This change had major implications for the outcome of Hebrang's efforts to increase the autonomy of regional party and political organizations.

With the Tito-Šubašić Agreement of June 19, the Partisans took a huge step toward gaining Allied recognition of their political objectives. After withdrawing their support from Mihailović in the spring of 1944, the British had pressured King Peter to appoint a new prime minister who could reach a political accommodation with the Partisans. As a Croat with strong Yugoslavist views who had advocated cooperation with the Partisans early on in the war, Ivan Šubašić, former Ban of Croatia, was a logical choice.[183] Šubašić was initially reluctant to head the new government; he believed that the Partisans' federal plan would divide and weaken Serbia and that a Serb should be prime minister. But the pleas of his CPP colleagues and the Allies finally prevailed.[184] On May 17, King Peter dismissed Prime Minister Purić, and Šubašić began negotiations

---

183. Šepić, *Vlada Ivana Šubašića*, 147-155. The Americans first suggested Šubašić as the new head of government; but the State Department was actually lukewarm about this idea. It believed that the CPP still had the potential to be the dominant political force in Croatia after the war and therefore that a prominant CPP leader such as Šubašić should not risk losing his prestige by reaching an agreement with Tito. Nor were the Americans fully committed to a united Yugoslavia. Roosevelt still thought that three separate states in a Balkan Federation might be the best solution to the problem of Croatian statehood. For moreon Šubašić's activities in the first two years of the war, see Šepić,*Vlada Ivana Šubašića*, 1-167.
    184. *Ibid.*, 147-155.

with Tito about the composition and platform of the new government. Finally, on June 16, Šubašić and the National Committee signed an agreement in which Šubašić consented to recognize AVNOJ and the National Liberation Army. He further agreed that the "main duty" of the new government would be to support the struggle for national liberation and that details of the final state arrangement would be left until the end of the war.[185]

Although the Tito-Šubašić Agreement did not treat Croatia separately, its impact there was tremendous. In his negotiations with Tito, Šubašić conceded on a number of issues which resulted in a weakening of the CPP's power in Croatia. Faced with the Partisans' strong position at this point in the war, Šubašić showed himself all too willing to be swayed by Tito's shrewd negotiating tactics. Schooled in the long years in which first Radić and then Maček dominated the Peasant Party, Šubašić adulated Tito in much the same way that CPP leaders before him had revered Radić. Moreover, he underestimated Tito's abilities, possessing a naive belief that, as he put it, Tito's "blue Zagorje eyes could never deceive him."[186] The Croat Peasant Party had precious few cards left to play at this point in the war; its leadership was in disarray at home and discredited abroad, and many CPP members had drifted into Partisan ranks. Nevertheless, the Peasant Party was still a formidable opponent and the Communists feared it greatly. Maček had tremendous prestige among Croat peasants, and the Allies, especially the Americans, considered his participation essential to any postwar political settlement in Yugoslavia. Although Šubašić was convinced that a deal must be made with the Partisans, he proved unable to preserve a viable political position for the CPP in the last months of the war.

Šubašić intially made an effort to consider the advice and concerns of CPP leaders in Croatia in his negotiations with Tito. But confident of his own powers and mistrusting theirs, he soon made the decision to go it alone in striking the best deal with the Partisans. When preparing for his meeting with Tito in mid-June, Šubašić originally requested that Tito include a prominent Peasant Party member in his negotiating party. Unwilling to jeopardize the negotiations, however, the British vetoed this

---

185. For a complete text of the Agreement see Tito, *Sabrana djela,* vol. 20, 250.

186. Many CPP leaders abroad and British observers soon came to feel that Šubašić was temperamentally unsuited to the task of holding his own in tough negotiations with Tito. He was a diabetic and reputedly subject to wild mood swings. For an unfavorable portrait of Šubašić by a former deputy foreign minister, see Jukić, *The Fall of Yugoslavia.*

request and no CPP leaders attended the meetings.[187] Šubašić did meet
with CPP members Colonel Babić and Tomo Jančiković, who were still
being held in British custody, and they attempted to persuade him to
make some provisions for the Home Guard in his negotiations with Tito.
At a June 13 meeting with Jančiković in Bari, Šubašić appeared hopeful
that the Home Guards would play an important part in the resistance
movement in cooperation with the Partisans and thus preserve a significant military and political role for the CPP. As Šubašić put it to
Jančiković: "Colonel Babić is now the most important person not only as
far as solving the Croat question goes, but as far as solving the question
of Yugoslavia as a whole."[188] Šubašić also expressed the hope that he
could establish contact with CPP leaders in Zagreb through Babić.

Conversations with Tito over the next several days quickly convinced
Šubašić that Tito would not tolerate any separate role for the Home
Guard in the resistance movement.[189] Consequently, by the time he met
with Babić several days later, Šubašić was considerably less enthusiastic
about the former Home Guard colonel. Babić expressed fears that the
Communists were seeking to control completely the national liberation
movement and urged Šubašić to reach an agreement with the Allies
about the Home Guard. Šubašić refused to take this suggestion seriously,
and told Babić that his fears of the Partisans were exaggerated.[190] After
their conversation, Šubašić made it clear to Tito that he had nothing
against the idea of returning the Colonel to prison. And, though CPP
leaders in Croatia continued to seek an agreement with the Allies over
the disposition of Home Guard forces, Šubašić did not raise this point
seriously with Tito again.

Šubašić was more firm in pressing Tito on the CPY's hostile stance
toward Maček and the Peasant Party. On this matter, Tito avoided a flat-
out rejection of Šubašić's demands, assuring Šubašić that the Partisans
were about to conclude an agreement with CPP leader August Košutić
which would affect positively their attitude toward the CPP. Košutić's
arrival at the Supreme Staff was expected momentarily, Tito told
Šubašić, and an agreement could be reached "within a few hours."[191]
Although the Partisans had taken a strong course against Maček, he
continued, "the truth is that he has been a prisoner of the Germans, and if

---

187. Šepić, *Vlada Ivana Šubašića*, 180.

188. *Ibid.*, 184.

189. *Ibid.*, 197-198.

190. *Ibid.*, 198. For Babić's account of this meeting see "Moja misija kod
saveznika godine 1944," *Hrvatska revija*, jubularni broj, (1951-1975): 276-278.

191. Šepić, *Vlada Ivana Šubašića*, 198.

an agreement is reached with the CPP through Košutić, then the situation concerning Maček will probably change."[192] Tito certainly knew that an agreement with Košutić was nowhere near being concluded; but negotiations with the Peasant Party leader would help placate Šubašić and convince the Allies that the CPY would not attempt to establish communism after the war.

Košutić was also under pressure from British Foreign Minister Eden to reach some kind of accommodation with the Partisans, and in April 1944 he drafted a proposal which suggested a basis of cooperation between the two groups. Focusing primarily on CPC plans for the postwar political order, the proposal called for a federal Yugoslavia in which Croatia would retain an independent army and foreign policy. A constituent assembly would be elected within three months of the end of the war to define the constitutional order.[193] This proposal, delivered to CPC leaders in April, was intended to provide a formal framework for negotiations over future cooperation.

Since Košutić was essential to Tito's strategy of negotiating with Šubašić, Tito was determined to procure the CPC's cooperation in this matter. Consequently, he instructed CPC leaders to begin talks with the Peasant Party leader under the direct supervision of the central party leadership; Kardelj was put in charge of this task.[194] Hebrang, who had refused Košutić's overtures the previous winter, appears to have had some reservations about renewing these contacts. But he received a delegation from Košutić "warmly," as he put it to Tito, and instructed Executive Committee members to be more "elastic" in their relations with these Peasant Party envoys.[195] Negotiations did not proceed quickly, however, since in fact the CPC was unwilling to approach Košutić on anything less than its own terms.[196] In these circumstances, Košutić continued to hold out to see which way the wind would blow.

Meanwhile, Hebrang grew increasingly uneasy over Tito's negotiations with Šubašić. Tito attempted to reassure Hebrang that an agreement with Šubašić was largely for external consumption and would have no significant impact on the CPC's position in Croatia, but Hebrang's fears were not assuaged. He was angry that an agreement of utmost

---

192. *Ibid.*, 198.

193. For the text of the proposal, see Jelić-Butić, *Hrvatska seljačka stranka*, 376-377.

194. AIHRPH NOV-2/130, Tito to Hebrang, 4/4/44. See also AIHRPH NOV-2/140.

195. AIHRPH HSS-2/111, Hebrang to Supreme Staff, 4/14/44.

196. AIHRPH KP-37/2438. See also AIHRPH KP-42-XI/3894.

importance to the CPC's relations with the Peasant Party, and hence Croatia's entire future, had been concluded without any participation from CPC leaders or members of the CPP Executive Committee. Rather, in the weeks preceding the conclusion of the agreement, Tito had specifically instructed the CPC to refrain from commenting on this matter.[197]

After the Agreement was signed, Hebrang felt that his hands were even more tightly tied. Tito and Šubašić had agreed not to publish the text of the Agreement until Šubašić formed a new government in London. But Krnjević and other CPP leaders in the government in exile soon began to leak word of the Agreement to the press, emphasizing the CPP's role in the new government. Hebrang complained to Kardelj that this put him in the difficult position of not being able to explain the particulars of the yet unpublished Agreement, which had created "fear and confusion" among many Partisans in Croatia. "We were in a very unpleasant position," Hebrang wrote, "because many suspected that we knew what had happened but that for some reason we were hiding it."[198] This situation must have been especially troubling for Hebrang, who had tried to create the image of a Partisan leadership concerned with Croatia's interests, a leadership that now looked either duplicitous or impotent.

Hebrang was greatly relieved when the Agreement was finally published in July and he lost no time in presenting it in the most favorable light. In an article in *Naprijed* on July 17, he emphasized that far from capitulating to the government in exile, the Agreement fully preserved the political gains of the Partisans thus far.[199] Although he attempted to present the Agreement as a triumph for the Partisans, Hebrang was concerned that it might hurt the movement in Croatia since, as he put it, Šubašić was so "unpopular among the masses." He was also unwilling to allow Tito's negotiations with Šubašić to supersede completely his own efforts to create an alternative CPP leadership through the Executive Committee. Consequently, Hebrang instructed party organizations to avoid trying to popularize Šubašić and to concentrate instead on rallying support for the CPP Executive Committee and its leaders in ZAVNOH.

Not only was Hebrang chagrined at not being fully informed of the contents of the Agreement, he was unhappy that the CPP Executive Committee had been excluded from the negotiations. During the previous several months he had attempted to create a CPP organization that could be touted as a viable alternative to the old Peasant Party leadership

---

197. AIHRPH NOV-2/143. Tito to Hebrang, 5/20/44.
198. AIHRPH KP-38/2514, Hebrang to Kardelj, 8/18/44.
199. *Naprijed*, 7/17/44, 1.

associated with Maček. Although he was determined to control this group, it was essential that the Executive Committee not appear to be an organizational stooge of the Communists. Hebrang feared that the Committee's exclusion from the negotiations with Šubašić would create just such an impression. Members of the CPP Executive Committee, Hebrang wrote Tito at the end of June, "regard it unfavorably that not one of them participated in the negotiations with Šubašić."[200] Not only would they have been able to express things to Šubašić that Communists might have found inexpedient to do themselves, their participation was essential if they were to appear more than an "ornament" of the Partisans.[201] Hebrang suggested that in order to dispel this impression, Tito should invite Frol to participate in future negotiations with Šubašić. Tito rejected this idea, however, with the somewhat spurious explanation that he did not intend to negotiate with Šubašić again.[202]

In addition to his dissatisfaction at the Executive Committee's exclusion from negotiations with Šubašić, Hebrang also worried that the agreement would strengthen CPP leaders in Croatia. The Tito-Šubašić Agreement had caught CPP leaders in Croatia off guard, and their initial reactions were mostly negative.[203] Farolfi, Jančiković, and Košutić had deep reservations about the Agreement which they felt did not safeguard the CPP's position in the postwar political order. Complaining that Šubašić had behaved too much like a prime minister and too little like a representative of the CPP, Košutić argued that the Agreement should be supplanted by one that would give more explicit political guarantees to the CPP.[204] Publicly, however, CPP leaders in the country took a more optimistic tone and proclaimed the Agreement a great victory for the CPP. Peasant Party publications emphasized that for the first time the "Great Serbian" government in exile had been forced to bend to Allied

---

200. AIHRPH KP-36/2411.

201. AIHRPH KP-36/2411, Hebrang to CC CPY, 8/25/44.

202. AIHRPH NOV-2/147, Hebrang to Supreme Staff, 7/13/44. In a letter to the CC CPC on August 8, Kardelj explained that the Executive Committee had not been invited to attend the negotiations because then the CPY would have been obliged to invite other members of the National Committee, which was logistically impossible. AIHRPH KPJ-2/51a.

203. Reactions from former ministers of the government in exile were varied. While Krnjević rejected Šubašić's terms of agreement, Šutej and Bićanić agreed to join the new government formed by Šubašić in July. For Krnjević's reaction to the Agreement see Krnjević, "Dvije umišljene i bijedne veličine u hrvatskoj emigraciji," *Hrvatski glas* 6, XII (1974).

204. Jelić-Butić, *Hrvatska seljačka stranka*, 253.

pressure and to appoint a Croat as head of government.[205] They applauded that fact that the British had finally recognized three separate peoples in Yugoslavia.[206] Peasant Party leaders also expressed hope that the Agreement was the first step in working out an arrangement with the Allies concerning the disposition of Home Guard troops.[207]

As word of the Tito-Šubašić Agreement leaked, Hebrang became alarmed that CPP leaders would use it to discredit the Executive Committee and seize the initiative from the Partisans. The various factions in the CPP leadership might still put aside their differences and launch a united campaign against the CPC. Hebrang was particularly worried that Magovac and other Maček supporters might yet make a bid to infiltrate ZAVNOH and the CPP Executive Committee.[208] Consequently, he once again took the offensive against Magovac, who had been crippled but not destroyed as a power in the Executive Committee. At the end of June, Hebrang complained to the CC CPY that Magovac was attempting to bolster the popularity of Maček and other CPP leaders by touting the Agreement as a sign of CPC failure, and that he had become "completely impossible" for the CPP Executive Committee.[209]

In order to minimize the possibility that Hebrang might create problems in his relations with the Allies by taking steps against Magovac, Tito ordered Hebrang to send the Peasant Party leader to the National Committee on Vis.[210] He also instructed Hebrang that no action should be taken against Magovac until AVNOJ had made a decision on this matter. While Magovac was on Vis, however, the CPC began to investigate his activities with the intention of charging and executing him for betraying the Partisans. The CPC sent the results of this investigation with Gaži and Frol who met with Tito on Vis at the end of July. At this meeting, CPY leaders agreed to withdraw their support from Magovac, as they were strongly urged to do by these Executive Committee members. But Hebrang was informed that he should not publicly denounce or arrest Magovac, and that CPY leaders would decide upon the timing of his removal from the National Committee.[211] Still, Hebrang persisted.

---

205. AIHRPH HSS-1/61.

206. *Ibid.*

207. AIHRPH HSS-1/33, CPP publication *Hrvatska i Hrvati.* See also CPP order to the Home Guard, 7/15/44 , AIHRPH HSS-1/32.

208. AIHRPH KP-42-XI/3899. Hebrang to Supreme Staff, 7/14/44.

209. AIHRPH KP-36/2411.

210. AIHRPH KP-42-XI/3954.

211. AIHRPH KPJ-2/51a, Kardelj to Hebrang, 8/8/44.

"We must resolve this matter of CPP infiltrators quickly," he wrote Kardelj several days later, and we cannot arrest and execute some CPP suspects and not their leader, Magovac. Since it is necessary for "some heads to roll," it would be much simpler if Magovac's head could go with theirs.[212] Hebrang did not succeed in persuading Tito to hand Magovac over to the CPC. Nevertheless, the former head of the Executive Committee found himself in an increasingly difficult position. At the end of August, he was forced to resign from the National Committee and he was placed under house arrest shortly thereafter.

Despite Tito's fears that Magovac's removal would upset Šubašić and the Allies, Šubašić did little to protest when Magovac was forced to resign from the National Committee and imprisoned shortly thereafter. The new prime minister did not think much of Magovac, though they shared similar views about the role of the CPP in the Partisan movement. When they met in mid-August on Vis, they discussed this question at length, and Magovac undoubtedly painted the situation in the Executive Committee in an unfavorable light.[213] Nevertheless, Šubašić does not appear to have raised this matter seriously with Tito, placing his hopes instead on the negotiations being conducted with Košutić.[214]

Given the obvious benefits negotiations with Košutić had in deflecting Šubašić's criticism of other matters, Tito pressed CPC leaders to continue their efforts to lure him to liberated territory.[215] At the end of July after weeks of half-hearted contacts, Košutić's delegate Krbek appeared in Partisan territory, where he was informed by Hebrang that the National Liberation Front of Croatia had rejected Košutić's proposal for cooperation. Košutić would be permitted to join the movement if he agreed to accept its goals (outlined in the second meeting of AVNOJ and the second and third meetings of ZAVNOH) to denounce the Ustashas and all CPP members cooperating with them, and to call upon all CPP members to join the Partisan movement.[216] Knowing full well the Executive Committee would refuse his membership (as indeed it did), Hebrang also informed Košutić that his relations with the Committee were an

212. AIHRPH KP-38/2514, Hebrang to CC CPY, 8/18/44.

213. Šepić, *Vlada Ivana Šubašića*, 263.

214. *Ibid.* 268.

215. AIHRPH KPJ-2/51a. Nevertheless, CPY leaders did not believe that at this point Košutić's decision to join the Partisans would increase substantially Croat support for the movement. Consequently, Kardelj informed Hebrang that it was not necessary to give Košutić's appearance in liberated territory any "great significance."

216. Jelić-Butić, *Hrvatska seljačka stranka*, 379-381. For Hebrang's report to Tito on the CPC's rejection of Košutić's proposal see AIHRPH NOV-2/151.

internal party matter to be worked out between them once Košutić joined the Partisans.[217]

Still Košutić waited, probably to see the outcome of CPP negotiations with Ustasha leaders. In mid-summer, Ustasha Minister of Police Mladen Lorković and Minister of Defense Ante Vokić initiated discussions with CPP leaders about reconstructing the Croatian government.[218] Convinced that the Germans would ultimately lose the war, they wanted Peasant Party leaders to join the current government so that Croatia would be treated mildly and allowed to retain its independence after Allied victory. From the end of July to mid-August, Lorković and Vokić contacted Košutić and Farolfi several times and, though Košutić met them with reserve, Farolfi agreed to talk. The negotiations failed suddenly in August, however, when Pavelić arrested the two Ustasha officials and numerous CPP leaders. What remained of a coherent Peasant Party leadership in Croatia was effectively destroyed.[219] Consequently, at the end of August when the CPC informed Košutić that he had three days in which to make up his mind, Košutić apparently felt he had no choice but to throw in his lot with the Partisans; he crossed into liberated territory shortly thereafter.

By the end of the summer 1944, the CPY's foreign policy initiatives appeared to have paid off. In his second round of negotiations with Tito in August, Šubašić appeared so compliant that even the British were upset by his solidarity with the Partisans. Although the British still had not formally recognized the Yugoslav National Committee, by the time Tito met Churchill in Italy in August, they had become wholly committed to military and political support for the Partisans.

The Tito-Šubašić Agreement and Tito's negotiations with Churchill marked the end of a phase that had begun with the first meeting of AVNOJ nearly two years before. During this period, the CPY succeeded in laying the foundation of a postwar political order and in gaining at

---

217. Jelić-Butić, *Hrvatska seljačka stranka*, 379-381.

218. The Lorković-Vokić affair ended with a strange twist. Pavelić was apparently informed of these negotiations, but at the end of August, partially in response to the attempt made on Hitler's life, he decided to move against the participants in this plot to take over the Ustasha government. See Jelić-Butić, *Hrvatska seljačka stranka*, 245-247; Bogdan Krizman, *Ustaše i Treći Reich* (Zagreb, 1983), vol. 2, 78-139.

219. According to Maček, of the CPP leaders arrested at the time—Pernar, Torbar, Farolfi, Pešelj, Tomašić and Smoljan—only Tomašić and Farolfi were involved in the Vokić-Lorković affair. All of these men, except Pešelj, were killed by the Ustashas at the end of the war. For Maček's account of these events see Maček, *In the Struggle for Freedom*, 255-256.

least *de facto* recognition from the Allies. Tito's efforts to gain this recognition brought him into conflict on numerous occasions with Hebrang, who was motivated by interests more specific to the movement in Croatia. Hebrang's emphasis on the autonomy of Croatian political institutions at a time when Tito was attempting to centralize the movement further exacerbated this conflict. Tito tolerated these clashes for a number of reasons, probably including his old personal ties to Hebrang. He may also have felt that Hebrang's tactics of emphasizing Croat concerns were successful and even necessary to gain the support of Croats loyal to the CPP. In addition, AVNOJ was not strong enough yet to function as an effective central political body and to prevent ZAVNOH from filling this gap. With the Tito-Šubašić Agreement, however, the position of the CPY and AVNOJ was strengthened greatly. Consequently, Tito no longer felt it necessary to tolerate Hebrang's approach to the Croat question, which he felt threatened the centralization of the party and the state. As Hebrang and ZAVNOH challenged the Politburo's authority anew, Tito determined to move against the leader of the Communist Party in Croatia.

Hebrang Removed

As the summer of 1944 drew to a close, ZAVNOH passed a series of measures which convinced Tito that Hebrang had strayed unacceptably from the CPY line. During the last year, Tito had emphasized repeatedly to the Allies that the Partisans did not intend to introduce Communism after the war. He had also warned the CPC on numerous occasions not to attack non-Communist political groups like the CPP. Nevertheless, Tito did not want the CPC to concede to non-Communists on issues of fundamental political or ideological significance to the Partisan movement. Several decisions taken by ZAVNOH at the third meeting of its presidency at the end of August he considered just such fundamental concessions, and he was determined to prevent their realization.

As ZAVNOH's authority began to touch on all major areas of social and economic life, it also began to intrude on areas traditionally regarded as the domain of the Catholic Church. Possible opposition from the church posed enormous problems for Communist leaders in Croatia. Not only was the church an extremely powerful institution, its strength and popularity had not been badly damaged by the war.[220] And, as the Peasant Party weakened, the church began to assume at least part of the

---

220. AIHRPH KP-42-XI/3918, Hebrang to Tito, 9/3/44.

CPP's political role as defender of Croat national interests. With its highly developed organizational structure, the church could prove a formidable opponent indeed. Hebrang appears to have become convinced that the CPC and ZAVNOH should not undertake any social or political changes the church would perceive as a direct challenge to its interests. In order to give the CPC time to solidify its position, he sought to avoid direct confrontation with church authorities at this point in the war.

The church considered the question of divorce and civil marriage to fall within its exclusive domain. Hebrang was therefore reluctant to introduce radical reforms in this area. Virtually inundated with requests for divorce, however, ZAVNOH authorities felt compelled to take action on this extremely sensitive issue, though they had different opinions about how ZAVNOH should respond.[221] In February 1944, a proposal was put before ZAVNOH to permit civil as well as church marriage, but it was tabled for fear of alienating church authorities and provoking their opposition. Nevertheless, it was adopted informally in some places like Dalmatia.[222] In mid-June, the head of the ZAVNOH Department of Justice, Ferdo Čulinović, proposed a progressive set of procedures for handling marriage and divorce.[223] Allowing for divorce only in "cases in which it is impossible for the marriage to continue," the legislative proposal took great pains to stress that ZAVNOH did not intend to interfere with the view the church held toward marriage, and that the church could continue to view a marriage as viable even if the state declared it void.[224]

Responding to opposition from the church and the Partisan women's organization (Antifascist Front of Women), Hebrang vetoed this proposed legislation at the third meeting of the ZAVNOH presidency in August. He further instructed the legislative commission to draft a proposal that would forbid the possibility of divorce.[225] Although ZAVNOH did permit national liberation committees to authorize "temporary separation from bed and table," these committees were instructed to "carry out a lively campaign against divorce and to emphasize the enormous service our women have rendered the national liberation movement."[226] According to Kardelj, who was present at the meeting,

---

221. *ZAVNOH, Zbornik dokumenata*, vol. 3, 69.
222. *Ibid.*, 60.
223. *Ibid.*, 77-80, 86-93.
224. *Ibid.*, 87.
225. *Ibid.*, 259.
226. *Ibid.*, 259.

Hebrang was prepared to go further and pass legislation requiring church marriages, even though most CPP members opposed this legislation. Kardelj claimed that only his presence at the meeting had prevented the ZAVNOH presidency from passing such legislation.[227]

A more dramatic move taken at the third meeting of the ZAVNOH presidency concerned the question of religious instruction in schools. This question had become more pressing as ZAVNOH increased the number of its schools in liberated territory. Indeed, a good portion of ZAVNOH's attention was occupied by the problems of recruiting and training teachers and guiding their courses of instruction. Religious instruction had been an obligatory subject in the interwar years and the church guarded this prerogative jealously. Apparently unwilling to spark a confrontation with church authorities on this matter, Hebrang decided to endorse obligatory religious instruction.[228]

This time Kardelj did not succeed in thwarting Hebrang's moves and the ZAVNOH presidency adopted legislation requiring religious instruction in all schools operating in Partisan territory.[229] Having previously instructed the CPC not to introduce such legislation, Tito must have felt this to be a direct challenge to his authority. His reponse was swift and furious. "It really surprised me," he wrote to Hebrang, "that you should have given the decision in ZAVNOH to introduce religious instruction as [an] obligatory [subject] in Croatia. This is a very serious error for which you are responsible, you and the other comrades. Attempt in every way to rescind this order...With such a rotten concession you will not help our national liberation movement and our sons in the least, rather you bring reactionary elements into our struggle."[230]

A third subject discussed by the ZAVNOH presidency in August was CPC policy for promoting Serb culture in Croatia. Serbs in Croatia considered the use of the Cyrillic alphabet a prerequisite for their national equality. The CPC had taken steps to promote Serb culture by facilitating the use of Cyrillic type for *Prosvjeta* and other publications. At the second meeting of the ZAVNOH presidency in the summer of 1944, Hebrang proposed that Cyrillic and Roman alphabets be used in all schools in Croatia. Where the majority of students were Serbs, they would learn the Cyrillic alphabet first; where the majority were Croats, they would begin

---

227. *Naša reč* XXXIII 313 (March 1980): 10-12, Kardelj to Tito, 9/30/44.

228. *Ibid.*

229. Despite Tito's intervention, this decision was popularized in the Partisan press in Croatia. For example, see *Naprijed*, #69, 8/24-25/44.

230. *Zbornik dokumenata NORa*, II/4/113-124, Cited in Jelić, *Komunistička partija Hrvatske*, vol. 2, 313.

with the Roman alphabet.[231] At a conference on literary language held in August, a commission was formed to work out regulations for the use of language in ZAVNOH and Partisan publications.[232] Roman and Cyrillic alphabets were to be considered equal and writers were free to choose which spelling they would use. The third meeting of the ZAVNOH presidency pledged to enforce the equality of both Cyrillic and Roman scripts in all Partisan publications and to take steps to "fix" the language in ZAVNOH documents.

Although ZAVNOH had taken consistent measures to facilitate the use of Cyrillic type in various publications, including children's books, there is evidence that at least some members of ZAVNOH attempted to impose a more rigid standard of Croatian orthography. Prvoslav Vasiljević, who was working on a bulletin for the foreign press, described an incident in a letter to Milovan Djilas at the end of September in which he was called into Vladimir Nazor's office and told not to use Serbian in bulletins published in Croatia. When Vasiljević protested that this was not current ZAVNOH policy and that some Serbs in Croatia did not know how to write in Croatian, Nazor informed him that in that case they wouldn't be permitted to work in Croatia.[233] These complaints added to the growing dissatisfaction of CPY leaders with Hebrang's policy toward Serbs in Croatia; alleged pressure to use Roman script in ZAVNOH publications was just one more indication of his neglect of, or even hostility toward, Serb rights. In sending Vasiljević's letter on to Ranković Djilas added curtly: "Put an end to these attacks and find those who inspired them, that is my opinion."[234]

The CPC's decision to establish a separate telegraph agency also increased Tito's alarm that Hebrang had diverged unacceptably from the CPY's line. In mid-September, ZAVNOH announced the formation of an independent telegraph agency for Croatia and instructed all national liberation committees to send regular information to the agency about developments in their areas.[235] Although this decision was not a radical departure from ZAVNOH's general practice of establishing departments in areas where AVNOJ was not functioning fully, Tito saw it as a direct challenge to the centralization of the movement. Control over the dissemination of information and the media was essential to the Communist Party's control over the new government and its citizens.

---

231. *ZAVNOH, Zbornik dokumenata,* vol. 3, 100-102.

232. *Ibid.,* 237-238.

233. Dedijer, *Novi prilozi za biografiju Josipa Broza Tita,* vol. 2, 842-843.

234. *Ibid.,* 842-843.

235. *ZAVNOH, Zbornik dokumenata,* vol. 3, 301, 316.

Delegating this function to regional party organizations would deprive the central party leadership of a crucial tool for executing its policies countrywide and for controlling the party organization in that region. Tito was not prepared to relinquish this mechanism of control.

Shortly after ZAVNOH announced the formation of the telegraph agency in Croatia, Tito issued a sharp reprimand to Hebrang. "Halt immediately the work of your so-called telegraph agency TAH," he wrote. "What does this really mean? You are entering with all your might into separatism. Why don't you see that a federal state order has one official telegraph agency? If no one else will do, let your example be the Soviet Union."[236] This last sentence was extremely revealing, for Tito made it clear that the greater degree of autonomy regional party leaders had possessed during the war was not permissible in the centralized "federal" order the CPY was now establishing. Tito was determined to centralize the new state, even if this meant removing some regional Communist leaders. If Hebrang couldn't be convinced to follow the CPY's line more closely and to acquiesce to the centralization of power in AVNOJ and the CPY, then he would have to go. On September 18, Tito instructed Kardelj to travel quickly to Croatia and to evaluate the situation there. "Unbelievably stupid things are being done there," he wrote. "All of this shows that separatist tendencies are very strong and that they appear among our comrades. Look into this and if Andrija holds on to these views, then we must remove him as secretary of the CC."[237]

Kardelj did not need any further investigation to arrive at his opinion about the situation in Croatia. He was convinced that Hebrang must be dismissed. In a scathing letter to Tito on September 30, he outlined his views on Hebrang's mistakes and the reasons why he should be removed.[238] First, Kardelj faulted Hebrang for his "nationalist proclivities" which he believed had led to increasingly serious errors in Croatia. Although the CPC talked a lot about Yugoslavia, Kardelj wrote, "I don't think I would exaggerate if I say that Andrija doesn't like Serbs or Slovenes and that he regards Yugoslavia more or less as a necessary evil....The CPC will never improve as long as Andrija is secretary here. His whole mentality and outlook are such as to minimize Croatia's con-

---

236. AIHRPH NOV-2/162.

237. Dedijer, *Novi prilozi za biografiju Josipa Broza Tita*, vol.2, 1098.

238. The complete text of this letter has been published in *Naša reč* XXXIII 313 (March 1980): 10-12. A less complete version is in Zatezalo, *Četvrta konferencija Komunistička partija za okrug Karlovca 1945*, 61-64. Zatezalo gives the following archival citation: Arhiv CK KPJ, 1944/576. This author was not able to locate the document in the archives at the IHRPH.

nection to Yugoslavia."[239] Moreover, Kardelj charged that under
Hebrang's leadership, CPC relations with the CPY had been "exceptionally lax"; the CPC put into effect "only those instructions that it wants to,"
he wrote, "or which we directly pressure it to—it does not take into
account the CC CPY." According to Kardelj, this improper attitude had
been displayed on a number of occasions. Hebrang had ignored Tito's
instructions not to introduce compulsory religious education and he had
continued to take harsh measures against the Dalmatian party leadership
after the CPY Central Committee had expressed satisfaction with its
progress. "I have no proof," Kardelj wrote, "but I suspect Hebrang is
against Dalmatia because Dalmatia has more correct relations toward
Yugoslavia, and [because] the Regional Committee for Dalmatia has
more correct relations toward the CC CPY than Hebrang."[240]

Kardelj also criticized Hebrang's policies toward Serbs, which he
believed were driving them from the movement. Based on conversations
with Pribićević and CPC leader Opačić-Ćanica, Kardelj concluded that
Hebrang had obstructed Serb Club publications because he feared that
popularizing the club would undermine the unity of ZAVNOH.
Moreover, he had taken unnecessarily harsh measures against Serbs in
Kordun, punishing Partisans loyal to the movement. Kardelj warned that
Hebrang's failure to give Serbs adequate assurances about their political
position in the new state could lead to a resurgence of the Independent
Democratic Party. In short, his policies were endangering Partisan popularity among Serbs in Croatia. Kardelj also objected to Hebrang's negative attitude toward Slovenes which had resulted in unnecessary squabbling over jurisdiction in Gorski Kotor.

Finally, Kardelj faulted Hebrang for his autocratic style of rule, which
he believed had prevented the CPC from recruiting cadres and creating a
strong leadership within the party. According to Kardelj, Hebrang had
an excessive need to dominate those around him and was extremely
hostile to men like Bakarić and Krstulović whom he couldn't bend to his
will.[241] Moreover, his autocratic style of leadership within the party was
mirrored in the CPC's relations with the populace. Instead of leading, it
ruled, and often by fear. Such tactics would only hinder the CPC's ability
to attract Croat support.

Kardelj concluded his letter by recommending that Tito remove
Hebrang and replace him with Vladimir Bakarić as secretary of the CPC.

---

239 *Naša reč* XXXIII 313 (March 1980).
240. *Ibid.*
241. Kardelj also mentioned that Hebrang's wife was an "alien element" and
had aroused a great deal of bad feeling among other Partisans. See *ibid.*

Given his own dissatisfaction with Hebrang's policies, Tito decided to heed this recommendation. Djilas and Kardelj were sent to Croatia to inform Hebrang of his appointment to a post in the new government in Belgrade. According to Djilas, Hebrang continued to defend his policies, insisting that any errors arising under his leadership were temporary phenomena due to external causes.[242] In any case, Hebrang's removal was presented in a favorable light publicly and the Partisan press in Croatia lauded his appointment as the new minister of industry. Before he departed for Belgrade, Hebrang was presented with an award for services rendered the national liberation movement in building the new government in Croatia and in strengthening unity between Serbs and Croats.

Aftermath

Since Hebrang's wartime activities have been viewed largely through the prism of his arrest and accusation (never formally raised) as a spy in 1948, it is necessary to consider briefly some of the events that occurred after he left Croatia in October 1944.[243] After his removal as CPC secretary, Hebrang appears to have enjoyed Tito's full confidence and he briefly assumed a number of powerful positions in the new government, including minister of industry.[244] By the beginning of 1946, however, Hebrang's star was once again in decline as tensions arose between him and other Communist leaders over the pace and method of economic development.[245] These disagreements came to a head in the spring of 1946 when Hebrang complained to Kardelj that he had been excluded

---

242. Djilas, *Wartime*, 410.

243. For a more thorough treatment of Hebrang's activities during this period see Ivo Banac, *With Stalin against Tito, Cominformist Splits in Yugoslav Communism* (Ithaca, New York: Cornell University Press, 1988).

244. In the spring of 1945, Hebrang was appointed minister of industry and president of the Economic Council in the new government established with Šubašić. The following fall he was elected as representative to the Sabor and served as representative from Croatia to the Presidency of the Constituent Assembly.

245. In his speech to the Second Congress of the CPC, Vladimir Bakarić charged that when the government was attempting to work out a general plan, Hebrang wanted first to establish a five year plan, and when the government decided to work out a five year plan, Hebrang then began to argue for a one year plan. Hebrang was also charged with adopting harsh policies toward peasants. See *Drugi kongres Komunističke partije Hrvatske* (Zagreb, 1949), 71-72.

from a recent trade delegation to the Soviet Union because of Tito's personal animosity toward him.[246] At a CPY Central Committee meeting shortly thereafter, Hebrang was expelled from the Politburo and relieved of his position as minister of industry and president of the Economic Council. He retained his post as president of the Planning Commission until January 1948, when he was further demoted to minister of light industry.[247]

The CPY's split with Stalin in 1948 was the occasion of Hebrang's final fall from grace. As tension increased between the two Communist parties in the spring of 1948, suspicion grew that Hebrang might side with the Soviets or that the Soviets might support him as an inside candidate against Tito. In any case, Hebrang was placed under house arrest in April 1948, and in a plenum of the CPY Central Committee shortly thereafter, Tito charged that Hebrang had misinformed the Soviets about the CPY.[248] At the beginning of May, along with Politburo member Sreten Žujović, Hebrang was removed to prison, where he was when the Cominform Resolution reached Yugoslavia in June.

During the next several weeks various accusations were made against Hebrang, not only about his attitude toward the Soviets but about his behavior during the war. At the Fifth Party Congress of the CC CPY in July 1948, Tito charged that Hebrang, along with Žujović, had sided with the Cominform, describing them as "vacillators" and "enemy elements."[249] He also charged that Hebrang had created an "unhealthy" situation in Croatia while he was secretary of the CPC. According to Tito, he had maintained "incorrect" relations with other members of the Central Committee and had adopted "a chauvinist stand which brought dissatisfaction to Serbs in Croatia."[250] Bakarić elaborated these charges in his speech to the Second Congress of the CPC shortly thereafter, accusing Hebrang of pursuing incorrect policies toward the Croat Peasant Party and of displaying anti-Serb, chauvinist tendencies. According to Bakarić, Hebrang had "hindered [Serbs] from their national and cultural

---

246. This letter has not been published in full, but was referred to at the April 19 CC CPY meeting. See Savo Kržavac and Dragan Marković, "Informbiro i Goli Otok," *NIN* 3/21/82, 54.

247. For a description of this meeting see *ibid.*

248. According to Tito, on his trip to Moscow Hebrang had given the Soviets inaccurate information about the CPY, charging that it did not operate in a democratic fashion, that the CC CPY never met, and similar things. Tito also hinted of more ominous accusations against Hebrang when he said that Hebrang was now under investigation concerning his behavior in Ustasha camps in 1942.

249. *Peti kongres Komunističke partije Jugoslavije* (Belgrade, 1949), 110.

250. *Ibid.*, 89.

development" by destroying Serb monuments and discouraging the use of Cyrillic. Almost as an afterthought, Bakarić added the ominous charge that "when [Hebrang] was removed as party secretary in 1944 it was not known that in Ustasha prison he had betrayed the party and that he was exchanged so he could be sent to liberated territory."[251] This charge, which implied that Hebrang had agreed to work for the Ustashas after his exchange, was to color all subsequent examinations of Hebrang's role during this period.

Much of what has been revealed about the ensuing investigation into charges that Hebrang cooperated with Ustasha authorities comes from an account published in 1952 by Mile Milatović, head of the Secret Police (UDBA) in Serbia, who was responsible for Hebrang's interrogation.[252] According to Milatović, Ranković asked him to initiate the investigation in June 1948 and, while admitting that the current evidence against Hebrang was slim, instructed Milatović to flesh out the story of Hebrang's treacherous behavior in Ustasha prison in 1942. Milatović constructed the following account. According to him, when Hebrang was in the Ustasha camps Jasenovac and Stara Gradiška in May and June 1942, he gave way under torture and betrayed essential information concerning party members and plans. Indeed, the extent of his knowledge and confession so impressed Ustasha official Eugen Kvaternik that he informed Pavelić that Hebrang would be extremely useful for their plans to infiltrate and divide the Communist Party of Croatia. Milatović further suggested that when faced with this plan, Hebrang agreed to cooperate with the Ustashas in exchange for his freedom. During the several months of his interrogation, Hebrang steadfastly denied these charges, insisting that he had never been in Jasenovac or subject to torture. But according to Milatović, the weight of the prosecutor's documentary evidence and eyewitness accounts contradicting his story eventually convinced Hebrang that he could no longer conceal his guilt. As a consequence, he took his own life in prison in 1949.

This is where the case of Andrija Hebrang stood for almost the next two decades. However, as is frequently true when a regime tries to bury important figures by destroying or altering the historical record, the case of Andrija Hebrang refused to die. Indeed, in the past fifteen years, an entire literature has been produced both questioning and defending the official account of Hebrang's actions and death rendered by Milatović.[253]

---

251. *Drugi kongres KPH*, 71-72.

252. Mile Milatović, *Slučaj Andrije Hebranga* (Belgrade, 1952).

253. Several works in recent years have reexamined the Hebrang case. For the pro-Milatović point of view see Dragan Kljakić, *Dosije Hebrang* (Ljubljana,

Since none of these authors has had access to any more reliable documentation, much of the discussion about the former CPC secretary still lies in the realm of speculation. Nevertheless, many of these works cast important doubts on Milatović's and subsequent accounts.

There is currently no definitive proof that Hebrang's actions during this period can be explained by any treacherous relations with the Ustasha or Gestapo police. Rather, Hebrang's disagreements with other Communist leaders were based on substantive issues concerning the process of building new political institutions in Croatia and Yugoslavia. The charges that were made against Hebrang at the time of his removal as CPC secretary and repeated on subsequent occasions—that he was a nationalist and an anti-Serb chauvinist, and that he pursued a sectarian policy toward the CPP—grew out of these disagreements over state-building strategies. In order to understand the veracity of these charges, it is essential to examine them in this larger context.

Was Hebrang a Croat nationalist? Yes, in the sense that he put the concerns of the Partisan movement in Croatia above the Partisan movement in Yugoslavia as a whole. Hebrang sought to build a strong party and to secure his position as leader of it. He believed that the CPC should be given leeway in matters pertaining to Croatia and tried to forge his own policies on such matters as relations with the Croat Peasant Party. He was convinced that in order to attract more Croats to the movement, the CPC must appear to fulfill their national aspirations. Hence, he adopted a state-building strategy that stressed Croatian autonomy and Croatian political institutions. Despite his emphasis on Croatian political autonomy, however, Hebrang was not a separatist. Though he sought Croatian autonomy in the new Communist state, he did not seek an independent Croatian state. Indeed, he stressed on numerous occasions the importance of a united Yugoslavia for achieving Croat national goals, and the necessity of fighting for its survival. Nor did he question the necessity for a unified Yugoslav Communist party and the ultimate authority of the central party leadership, though he may

---

Belgrade, 1983); Milomir Marić, *Deca komunizma*, Berislav Žulj, "Točka na slučaj Hebrang," *Nedjelnja Dalmacija*, 10/6/85, 11; and Mile Milatović, "Činjenice i slučaj Hebrang," *NIN*, 4/4/82, "Zašto Hebrang ne počiva u miru," *NIN*, 8/4/85. For works challenging Milatović's account see Milenko Doder, *Kopinič bez enigme* (Zagreb, 1986); excerpts of this book may be found in *Slobodna Dalmacija*, 5/15/85 to 6/4/85. See also Doder interview in *Slobodna Dalmacija*, 4/30/85, 5/1-2/85, and *Start*, 6/29/85. See also Ivan Supek, *Crown Witness against Hebrang* (Chicago: Markanton Press, 1983); Zvonko Ivanković-Vonta, *Hebrang* (Zagreb, 1988), and Ivo Banac, *With Stalin against Tito, Cominformist Splits in Yugoslav Communism* (Ithaca, New York: Cornell University Press, 1988).

have understood its prerogatives differently from Tito and other Politburo members.

Hebrang's state-building strategy caused apprehension and dissatisfaction among Serb Partisans in Croatia, but it cannot be inferred that he was therefore anti-Serb. Responding to the concerns of Serbs in Croatia does not appear to have been Hebrang's first priority. Nevertheless, there is no evidence that he pursued explicitly anti-Serb policies. Indeed, he was quite vocal in his defense of Serb rights in Croatia and visible in his support of the two Serb members he brought into the CPC leadership— Dušan Brkić and Rade Žigić. During this period of state-building, it was natural that the question of Serbs' place in Croatia would be raised once again. The CPC's increasing emphasis on Croatian political autonomy undoubtedly sharpened this question, especially since Serbs in Croatia were likely to feel more secure in a unitary political system. In any case, it is unlikely that dissatisfaction and apprehension among Serb Partisans could have been avoided altogether while the Partisans were attempting to increase Croat support for the Partisan movement.

Finally, Hebrang has been accused of myriad mistakes in his approach to the Croat Peasant Party, from seeking to join it in a political coalition to pursuing a dangerously "sectarian" policy toward it. In his speech to the CPC Second Party Congress in 1948, Bakarić dwelt longest on Hebrang's mistakes in this realm and suggested in the same breath that Hebrang was both too harsh and too conciliatory toward the Peasant Party.[254] Relations with the CPP were a crucial part of state-building efforts in Croatia and Hebrang focused a great deal of attention on this problem. As we have seen, there were elements both of coalition-building and "sectarianism" in his policy. On the one hand, he attempted to create a coalition with the CPP Executive Committee, though one which the CPC would completely dominate. On the other hand, he launched virulent attacks against Maček and other "speculators" in Partisan ranks, even as he attempted to prevent indiscriminate hostility toward the Peasant Party. That other Communist leaders objected to various aspects of this policy is indisputable. The real source of disagreement between them, however, was Hebrang's unwillingness to act according to their views in determining policy toward the CPP. To Tito, who frequently felt that Hebrang's policy toward the CPP was jeopardizing the interests of the Partisan movement as a whole, Hebrang's reluctance to follow his instructions or to accept a larger framework for his actions in Croatia ultimately became cause enough to remove him from this crucial area of the country.

---

254. *Drugi kongres KPH*, 71-72.

5

Building a Party-State, 1945

In the fall of 1944, the CPY entered a new phase of state-building and a new phase in its approach to the Croat question. When Partisan troops liberated Belgrade in October, the CPY leadership gained a stable base from which to direct political and military activities in the entire country. No longer harassed and on the run, AVNOJ rapidly expanded its administrative and governmental apparatus. The process of centralizing Partisan institutions intensified. CPY leaders faced several tasks in their attempts to consolidate new state structures in Croatia. The first was to subordinate ZAVNOH, which was the most highly developed of the regional councils, to the central authority of AVNOJ. The second was to neutralize forces like the Croat Peasant Party and the Catholic Church, which might challenge the Communists' new state order or provide a political base for decentralizing power. Finally, Communists needed to work out the sensitive issues concerning the delineation of borders of the republics and the status of Serbs in Croatia that had been left until this point in the war.

With Hebrang removed, Tito had a more loyal instrument for achieving these goals in the new CPC secretary Vladimir Bakarić. Bakarić was the right man to be CPC secretary in the period of consolidation and centralization the CPY was now entering. Like Djilas and Ranković, he lacked the equal footing that Communist veterans Kardelj and Hebrang had with Tito. Consequently, he was less likely to pursue an independent course in Croatia. In the prewar period, Bakarić had shown himself much less susceptible to Zagreb "revisionist" tendencies, and as leader of the Communist youth group had adhered closely to Tito's line. During the last year and a half, Bakarić had spent most of his time with the central CPY leadership in Drvar and then Vis, where he had established a good working rapport with Tito. Indeed, his views more often paralleled

Tito's than Hebrang's, with whom he frequently clashed.[1] Though his ties to Croatia were strong, his first loyalty appears to have been to the central party leadership, not the CPC.

Bakarić also did not possess the personal traits that would allow him to become a charismatic leader in his own right in Croatia. In contrast to the powerful, if not always flattering, impression Hebrang made on his followers, Bakarić seemed a cautious and almost bland man. Nicknamed "the corpse" for his curiously impassive demeanor, he had a knack, conspicuously absent in several more flamboyant Partisan leaders, of never drawing attention to himself at the wrong time over the wrong issue. Already the consummate bureaucrat, he managed to avoid expressing objectionable opinions without appearing to be weak-willed. In marked contrast to Hebrang's polemical and often abrasive style of leadership, Bakarić was a conciliator and an adept manager. Though he never inspired the loyalty that Hebrang did, he soothed many grievances among CPC leaders that had ignited under Hebrang's leadership, and created an obedient party more suitable to the new phase of political consolidation.

The Second Tito-Šubašić Agreement

As the months elapsed after the conclusion of the first Tito-Šubašić Agreement in June 1944, pressure mounted on Tito to reach a second agreement for establishing a joint government composed of ministers from the government in exile and AVNOJ. After major German defeats in the European theatre, there was a sense of urgency in London that a political settlement was needed to delineate more clearly the shape of the provisional government and to set procedures for drafting a new constitution.[2] In spite of pressure from Šubašić and the British, however, Tito dragged his feet. He was unwilling to negotiate a second agreement until the Partisans had secured their military position in Serbia and eradicated Chetnik forces operating there. Unless they controlled Serbia, the Partisans could not claim to be the dominant political force countrywide

---

1. It was rumored that Hebrang had gotten Bakarić out of his way by sending him to the National Committee in the fall of 1943.

2. For a discussion of the activities of the government in exile during this period see Branko Petranović, *Jugoslavenska vlada u izbeglištvu* (Zagreb, 1981); and Dragovan Šepić, *Vlada Ivana Šubašića* (Zagreb, 1983).

and were therefore susceptible to British pressure to permit King Peter's return to the country.[3]

At the beginning of September, the military situation in Yugoslavia altered drastically in the Partisans' favor. Axis forces had suffered heavy military defeats in the Balkans in the summer of 1944 as first Romania, then Hungary, and finally Bulgaria fell to Soviet advances. Although German troops were still operating extensively in Serbia, using this area to pull back troops from elsewhere in the Balkans, Chetnik forces proved no match for the Partisans' superior strength. In mid-September, the National Liberation Army thrust deep into Serbia and completely dispersed Chetnik forces there. Joint Soviet-Partisan military activities began shortly thereafter, resulting in the liberation of Belgrade on October 20. In mid-November, the Red Army veered toward Budapest and the Partisans established a line dividing the Axis troops in the north from the Partisan-occupied area to the south. When winter arrived, both sides settled in for a long and bitter stalemate at the Srijem Front.[4]

As Partisan military successes against Axis and Chetnik forces increased in the fall of 1944, relations with the British deteriorated. Churchill's enthusiasm for Tito had soured after Tito secretly left his headquarters on the Adriatic island Vis in August 1944 and flew to Moscow to meet with Soviet leaders. It continued to wane over the next few weeks as the Partisans took an increasingly harsh stance toward the British presence in Yugoslavia. Shortly after a joint British-Partisan military exercise, "Operation Ratweek," at the beginning of September, Tito issued an order forbidding members of the British and American military missions accredited to the Supreme Staff to circulate beyond corps headquarters.[5] He was particularly anxious to discourage Allied activity along the Adriatic coast, and instructed Partisan commanders in Croatia

---

3. As early as the spring of 1944, Tito began to formulate his own strategy for the final liberation of the country. He decided to shift the focus of military operations to Serbia in order to destroy Chetnik forces there and to liberate Dalmatia in order to preclude any Allied operations on the Adriatic coast. See Fabjan Trgo, "Military Strategy and the Liberation of Yugoslavia, 1944-1945" in *War and Revolution in Yugoslavia 1941-1945*, Branko Prnjat, ed., (Belgrade, 1985), 245-284.

4. During the fall of 1944, Partisan troops also completely liberated Dalmatia. The Germans suffered tremendous losses with about 12,000 dead. The Partisans also broke up a main Chetnik group under Djujić, which fled to the northwest part of the country. See Trgo, "Military Strategy and the Liberation of Yugoslavia 1944-1945."

5. In Operation Ratweek, the British supplied the bombing and air cover and the Partisans launched an attack on German lines of communication from Belgrade to Zagreb.

to deny Allied troops access to the mainland without the express consent of the Supreme Staff.[6] At the end of October, Churchill approved the dispatch of several Allied divisions to Zadar, Split, and Dubrovnik, but Tito refused to open these ports.[7] The British were particularly annoyed when the Partisans refused to accept British personnel accompanying the heavy artillary sent in October and November. British intelligence was undoubtedly accurate in its speculation that Tito no longer needed to solicit Allied support now that he had the civil war "in the bag."[8] Unwilling to tolerate British interference in his actions against the Chetniks and other domestic political foes, Tito was no longer forced, as he had been a year earlier, to make political concessions for Allied aid. The British had chosen to back the Partisans over the last year; they would now pay the political price for it.[9]

With his position in Serbia secure, and his hand against the British strengthened, Tito was ready to begin negotiations with Šubašić on the terms of a second accord. After settling in October the terms of Soviet participation in the liberation of Belgrade, Tito invited Šubašić to return to Yugoslavia to work out the particulars of further cooperation. On November 1, 1944, after less than one week of talks, the British and

---

6. Trgo, "Military Strategy and the Liberation of Yugoslavia 1944-1945," 257.

7. At a meeting of the Mediterranean Command in Naples on October 21, General Wilson proposed that instead of a direct assault on Istria, Allied troops be used along the Dalmatian coast. Allied forces had become bogged down and an early advance upon Vienna through the Ljubljana Gap, as previously planned, was looking less likely. Washington objected to Wilson's proposal with the reasoning that it would be unable to accomplish anything until February 1945. Walter Roberts, *Tito, Mihailović and the Allies* (New Brunswick: Rutgers University Press, 1973), 284-286.

8. OSS report from Bari, 9/20/44, cited in *ibid.*, 261-262.

9. It is clear, in retrospect, that the Churchill-Stalin agreement which divided Yugoslavia into equal British and Soviet spheres of influence was an illusion, given Partisan military dominance of the country. At a meeting on October 9, 1944 at which this agreement was reached, Stalin and Churchill agreed they should work together to bring about a strong federation in Yugoslavia. If this proved impossible, then Serbia would be established as an independent country. Meanwhile, the Americans continued to resist all efforts to involve them politically in the Balkans. Although they withdrew their last observers from Mihailović's headquarters in early December, they refused to sanction the Tito-Šubašić Agreement in November. For more on Allied policy toward Yugoslavia at this stage of the war see Roberts, *Tito, Mihailović and the Allies*, 267-286; Šepić, *Vlada Ivana Šubašića*, 320-346; Ilija Jukić, *The Fall of Yugoslavia* (New York: Harcourt Brace Jovanovich, 1974).

Soviet mission chiefs were invited to witness the signing of a draft agreement, with final ratification pending King Peter's approval. According to the agreement, a unified government would be formed by members of AVNOJ and the Royal Government in London. Tito would be prime minister and Šubašić minister without portfolio. Of the six members included from the Royal Government, two were Partisan representatives and a third was pro-Partisan, thus ensuring the CPY's political dominance. Yugoslavia would theoretically remain a monarchy but the king would actually be represented in Yugoslavia by a council of three regents. Until the new government could hold elections for a constituent assembly, AVNOJ would continue to function as the supreme legislative body.[10]

With this agreement signed, the CPY prepared to establish a united government for Yugoslavia. By ensuring their predominant role in this body, the Communists were well positioned to complete their state-building efforts and their solution to the Croat question. There was considerable opposition to the Agreement, however, both from the king and from CPP leaders abroad. King Peter refused to sign this "unconstitutional agreement" and, in a meeting with Churchill at the end of December, insisted that he must be permitted to name the regents.[11] The king dismissed Šubašić several days later. After the British continued to back the former prime minister, however, the king agreed to the formation of a new government under Šubašić with wider representation. Shortly thereafter, Šubašić invited Tito to form a "temporary Parliament" by including former members of the Yugoslav Parliament in AVNOJ.[12] Though the king still refused to endorse the Tito-Šubašić Agreement, his field of maneuver was becoming increasingly narrow, and the formation of a united government was only a matter of time.

---

10. For the text of the Agreement see Petranović, *Jugoslavenska vlada u izbeglištvu*, #290, 400-401. See also Šepić, *Vlada Ivana Šubašića*, 324-330.

11. King Peter further outlined his objections to the agreement on December 29 and January 4. See Petranović, *Jugoslavenska vlada u izbeglištvu*, #300, 414-419.

12. *Ibid.*, #305, 423. This stipulation was insisted upon by the Big Powers at the Yalta conference at the beginning of February. The Soviets, who up until this time had taken a relatively reserved stance toward the National Committee, now began to push hard to implement the Tito-Šubašić Agreement. They attempted to have this question resolved quickly at Yalta by arguing that the two December amendments concerning elections and the regency should not be included; but they eventually agreed to a compromise whereby Tito would be asked to endorse these amendments in advance and to put them into effect once the principal agreement was in force. The Americans, as was usually the case when discussion about Yugoslavia arose, played a relatively minor role.

CPP leader Juraj Krnjević also adamantly opposed the second Tito-Šubašić Agreement, which he feared would completely negate CPP influence on the final determination of the Croat question. Having rarely supported the monarch in the past, Krnjević suddenly found himself in league with King Peter in a desperate attempt to block the Agreement. At the end of December, he protested to Churchill that the Partisans could not possibly be considered the main representative of the Croat people, as the Agreement appeared to suggest.[13] However, the Foreign Office dismissed this protest with the argument that Krnjević was in no better position to speak for Croats, since he had been out of the country for so long.[14] Thoroughly disgusted with Šubašić, especially after his failure to consult CPP leaders and the king before going to Moscow in mid-November, Krnjević placed his faith in August Košutić, whom he hoped would be able to negotiate more favorable terms of cooperation with the Partisans. When Šubašić left for Yugoslavia in October, Krnjević urged him to support Košutić's efforts to reach a settlement with Communist leaders in Croatia. But Šubašić proved as unwilling to support Košutić as he had Magovac before him.[15] As the Communists moved against Košutić in the next several weeks, Košutić found himself increasingly isolated and ineffective.

Košutić in Liberated Territory

When Košutić crossed into liberated territory at the beginning of September 1944, he was the last well known, pro-Maček leader in a position to defend Peasant Party objectives in Croatia. Communist leaders were therefore determined to muzzle him. As the Partisans' political and military position improved during the next several weeks, there were fewer reasons to speak softly to Košutić or behave circumspectly toward the CPP. Consequently, with Tito's blessing, Bakarić launched a campaign to isolate and intimidate Košutić (similar to the campaign against Magovac a year earlier), which ended in Košutić's total eclipse.

Despite his precarious position in liberated territory, Košutić was initially hopeful that he was making genuine progress in negotiating a

---

13. AIHRPH HSS box 2/37.

14. Šepić, *Vlada Ivana Šubašića*, 361.

15. *Ibid.*, 358. See also Fikreta Jelić-Butić, *Hrvatska seljačka stranka* (Zagreb, 1983), 254.

favorable political settlement with the Partisans.[16] In a series of communications with CPC leaders in October and November, Košutić outlined his views on cooperation with the Partisans and on the resolution of the Croat question in the postwar state.[17] Although he accepted the reality of Communist political and military strength, he continued to view the Peasant Party as the most powerful political force in Croatia. Like Maček and Krnjević, he was convinced that no resolution of the Croat question could be reached without the CPP. Indeed, he believed that precisely because the CPP was so firmly entrenched, it could afford to cooperate with the Partisans since, as he put it, "in order to swallow the Peasant Party, one would have to swallow the entire Croat people."[18] Although Košutić accepted that cooperation with the Communists was a tactical necessity, he left no doubt as to who would ultimately be senior partner in this arrangement.

In his communications with Communist leaders, Košutić attempted to defend the Peasant Party from accusations that by not actively resisting the occupying powers it had lost its right to lead the Croat national movement. Košutić knew that the CPP's reputation had been damaged at home and abroad by its failure to mount a resistance effort. He also feared that Communists would translate their leadership of the Partisan movement into postwar political legitimacy. Consequently, he attempted to paint the CPP's wartime role in a more favorable light. According to him, Peasant Party members had formed an "internal front" of passive resistance to the occupying forces that had contributed significantly to Axis defeats in Yugoslavia.[19] By emphasizing the Peasant Party's different but important role in the resistance movement, Košutić hoped to deprive the Partisans of exclusive claim to the moral high ground and to assert the CPP's right to equal partnership in determining the postwar political settlement.

Košutić presented a deliberately vague outline of the postwar state in order to stress the points of agreement between the CPP and the CPY. Nevertheless, the differences in their views could not be concealed.

---

16. Stephan Clissold, "Britain, Croatia and the Croat Peasant Party, 1939-1945," unpublished article, 1979, 22-24. At the beginning of September, Košutić sent a letter to Randolph Churchill saying that he "had achieved remarkable progress" in his negotiations with the Partisans.

17. AIHRPH HSS box 1/3, "Nacrt," 10/44; AIHRPH HSS box 1/9, "Košutić Answers Partisans' Questions," 10/14/44; AIHRPH HSS box 1/6, "Izjava," 11/15/44; AIHRPH HSS box 1/15, "Supplementary Statement," 11/15/44.

18. AIHRPH HSS box 1/13.

19. AIHRPH HSS box 1/13, AIHRPH HSS box 1/5.

Calling the CPY leadership "the Piedmont of the south," Košutić praised its role as state-builder and its federal political program.[20] The Communists, he wrote, had consistently fought against centralized state arrangements; for example, Stalin had rejected Serbian centralism and had encouraged the establishment of a separate Communist Party of Croatia.[21] Košutić also praised the Tito-Šubašić Agreement as providing the basis for the future state arrangement in Yugoslavia. It was not clear, however, how Košutić could reconcile this Agreement or the CPY's federal program with his own conception of the postwar Yugoslav state.

Košutić diverged considerably from the CPY view of the postwar state on two major points. First, he believed the Peasant Party should join the Partisans as coalition partner in Croatia. Elaborating on his ten points of cooperation presented the previous spring, he argued that ZAVNOH and members of the pre-1941 Parliament should form a joint constitutional body called the "Supreme Council of the Republic of Croatia." This body, with a majority of CPP representatives, would constitute the legitimate government of Croatia. The Home Guard would also merge with Partisan forces under a joint military command. It was not clear exactly what role the CPP Executive Committee would play in the Council. Though Košutić praised its members as "pioneers" who had furthered the Croat cause, many of their policies toward Maček, for example, were clearly unacceptable to him.[22]

Košutić also envisioned a significant role for the CPP at the federal level and argued that the 1939 *Sporazum* should provide the basis of the future federal system and the resolution of the Croat question. In conjunction with other political parties, Tito and Maček would work out the particulars of a new federal arrangement in which Croatia would be granted extensive autonomous powers, including an independent army and foreign policy.[23] Elections would be held shortly after the end of the war to ratify this Tito-Maček agreement. Although Košutić did not rule out the possibility of the king's return, he emphasized that the Peasant Party had long preferred the republican form of government. Predicting a CPP electoral landslide in Croatia, Košutić was confident the Peasant Party would easily retain its predominant political position in this part of the country.[24]

---

20. AIHRPH HSS box 1/13; AIHRPH HSS box 1/9; AIHRPH HSS box 1/3; AIHRPH HSS box 1/16.

21. AIHRPH HSS box 1/9.

22. AIHRPH HSS box 1/13; AIHRPH HSS box 1/9.

23. AIHRPH HSS box 1/15; AIHRPH HSS box 1/9.

24. AIHRPH HSS box 1/15.

Košutić's political "sketch," patently unrealistic given the Communists' powerful political position, was completely unacceptable to CPC leaders. Consequently, during the next several weeks they sought to discredit Košutić and his views. In a series of articles in *Naprijed* and *Slobodni dom* in November and December 1944, Bakarić rejected the idea that the CPP might serve as an equal partner in the postwar state. Though he endorsed "sincere and lasting" cooperation between the CPC and the Peasant Party, Bakarić argued that the CPP was not as united or powerful as it had been during the previous decade; therefore it would not continue to play as significant a political role.[25] While recognizing the Peasant Party's past accomplishments, Bakarić deplored its largely passive wartime role and derided the idea of an "internal front" of CPP resistance.[26] He accused Košutić of being interested only in the division of power after the war, not in the resistance movement. "How could we justify to the populace," he wrote, "cooperation with individuals who for the liberation of the people (at the very least) have done nothing and wish to do nothing but [focus on] questions regarding the division of power which are not essential today."[27] Bakarić insisted that the Communist Party had demonstrated during the war that it could lead the Croat people in their struggle for national emancipation and that it would continue to lead them in the years to come.

CPC leaders also attempted to discredit the idea that the 1939 *Sporazum* could provide the basis for resolving the Croat question in the postwar state. Numerous articles in the Partisan press praised Communist state-building achievements and faulted Peasant Party leaders for their own previously misguided efforts in this direction. The 1939 *Sporazum* was described as a "trick of the bourgeoisie" which had failed to give Croats the republic they desired. Due to their political immaturity, Croats had initially accepted this state but they were now mature enough to support the truly federal institutions established by ZAVNOH.[28] In an article at the beginning of January titled "Nothing Can Hinder Us on the Path toward Building a New Yugoslavia," Bakarić emphasized that only Communists had a viable solution to the Croat question which, in contrast to CPP policies in the interwar years, could effectively counter Great Serbian hegemony.[29] Whether the flawed

25. *Slobodni dom*, #19, 11/19/44, 1.

26. *Naprijed*, #80, 11/21/44, 1.

27. *Naprijed*, #77, 10/31/44, 1.

28. *Slobodni dom*, #6, 3/8/44, 2.

29. *Naprijed*, #86, 1/2/45, 2. See also *Naprijed*, #87, 1/9/45, 1; *Vjesnik*, #2, 1/8/45, 2.

Sporazum could have provided the foundation for any postwar political settlement is debatable. In any case, Košutić's demand that it provide the basis of discussion challenged the CPY on two cardinal points—the Communists' monopoly of political power and the CPY's efforts to centralize the new state structures—and party leaders were not prepared to consider it.

Košutić attempted to defend himself from the harsh criticism directed at him by CPC leaders, but he was hampered by increasing restrictions on his movements. At the beginning of October, he was placed under house arrest and his access to Peasant Party members was curtailed severely.[30] Complaining about his treatment to Bakarić, he pleaded for a personal meeting with the new CPC secretary to argue his case.[31] The conciliatory tone of his communications, strikingly similar to some of Magovac's letters to Hebrang the year before, gradually gave way to more bitter complaints in the face of Bakarić's persistent indifference. With no end to his confinement in sight, Košutić finally lodged a vehement protest concerning his treatment in Partisan custody.[32] Charging that the CPC had involved him in a "disloyal" discussion with a preconceived purpose, Košutić demanded that the restrictions on his political freedom be lifted and that he either be allowed to participate in the military as a regular engineer or be brought to trial.[33] Communist leaders had no intention of releasing him, however, and made sure he was effectively isolated before the Provisional Government was established in the spring.

In addition to confining Košutić, Bakarić also took steps to minimize the negative effect that Krnjević's opposition to the Tito-Šubašić agreement might have on public opinion in Croatia. In mid-January, he instructed party organizations to "unmask" Krnjević's efforts in London to bolster Maček's position.[34] This hardline policy was very similar to Hebrang's previous approach to the CPP. Bakarić began to warn of CPP speculators in Partisan ranks and demanded that Peasant Party members

---

30. For Randolph Churchill's description of Košutić's arrest see Clissold, "Britain, Croatia and the Croat Peasant Party, 1939-1945," 23.

31. AIHRPH HSS box 1/17, Košutić to Bakarić, 12/14/44; AIHRPH HSS box 1/19, Košutić to Bakarić, 12/19/44; AIHRPH HSS box 1/20, Košutić to Bakarić, 12/31/44.

32. AIHRPH KP-42-X/3941, Ivan Krajačić to Bakarić, 3/20/44.

33. *Ibid.*

34. AIHRPH KP-42-I/2980, CC CPC meeting, 1/20/45.

joining the Partisans confess their mistakes publicly.[35] He also instructed party organizations to make greater efforts to popularize the CPP Executive Committee and to stress the continuity between Communists' views and those of Stjepan Radić.[36]

The vituperative campaign against Krnjević in the Partisan press which followed described him as "a diplomatic representative of the reactionary circle around Maček and a man of strong pro-German views."[37] He was accused of supporting the king's attempts to reassert Serbian hegemony in the postwar Yugoslav state, a position which CPC leaders stressed was "against the politics and program of the CPP," and of falsely charging the Communists with attempting to dominate the Partisan movement.[38] In addition to their anti-Krnjević tone, these articles in the Partisan press also attempted to translate CPP republicanism into opposition to the king.[39] Combined with British pressure, they ultimately proved successful in forcing the acceptance of the Tito-Šubašić Agreement by Yugoslav leaders in London. By March 1945, the CPY leadership was ready to establish a provisional government largely of its own making.

The Provisional Government: Tito, Šubašić and the Future of Croatia

The founding of the Provisional Government on March 7, 1945 had crucial implications for the resolution of the Croat question in the postwar Yugoslav state. According to the agreement reached between Tito and Šubašić the previous November, the shape of the new state and relations among its national groups were to be decided by a constituent assembly at the end of the war. In fact, the composition of the Provisional Government affected the outcome of these questions in two important ways. First, the CPP's weak position in the government meant that it would play a negligible political role in the postwar state. Second, the CPY's predominance in the new government permitted AVNOJ to continue its centralizing efforts unhindered and to consolidate its political gains before a constituent assembly could be convened in the fall.

---

35. *Zbornik dokumenata NORa*, IX/7/331-335, cited in Jelić-Butić, *Hrvatska seljačka stranka*, 337; and *Slobodni dom* #22, 12/10/44, 1.

36. AIHRPH KP-42-I/2980)

37. For example, see *Naprijed*, #89, 1/23/45; *Naprijed*, #88, 1/16/45; *Naprijed*, #90, 1/30/45.

38. AIHRPH KP-42-I/2960, statement by Rudolf Bićanić, 1/15/45.

39. For example, see *Naprijed* #90, 1/30/45, 1.

The Provisional Government established on March 7 effectively sealed the fate of all non-Communist political groups in Yugoslavia. In accordance with the Tito-Šubašić Agreement, the Provisional Government was composed of twelve members of the National Committee and eight members of the Royal Government, four of whom were pro-Partisan.[40] Tito was designated prime minister and Šubašić foreign minister. Despite the king's persistent attempts to include CPP leader Juraj Šutej in the Regency, he was forced to agree to the appointment of pro-Partisan Ante Mandić. In any case, after endorsing the new government, the Regency retired from all meaningful participation in public affairs. The distribution of portfolios and the Provisional Government's full support for the Partisan program made it clear that there would be no "third way" in Yugoslavia for non-Communist reformers or a resurrection of the 1939 *Sporazum*.[41]

After the formation of the Provisional government, AVNOJ continued to act as the supreme legislative body in Yugoslavia. As its activities expanded rapidly in the spring of 1945, it attempted to subordinate the regional councils, especially ZAVNOH, to its authority.[42] AVNOJ ministries began to pass laws and regulations on matters that had previously been initiated by ZAVNOH. A uniform currency, tax rates and property laws were established, superseding the regulations previously effective in Croatia.[43] The central authorities used stringent laws on economic sabotage and property confiscation to control the activities of economic enterprises, including both the increasing number of state owned firms and those in private hands.[44] They even began to direct the harvesting and planting of crops. AVNOJ also introduced laws allowing it to move resources among republics, for example, sending medical personnel from

---

40. Non-Communist members of the government were Milan Grol (Democrat), Sava Kosanović (Independent Democrat), Jaša Prodanović (Republican), Frane Frol (CPP Executive Committee), Ante Vrkljan (CPP Executive Committee), Šubašić (CPP), Šutej (CPP), and Kocbek (Slovene Christian Socialists).

41. For the text of the statement released by the Provisional Government several days after its formation see Branko Petranović, *Političke i pravne prilike za vreme privremene vlade DFJ* (Belgrade, 1963), 88-89.

42. Four organs were responsible for governing at this time: AVNOJ, the AVNOJ Presidency, the Regency, and the Provisional Government. Of the four, the first two were the most powerful.

43. *Zakonodavni rad Pretsedništva Antifašističkog veća narodnog oslobodjenja Jugoslavije i Pretsedništva Privremene narodne skupštine DFJ (19 novembra 1944-27 oktobra 1945)* (Belgrade, 1951), 106, 190-195, 458-478.

44. *Ibid.*, 150-159, 330-340.

Croatia to other republics where their services were needed.[45] The Ministry of Construction meted out stiff punishments to anyone hindering its efforts to send individuals to other parts of the country "for physical and intellectual work."[46]

As AVNOJ expanded its functions, it clashed frequently with ZAVNOH ministries concerning the distribution of authority between them.[47] AVNOJ ministries were particularly intolerant of local displays of resistance to central economic planning.[48] Ironically, Hebrang, who had done so much to augment the power of ZAVNOH, showed himself in a different light as minister of industry. He remained sensitive to Croat national sentiment and resisted measures he believed would arouse hostility toward AVNOJ in Croatia. For example, he vehemently opposed proposals which offered Croats a poor rate of exchange for the Kuna, the currency used in Croatia during the war.[49] Nevertheless, he consistently argued in favor of strong central intervention in the economic affairs of local enterprises. As minister of industry, his first act was to establish a central accounting department which would "allow for central control over all state and economic enterprises."[50] Convinced that the state must position itself on "the commanding heights of the economy," he opposed granting greater decision-making authority to workers because it would interfere with the plan.[51] Nor did he favor delegating this authority to ZAVNOH; rather, he ardently supported rapid centralization of the economy and reliance on central planning at the ministry level.

How can one account for this apparent change in Hebrang's state-building strategy? His previous efforts to carve out the maximum sphere of autonomy for ZAVNOH were replaced several months later by equally strenuous efforts to intervene in that sphere. To a certain extent, this shift in strategies reflects the maxim that where you sit in the bureaucracy is where you stand. Hebrang's motives appear consistently tied to strengthening his own political and bureaucratic turf, whether his job was at the regional or federal level. As CPC secretary and effective head of ZAVNOH, Hebrang fought to augment ZAVNOH's authority; as

---

45. *Ibid.*, 145-153.

46. *Ibid.*, 278.

47. Petranović, *Političke i pravne prilike za vreme Privremene vlade DFJ*, 94-95.

48. *Ibid.*, 95.

49. *Zakonodavni rad pretsedništva AVNOJ-a*, 106.

50. *Ibid.*, 37.

51. *Ibid.*, 458-478. See also *Narodna skupština FNRJ, Ustavotvorni odbori savezne skupštine i skupština naroda* (Belgrade), 169-177.

minister of industry, he sought to increase his ministry's effectiveness and control over the planning process. His personal assertiveness undoubtedly enhanced this tendency since he was a man who sought to maximize his control over all areas within his purview. Tito apparently calculated correctly when he assumed that removing Hebrang from Croatia would reduce his "nationalist proclivities." Though Hebrang's sensitivity to Croat national sentiments did not disappear, his perspective and priorities changed with his new vantage point in the state structure.

In fact, something similar to Hebrang's change of perspective can be observed in many of Yugoslavia's postwar Communist leaders. When decentralized conditions prevailed, regional Communist leaders tried to maximize their authority; they also became more susceptible to local political pressures. Hence republic party organizations in Yugoslavia after the reforms of the late sixties and early seventies operated largely independently of one another and often at cross purposes. When power resided with central political institutions, as it did in Yugoslavia at the end of the war and in the years immediately following it, Communist leaders sought to increase the power of these institutions; at these times a post in the central party or state apparatus in Belgrade was most coveted. Thus depending on the conditions in which they operated, the same leaders often endorsed two different state-building strategies, both within a nominally federal framework; the first led toward the kind of federalized state Hebrang pursued as CPC secretary, the second toward the centralization achieved by Tito at the end of the war.

Shortly after the Provisional Government was established in March 1945, it released guidelines for forming governments in the federal units. These instructions, which the CPC followed in establishing the Croatian government in April, were put forward as "suggestions," since it was felt that regulating this matter by law "would not be in the spirit of federalism."[52] Nevertheless, the very fact that AVNOJ instructed the antifascist councils to form republic governments only after the Provisional Government was formed signified an important change from the previous fall, when Hebrang was ready to establish a Croatian government without the initiative and guidelines of the central government. ZAVNOH was instructed to form a government that would execute all business not specifically assigned to the federal government.[53] In spite of

---

52. *Zakonodavni rad pretsedništva AVNOJ-a*, 73.
53. *Ibid.*, 70-74. See also Slobodan Nešović and Branko Petranović, *AVNOJ i revolucija* (Belgrade, 1983), 707.

this federal formula, however, important matters were regulated increasingly by the central authorities.

The CPC faced three important issues concerning the formation of the Croatian government which would bear importantly on its resolution of the Croat question. First, it had to determine the role of the CPP in the new government. Would prewar CPP leaders or the CPP Executive Committee have independent decision-making authority? How much independence the Peasant Party retained would determine the extent to which Communist leaders were pressured by Croat national concerns. Second, the CPC had to delineate Croatia's borders and the character of its relations with other republics. Jurisdictional battles over areas like Bosnia and Vojvodina had hindered a federal solution to the Croat question in the interwar years and posed a potential threat to the reconstituted Yugoslav state. Finally, CPC leaders had to define Serbs' place in the Croatian republic, a question that had also caused serious friction in the interwar years. Would Serbs be granted any kind of autonomous status within the Croatian republic and, if so, how would this status be determined?

The most immediate question concerning the CPP's future political role related to the composition of the Croatian government. With Košutić effectively neutralized, there were no important pro-Maček leaders available to participate in the new government. Consequently, its CPP members were drawn exclusively from the Executive Committee. This appeared to make the Communists' task much easier since it held a tight grip over "its" peasant organization. Despite its loyalty to the Communist Party, however, the Executive Committee displayed some unexpected resistance to its subordinate role in the new government.

At a CPC Politburo meeting on March 28, 1944, Bakarić suggested that he be named president, Rade Pribićević first vice-president, and Franjo Gaži, second vice-president of the Croatian government.[54] However, CPP leader Gaži, a ZAVNOH member and Partisan supporter, had become increasingly aggravated by the CPC's "derogation of the Executive Committee" in recent weeks, and he was unhappy with his designation as second vice-president.[55] Convinced that the Peasant Party must play a more visible role in the Croatian government, he proposed that a CPP Executive Committee member be appointed president. Bakarić rejected this suggestion with the argument that choosing a CPP member for president might look like the CPC was attempting to camouflage itself or that the CPP Executive Committee was simply a "mari-

---

54. AIHRPH KP-42-II/3196.
55. AIHRPH-42-II/3244. See also Jelić-Butić, *Hrvatska seljačka stranka*, 288.

onette" in Communist hands.[56] CPC leader Marko Belinić echoed this
sentiment and pointed out that "political developments in Croatia did
not require that some sort of compromise be reached between the CPC
and the CPP."[57] Nevertheless, Gaži's position was upgraded from second
vice-president to first vice-president and an effort was made to reconcile
the Executive Committee to the new arrangements.[58] Placated for the
time being, Committee members threw their efforts behind popularizing
the Provisional Government and the new government of Croatia.[59]

The Borders of Croatia

Another problem the CPC faced in forming the new Croatian government concerned the borders of the republic this body would govern.[60]
With the establishment of the Antifascist Council of Bosnia-Hercegovina
in the fall of 1943, many divisive questions about the size and character
of the new Croatian republic had been settled. Although Hebrang had
expressed his desire to see at least portions of this territory included in
Croatia, he had ceased pressing this point when the CPY leadership had
declared its support for forming the new republic of Bosnia-
Hercegovina.[61] The Peasant Party's vision of a Croatian political unit
which included at least portions of Bosnia and Hercegovina was
effectively ruled out. Nevertheless, several thorny problems with
Croatia's borders remained, especially concerning the disposition of the
largely Croat inhabited areas of Vojvodina. Communist leaders were

56. Cited in Jelić-Butić, *Hrvatska seljačka stranka*, 288.

57. *Ibid.*, 288.

58. For the composition of the new Croatian government see *Naprijed*, #102, 4/18/45.

59. Members of the Executive Committee enthusiastically praised the Provisional Government and repeatedly described the new political institutions as
reflecting the federalist ideals of Stjepan Radić. See *Slobodni dom*, #8, 3/22/45, 1-
2; *Slobodni dom* #5, 3/1/45, 1-2.

60. For a thorough discussion of this question see Banac, *With Stalin against
Tito*, 103-110.

61. Borders between the republics of Croatia and Bosnia-Hercegovina continued to be adjusted during and after the war. For example, Croats gave up the
country of Livno in southwestern Bosnia (71% Croat) whose Communist leadership had operated under the jurisdiction of the CPC. Bosnia-Hercegovina gave
up the county of Dvor (88% Serb), which had been under the command of the
Hercegovinian operational staff. See *ibid.*, 106.

anxious to delay these difficult questions as long as possible, but by the spring of 1945 they could no longer be ignored.

Jurisdiction over areas of Vojvodina heavily populated by Croats had posed difficult problems for settling the Croat question in the interwar years, and it continued to vex CPY leaders during the war. This area between the Danube and Sava rivers, in which Serbs, Croats and Hungarians lived side by side, resembled Bosnia-Hercegovina in many ways. Although possessing a distinct historical identity, large parts of it were also claimed by both Serbia and Croatia. Before the war, the CPY recognized the unique character of this region and supported its autonomous status within a federal state. As with Bosnia-Hercegovina, however, the particulars of this autonomy remained undefined. Consequently, when war broke out tensions arose among Partisan leaders from Vojvodina, Croatia and Serbia as they all sought to establish control over this area.

Relations between the Provincial Committee for Vojvodina and the CC CPC were strained from the beginning of the war over Srijem (Srem). Although the majority of this region's inhabitants was Serb, it had historically been a part of Slavonia. Most Croat leaders considered this area a rightful part of Croatia.[62] The Independent State of Croatia established jurisdiction over it in 1941.[63] When the Regional Committee for Vojvodina was decimated by arrests in the early months of the war, the CPC instructed Slavonian Communists to organize resistance activities in Srijem.[64] After the Regional Committee for Vojvodina was reestablished in mid-1942, it also began to operate in Srijem. Before long, Vojvodina Communists became frustrated by their encounters with Slavonian party officials, and they complained to CPY leaders that the CPC was encroaching on their sphere of authority.[65] Unwilling to antagonize Croat Communists over this issue, CPY leaders instructed the Regional

---

62. The five Srijem counties of Ilok, Šid, Vinkovci, Vukovar and Županja (Serb population 31%) had been part of the Croatian Banovina in 1939; the remaining counties of Irig, Ruma, Sr. Mitrovica, Stara Pazova and Zemun, and the city of Zemun (Serb population 64%) remained outside the Banovina. See *ibid.*

63. At the beginning of the war, Vojvodina was divided between Germany (Banat), Hungary (Bačka and Baranja) and the Independent State of Croatia (Srijem).

64. For a general discussion of the Partisan movement in this area see Jelena Popov, "Politika KPJ u Vojvodini na stvaranje masovne osnove narodnooslobod-ilačkog rata i revolucije," *Zbornik za istoriju* 16 (1977): 7-26.

65. Ranko Končar, "Problem autonomije Vojvodine u kontekstu odluka drugog zasedanje AVNOJ-a," in Nikola Babić, (ed.), *AVNOJ i narodnooslobodilačka borba u Bosni i Hercegovini (1942-1943)* (Belgrade, 1974), 623.

Committee to coordinate the work of the Srijem party organization with the CPC Commissariat for Slavonia and the Regional Commissariat for Banat (which to make matters more complicated was to maintain contact with Belgrade).[66] Problems between Vojvodina and Slavonian Partisans continued to fester.

At the beginning of 1943, the Regional Committee for Vojvodina stepped up its effort to wrest control of this area from the CC CPC. At the end of January, it informed the Commissariat for Slavonia that since Vojvodina had been accorded a status similar to that of Bosnia-Hercegovina, Slavonian party leaders must coordinate their activities with the Regional Committee for Vojvodina, not the other way around.[67] The CPC completely disregarded these admonitions, however, and instead changed the name of the Commissariat for Slavonia to the Commissariat for Slavonia and Srijem. By now thoroughly exasperated, the Regional Committee for Vojvodina protested about this action to the CC CPY and asked it to clarify the status of Srijem.[68]

CPY leaders were still reluctant to tackle this complicated issue head-on. While determining that this area was formally under the jurisdiction of the Slavonian party organization, the CC CPY informed the Regional Committee for Vojvodina that the eastern portion of Srijem (the line was drawn through Vukovar, Vinkovci, and Županja) would be placed under the jurisdiction of the Regional Committee for Vojvodina.[69] At the same time, it insisted that larger discussion of Srijem's status await the end of the war. Until then, Vojvodina leaders were to refrain from pressing this issue since it might "drive Croat elements away from the national liberation movement."[70] Although squabbles over this matter continued, it was not taken up officially again until the spring of 1945.[71]

---

66. *Ibid.*, 624.

67. *Ibid.*, 625. The Serbian Regional Committee apparently also was uncertain about the status of Srijem at this time since it referred to the Committee for Vojvodina as both cooperating with and falling under the jurisdiction of the CC CPC.

68. *Ibid.*, 626.

69. Tito, *Sabrana djela*, vol. 16, 15.

70. Končar, "Problem autonomije Vojvodine u kontekstu odluka drugog zasedanja AVNOJ-a," 627.

71. Although AVNOJ did not treat the question of Vojvodina separately in its documents, Secretary of the Vojvodina Regional Committee Jovan Veselinov-Žarko in his memoirs *Svi smo mi jedna partija* (Novi Sad, 1971) asserts that Vojvodina was discussed at the second session of AVNOJ and that in the absence of any representatives from Vojvodina it was decided that an autonomous Vojvodina should be part of Serbia after the war.

On April 6, 1945, four days before the new government of Croatia was proclaimed, the Regional Committee for Vojvodina announced that Vojvodina would be included in the republic of Serbia.[72] The Antifascist Council of Serbia approved this announcement shortly thereafter, pending approval by the national liberation committees the following month.[73] Local elections in July "officially ratified" the decision to include Vojvodina in Serbia and in August the decision was approved by AVNOJ.[74] Confusion over Vojvodina's borders remained, however, and CPY leaders decided to form a commission headed by Milovan Djilas to determine the exact delineation of borders in the disputed areas.[75] Although the commission deliberated quietly in order to minimize conflict, the potential for bitter feelings among the populace and among Communist leaders continued to make the determination of Vojvodina's borders a sensitive subject.[76] Ultimately this issue was settled by the innermost circle of CPY leaders, with little party or public discussion and debate.

With the announcement that Vojvodina would be included as an autonomous federal unit within Serbia, CPY leaders took a major step toward resolving one of the most difficult aspects of the Croat question in the interwar years.[77] Tito had vowed repeatedly in previous months

---

72. Nešović and Petranović, *AVNOJ i revolucija*, 717-734.

73. Questions remained about whether the large numbers of Croats in northwest Bačka and Subotica, in which Croats were a majority, should be included in Serbia or Croatia. The county of Vukovar was a part of Croatia geographically and economically, though the majority of its citizens were Serbs, while that part of Vukovar which had fallen to Vojvodina, with the justification that it had been organized and liberated by the National Liberation Army from Srijem and Vojvodina, was inhabited largely by Croats.

74. Elections to the national liberation commiteees proved difficult to organize, however, and the Main National Liberation Committee of Vojvodina sought to have them delayed because of confusion over Vojvodina's borders.

75. The decision to establish a border commission was prompted by instructions from the Soviets to the CPY in March to form a commission for deciding upon internal borders and borders with other countries (AIHRPH KP-42-II/3196, CC CPC meeting 3/28/45).

76. For a description of the commission proceedings by one CPP member see Jerko Zlatarić, "Kako se krojila hrvatska istočna granica," *Nova Hrvatska*, 15: 6 (June 1973): 10-13.

77. Another less serious border question concerned the disposition of Boka Kotorska in the southern region of the Adriatic coast. This area had historically been part of Dalmatia, but since it was inhabited largely by Montenegrins the decision was made to include it in the republic of Montenegro.

that the citizens of Vojvodina themselves would decide whether to affili-
ate with Serbia or Croatia after the war. But by the spring of 1945, party
leaders were in a position to resolve this question by *fiat*, though they
took pains to handle this matter as circumspectly as possible. Not only
could they impose their solution upon the populace, since the Croat
Peasant Party was too disorganized to resist such measures, they were
also able to enforce it upon previously recalcitrant regional party leaders.
Although CPC and Regional Committee leaders had hitherto resisted
CPY efforts to diminish their authority over this area, they appear to
have accepted the decision of April 6 without serious opposition.[78] Given
the degree of centralization that was being imposed at this point in the
war, the delineation of borders did not matter as much as it did when
ZAVNOH possessed some real measure of autonomy. But disputes
about the disposition of various areas of Vojvodina, and resentment over
the seemingly arbitrary nature of their assignment to Croatia or Serbia,
would resurface whenever Croat leaders attempted to assert a greater
degree of autonomy.

In 1945, Communists in Croatia were concerned, however, about how
establishing Vojvodina as an autonomous unit within Serbia would
affect their popular standing. Including parts of Bosnia, Hercegovina and
Vojvodina in a Croatian political unit had been an essential part of the
CPP (and Ustasha) program in the interwar years and was still widely
supported by the Croat population. The sectarian violence accompanying
the inclusion of Bosnia-Hercegovina in the Independent State of Croatia
had at least partially discredited the idea of a Great Croatian state. But
relinquishing Croatia's claims to large portions of territory was not likely
to enhance the CPC's popularity or to bolster its claims to being the only
political force capable of achieving Croat national aims.

Consequently, CPC leaders took pains to emphasize that the Partisans
had regained control over the Italian annexed territories of Dalmatia and
Istria. They highlighted the fact that the new Croatian government had
first convened in April 1945 in the Dalmatian city of Split. As Bakarić
wrote in an article in *Naprijed* in the spring 1945: "Dalmatia is proof today
to every Croat that the Croat people in this war has achieved its right to

---

78. There was further squabbling over this area, especially within the border
commission, but until the commission documents are released, it is impossible to
know how seriously decisions concerning the disposition of Vojvodina territory
were resisted by regional party leaders. Milovan Djilas asserts that Hebrang argued vigorously for the borders of Croatia to incorporate much of this region, by
extending south to Zemun.

independence and national freedom."[79] Members of the CPP Executive Committee similarly expressed their joy at "the return to us [of] those areas that were taken from us."[80] Though it may not have compensated entirely in the minds of the populace for the loss of territory in Bosnia and Vojvodina, the liberation of Dalmatia in the fall of 1944, and later of Istria, was essential to bolstering the Communist Party's popularity in Croatia.[81]

Nevertheless, not all Communists in Dalmatia were happy about its inclusion in the new Croatian republic. Tensions which had existed throughout the war persisted between the central CPC leadership and Communists in Croatia as some Communists in Dalmatia continued to press for more autonomy for Dalmatia. Bakarić and other CPC leaders continued to resist fiercely any idea of Dalmatian autonomy as an unacceptable step toward the federalization of the new Croatian republic. While Tito and CPY leadership had chastised Hebrang for his efforts to curb "autonomists" in Dalmatia, they were not sympathetic to the idea of a formally autonomous status for Dalmatia, and discussion of this matter was eventually dropped.

Serbs in Croatia

The final problem CPC leaders faced in forming the new Croatian government was defining the status of Serbs in Croatia. As was discussed in the last chapter, CPY leaders had become increasingly concerned that CPC emphasis on Croatian political autonomy was diminishing Partisan popularity among Serbs in Croatia. Even after Hebrang's dismissal, they continued to worry that Serbs' apprehension about their political future in Croatia would translate into support for King Peter. Consequently, they attempted to reassure Serbs in Croatia by stressing the more unitary features of the new state and the strong ties Serbs would have with their brethren in the republic of Serbia. They also instructed CPC leaders to form new political and cultural organizations to champion the equal status of Serbs in Croatia.

---

79. *Naprijed*, #86, 1/2/45.

80. *Slobodni dom*, 3/22/45.

81. Many Istrians did not, however, perceive their incorporation into Croatia as an entirely positive event. There have traditionally been strong forces for autonomy in Istria, which were evident during the Partisan struggle. These forces resurfaced after the election of a non-Communist government in 1990.

The existence of large numbers of Serbs in Croatia had always posed a difficult problem for the Croat national movement. What kind of status and protection to grant Serbs had been hotly contested in the interwar years, and both the Croat Peasant Party and the Independent Democratic Party had changed their position on these matters several times. The fact that Ustashas had massacred a large number of Serbs in attempting to "solve" this problem had made it an even more sensitive issue. With the founding of the Croatian government, questions naturally arose about the kind of guarantees Serbs would be given in the new state. Would Croatia be considered a Serb and Croat homeland or only a Croat home- land? If the latter, what kind of minority rights would Serbs have in Croatia? What would be their relationship with Serbs in Serbia? The answers to these questions would have a crucial effect on the CPY's reso- lution of the Croat question.

Bakarić addressed CPC policy toward Serbs shortly after becoming the new party secretary in October 1944. In addition to greatly diminish- ing CPC emphasis on Croatian autonomy, he frequently mentioned Serbs' special needs and interests. At CC CPC meetings throughout the fall and winter, he repeatedly exhorted party organizations to pay more visible attention to Serb concerns and referred them to various articles by Kardelj, Djilas and especially CPY Central Committee member Moša Pijade on this subject. After bitter complaints from Dušan Brkić that Slavonian Communists were neglecting Serbs' needs, Bakarić removed Slavonian party leader Dušan Čalić and reorganized the party committee there.[82]

The CPC also responded to complaints by Serbs that not enough had been done to promote their cultural life in Croatia. In November 1944, it founded a new Serb cultural organization, Prosvjeta (whose mouthpiece would be the journal of the same name), to further the development of Serb education and culture. At the founding meeting of Prosvjeta, CPC leader Dušan Brkić emphasized that brotherhood between Serbs and Croats in Croatia was the cornerstone of the new federal system. He pledged that the CPC would address the issue of Serbs' education, which had been seriously neglected since the nineteenth century in Croatia.[83] Prosvjeta would receive funds from the Croatian government to publish books in Cyrillic about the history of Serbia and to publicize Serb cus-

---

82. AIHRPH KP-40/2669; AIHRPH KP-42-I/2955.

83. *Naprijed*, #80, 11/18/44. At the founding meeting of Prosvjeta, an adminis- trative board was chosen with Dane Medaković as president, and Petar Drapšin as vice-president. Also included among its members were Dušan Brkić and Rade Žigić.

toms and heroes.[84] In a speech in Kordun shortly thereafter, Bakarić also lamented the lack of instruction of Serbian history and "the glorious Serb traditions" in Croatia and promised that henceforth Serbs would be given the means to foster their national culture. [85]

In addition to founding Prosvjeta, the CPC also called for the establishment of a new Serb political organization, or Main Committee. Kardelj had urged Tito in September 1944 to form a larger political organization for Serbs in Croatia, and he appears to have been a driving force behind this effort in the next several months. The need for a new political organization of Serbs in Croatia was first mentioned publicly at the beginning of November by the head of the Serb Club Rade Pribićević. Pribićević argued that the Serb Club had been very successful in helping to "destroy the remnants of Great Serbian tendencies" but that as an organization of ZAVNOH delegates it was too narrowly conceived to answer all the needs of Serbs in Croatia.[86] Consequently, it was necessary to establish "a wide political organization of Serbs," which "together with Croats would solve the major political questions in Croatia."[87]

The first step toward founding this organization was taken at a meeting of Serbs in the coastal town of Šibenik at the end of February 1945. Concerned about King Peter's hostility toward the second Tito-Šubašić agreement, the CPC called this gathering to generate support for the Partisan regime. After general discussion about federalism and denunciations of the king, a decision was made to establish an organizational committee which would begin preparations for founding a "Main Committee of Serbs in Croatia."[88] This Main Committee was to be a "unified organization of all Serbs in Croatia" which would articulate Serb interests and concerns. According to Prosvjeta President Dane Medaković, it would not be a political party in the strict sense of the word but it would carry initiatives from "the most remote Serbian village" to the highest ZAVNOH officials.[89] It was also decided that a Congress of Serbs from all parts of Croatia would be held in May to

---

84. *Srpska riječ*, #28 11/28/44.

85. *Srpska riječ* #31, 12/15/44.

86. *Ibid.* Interestingly, he lauded Hebrang's role in establishing and supporting the Serb Club.

87. *Srpska riječ*, #25, 11/1/44.

88. *Srpska riječ*, #40, 3/4/45, 1. The Organizational Committee was composed of Rade Pribicévić, Dušan Brkić, Rade Žigić, Pavle Jakšić, Mile Počuca, Dušan Čalić, Dane Medaković, Stanko Opačić-Ćanica and several others.

89. *Srpska riječ*, 2/25/45.

establish the Main Committee and to discuss the character of federalism as it related to Serbs in Croatia.[90]

The Main Committee was intended to publicize Communist concern for the welfare of Serbs in Croatia. However, the character of the committee and the nature of its ties to Serbs in Serbia were not entirely clear. As with the CPP Executive Committee, Communist leaders were anxious to use the Main Committee to convince the Allies and the populace that a one party system was not being established in Yugoslavia. They had no intention of permitting the Main Committee to function as a political party, however, or to play an independent political role. Nevertheless, though they were agreed on this point, there was less agreement about how the Committee would operate and about its relations with similar organizations in Serbia.

Pribićević conceived of the Main Committee primarily in political terms as an organization that would defend the interests of Serbs in Croatia. According to him, the Main Committee would "concern itself with Serb matters and ensure the equal participation of the Serb people [in Croatia] in the execution of state and social affairs."[91] As the most powerful leader of the Serb Club, Pribićević may also have seen the Main Committee as an opportunity to expand his own influence within the Partisan movement. Medaković similarly viewed the Main Committee as a "political instrument" for defending Serb interests and advocated a wide interpretation of its powers.[92]

This highly political conception of the Main Committee made some CPC leaders uneasy. They feared it would provoke "Serbing it up" tendencies and send the wrong message to Serbs already disenchanted with Partisan policies. Moreover, they may have worried that creating a political instrument for defending Serb rights would raise concern among Croats for whom Croatian sovereignty over this territory was essential. These leaders believed the Committee should serve a primarily cultural function and concentrate on disseminating the Partisan message in the villages.[93] In an article in *Naprijed* in mid-April, CPC member Ivo Sarajčić argued that the Committee could best serve its purpose by preventing

---

90. AIHRPH KP-42-XI/3942. According to these instructions, 700 delegates would attend the Congress which would pick a Main Committee of about 300 members and an Executive Committee of 50 members.

91. *Naprijed*, #103, 4/25/45, 2.

92. *Srpska riječ*, #44, 4/1/45, 1.

93. *Ibid.*

harmful party bickering and working for the national and cultural education of Serbs in Croatia.[94]

Even this minimalist definition of the Main Committee as a primarily cultural organization did not resolve uncertainties about its ties to Serbs in Serbia. The question of where Serbs in Croatia would place their primary loyalty was of utmost importance for resolving the question of Croatia's status within the Yugoslav federation after the war. Toward the end of the war, Moša Pijade and other Serb Communists began to advocate the establishment of an autonomous region of Serbs in Croatia.[95] This proposal met with fierce opposition from Croat Communists, and realizing that it would be extremely unpopular among Croats in general, Tito rejected the idea. Nevertheless, Pijade and other CPY leaders continued to advocate strong ties between Serbs in Croatia and Serbia. In an article in *Politika* in the fall of 1944, Pijade appeared to endorse some kind of cultural autonomy for Serbs in Croatia and the establishment of formal organizational ties with Serbia. "The Serb and Croat nations," he wrote, "have and will have in federal Yugoslavia all possibilities and all the means necessary to organize their national life as complete national entities. The borders of the federal units will not be and cannot be any kind of obstacle to this."[96] The implication for Serbs in Croatia of this more centralized notion of the state was obvious: if republics were not to be accorded real autonomy, then the establishment of the new republic of Croatia was not to be greatly feared.

Medaković elaborated this theme in an article about the Main Committee in *Srpska riječ* at the beginning of April. According to Medaković, Serbs would have strong cultural ties to Belgrade, though their political loyalty would be to Zagreb. He wrote: "Our first cultural center, as our political [center] will be Zagreb, where the government and Sabor and all the other lower institutions of Croatia will be located, as well as the Serb Club, the Main Committee of Serbs, the center of the Serb Cultural Society and others. But the wider cultural center for all Serbs in federal Yugoslavia will be Belgrade, as for all Croats, Zagreb will be the center in this regard."[97] This solution, like Pijade's, also failed

---

94. *Ibid.*

95. Moša Pijade apparently first proposed the establishment of a Serb autonomous province in Croatia in late 1942. According to Dedijer, Pijade drew up a map of the borders of such an autonomous region. When he went off to present this idea to Tito, however, "he returned faster than he went." *Novi prilozi za biografiju Josipa Broza Tita,* vol. 2, 903, cited in Banac, *With Stalin against Tito,* 106.

96. Moša Pijade, *Izabrani govori i članci, 1941-1947* (Belgrade, 1948), 270.

97. *Srpska riječ,* 44, 4/1/45, 1.

to resolve decisively the question of Serbs' status. While ruling out any specific arrangements for granting Serbs cultural autonomy in Croatia, Medaković appeared to designate both Zagreb and Belgrade as the main cultural center for Serbs in Croatia. Just how Belgrade would serve as the "wider" cultural center for all Serbs in Yugoslavia was not clearly defined.

In contrast to Medaković's emphasis on Serbs' national concerns, Ivo Sarajčić conceived of a special role for Serbs in Croatia in fostering a supra-national Yugoslav consciousness. Sarajčić argued that the problems posed by the large number of Serbs in Croatia could be resolved not by strengthening their ties with Serbia but by diminishing their national consciousness and, ultimately, the consciousness of all national groups in Yugoslavia. These various national sentiments would be replaced by a Yugoslav patriotism that would diminish sectarian differences among Serbs and Croats. Sarajčić wrote:

> The purpose of the Main Committee is to form and strengthen a new Yugoslav patriotism, which has arisen in the struggle of the people for complete freedom and which is founded on love toward a common fatherland, freedom, and the equality of individuals...As far as the new Yugoslav patriotism is concerned, whose carrier is the Serb people in Croatia and which the Main Committee will place among its tasks, it is sufficient to emphasize the well known fact that Serbs in Croatia (along with Serbs in Bosnia-Hercegovina) were the carriers of brotherhood and unity to all nations of Yugoslavia. Today it is not necessary to add that Serbs in Croatia through their Main Committee will disseminate the new Yugoslav patriotism. That fought-for patriotism, which arose during the struggle against Great Serbian and Great Croatian chauvinism, will prevent the return of the old understanding of the "Yugoslav integral indivisible nation'"which hindered the drawing closer together of the nations of Yugoslavia, and instead will develop love toward the new fraternal Yugoslav community of equal nations.[98]

This description of Yugoslav patriotism foreshadows the CPY's vigorous promotion of this concept in the early 1950s. What makes it significant is the special, almost messianic role assigned to Serbs in Croatia as repositories and conveyors of this sentiment, a role that was mitigated when the CPY introduced this concept in earnest several years later. Although it has the great theoretical advantage of reinforcing a more centralized state, the creation of a new Yugoslav national consciousness

98. *Naprijed*, #103, 4/25/45, 2.

was shown later to be almost impossible to achieve in practice. In any case, it clearly went too far for CPY leaders at this point in their war for "national liberation." Despite the fact that Sarajčić published his article in *Naprijed*, there is no evidence that Bakarić or any other important Communist leader ever publicly endorsed this concept. Rather, it was allowed to fade away during the next several weeks as CPC leaders turned their attention to other matters. When the Congress of Serbs was finally held in Zagreb the following September, this kind of far-reaching discussion about the character of the Main Committee was a thing of the past.

With the end of discussion about the role of the Main Committee, questions about the status of Serbs in Croatia were for all intents and purposes dropped. As a result of its more powerful political position, the CPY felt itself to be in a better position to resist the national sentiments of the Serb as well as the Croat population. The decision to accord the Main Committee no meaningful political role meant that Serbs would be encouraged to realize their cultural and political aims within the larger development of the Croatian republic, which, it was emphasized, would occur under the centralized conditions of the Yugoslav party-state. There would be no separate Serb newspapers or programs of instruction in schools. Nevertheless, the lack of explicit guarantees of Serb cultural and political autonomy was accepted by Serbs only as long as centralized arrangements prevailed. When Croatia was accorded greater political autonomy in the 1960s and again in the 1980s, Serbs began to seek more explicit guarantees; their memory of Ustasha massacres heightened their fears about their situation in an independent Croatian republic. Croats, however, continued to resent Serb predominance in Communist Party organizations that had been established by the end of the war.[99] Long-standing tensions between Serbs and Croats in Croatia, compounded by the legacies of the war, remained unresolved.

Victory at Hand: The NDH Falls and Maček Leaves the Country

Less than four weeks after the new Croatian government was established in April 1945, Partisan troops entered Zagreb. The weeks preceeding the liberation of Zagreb on May 8 saw a frenzy of activity as Ustashas, Chetniks, Peasant Party leaders and Slovene anti-Communists

---

99. At the end of the war, Serbs constituted over one quarter of CPC membership or 543,795 out of a total of 2,975,399 members. See Shoup, *Communism and the Yugoslav National Question*, 266.

maneuvered to surrender their military troops to the advancing Allies, and to procure Allied support for further military and political struggle against the Communist-led Partisan forces. Although they had various ideas about how to approach the Allies, all political groups outside the Partisan movement shared a fervent desire to prevent the establishment of the postwar state proclaimed by AVNOJ.

The temporary optimism of many Ustasha and CPP leaders after the front stabilized at Srijem in November 1944 was abruptly shattered when Partisan forces began their spring offensive in March 1945. Despite the intense military pressure applied from all sides, the Germans were determined to defend Croatia to the bitter end in order to make a last stand at the Alpine Fortress (Bavaria, parts of Czechoslovakia, Austria, northwest Yugoslavia and the Italian Alps).[100] Consequently, the NDH military, which Pavelić had reorganized in December by uniting the previously separate Ustasha and Home Guard troops, was completely subordinated to Germany's needs.[101] The final strike against these forces began on March 20, when Partisan troops breached the front at Lika and Srijem and began to move northward toward Trieste. It quickly became obvious that the combined German-NDH forces, which suffered heavy casualties, could not stave them off for long.

As Partisan troops advanced, anti-Communist leaders began a belated effort to salvage their own position. A plan was devised by members of the Slovenian Alliance, in contact with the government in exile, Mihailović, and the Vatican, to create a united political body, including the CPP, the Chetnik's Central National Committee and the Slovene National Committee (a political body founded by the Slovene Alliance, a coalition of anti-Communist political forces).[102] This Assembly would meet as soon as was feasible and proclaim a provisional government in Yugoslavia under a federal Yugoslav monarchy. It would invite King

---

100. For more on German military strategy in Yugoslavia in 1945 see Trgo, "Military Strategy and the Liberation of Yugoslavia 1944-1945."

101. Fikreta Jelić-Butić, "Snage kontrarevolucije u Hrvatskoj u 1945 godini," in Mira Kolar-Dimitrijević, ed., *Oslobodjenje Hrvatske 1945 godine* (Zagreb, 1986), 267. At the beginning of 1945, the Germans had nineteen divisions in Yugoslavia operating in conjunction with another sixteen divisions of approximately 150,000 Croat soldiers of the "Croatian Military Forces."

102. Jelić-Butić, "Snage kontrarevolucije u Hrvatskoj u 1945 godini," 272-273. It is not clear whether there were one or two plans for a general retreat through Slovenia. According to Jelić-Butić, there was only one plan, which was proposed by Mihailović's envoys in Slovenia and conveyed to Pavelić and Maček. Most scholars have described this as a second, separate plan. For example see Petranović, *Političke i pravne politike za vreme Privremene vlade DFJ*, 102.

Peter to come to Ljubljana and assume command of the Home Guard, which would operate in conjunction with Chetnik forces in Slovenia under General Damjanović. King Peter would then ask the Allies to send troops into Yugoslavia "to end the civil war."[103]

In accordance with this plan, on May 3, the Slovene Alliance called upon these united political forces to convene an assembly in Ljubljana and to proclaim the new provisional government. The German Commander in Ljubljana refused to hand over authority, however, and Assembly members soon learned that Damjanović's Chetnik forces had been interned by the British. In a state of frantic dismay, they retreated with the Home Guard to the Austrian border where they were also taken into British custody. Prevented from further political activity, they waited for what they hoped would be energetic measures taken by the Allies on behalf of their cause. So ended the main attempt by non-Communist political forces to prevent a Communist victory in Yugoslavia.

Meanwhile, Ustasha authorities attempted to reconstitute their government in the hopes of staving off a Communist bid for power. In early May, they approached Archbishop Stepinac and asked him to assume leadership of a temporary regency which would represent the legitimate political authority in Croatia to the Allies. Refusing on the grounds that the clergy should not engage in partisan political activity, Stepinac suggested that Ustasha authorities approach Maček with this proposal.[104] Maček appears to have been equally reluctant to become involved in such a dubious adventure, however, and he also refused. In any case, by this time, Ustasha authorities were preparing to flee Zagreb and they urged Maček to do the same.[105] Concerned for the safety of his family, on May 7 Maček left Zagreb for Austria where he made contact with the Americans. From there he went to Reims, France, the seat of the Supreme Headquarters of the Allied Expeditionary Force, and then on to Paris.

Shortly after his arrival in Paris, Maček attempted to visit London to talk with Krnjević and other political leaders. Concerned about how this visit would affect their relations with the new Yugoslav government, the

---

103. That even Pavelić was willing to contemplate cooperation with Mihailović is evident from his reception in the spring of Mihailović's emissaries, who were attempting to contact Maček about cooperation against the Communists.

104. Stella Alexander, *Church and State in Yugoslavia since 1945* (Cambridge England, New York: Columbia University Press, 1979), 108-110.

105. Vladko Maček, *In the Struggle for Freedom* (New York: Robert Speller & Sons, Inc., 1957), 258-260.

British denied Maček permission to enter the country and encouraged him instead to meet with the king during his upcoming trip to Germany.[106] The Peasant Party leader appears to have made an unfavorable impression upon the British who viewed him, as one foreign service officer put it, "of limited Balkan mentality."[107] Maček became increasingly critical of the "Communist dominated" government in Yugoslavia, but he decided to refrain from more concrete political actions to undermine the regime until he consulted with other political leaders. Although it is questionable whether he could have done anything to weaken the CPY's position in Yugoslavia, this period of inactivity gave the Communists precious time to consolidate their hold in Croatia.

While Maček and Pavelić escaped across the border to safety in early May, the bulk of the NDH troops did not. Although many managed to reach the Allies at the Austrian border, their illusion that they had surrendered to safety proved short lived. Since the Allies had previously agreed that all Axis troops must surrender to the countries against which they had fought, the British returned to the Partisans those Yugoslavs who had placed themselves in their hands.[108] Most of these soldiers and many civilians were killed over the next several weeks.[109] Despite protests from abroad, Communist leaders insisted that Home Guards

106. Ljubo Boban, "Plan Ivana Šubašića za sastanak s Mačekom u ljeto 1945 godine," in *Oslobodjenje Hrvatske 1945 godine*, 245. In answer to Churchill's request for information about Maček in mid-May, Foreign Secretary Eden responded that although Maček had not collaborated with the Germans and was still an important person in Croatia, he should not be granted asylum in Britain, which had its hands full with King Peter, Prince Paul, Stojadinović and numerous other Yugoslavs.

107. *Ibid.*, 246.

108. The question of British responsibility for the massacre of these returned troops has been hotly debated. While they could not have known for certain what would be the fate of these troops, they had a clear understanding at this point of the Partisans' political objectives, which included the eradication of Chetniks, Ustashas, Peasant Party members and other non-Communist military and political forces.

109. Although it is difficult to gauge the exact number of Home Guard troops killed, it almost certainly ran into the tens of thousands. The Yugoslavs have never provided any specific data on the number of NDH troops killed at the end of the war. According to Bakarić, at the end of the war the Partisans captured more than 11,000 "agents and spies" and killed more than 12,000 individuals opposed to the new regime. For a discussion of this question see Jozo Tomasevich, "Yugoslavia during the Second World War," in Wayne Vucinich, ed., *Contemporary Yugoslavia*. (Berkeley: University of California Press, 1969), 114.

were to be treated as common collaborators, and the eradication of non-Communist forces continued throughout the summer.[110] The large number of those killed greatly reduced the strength of political opposition in Croatia and allowed the CPC to secure more easily its predominant political position there.

The CPC also launched a campaign to round up Ustasha and Peasant Party sympathizers in the newly liberated areas of Croatia, especially Zagreb. Shortly after Partisan troops entered the city to a lukewarm reception, slogans began to appear of the walls pledging "no mercy for those who have collaborated with the enemy."[111] Articles in the Partisan press like the one by CPC leader Karlo Mrazović in *Naprijed* exhorted individuals as "a duty to your fallen comrades" to capture for the authorities all Ustasha sympathizers. "The unpunished wrongdoer is a very big danger," he wrote, "especially in Zagreb where so many are trying to camouflage themselves."[112] The message of these articles was clear and effective, and anyone, including CPP sympathizers, who appeared to pose a political threat was liable to fall under its injunction. Although it is impossible to say with any reliability how many CPP followers were arrested and imprisoned during the summer of 1945, large numbers of them were certainly prevented in this way from engaging in any political activity that might hinder the process of Communist political consolidation.[113]

CPC leaders also took steps to further discredit Maček by portraying his departure from the country as an act of personal cowardice and a sign of his collaboration with Ustasha authorities. Attempting to counter rumors that Communists had forced Maček to leave Yugoslavia, Bakarić in his speech to the fourth session of ZAVNOH insisted that Maček had fled even after receiving guarantees for his personal safety from Zagreb

---

110. *ZAVNOH, Zbornik dokumenata,* vol. 4, 713.

111. Boban, "Plan Ivana Šubašića za sastanak s Mačekom u ljeto 1945 godine," 247. At the beginning of June, British Ambassador Stevenson reported a conversation he had with CPP member M. Martinović (then Yugoslav envoy in Cairo and a Partisan sympathizer), who said that Šutej had just returned from Croatia and reported that the Yugoslav Army had been coldly received there. According to Šutej, CPP Executive Committee members Frol and Gaži had not gone to Zagreb yet because they could not be sure of their reception there.

112. *Naprijed,* #106, 5/18/45, 2.

113. Boban, "Plan Ivana Šubašića za sastanak s Mačekom u ljeto 1945 godine," 251. Šubašić was reportedly depressed after his return from a trip to Croatia in August by the number of former CPP colleagues whom he found had been arrested or jailed.

party members.[114] Whatever the reasons for his departure, there is no doubt that Maček's absence had a more demoralizing effect on the CPP than had constant hammering by the Partisan press during the previous four years. As long as Maček was in Croatia, he was a powerful reminder of the prewar strength and vitality of the Croat Peasant Party. After his departure, the remnants of the party appeared to crumble with astonishing speed.

With Maček out of the way and many CPP sympathizers killed or imprisoned, Communist leaders were in a strong position to realize their solution to the Croat question and complete the process of political centralization. CPC leaders had been forced previously to compromise with the powerful Peasant Party. This accomodation had often caused them to adopt more federalist political solutions than those endorsed by the central party leadership, creating tension within the Yugoslav Communist party. The steady erosion of CPP strength during the war, completed by the decimation of the Home Guard in the summer of 1945, meant that Communists were finally able to resist pressure from the CPP and to impose their own solution to the Croat question.

The Croat Question and the Catholic Church

When Maček fled Zagreb in April 1945, there was one powerful Croat left who quickly became the focus of the political aspirations of all those who opposed the Partisans in Croatia: Archbishop Alojzije Stepinac, Metropolitan of Zagreb, senior Catholic prelate in Croatia, and outspoken advocate of Croat national aims before the war. Ironically, Stepinac's pro-Yugoslav views and his service at the Salonika Front in the First World War had prompted King Aleksandar to support his appointment to the see of Zagreb. Stepinac's attitudes were transformed during his rapid rise in the church hierarchy, however, and by the time he became Archbishop in 1937 at the age of thirty-nine, he was deeply opposed to Serbian domination of Yugoslavia. A staunch supporter of Maček, he became a forceful spokesman for the Croat cause in the years before the war.

The Communists faced a formidable foe in Stepinac in their approach to the Croat question. The Catholic Church in Croatia and the Archbishop himself were powerful national symbols, especially since the Croat Peasant Party had been fatally weakened. With Maček gone, Stepinac's role as defender of Croat national aims, as much as his reli-

---

114. *ZAVNOH, Zbornik dokumenata*, vol. 4, 709.

gious authority, made him a potential threat to the political goals of the CPY. His support for Croatian political autonomy and the CPP made him a rallying point for the opposition. It was with this fact in mind that Communist leaders approached Stepinac in the summer of 1945.

The CPC had taken pains during the war not to alienate the peasantry by hostile manifestations toward the church. Clergymen who could be persuaded to join the Partisans were generally permitted to celebrate mass with the troops and peasants in Partisan occupied villages. Some well known priests, like Monsg. Rittig, rector of the Church of St. Mark in Zagreb's upper town, joined the Partisans and became ardent spokesmen for their cause.[115] Nevertheless, CPC leaders were well aware that most of the Catholic clergy was vehemently anti-Communist, if not openly sympathetic to the Ustasha regime.[116]

As the end of the war approached, tensions between church and Partisan leaders increased dramatically. Alarmed by the anti-Communist political activity of many priests, the CPC began to criticize church authorities. While disclaiming any general anti-religious intent, various articles in the Partisan press deplored the collaborationist role played by many clergymen and their failure to take decisive actions to prevent the massacre of Serbs in Croatia.[117] The CPC reacted particularly strongly to a statement released by Catholic bishops on March 24, 1945 which denounced "materialistic communism" as an enemy of the Croat nation and defended the "desire and right" of the Croat people to establish an independent state.[118] While prepared to tolerate some religious autonomy, Communist leaders were not prepared to condone such explicitly political statements or interference in their efforts to determine the resolution of the Croat question.

Despite this increase in hostility toward church authorities, Tito was anxious to avoid completely antagonizing the Archbishop, and he took

---

115. Rittig was one of the few higher clergy who joined the Partisan movement early in the war. Consequently, he was accorded special treatment, holding a series of posts first as a member of the ZAVNOH presidency and then as minister for religion in the new Croat government.

116. Many Catholic clergymen, particularly in Bosnia-Hercegovina, were strongly sympathetic to the Ustasha regime, and some priests participated in the forced conversions and massacres of Serbs in the Independent State of Croatia. Several Ustasha leaders such as Artuković were educated at the Franciscan monastery at Široki Brijeg in Hercegovina and retained strong ties to their former teachers.

117. For example, see *Naprijed*, #107, 5/26/45, 4.

118. Richard Pattee, *The Case of Cardinal Aloysius Stepinac* (Milwaukee: The Bruce Publishing Company, 1953), 418.

several steps during the summer of 1945 to procure Stepinac's cooperation. Bakarić followed suit and, putting aside his strong antipathy
toward Stepinac, toned down the CPC's escalating rhetoric against
church officials.[119] Several days after Stepinac was taken into "protective
custody" in mid-May, Vicar-general Bishop Salis-Seewis was invited to
talks with Bakarić and Tito on important matters pertaining to the
relationship between church and state. At this meeting, and at a meeting
two days later with Stepinac himself, Tito indicated that his main concern was the manner in which the church's attitude toward the Croat
question would affect "the work of consolidating the state."[120] Indeed,
Tito focused almost exclusively on national concerns, instead of the
purely political question of how to divide authority between church and
state.

"Speaking as a Croat and as a Catholic," Tito began, he was not satisfied with one part of the clergy who had turned away from the ideas of
Strossmayer and embraced a virulent Croat nationalism during the
war.[121] This view was contrary to the church's mission and harmful to
the interests of the state. Instead of fostering separatism and chauvinism,
the church should guide Croat national sentiment in the more moderate
direction of Yugoslavism. Equally worrisome, according to Tito, was the
fact that the Catholic Church in Croatia was tied so closely to Rome,
which had always been more inclined toward Italy than toward the
Slavic nations. These ties, he pointed out, meant that the church could
not possibly act in the best interests of Croatia or Yugoslavia. "I would
say for myself," Tito concluded, "that our church should be more
national, that it should be more adapted to the nation; though perhaps
you are surprised that I approach the subject of nationality with such
emphasis."[122]

The reply that Tito received from Salis-Seewis and Stepinac could
hardly have been satisfying to him. Both men hastened to assure the CPY

---

119. Bakarić later told Dedijer that he thought Stepinac a very difficult character, a "raging nationalist, [who is] pro-Ustasha and anti-Serb," but that he avoided
any kind of conflict with him in the spring of 1945 because that was Tito's
approach. Dedijer, *Novi prilozi za biografiju Josipa Broza Tita*, vol. 2, 563-564.

120. Pattee, #64, 422.

121. *Ibid.*, #64, 422; *Slobodni dom*, #17, 6/9/45, 4. According to Bakarić, Tito
originally said "speaking as a Croat and as a Catholic" but that "as a Catholic"
was removed from the text when it was published. Dedijer, *Novi prilozi za
biografiju Josipa Broza Tita*, vol. 2, 563-564.

122. *Slobodni dom*, 6/9/45, #17, 4. This suggestion was also made in an article
in *Naprijed* several days earlier. *Naprijed*, #107, 5/26/45, 4.

leader that the Vatican's policy toward the Croat question had always been "discreet and judicious."[123] They argued that the Vatican had refused to put Medjumurje under Hungarian jurisdiction during the war and had also refused Italian requests to transfer Dalmatia to Italian control. Moreover, Salis-Seewis insisted that the Holy See was very supportive of the Slav idea and pointed out that it had proclaimed Cyril and Methodius as patron saints of the Croatian Catholic Church.[124]

Behind these friendly protestations lay Stepinac's unequivocal rejection of Tito's suggestion that the Catholic Church in Croatia sever its ties to Rome. Instead, he advised that if Tito really desired to consolidate the new political order, he should sign a concordat with the Vatican which "would have a very great significance for the new state that has just been created."[125] Moreover, Stepinac made it clear that he had no intention of denouncing all non-Communist political forces in Croatia as Croat chauvinists. Rather, he urged Tito to meet "frankly and courageously" with representatives of the Croat Peasant Party and with "honest" adherents of the Ustasha movement in order to arrive at some wider political consensus.[126]

Tito's request to Stepinac that he sever ties to Rome is at first glance perplexing. Was Tito seriously trying to make a deal with Stepinac that he would not take repressive measures against him if the Archbishop recognized the political authority of the CPY? And why, if the Catholic Church was already a potent national symbol, did Tito suggest it play a more national role in Croatia? It does appear that Tito seriously hoped that by "cutting a deal" with Stepinac he could deprive the Catholic Church of its external support, thereby making it more susceptible to Communist control. [127] Though he must have known there was little chance that Stepinac would concur in loosening the church's ties with the Vatican, had the plan succeeded, casting the Catholic Church as a Croat national symbol would have been a small price to pay. The Catholic Church posed the greatest threat to the CPY's solution to the Croat question because it was an independent, quasi-political force, not because it

---

123. Pattee, #64, 420.

124. *Ibid.*

125. *Ibid.*, 424.

126. *Ibid.*, 425.

127. The implications of this "deal" for the subsequent trial and imprisonment of Stepinac for war crimes are obvious. It was for this reason that there was such an uproar over the insistence by Jakov Blažević, who was public prosecutor in Croatia at the time, that this was precisely what Tito had in mind. See *Danas* 159 (May 3, 1985): 26-27.

was a national symbol as such. As it was, however, Tito's attempts to reach an "understanding" with Stepinac were unnecessary. As elsewhere in Eastern Europe, the church's ties with the Vatican ultimately could not keep it from being thoroughly undermined by the new Communist regime. As Stepinac attempted to hold his ground over the next several weeks he found himself increasingly isolated and impotent.

Although Tito and Bakarić continued to avoid a major confrontation with the church, relations between them became further strained. After his initial refusal to cooperate with Tito, Stepinac showed himself no more willing to modify his positions in order to maintain amiable relations with the CPY. During the summer, he protested to Bakarić several times about new legislation concerning civil marriages, religious instruction in schools, and agrarian reform, which would result in the confiscation of the vast majority of church property.[128] Although Bakarić generally maintained a noncommittal and polite tone in his responses to these letters, he criticized Stepinac publicly on a number of occasions for his political "obstructionism."[129]

Relations between them took a turn for the worse after a meeting of the Bishops Conference in mid-September 1945. A "Pastoral letter to the Faithful" and a circular to the clergy published after the Conference adopted an uncompromising tone toward the new regime. Objecting to the government's harsh treatment of the church, the bishops demanded complete freedom for the Catholic press, freedom of religious instruction in primary and secondary schools, the return of confiscated property, respect for the church's authority over marriage, and freedom for Catholic charitable organizations. They concluded with a demand that the political authorities reach an understanding with the church as an "independent and equal party."[130]

In the tense atmosphere in Croatia preceding elections to the Constituent Assembly, Communist leaders were not prepared to tolerate these demands and especially the church's insistence that it be treated as an equal partner in certain political matters. Nevertheless, they were still reluctant to risk antagonizing large numbers of Croats by taking the offensive against the church. Consequently, Bakarić's initial reaction to the Pastoral letter in an interview with *Vjesnik* was to deny that the

128. Pattee, #66, 426-452, Stepinac to Bakarić, 7/21/45; #66, 443-446, Stepinac to Bakarić, 8/2/45; #67, 452; Stepinac to Bakarić, 8/11/45; #68, 456-462, Stepinac to Tito and Bakarić, 8/17/45.

129. For example see Bakarić speech to the fourth session of ZAVNOH. *ZAVNOH, Zbornik dokumenata*, vol. 4, 715-716.

130. Pattee, #70, 470-480.

Catholic Church was subject to repression in Croatia and to insist that relations between the church and the state were improving steadily.[131] Tito appears to have decided that a clash with Stepinac was unavoidable, however, and in his response to Stepinac's letter three weeks later, he took a noticeably sharper tone. Charging that the letter had attempted to spread hatred not only among the clergy but among the Croat population, Tito criticized it for hindering the "process of consolidation." He concluded with a thinly veiled threat that everyone was obliged to obey the laws forbidding the propagation of chauvinism.[132] This appears to have been a clear enough signal that the Archbishop no longer enjoyed the protection of the regime. Within a week, he was attacked by a mob on his way to open a new church at Zaprešić. Shortly thereafter, he was confined to his house where he remained until he was tried and imprisoned the following fall.

With Stepinac muzzled, another important obstacle to the process of centralizing the new state structures was removed. Within a few short months, the Communists had succeeded in squashing the independent power of their main rivals for political power in Croatia. With their destruction of the Croat Peasant Party and their repression of the Catholic Church, the Communists had effectively silenced voices in Croatia which supported either a separate state or more autonomy within the Yugoslav federation. As they prepared for elections to the Constituent Assembly in the fall of 1945, they were thus in an excellent position to achieve their state-building aims in Croatia.

Elections to the Constituent Assembly

Elections to the Constituent Assembly, agreed upon by Tito and Šubašić the previous November, were announced on September 6 and held on November 11, 1945. The elections were the crucial next step in the CPY's plans to remake the state and to resolve the Croat question in the framework of a centralized political order. They presented opportunities, but also many dangers. Despite the Communists' strength in Croatia, there was still a real threat that the Allies might intervene in support of the CPP. Nor was the mostly compliant Šubašić an entirely known factor, for he did not wish to see the Peasant Party's political influence entirely eradicated by a Communist landslide. The stakes were

---

131. *Borba*, #241, 10/7/45, 3.
132. *Borba*, #259, 10/25/45, 1.

high, and the Communists did not intend to leave themselves vulnerable
to a victory of the CPP old guard in the upcoming elections.

In the weeks preceding the call for elections, the Communist Party of
Croatia had upgraded the status of the CPP Executive Committee so that
it could appear to run as a separate political party. An Executive
Committee meeting in June expanded the goals and structure of the
organization. In a highly symbolic move that stressed its claim to being
the "true" peasant party, the Committee announced that it would take its
old name of the Croat Republican Peasant Party, "which in truth it had
never rejected."[133] Although the CRPP was not formally declared a
political party, the term "Executive Committee" was now used to refer
specifically to the Committee (which was expanded to include eighty-
seven members), not the entire group of Peasant Party sympathizers
cooperating with the Partisan movement. More importantly, the con-
stituency of the CRPP was now broadly defined to include representatives "from all federal units in which Croats live." Many of the new
members included in the Executive Committee were from Bosnia-
Hercegovina and a new business secretary for Bosnia-Hercegovina was
established.[134] The CRPP was also permitted to expand its organizational
network by renewing its peasant cooperatives and educational groups.[135]
By granting the CRPP these privileges and the virtual status of a separate
political party, Communist leaders hoped to fill the political vacuum that
had been created in Croatia by the disintegration of the CPP and to
effectively preclude its resurrection.[136]

The CRPP occupied a strong position in the new Provisional
Assembly created in August 1945. According to the recommendations of
the Yalta Agreement, the Assembly was to be formed by expanding
AVNOJ to include all members of the pre-war Skupština who had not
cooperated with the Ustasha regime. But in an effort to exclude as many
anti-Communists (including CPP members) as possible, the CPY incorporated only fifty-three members of the prewar Skupština and then
added another sixty-five people, most of whom were sympathizers of the
Communist movement.[137] With the large number of CRPP members
included in the new Assembly, the small group around Ivan Šubašić had
little political influence.[138] Moreover, the CRPP Executive Committee

---

133. AIHRPH IO HSS/85.
134. *Slobodni dom*, #10, 4/21/45, 1.
135. *Borba*, #226, 9/16/45, 1-2; AIHRPH IO HSS/85.
136. *Borba*, #218, 9/8/45.
137. Petranović, *Političke i pravne prilike za vreme Privremene vlade DFR*, 142.
138. *Ibid*.

managed to exclude such relatively well known CPP leaders as Tomo Jančiković with the argument that he was "too closely associated with Maček and other collaborators."[139]

As CPP leaders in Croatia considered their strategy for entering the elections, a split developed between those like Šubašić who planned to run as a member of the Communist-sponsored mass political group, the Popular Front of Yugoslavia (PFY), and a group gathered around Marija Radić, the widow of Stjepan Radić, who insisted on campaigning outside of the PFY.[140] Šubašić believed the CPP would be permitted to retain its separate party identity within the confines of the PFY. He envisioned a kind of two-party system in Yugoslavia composed of workers, on the one hand, and peasants on the other; he would organize a coalition of agrarian parties from Serbia, Croatia and Slovenia, and the workers party would be based on trade union organizations.[141] Hoping to elicit a mandate from Maček and CRPP leaders for his activities in the Front, Šubašić joined the PFY at the beginning of August and was elected to its Executive Committee.[142]

During the next few weeks, Šubašić attempted to put his strategy for the upcoming elections into action. In mid-August, he met in Zagreb with a group of CPP members, including Šutej and Jančiković, who were anti-Communist, and Gaži, who was pro-Communist. While some present at the meeting, such as Jančiković and Gaži, generally agreed with Šubašić's approach, an equal number adamantly opposed Šubašić's membership in the Popular Front and endorsed Marija Radić as the main representative of the opposition. However, they all agreed that Šubašić should go to Paris and seek guidance from Maček about the best way to proceed. Šubašić was demoralized by his failure to procure a strong

---

139. *Zakonodavni rad pretsedništva AVNOJ-a*, 567.

140. The Popular Front of Yugoslavia, founded the previous December, was officially conceived of as a "coalition of individuals working toward the political and economic reconstruction of Yugoslavia." This ambiguous description led some CPP leaders like Šubašić to argue that they would be able to retain their separate programs within its confines.

141. Petranović, *Političke i pravne prilike za vreme Privremene vlade DFJ*, 147. There does not appear to have been a great deal of contact between Šubašić and Milan Grol, head of the United Opposition. (The United Opposition included representatives of the Democrats, the Radicals and the Agrarian Party.) Nevertheless, the United Opposition's publication, *Demokratija*, displayed sympathy toward the CPP on a number of occasions and described it as being in an exceptionally difficult position.

142. Boban, "Plan Ivana Šubašića za sastanak s Mačekom u ljeto 1945 godine," 249.

mandate from the remnants of the Peasant Party leadership. He was further frustrated after his return to Belgrade by his inability to elicit support from the Serb agrarian parties for presenting a united list in the elections. Nevertheless, he made plans to go to Paris where he hoped to receive Maček's support for his political strategy.

Maček had become more politically active as the elections approached, and he attempted to rouse Allied interest in the situation in Yugoslavia. At the beginning of September, he endorsed a memorandum prepared by several former Serb members of the government in exile for the Conference of Allied Ministers of Foreign Affairs to be held in London the following week. Charging that the Yugoslav regime was completely dominated by Communists, the memorandum called upon the Allies to establish a government in Yugoslavia composed of all political parties, including the Communist Party, and to supervise free elections. It also requested that an Allied military mission be sent to Yugoslavia to help form a "nonpolitical" army and police.[143] In an interview in the *New York Times* in mid-September, Maček repeated these requests, with the warning that fundamental reforms should be carried out in Yugoslavia before holding western-style elections.[144] He also denounced the Tito regime for treating Home Guard soldiers like war criminals and charged that in some areas up to sixty percent of the voters had been denied the right to vote.[145]

Surprisingly, when Šubašić first informed Tito and Kardelj of his plans to visit Maček in Paris he encountered no resistance, other than a wry observation from Kardelj that the trip would accomplish little of substance.[146] Consequently, Šubašić decided that he would also like to go to London to talk with political figures there, and he requested British Ambassador Stevenson to provide British air transportation to the capital. Despite instructions from London that Stevenson should convince Šubašić to postpone his trip, which coincided with the conference of Ministers of Foreign Affairs, British air transportation was arranged. But at the last minute, Šubašić was prevented from leaving the airport by Communist authorities.[147] The next day an announcement appeared in

143. Petranović, *Političke i pravne prilike za vreme Privremene vlade DFJ*, 191.

144. *New York Times*, 7/23/45, 6.

145. *Ibid.*

146. Boban, "Plan Ivana Šubašića za sastanak s Mačekom u ljeto 1945 godine," 252.

147. *Ibid.* According to one participant at the Politburo meeting that day, someone came into the room and whispered to Ranković that Šubašić was at the

the newspapers that Šubašić had suddenly taken ill and was confined to his bed.[148] Heavily guarded, the former prime minister was prevented from further contacts with British officials.[149]

Although it is not entirely clear why CPY leaders had a change of heart concerning Šubašić's travel plans, relations between Šubašić and Communist authorities had deteriorated steadily during the past several weeks because of disagreements about the upcoming elections. CPY leaders may have decided by this time that it was simply too great a risk to allow Šubašić to confer with Maček abroad. Šubašić's plans to extend his trip to London must have heightened their fears that he would seek political support for an independent election campaign. Moreover, though he had not made arrangements to take his wife, there was always the chance that he might decide to stay abroad, thus depriving the regime of an essential source of legitimacy at this crucial time.[150]

Whatever the exact reasons, CPY leaders clearly decided that Šubašić could no longer be trusted and must be closely confined. After languishing under virtual house arrest for several days, the frustrated and demoralized Šubašić charged that Tito had failed to carry out the provisions of the Tito-Šubašić Agreement and offered his resignation.[151] Along with other oppositional groups, he also called upon CPP members to abstain from the elections or to vote for the "box without a list," a reference to the fact that voters were permitted to register a vote of no confidence in the single list offered by the Popular Front. Tito was plainly relieved to see Šubašić go. Charging that Šubašić was "in league with the forces of reaction which are trying to sabotage the election," Tito quickly accepted his resignation.[152]

In retrospect it seems that the plaintive words Mihailović used to describe his plight during the war could be applied equally well to Šubašić. "I wanted much, I began much," Mihailović stated at his trial in 1946, "but the whirlwind, the world whirlwind, carried me and my work

---

airport with the British ambassador and was preparing to leave the country. Tito instructed that Šubašić was to be prevented from leaving, by force if necessary.

148. *Borba*, 10/9/45, 2.

149. Boban, "Plan Ivana Šubašića za sastanak s Mačekom u ljeto 1945 godine," 254. Stevenson's efforts to see him proved fruitless and Gaži and Jančiković observed that Šubašić was heavily guarded when they visited him shortly thereafter. Šubašić told them he had tried to contact Tito and Ranković about his situation but had been unable to reach them.

150. For a discussion of this question see *ibid.*, 55

151. Šutej and Jančiković also submitted their resignations at this time.

152. *Borba*, #248, 10/13/45, 1.

away."[153] Šubašić also sought to accomplish much. He hoped to take on the CPY almost singlehandedly, and by cooperating with it, buy Maček enough time to regain his former political stature. Refusing to protect those CPP leaders like Magovac and Košutić who shared many of his goals and could have provided essential political support, he ultimately found himself in the same unenviable position as they. Isolated and impotent, he waited until the elections to the Constituent Assembly to make his move when it was already too late. By then he was, as Tito scornfully remarked, like a "general without an army," and his last-ditch effort to preserve some political independence for the CPP proved starkly ineffective.

The efforts of Peasant Party leaders operating outside the People's Front to run independently in the elections were also ineffective. This group gathered around Radić's widow in the hopes that the prestige of her name and her opposition to the CRPP Executive Committee would undermine the CPC's efforts to portray "its" peasant party as the true follower of Radić.[154] At the beginning of September, Marija Radić released a statement in which she warned against the "wolves in sheep skins" who comprised the CRPP Executive Committee and who, having abandoned the CPP, were using Radić's name to bad purpose.[155] One of the numerous flyers released by this group in the fall of 1945 had this to say about the CRPP: "Where are the Communists leading us?...Now they are trying to deceive the Croat people [into thinking] that they are followers of the ideology of the Radić brothers. Communist servants Franjo Gaži, Tuna Babić and their fellow travellers have voluntarily founded some 'executive committee' on the basis of some new Communist party, to which they have deceptively given the name 'CRPP,' drawing in this way on the memory of our leader and teacher, Stjepan Radić, who was never a Communist or a Partisan."[156] These publications also attempted to defend Maček's policies during the war and to convince the population he was doing everything he could abroad to "improve the fate of the Croat people."[157] They warned that, once in power, the Communists

153. *The Trial of Draža Mihailović* (Belgrade, 1946), cited in Jozo Tomasevich, *The Chetniks, War and Revolution in Yugoslavia, 1941-1945* (Stanford: Stanford University Press, 1975), 47.

154. This group included such well known CPP members as Mira Košutić and Ivan Bernardić.

155. AIHRPH HSS box 1/42.

156. AIHRPH HSS box 1/39.

157. AIHRPH HSS box 1/41; AIHRPH HSS box 1/44.

would seize land from the peasants, collectivize agriculture and pursue an anti-peasant, anti-Croat platform.[158]

Despite these publications, CPP attempts to organize an electoral opposition foundered in the face of Communist harassment and the CPY's tremendous organizing abilities. Communist leaders in Croatia took a variety of actions to ensure that the CPP would be unable to mount a serious challenge on November 11. They had a particularly effective tool in their hands by denying anyone who had "cooperated" with the Ustasha regime the right to vote.[159] Although this method of controlling voters was used everywhere in the country, it appears to have been employed most extensively in Croatia, where in some areas an estimated thirty to forty percent of the electorate was kept from the polls.[160] This rule was used not only against Ustasha supporters but against all opponents of the CPC, and was applied heavily in entire regions which were known to be strongly pro-CPP.[161] The CPY also moved swiftly against the first issue of *Narodni glas* put out by supporters of Marija Radić. The paper, which called for a boycott of the elections and guarantees of Croatian sovereignty in the new state, was banned almost immediately and prevented from further publication.[162]

Communist leaders also stepped up their campaign in the press and at election rallies to discredit the Peasant Party and the Cvetković-Maček Agreement. For example, in an article in the CPY organ *Borba*, Milovan Djilas criticized the Agreement for failing to fulfill Croat national demands and as a hindrance to the "national renaissance" which Yugoslavia was now said to be experiencing.[163] Denouncing Maček for "spreading lies abroad" that there was a dictatorship in Yugoslavia, another article insisted that if Maček were to gain power he would keep Croats in poverty and hunger.[164] As Communist rhetoric escalated,

---

158. AIHRPH HSS box 2/45.

159. *Borba*, #213, 9/2/45, 2. This article lauded several recent voters' conferences in which "the people demonstrated that they were not ready to allow those to vote who had cooperated with the occupier." The article did admit, however, that some individuals had been unfairly deprived of the right to vote and promised that a commission would be established to review their cases.

160. Petranović, *Političke i pravne prilike za vreme Privremene vlade DFJ*, 189.

161. *Ibid.*, 202. CPP resistance to the elections in the fall was strongest in Zagreb, Podravina, Slavonia, parts of the Croatian Littoral, Pokuplje and Karlovac.

162. Vojislav Koštunica and Kosta Čavoški, *Stranački pluralizam i monizam Društveni pokreti i politički sistem u Jugoslaviji, 1944-1949* (Belgrade, 1983), 59.

163. *Borba*, #230, 9/22/45, 1.

164. *Borba*, #227, 9/19/45, 3. See also *Borba* #238, 10/1/45, 1.

Maček was portrayed as an enemy of ordinary working people. As Croat Communist leader Anka Berus put it at a rally in Zagreb, Maček's followers were "old people" who had one main enemy in Croatia—the working class."[165] Communist leaders warned that since the CPP was not a loyal opposition such as existed in England and America, it could not expect to be treated in the same way.[166]

The CRPP Executive Committee also continued to denounce Maček and, at its Second Congress in Zagreb in mid-September, endorsed the Popular Front in the elections.[167] In his speech to the Congress, Executive Committee President Franjo Gaži spoke of Tito in the same glowing terms that had previously been reserved for Radić. He compared the current congress to the CRPP congress in December 1920 which had adopted a strong anti-regime, pro-federalism platform, and reminded his listeners that the CRPP had much in common with the Communists since the 1921 *Obznana* had been directed against them both. A CRPP election announcement released shortly thereafter expressed its disapproval of a multiparty political system and denounced all political activity outside the Popular Front.[168]

The CPC also attempted to use the Main Committee of Serbs in Croatia, founded at the end of September, to popularize the Popular Front platform.[169] At its founding congress, questions raised the previous spring about the character of the Main Committee were smoothed over as its primary purpose of organizing Serb support for the PFY became clear. Designating the Main Committee as the highest organ of Serbs in Croatia, the congress adopted a resolution pledging to guard the unity of Serbs in the political and cultural sphere. The committee quickly began to campaign for Popular Front candidates in the elections. In an election announcement issued shortly thereafter, the Committee called upon Serbs in Croatia to vote on "an ordering of our state that will ensure the harmony and equality of Serbs and Croats in Croatia."[170] Pijade's confusing formulation about the unimportance of republic borders was

---

165. *Borba*, #244, 10/8/45, 1.

166. *Borba*, #246, 10/10/45, 1.

167. *Borba*, #226, 9/18/45, 2. CPY leaders estimated that aproximately 100,000 people attended this meeting. While this estimate is probably too high, aerial photographs indicate that a good sized crowd was present.

168. *Politika*, 10/21/45, cited in Koštunica and Čavoški, *Stranački pluralizam i monizam*, 34.

169. At this congress, a seven member secretariat and fifty-four member executive board were formed.

170. *Borba*, #256, 10/22/45.

also included in an effort to counteract the growing support among some Serb Partisans for the establishment of an autonomous region of Serbs in Croatia. The resolution stated that "the borders of the federal republics do not sever or divide the Serb people but are a firm basis [on] which to connect all Serbs in Yugoslavia."[171]

By the end of September 1945, it was clear that Peasant Party leaders would be unable to organize an effective opposition to the Communists, either within the Popular Front or outside it. Consequently, along with the rest of the opposition in Belgrade, they began to call for a boycott of the elections. CPY leaders attributed this boycott to CPP weakness and denied any harassment on their part; but they were not entirely indifferent to its effect on Allied opinion abroad.[172] Consequently, the election laws were changed to allow for a "box without a list." According to Hebrang, this method of voting would prevent the opposition from using the current system to their advantage and claiming a larger number of abstainees than was actually the case.[173] With the opposition paralyzed, the elections proceeded relatively smoothly. Not surprisingly, the CPY reported that ninety-five percent of the votes were cast for the Popular Front. Although it is impossible to know how many Peasant Party members abstained from voting, the CPP was unable to capitalize on anything resembling an organized boycott of the elections. By carefully controlling all aspects of the elections, the CPY captured complete control of the Constituent Assembly. With their position secure, the Communists set out to produce a formal constitutional arrangement that would legitimize the new party-state.

A little more than two weeks after the elections, and exactly two years after the second meeting of AVNOJ, the Constituent Assembly proclaimed the founding of the Socialist Federal Republic of Yugoslavia. This proclamation, which denied King Peter the right to return to the country, signaled the Communists' victory in fundamentally remaking the political order of Yugoslavia and with it a new solution to the Croat question. During the several weeks after the elections, a constitutional committee of the Constituent Assembly met to work out the particulars of the new constitution which, patterned closely after the Soviet model, was adopted unanimously in April 1946.[174] The framework of the new

---

171. *Ibid.*

172. *Borba*, #230, 9/22/45, 1.

173. *Zakonodavni rad pretsedništva AVNOJ-a*, 625.

174. Sweeping rights were granted to the republic units, although they were not permitted, as in the Soviet Union, to maintain separate armies or foreign offices. The federal government was granted authority to pass laws on most

political system had been put into place piece by piece during the war, beginning with the foundation of local political organizations, followed by the establishment of AVNOJ and the various regional antifascist councils, and culminating in 1945 in the creation of a centralized governmental structure based on a highly unified Communist party.

Conclusion

By the end of 1945, the Communist Party of Yugoslavia was in firm control of Yugoslavia's political life. During the previous four years it had succeeded in rebuilding the Yugoslav state and placing itself at its helm. To do this, it had mobilized an enormous segment of the population into the Partisan movement which, in addition to fighting the occupying forces, served as a springboard to Communist power. In the earlier stages of the war, as the CPY attempted to build the Partisan movement, it was forced to respond to the national aspirations of the populace. These aspirations often interfered with the CPY's aim to build a highly centralized state based on a monolithic Communist party. This was particularly true in Croatia, where a large portion of the population desired greater political autonomy within Yugoslavia or an independent state. In an effort to channel these national aspirations into support for itself, the Communist Party of Croatia adopted a federalist strategy that provided real autonomy to party and state organizations.

By the last year of the war, however, the CPY had achieved a more powerful political and military position. Although Communist leaders continued to emphasize the state's nominally federal framework, they focused on consolidating and centralizing its institutional structure. In the process, Hebrang was replaced by Bakarić, who did not pose a challenge to party unity, and ZAVNOH was subordinated to AVNOJ. Most importantly, Communist leaders eradicated the Croat Peasant Party, which had exerted enormous decentralizing pressures on state-building elites in the interwar period and on the CPY during the war. With the

---

subjects, but the right to legislate in areas not specified by the constitution lay with the republics, which were supposed to exercise responsibility over their own administrative organs. The legislature, like the Soviet one, was composed of one house, the Chamber of Nationalities, which was designed to articulate the interests of the republics. The administrative apparatus was also based on the Soviet system in which all-union, union-republic and republic ministries share powers. For more on this subject see Shoup, *The National Question in Yugoslavia,* 114-117.

Peasant Party and the Catholic Church in Croatia effectively supressed, Croat national demands no longer posed a threat to the political consolidation and centralization of the new party-state.

The imposition of a highly centralized state in 1945, which was maintained by a high degree of coercion and repression, meant that many sensitive questions concerning the resolution of the Croat question were addressed within the framework of a unitary state. Questions about cultural and political autonomy of Serbs in Croatia were answered by emphasizing the unimportance of republic borders, which rendered any protection for minority rights unnecessary. Similarly, the delineation of borders between the republics was imposed without plebiscite or public discussion. Although questions lingered about the character of the multinational republic of Bosnia-Hercegovina, these were not publicly discussed.

Nevertheless, these questions only ceased to be of importance as long as the Bolshevik state-building strategy prevailed. When Communist leaders began to discuss a different distribution of power between the central and republic party and state organs, these questions arose again. The increase in national expression after the political liberalization in the 1960s forced Yugoslav leaders to contend again with the complexities of these problems and the way in which they were settled by the CPY during the Second World War.

6

Reflections on the Partisan Legacy

At the end of the war, the Communist Party of Yugoslavia imposed a centralizing state-building strategy modeled closely on the Bolshevik pattern. Declaring the national question resolved, the CPY settled down to the business of achieving rapid economic development through centralized state planning. By 1946, the Yugoslav state was consolidated sufficiently to launch an ambitious program of modernization which Soviet Communists had required almost a decade to undertake. Indeed, elated by their success in following the Bolshevik model of state-building, Yugoslav Communists boasted in the months after the war that Yugoslavia was more fully Socialist than the other people's democracies in Eastern Europe. Within a few years, however, the CPY began to pursue a very different course of development. With the introduction of self-management in the early fifties and the establishment of a confederal system in the late sixties, Yugoslavia evolved from a highly centralized polity into a more pluralist, federal state. In the process, the Bolshevik state-building model embraced so fervently at the end of the war was left behind.

The usual interpretation of this change in state-building strategy is that it was a response, first to the break with Stalin in 1948, and finally to the economic difficulties which beset the regime in the early sixties. According to this perception of Yugoslav political development, the federalization of the party and state, spearheaded by Communists in Croatia in the mid-sixties, was a response to immediate economic problems which only gradually took on more political overtones.[1] Representing a sharp break with previous practice, not only in Yugoslavia but in other Communist countries, this federalization had its roots in the situation and character of Yugoslavia at this time.

---

1. For example, see Pedro Ramet, *Nationalism and Federalism in Yugoslavia* (Bloomington: Indiana University Press, 1984).

This interpretation of recent Yugoslav history disregards the roots of the federalist state-building strategy which appeared in Yugoslavia during the war. While it is true that support for political reform among some League of Communists of Yugoslavia (LCY) leaders was at least partially a response to pressing economic needs, the contours of this reform were not new. Proponents of the federalist strategy in the 1960s appealed to the origin of this strategy in the policies adopted by ZAVNOH in 1944. According to them, the reforms were simply a return to the "true principles" of the revolution which had been abandoned after the war. Opponents of reform countered in a similar fashion by referring to the centralizing Bolshevik strategy adopted in 1945. In advocating reform of the federal system and in opposing it, both sides could point to the contending state-building strategies pursued during the formation of the Yugoslav socialist state. The struggle over these two visions of the party-state, inherited from the Partisan period, was a defining feature of the evolution of the Yugoslav state after 1945.

Self-Management and the National Question

Five years after the break with Stalin when the new Yugoslav constitution was promulgated in 1953, Yugoslav Communists announced that they were returning to the true path of Socialist development abandoned by the Bolsheviks. This new system, which the Yugoslavs called self-management, sought to correct the "deformations" of the centralized Soviet state by devolving decision-making power to workers' councils and municipal organizations and redefining the role of the Communist Party. In contrast to the Soviet system, which had created a large and oppressive state apparatus, self-management would lead to the eventual "withering away" of the state. The Communist Party of Yugoslavia was renamed the League of Communists of Yugoslavia in order to emphasize its new function as a guiding instead of directing force.

While the introduction of self-management resulted in significant political changes in Yugoslavia, including real decentralization of political power along functional lines, it did not revise fundamentally the Bolshevik solution to the national question imposed in 1945; the most important aspects of the Yugoslav federation introduced during the war remained in place. The locus of power continued to be found in the highly centralized party apparatus, and regional party leaders were expected to carry out central party directives. Although the municipalities gained more political control, the authority of the republics continued to decline. Furthermore, the regime embraced a policy of *jugoslavenstvo*, which attempted to create a supranational Yugoslav consciousness to replace the "outmoded" national identities of Yugoslavia's various national groups.[2]

Although the introduction of self-management in the 1950's did not mean a significant revision of the federal formula adopted at the end of the war, it did leave the door open for such change. Self-management provided the theoretical underpinning for the reduction of federal power and the articulation of pluralist interests, including national interests. Moreover, it signaled a definite break from the Bolshevik approach to all aspects of social engineering, including the construction of the federal system. As discussion about the character of this system intensified in the 1960s, liberal proponents of reform used self-management to justify their demands for greater political autonomy; they argued that self-management could only be achieved by decentralizing economic and political decision-making power to the republics.

At the Eighth Congress of the LCY held in December 1964, Tito officially sanctioned a more wide reaching discussion of measures for economic and political reform, including the federal model. In his speech to the Congress, he rejected the idea held previously that it was possible to create a single Yugoslav nation. According to him, this policy of *jugoslavenstvo* was tantamount to "assimilation and bureaucratic centralism, to unitarism and hegemony."[3] A series of policy decisions adopted after the Congress transferred significant responsibility for the administration of the economy from the federal government to the republics.[4] When Tito removed secret police chief Aleksandar Ranković in 1966 for obstructing these policies, he gave the green light to liberal forces in Croatia to restructure the centralized party-state.

Why Tito decided to endorse, within certain limits, a more federalist state-building strategy is an interesting question. Centralizing, anti-reform forces were strongest in the mid-sixties and would have triumphed if they had received support from Tito. The LCY leader appears to have believed that political decentralization was necessary both to achieve meaningful economic reforms and to manage national relations. Moreover, after Ranković was removed, resistance to decentralization and reform began to be seen as an expression of Serb chauvinism, some-

---

2. For a discussion of the policy of *jugoslavenstvo* see Paul Shoup, *Communism and the Yugoslav National Question* (New York and London: Columbia University Press, 1968), Chapter 5.

3. Ante Čuvalo, *The Croatian National Movement 1966-1972* (New York: Columbia University Press, 1990), 22.

4. For example, the General Investment Fund, which channeled funds from the more developed to the less developed republics, was abolished at this time.

thing Tito and other LCY leaders were anxious to avoid. Slovene party leader and chief constitutional architect Edvard Kardelj's ardent support for reform of the federal system appears to have been instrumental in helping Tito reach his decision. In any case, the character of the federal system became the focus of intense debate between 1965 and 1971 and led to a series of reforms which fundamentally restructured the Yugoslav political system.

The most persistent aim of the reformers in the League of Communists of Croatia (LCC) regarding the federal system was to increase the autonomy of Croatia's party organizations and political institutions. Like Hebrang in 1943, these reformers sought to maximize their own decision-making authority within the party and the state. Reformers in the LCC had long maintained that excessive federal intervention in the economy was adversely affecting the well-being of the country. By the mid-1960s, they began to argue forcefully that democratic centralism was designed to meet the conditions of Tsarist Russia and was unsuitable for Yugoslavia. Insisting that there could be no federalism in the state without federalism in the party, Croat Communists urged that the reality of the Yugoslav political system be brought more in line with its norms.

As a result of this pressure from Croat political leaders, various changes were made in the LCY in 1966 and 1967.[5] First, the leading bodies of the LCY were weakened by increasing their size and requiring them to meet less frequently. In an effort to minimize Serb numerical predominance in these organs, proportional representation according to nationality was replaced by parity in all party organizations. Most significantly, it was decided that the republican party congresses would meet before the Ninth Party Congress in 1969. They would be responsible for picking members of the LCY Central Committee and drawing up their own party statutes. These changes resulted in a fundamental shift in power and authority away from the central party leadership to the republican party organizations.

Concomitant with this push for federalization within the party, the LCC attempted to redistribute power from the federal to the republican government and state bureaucracy. Like CPC Communists during the war, LCC reformers emphasized the primacy of Croatian statehood and

---

5. For a thorough discussion of these reforms see April Carter, *Democratic Reforms in Yugoslavia: the Changing Role of the Party* (Princeton: Princeton University Press, 1982); Dennison Rusinow, *The Yugoslav Experiment, 1948-1974* (Berkeley and Los Angeles: University of California Press, 1977); Stephen Burg, *Conflict and Cohesion in Socialist Yugoslavia* (Princeton: Princeton University Press, 1983).

the importance of placing Croatian political interests above the interests of the Yugoslav state as a whole. In 1967-1968, nineteen constitutional amendments were adopted which trimmed the prerogatives of the federal government. In order to restrict the authority of federal institutions, they demanded that decisions be based on consultations among republican representatives, who were bound to uphold the interests of their republics. The use of the imperative mandate became particularly prevalent in the Chamber of Nationalities in the Federal Parliament, which was upgraded in status to an equal partner with the Federal Chamber. In April 1970, the LCY Presidium adopted the principle of unanimity in decision-making in party and state organizations.

The turning point in the LCC's role in redefining the Yugoslav state came at the LCC Tenth Plenum held in January 1970. Previously, LCC leaders had concentrated on introducing reforms at the federal level. Now, they began to implement important aspects of the federalist strategy within the republic itself and to seek popular support to bolster their efforts in this direction. The Tenth Plenum signaled that discussion of national issues and grievances would no longer be prohibited or even discouraged. LCC authorities further emphasized that they would be responsive to legitimate—and henceforth national was defined as legitimate—popular interests. Previously, the LCC leadership had made a point of opposing equally the forces of nationalism and unitarism. At the Tenth Plenum, apparently with Tito's blessing, the recently appointed head of the LCC, Savka Dabčević-Kučar, led the attack against the forces of unitarism since, as she put it, behind these forces "were hidden the hegemonistic tendencies of the largest and most responsible nation."[6] Vladimir Bakarić also warned against "unitarists of the romantic *jugoslavenstvo* variety" among Croats.[7] This apparent invitation to express national sentiments unleashed a mass movement (abbreviated as *maspok* by the Communists) which demanded the fundamental revision of the Bolshevik state-building strategy imposed in 1945.

---

6. Miko Tripalo, *Hrvatsko proljeće* (Zagreb: Globus, 1989), 112. Tripalo insists that Tito approved of the harsh tone against unitarists taken by the Tenth Plenum and that he was consulted by phone concerning the new line. See also *Deseta sjednica CK SKH* (Zagreb: Vjesnik, 1970).

7. Tripalo, *Hrvatsko proljeće*, 112.

The Maspok and the New Federal Formula

The events of 1971 were a dramatic episode in Yugoslav political life. During the course of this year, a popular movement emerged in Croatia which began to talk openly about national grievances and issues that had been repressed since 1945. The series of amendments to the federal constitution adopted in the summer of 1971, and the revision of Croatia's constitution in the fall, provided the backdrop for discussion of these issues. As popular agitation for Croatian autonomy increased, the struggle among LCC leaders over the aims and control of the popular movement grew. While Tito initially appeared to support (or at least acquiesce to) the activities of the LCC liberals, he became increasingly alarmed by the implications of the *maspok* for the centralization and political authority of the LCY. When students went on strike at Zagreb University in November 1971, Tito supported LCC conservatives who demanded the removal of the LCC liberals and the suppression of the mass movement.

In advocating reform of the federal system in 1971, LCC liberals—led by LCC Central Committee Secretary Pero Pirker, member of the Presidency of the LCY Executive Bureau Miko Tripalo, and LCC Secretary Savka Dabčević-Kučar—attempted to reappropriate the federalist state-building strand the CPC had adopted during 1943-1944. During the months after the Tenth Party Plenum, these leaders began to embrace a vision for ordering the state that was similiar to the one endorsed by Hebrang during the war, and they emphasized that the roots of this vision were to be found in the Partisan struggle. Indeed, though their position was not explicitly associated with Hebrang by name, it was no coincidence that there was an effort to rehabilitate him at this time.[8] LCC liberals declared that the Croat question had not been resolved in the way that had been promised by ZAVNOH and that the federation must be reorganized to more fully realize that promise. They put forth three important ideas, all of which they linked to the Partisan legacy: first, that national (Croat) sentiments were a legitimate expression of popular interests; second, that Communists should defend these interests; and third, that the Yugoslav state must be organized so that the republic, which was the political unit in which the national principle was embodied, had the most power.

In justifying the legitimacy of national sentiments, LCC leaders pointed out that the National Liberation Struggle, as its name suggested, had been a struggle for national as well as social liberation. According to

8. For a discussion of this matter see Tripalo, *Hrvatsko proljeće,* 211.

them, this fundamental aspect of the Yugoslav revolution had been negated in the period of centralism after the war; LCC reformers were attempting to return it to its rightful place in Yugoslav theory and practice. "Self-management reforms," Tripalo wrote, "also mean a reaffirmation of some principles concerning national relations which were established during the National Liberation Struggle and which were called into question during the period of administrative Socialism."[9] LCC leaders were particularly vociferous in their claims that the organization of the federation had hurt Croat economic interests and in demanding that Croatia acquire greater control over the dispensation of its revenues.

LCC liberals further emphasized their essential role in defending the particular national interests of the Croat population. Since 1945, official rhetoric had stressed the CPY's role in creating "brotherhood and unity" among the nations of Yugoslavia, especially among Serbs and Croats; its role in realizing the more particular national aspirations of these nations were seldom mentioned. LCC liberals returned, however, to the Croat national themes emphasized by the CPC during 1943-1944. In a statement echoing party pronouncements almost thirty years earlier, Tripalo argued that Communists had been the true defenders of the Croat nation because the NDH had abandoned Dalmatia, Istria and Medjumurje while the Communists had won the unity of Croatian lands.

In addition to their aggressive defense of Croatian economic interests, party leaders responded sympathetically to complaints by Matica Hrvatska—a cultural organization founded in the nineteenth century—that Croatian language, culture and history had been ignored or denigrated during the past two decades.[10] LCC leaders were also sympathetic to Matica charges that Serbs had assumed an unfairly predominant role in Croatian political life. As a result of their active participation especially in the crucial early stages of the Partisan struggle in Croatia, Serbs had retained a disproportionate influence—by virtue of their relatively higher numbers—in the Communist Party of Croatia and in the police and security apparatus.[11] CPC leaders had struggled with a similiar problem in 1943-1944, when they had attempted to reduce the visibility of Serbs in the Partisan forces and ZAVNOH in order to attract more Croats to the movement. At the beginning of 1971, LCC Secretary

---

9. Miko Tripalo, "Aktuelni politički trenutak i reorganizacija federacije," *Reorganizacija federacije i razvoj političkog sistema* (Zagreb: 1971), 26.

10. Tripalo, *Hrvatsko proljeće*, 153.

11. In June 1971, Tripalo complained to Tito that while Croats comprised 80% of the population, they represented only 60% of the LCC membership. Tripalo, *Hrvatsko proljeće*, 153.

Savka Dabčević-Kučar emphasized that this "sensitive" problem must be addressed "openly, publicly and ethically," and she called for "adequate proportional representation" in all social and political organizations.[12] Tripalo also expressed his concern about this problem on a number of occasions to Tito, who warned him to be "very cautious and patient [in his approach] because it involve[d] a very sensitive question."[13]

In defending the national interests of the populace, LCC leaders cast themselves as leaders of a mass movement like the one which had emerged during the Second World War.[14] Tito appeared to concur with this anaysis when he remarked on a trip to Croatia in the fall of 1971 that the enthusiasm he encountered among the populace there reminded him of the National Liberation Struggle.[15] LCC reformers further defended their willingness to permit the activities of Matica Hrvatska by the Communist Party's similar tolerance of widespread political activity during the war. And, they perceived themselves to be in an excellent position to control these forces since Matica Hrvatska did not appear to have the political power the Croat Peasant Party had once possessed. Hebrang had keenly appreciated the threat the Peasant Party had posed to the Communists' political position. Consequently, while wooing its members, he sought to discredit CPP leaders and to undermine the Peasant Party's organizational strength. Believing they had less to fear from Matica Hrvatska, LCC leaders took a less cautious approach. This strategy was clearly miscalculated, however, as Matica Hrvatska increasingly resembled a political party and used its popularity to pressure Communist authorities.

Since national interests, as defined by the LCC, were considered to be legitimate and the LCC their representative in the political arena, it followed that the republic should be the locus of decision-making power. LCC leaders argued that the LCY should return to the principle of self-determination embraced during the Second World War, which clearly meant the right to form national states. As the decisions of the third meeting of ZAVNOH had made clear, this right to statehood in the Yugoslav context meant states based on the republics. Tripalo emphasized in a seminar on the reorganization of the federation that republics must be regarded as "the purveyors of statehood, not as the repository of etatism" (one of the several "deformations" the self-management reforms

---

12. *Ibid.*, 165.

13. *Ibid.*, 154.

14. For example see Miko Tripalo, "Ovaj naš pokret izravno je nasljednik i nastavak masovnog pokreta iz NOB i socialističke revolucije," *Vjesnik*, 8/26/71.

15. Rusinow, *The Yugoslav Experiment*, 301.

were aimed at eradicating); unfounded fears of the disintegration of Yugoslavia should not prevent republics from assuming their correct position in the Yugoslav federation.[16] Although they embraced the notion of the withering away of the state in principle, LCC reformers believed this process of withering away should apply only to the central organs of the government and the party.

While the liberal faction of the LCC emphasized the importance of returning to the "correct" approach to national relations embraced during the war, hardliners in the leadership opposed this understanding of the Partisan legacy.[17] They challenged the liberals' attempt to return to the federalist strategy adopted by ZAVNOH and their renewed emphasis on Croatian autonomy. Interestingly, they received increasing support from the powerful Vladimir Bakarić, who had also opposed Hebrang's attempts to federalize the party in 1944. Charging that the decisions taken by ZAVNOH had a nationalist character, Bakarić disputed the focus on Croat sovereignty championed by the LCC reformers.[18] Bakarić asserted, not entirely consistently, that Communists in Croatia had not been concerned with national issues at the end of the war, and that they too were responsible for the imposition of a centralized state order.[19] LCC hardliners further objected that Matica Hrvatska had pressured the liberals into adopting positions on the national question that were not in line with central party directives. This question of LCC control over the popular forces led by Matica Hrvatska became the most serious point of contention between the liberal and hardline factions in the LCC.[20]

By 1970, Matica Hrvatska began to play a more active political role. At its annual assembly in November 1970, Matica Hrvatska launched a new membership drive and adopted a program which addressed various political and economic questions; its attention to these matters gave it an instantaneous and enthusiastic following. During the next year, its membership increased twentyfold, from 2,323 members in November 1970 to

---

16. Tripalo, "Aktuelni politički trenutak i reorganizacija federacije," 28.

17. The hardline faction of the LCC consisted roughly of the following leaders: Vladimir Bakarić, Milka Planinc, Josip Vrhovec, Milutin Baltić, Ema Derossi, Dušan Dragosavac, Jure Bilić and Jakov Blažević. In addition to Pirker, Dabčević-Kučar, and Tripalo, the liberals consisted of Ivan Sibl, Dragutin Haramija, Srećko Bijelić, Marko Koprtla and Ivica Vrkić.

18. Tripalo, *Hrvatsko proljeće*, 211.

19. *Hrvatski tjednik*, #21, 9/10/71, 1.

20. Tripalo, *Hrvatsko proljeće*, 165.

41,000 members in November 1971.[21] In response to the discussion of the Croat question opened by the Tenth Plenum, Matica publications began to tackle themes on Croatian history, culture and political life that had previously been taboo. [22] They addressed at length the ways in which Croatia was suffering from its current position in the Yugoslav federation: its punitively high payment of revenue to the central government, the unusually high rate of emigration from Croatia compared to other republics, the "denigration" of the Croatian language, and the lack of instruction about Croatian history in schools and universities. In a new publication launched in April 1971, *Hrvatski tjednik*, Matica Hrvatska became the widely accepted voice for the Croat national movement and a strong advocate of redressing Croat grievances.

In a series of articles about the proposed reform of Croatia's constitution in the fall of 1971, Matica Hrvatska presented its positions concerning the organization of the Yugoslav state and Croatia's position in it. For Matica Hrvatska, as for the LCC liberal leadership, Croatian cultural and political development could be addressed only within this wider framework. Matica Hrvatska strongly embraced the idea endorsed by LCC liberals that the reorganization of the federation meant a return to the original, guiding principles of the revolution. "The fact is that the reconstruction of the federation," *Hrvatski tjednik* wrote in September 1971, "is really the renewal of those ideals which were established and realized in the course of the National Liberation Struggle and the Socialist revolution."[23] Matica Hrvatska stressed that attaining Croat sovereignty was the fundamental principle of the Partisan struggle and that it remained the most important goal to be achieved in 1971. As Marko Veselica, a frequent contributor to *Hrvatski tjednik*, wrote in his article titled "From *Jugoslavenstvo* to a Modern Understanding": "The Croat nation, like the other nations of Yugoslavia, in the National Liberation Struggle for the new Yugoslavia, wanted to completely realize its national essence and to be completely sovereign within the framework of a federal Yugoslavia, not losing one part of its sovereignty and not recognizing any kind of advocate from outside in view of interpreting what is and what is not in its justifiable national interest.[24] Sovereignty meant a Croat Communist leadership not susceptible to interfering central authorities.

---

21. *Izvještaj o stanju u Savezu komunista Hrvatske,* 83-84, as cited in Ramet, *Nationalism and Federalism in Yugoslavia,* 128.

22. For a summary of these publications see Ivan Perić, *Suvremeni hrvatski nacionalizam* (Zagreb: August Cesarec, 1976).

23. *Hrvatski tjednik,* #21, 9/10/71, 1.

24. *Hrvatski tjednik,* #17, 8/3/71, 7.

Hrvatski tjednik argued that the decisions taken by ZAVNOH and its method of operation provided the legitimation of and the model for the independent functioning of Croatian political institutions. In an article by Franjo Tudjman celebrating the anniversary of the 1941 Partisan uprising in Croatia, *Hrvatski tjednik* featured an article glorifying the achievements of ZAVNOH, accompanied by a large picture of Andrija Hebrang (though Hebrang was still treated as a traitor and a spy by official party history).[25] On the front page of the next issue, Vladimir Bakarić and another old Partisan, Jakov Blažević, were charged with working against the decisions of the third session of ZAVNOH, which had proclaimed "the unification of all Croatian lands and the renewal of Croatian statehood."[26] The fact that this issue of *Hrvatski tjednik* was banned reflected the sensitivity not only of criticizing top party leaders like Bakarić and Blažević but of using their ostensible betrayal of the revolution to do it.[27]

In their attempt to base the current reorganization of the federation on the principles championed during the Communist revolution, contributors to *Hrvatski tjednik* also insisted that the historical record concerning ZAVNOH and the activities of the Communist Party of Croatia be set straight. As part of his series of articles on Croatian historical themes and personalities, Franjo Tudjman emphasized the importance of Croatia's contribution to the Partisan movement. His purpose was to refute what many Croats felt was the erroneous assumption (or accusation) that Croatia had been primarily passive or under the sway of fascist forces during the war.[28] As one author protested in an article on constitutional reform : "We Croats don't have a 'guilt complex,' we participated massively in the National Liberation Struggle [in which] we were the purveyors of a traditional Croat idealism."[29] Furthermore, these authors argued that there was a tendency toward a more democratic, pluralistic understanding of communism in Croatia than elsewhere in Yugoslavia; a tendency that was evident in the "attempt to radicalize the revolution in Croatia in 1971."[30]

This effort to highlight the pluralism present in Croatia under ZAVNOH and even to depict Hebrang as a kind of democrat was not, in fact, an accurate portrayal of the historical record. As this work has

---

25. *Hrvatski tjednik,* #15, 7/23/71, 13.

26. *Hrvatski tjednik,* #20, 8/30/71, 1.

27. For an explanation of the reasons why the issue was banned, see *Hrvatski tjednik,* #19, 8/27/72, 4-7.

28. See article by Tudjman in *Hrvatski tjednik,* #15, 7/23/71, 12-14.

29. *Hrvatski tjednik,* #31, 11/19/71, 2.

30. *Hrvatski tjednik,* #23, 9/24/71, 1.

demonstrated, Hebrang and the CPC never endorsed a coalitional arrangement with the Croat Peasant Party. Although the CPP Executive Committee founded by Hebrang in 1943 was invited to join ZAVNOH, Hebrang always sought to maintain firm control over the peasant organization and its leader. References to ZAVNOH by *Hrvatski tjednik*, however, emphasized its democratic character. In addition to placing Croat Communism in the most positive light by associating it with a more western, pluralist tradition, Matica Hrvatska was attempting to legitimize a more prominent political role for non-Communist political organizations. In October 1971, *Hrvatski tjednik* called for the formation of a National Congress of Social Forces in Croatia which would make decisions on all crucial political matters. In an obvious attempt to reduce the power of the LCC and its control over the Sabor, Matica Hrvatska called for the inclusion of the Sabor, the LCC, the Socialist Alliance, economic firms, cultural organizations, university organizations and municipal organizations in this Congress.[31]

While Matica Hrvatska advocated a return to the "true principles" of the revolution adopted by ZAVNOH, its attitude toward the revolution and the legacy of ZAVNOH was not entirely positive. Matica Hrvatska viewed ZAVNOH as providing a basis for modern Croatian statehood. It emphasized, however, that the National Liberation Struggle was not the defining moment in Croatian history. Rather, it was simply a continuation of the legal tradition of the Croatian state on a new, class basis. In a traditional state right argument, *Hrvatski tjednik* insisted that "the National Liberation Struggle signified the complete renewal and continuation—on a new basis—of the centuries-old Croatian legal continuity."[32] Matica further argued that certain positions adopted by ZAVNOH had given "an imprecise understanding and...inadequate feeling for Croat sovereignty."[33] These positions, which had negative consequences for Croatian statehood, must be overcome in the new constitution.

As part of its efforts to diminish Communist focus on the revolution as the legitimizing factor of Croatian statehood (even as it sought to legitimize its own goals by appealing to the revolution), in its first draft of the proposed constitutional amendments, Matica Hrvatska mentioned the National Liberation Struggle in article six instead of article one of the first amendment. It stated that in carrying out their right of self-determination in the National Liberation Struggle, the Croat people had "founded their state as a continuation of the centuries-long legal tradition

---

31. *Hrvatski tjednik*, #24, 10/1/71, 3.
32. *Hrvatski tjednik*, #21, 9/10/71, 2.
33. *Ibid.*, 1.

of the Croatian state."[34] As a result of strong negative reaction by Communist Party authorities to this dimunition of the role of the Partisan struggle, mention of the revolution was moved back up to article one of the first amendment in the final draft of the constitutional amendments published by Matica Hrvatska in November.[35] Nevertheless, Matica Hrvatska continued to emphasize that during the Second World War the Croat nation had simply been "guarding and perpetuating the historical continuity of the Croat state" and pursuing its "desire for complete national sovereignty."[36]

In discussing the attributes of Croatian statehood in the new Croatian constitution, Matica Hrvatska stressed the importance of two essential and interrelated aspects of sovereignty, both of which, it maintained, derived their legitimacy from the legacy of the Partisan movement; the first was the indivisible nature of sovereignty—that it must reside in the Croat nation and only in the Croat nation; the second was the unity of Croatian lands—that sovereignty must extend to all parts of Croatia. Matica's emphasis on these two aspects of sovereignty was troublesome because it raised questions about relations with Serbs in Croatia. CPC leaders had struggled with a similar problem in 1943-1944, as their emphasis on Croat concerns and autonomy had raised questions in the minds of Serbs about their status in Croatia and their protection as a minority group. This problem was resolved by the imposition of a highly centralized state in which the borders of the republics had signified very little. Since borders were not meaningful, Serbs did not need to fear the prospect of being separated politically or culturally from their brethren in Serbia. When LCC liberals and Matica Hrvatska began to champion a more far reaching sovereignty for Croatia, however, and to insist that this sovereignty was based solely upon the Croat nation, Serb apprehensions about their status in Croatia were raised again.

In the summer of 1971, the LCC put forth its proposed amendments to the Croatian constitution. In these proposals, Croatia was declared to be the "sovereign national state of the Croat nation, the state of the Serb nation in Croatia, and the nationalities that live in it."[37] Matica Hrvatska emphatically rejected this formulation, insisting that meaningful sovereignty could only reside in one nation. According to Matica Hrvatska, the indivisibility of sovereignty was the key to establishing Croat control over their historical lands. Consequently, in its own pro-

---

34. *Hrvatski tjednik*, #23, 9/24/71, 1.
35. *Hrvatski tjednik*, #29, 11/5/71, 12.
36. *Ibid.*
37. *Hrvatski tjednik*, #21, 9/10/71, 2.

posed amendments to the constitution, Matica Hrvatska stated simply that the Socialist Republic of Croatia was the sovereign state of the Croat nation. As the September issue of *Hrvatski tjednik* wrote: "We stand firmly on the position that the Socialist republic of Croatia is a unified, national state of the Croat nation and that Croatian sovereignty is one, indivisible, and inalienable."[38] Attempting to assuage Serb fears about this understanding of sovereignty, Matica Hrvatska emphasized that "only the most die-hard reactionary" could doubt that Serbs and other nationalities would be completely equal to Croats under the new constitution.[39]

At the end of October, Matica Hrvatska completed the final draft of its proposed constitutional amendments and presented them to the Sabor for discussion. In presenting these proposals, Matica Hrvatska maintained that they were based on the principles that had been fought for during the Socialist revolution. The concept of Croatian sovereignty presented in the amendments was far reaching and represented a fundamental change in the distribution of power in the Yugoslav federation. Croatia would have a separate monetary policy and complete control over its tax revenues. Croatian would be the sole official language. Perhaps the most striking aspect of this proposed constitution was its call for the formation of an independent defense force in Croatia. Matica Hrvatska argued that the Partisan struggle had endorsed the concept of separate national defense forces by having Partisans fight in their own republics and speak their own languages.[40] Consequently, under the new constitution proposed by Matica Hrvatska, Croat troops would speak Croatian and serve only in Croatia except during exceptional times; it elaborated the rules for joint command when these troops served elsewhere in the country. The constitution further stipulated that Croat representatives would advise the national defense council of the Socialist Federal Republic of Yugoslavia.[41]

Matica Hrvatska's focus on Croatian sovereignty, as part of a wider emphasis on Croat national concerns, soon aroused fear and dissatisfaction among Croatia's Serb population. The mouthpiece for these fears, and the counterpart to Matica Hrvatska, was the Serb cultural organization Prosvjeta, which had been formed by Vladimir Bakarić in 1944. Like Matica Hrvatska, Prosvjeta became increasingly politicized during 1971 as it began to champion more specifically political interests. At a meeting in March 1971, the Main Committee of Prosvjeta adopted several deci-

---

38. *Hrvatski tjednik*, #21, 9/10/71, 3.
39. *Ibid.*
40. *Ibid.*, 13.
41. *Hrvatski tjednik*, #29, 11/5/71, 12.

sions aimed at revamping the organization and changing what many members felt was a rather desultory mode of operation.[42] Most importantly, it declared that since the Tenth Plenum had opened up a discussion of national feelings, "and with this had come a growth in unclarity and uncertainty about the position of Serbs in Croatia," Prosvjeta must direct itself foremost to a discussion of this matter.

Prosvjeta complained that in the previous months the status of Serbs in Croatia had been called into question in a number of ways and that "certain actions had created unease among the Serb community."[43] Charging that the recent emphasis on Croat culture had threatened Serb cultural rights, Prosvjeta called for the convocation of an Extraordinary Congress at the end of the year which would discuss the protection of Serb culture.[44] Prosvjeta particularly objected to the proposed educational plan for elementary and middle school which was aimed at the "Croatinization" of instruction. The plan to require that 75% of instruction in history and literature treat Croat topics denied the fact that Serbs in Croatia had a separate language and history. Moreover, Prosvjeta complained that Serbs were never even consulted about this plan.[45] The Serb organization concluded from these actions that Croats intended to exert pressure on Serbs in Croatia to assimilate, which was a violation of their most fundamental political and human rights.[46]

Prosvjeta further objected to Matica's attempt to reinterpret the legacy of the Partisan struggle as it had been understood for the past two decades. This dissatisfaction with Croats' approach to the revolution was particularly evident in veterans' organizations, many of which were dominated by Serbs. Veterans objected to Croat attempts to deemphasize the theme of "brotherhood and unity" from the war, and even to question the enormous sacrifices Serbs had made for the Partisan cause. During the 1971 celebrations for the anniversary of the uprising in Croatia, there was evidence of unhappiness among Serbs, especially in the Lika region, and there were confrontations between Serb veterans and Croat youths.[47]

In the months after its March meeting, Prosvjeta began to articulate its positions concerning Serb cultural and political rights in Croatia. Prosvjeta reiterated that the national question had been resolved by the National Liberation Struggle, although the changing circumstances of

---

42. *Prosvjeta*, 4/71, 2.
43. *Ibid.*
44. *Prosvjeta*, #608-609, 7/10/71, 1.
45. *Prosvjeta*, #610, 9/71, 1.
46. *Ibid.*, 16.
47. Tripalo, *Hrvatsko proljeće*, 159.

recent months required a renewed examination of its tenets. Rejecting the attempt by Matica Hrvatska to emphasize the federalist state-building strand of ZAVNOH, Prosvjeta leader Milan Žalić insisted that while articulation of the separate national aims of Yugoslavia's national groups during the war may have been necessary at that earlier state of develop-ment, it was no longer necessary as the nations of Yugoslavia moved from a "provincial to a more national [Yugoslav] consciousness."

Prosvjeta also emphatically rejected the notion that sovereignty should reside only in the Croat nation in Croatia. Praising several state-ments by LCC hardliner Dušan Dragosavac which also rejected this notion of sovereignty, Prosvjeta denounced the one nation-one state message espoused by Matica Hrvatska. It warned that this position would lead to the dangerous conclusion that Serbs in Croatia could only realize their statehood in Serbia.[48] Prosvjeta explained that Serbs in Croatia must be extended not only the right to equality, but the right to preserve their national identity.[49] In order to do this, they must be certain that republic borders would not stand between them and Serbs in Serbia. "Since the unity of the Serb nation and its culture without regard to federal borders is indisputable," *Prosvjeta* wrote, Serbs in Croatia must look to Serbia to help them in their task of national preservation.[50]

Prosvjeta also argued that it was necessary for Serbs in Croatia to have greater political representation in Croatia, and at its March meeting hinted that it might play this more formal political role. The July issue of Prosvjeta called for the "formation of a Sabor committee which would follow and consider questions related...to the equality of nations and nationalities...."[51] This issue was initially banned on the grounds that Prosvjeta was attempting to obstruct Croat national aims and, by draw-ing on its wartime role, to operate autonomously of the LCC. [52] Although the issue was eventually permitted to circulate, its initial banning did little to assuage Serb fears about their position in Croatia, and Prosvjeta's demands began to escalate. Shortly thereafter, a functionary of Prosvjeta, Rade Bulat, called for the establishment of an autonomous region of Serbs in Croatia.[53] Calls were also heard from Dalmatia for granting greater autonomy to this area.

---

48. *Prosvjeta*, 4/71, 3.

49. *Prosvjeta*, #610, 9/71, 16.

50. *Prosvjeta*, 4/71, 16.

51. *Prosvjeta*, #608-609, 6/71, 2.

52. For the documents relating to the banning of this issue see *Prosvjeta* #610, 9/71, 6-7.

53. Tripalo, *Hrvatsko proljeće*, 168.

LCC leaders and Matica Hrvatska responded vehemently to demands for the establishment of an autonomous region of Serbs. An LCC meeting was convened with the purpose of expelling Bulat from the party, although Tripalo intervened to prevent this move.[54] Nevertheless, Tripalo himself firmly rejected Serb autonomy as did other LCC leaders from both factions. Matica Hrvatska insisted that any call for the federalization of Croatia was aimed directly against the positions adopted by the CPY during the war. As the September issue of *Hrvatski tjednik* wrote: "the constitutional concept of Croatia as a federation of nations... negates the Croatian revolution, Croatian history, and the Croatian right to self-determination."[55] The main aim of the LCC reformers, and to an even greater extent of Matica Hrvatska, was to achieve a greater degree of political autonomy for Croatia. LCC leaders wanted a more federal state, but under no circumstances did they accept a federal Croatia. While democratic centralism was not appropriate for relations between the central party organs and republic party organizations, it was to be strictly adhered to in intrarepublic party relations. And, reformers could point to the legacy of ZAVNOH and the Partisan struggle in Croatia to give weight to this position. The last few years, *Hrvatski tjednik* wrote, had "liquidated the historical speculation of autonomists and returned to Croatia the basis for resolving this question established by the revolution."[56]

The unity of Croatian lands as a precondition to achieving full Croatian sovereignty was, as we have seen, an historic theme of the Croat national movement. The division of what Croats referred to as the historic Croatian lands, and the large numbers of Serbs residing within these historic borders, had made the unity of Croatia a sensitive issue. The Communist Party of Croatia had emphasized these themes during the Second World War, proclaiming its role in reuniting Dalmatia and Istria to the Croatian state. But just as the CPC had struggled with "autonomists" and "unitarists" in Dalmatia, the increased emphasis on Croatian sovereignty in 1971 resulted in a push by Serbs for greater autonomy for this area. To be sure, the factional struggles within the party during the wartime period over the question of Dalmatian autonomy did not reappear. Nevertheless, LCC leaders perceived Dalmatian autonomism as a potentially serious threat. As *Hrvatski tjednik* described, attempting to split off Dalmatia, "the historical cradle of the Croatian state," was simply the first phase of a "master plan" to seek the autonomy

---

54. *Ibid.*

55. *Hrvatski tjednik*, #21, 9/10/71.

56. *Hrvatski tjednik*, 5/7/71, 7.

of Lika, Bania, Kordun, Istria and Slavonia.[57] Consequently, autonomism of any sort was a prospect that LCC leaders and Matica Hrvatska were not prepared to tolerate, and they made it clear they believed the Partisan struggle had clearly resolved this question in favor of the unity of Croatian lands.

Matica's emphasis on the unity of Croatian lands and Croatian sovereignty also began to raise questions about Croatia's borders and the status of Croats living in other republics. As during the Second World War, emphasis on Croat national aims raised old questions about the shape of the Croatian political unit. In 1945, borders between Croatia and Serbia's Vojvodina had been determined by a commission headed by the Montenegrin Communist Milovan Djilas.[58] Since that time, Tito had made it abundantly clear that this issue was not to be further negotiated. The discussion of previously taboo themes in 1971, however, inevitably led to talk about this sensitive question. Concern about the well-being of Croats in Bosnia-Hercegovina and Vojvodina was raised most insistently by Matica Hrvatska. Claiming that Croats in Bosnia were repressed by Serbs, especially under Ranković, and denied their rights in other republics, Matica Hrvatska made aggressive attempts to establish its organizations outside of Croatia. Before long, Matica members began to call for changes in the borders between Croatia and Bosnia-Hercegovina.[59] These claims to their territory were vigorously rejected by Communist leaders in Bosnia-Hercegovina who denied the existence of any serious discrimination against Croats.

While LCC liberals never formally raised the question of revising the wartime borders, they were not entirely unsympathetic to Matica Hrvatska claims. Tripalo relates an incident in mid-October 1971, when he was confronted by the former head of the Communist Party of Bosnia-Hercegovina. Djuro Pucar demanded to know why the LCC had failed to denounce Matica Hrvatska members such as the President of the Croatian society of novelists, Petar Šegedin, who were making claims on Bosnian territory. Tripalo replied that it "would take awhile" to correct some of the "injustices" in borders delineated after the war. And, he reminded Pucar that the Bosnian leader himself had offered to exchange Cazinska Krajina for Dubrovnik after the war.[60] Such remarks about the need for revising the current republic borders could only have increased the hostility of Croatia's neighbors to the escalating rhetoric of the mass

---

57. *Ibid.*
58. See chapter five, 227-231.
59. Tripalo, *Hrvatsko proljeće*, 163
60. *Ibid.*

movement. Indeed, Communist leaders in Bosnia-Hercegovina, who feared such claims on their territory, appear to have been instrumental in having the LCC liberals removed.

The growing clash between Serbs and Croats over the wartime settlement of the Croat question was averted by Tito's intervention in the situation in Croatia. During the summer and fall of 1971, Tito and several other LCY leaders had become increasingly concerned about the effect of the LCC's strategy on Serbs in Croatia. In July, Tito had issued a stern warning to LCC leaders that their toleration of Matica Hrvatska's nationalist activities was having a negative effect on the Serb population. "Do you want to see 1941 all over again?" he asked, warning of the possibility of civil strife.[61] Kardelj also warned LCC reformers in November that the way in which they had carried out the "mostly correct" reform policies had resulted in the awakening of a Great Serbian reaction.[62] Communist leaders in Bosnia-Hercegovina were also worried about the effect the LCC's policies might have on relations between Serbs and Croats in their multinational republic.

In his notorious Karadjordjevo speech on December 1, 1971, when Tito declared his intention to put a halt to the *maspok* in Croatia, he also made it clear that he rejected the LCC's and Matica Hrvatska's attempt to draw on the federalist strand of the revolution. Emphasizing that the political activity that had led up to the student strike was "counterrevolutionary," he emphatically rejected all further attempts by reformers to legitimize their activities by appealing to the National Liberation Struggle. Although he had initiated some of the reforms, Tito had become convinced that the attempt to revise the Bolshevik strategy had gone too far and must be stopped.[63] Tito believed the LCC had made two critical mistakes. First, it had lost control of popular political forces such as Matica Hrvatska and had been forced to go along with some of Matica's unacceptable nationalist positions. Second, and most importantly, the LCC had forgotten the dictates of democratic centralism and had begun to act as if it were responsible to no higher authority than itself. In a statement remarkably similar to one he had made to CPC leader Andrija Hebrang decades earlier, Tito adamantly denounced the Croat position that "no one, not even the Presidency of the LCY" had the right to inter-

---

61. *Ibid*, 155. See also *Izvještaj o stanju SKH*, 83-84, as cited in Ramet, *Nationalism and Federalism in Yugoslavia*, 129.

62. Tripalo, *Hrvatsko proljeće*, 169.

63. *Ibid*, 190. Tripalo says this was typical of the patterns of decision-making Tito had exhibited in previous years of introducing reforms at the urging of other Communist leaders and then balking at their possible ramifications.

fere in the affairs of the republican parties. Tito insisted that the LCY was the one organization that did had the right to intervene anywhere in Yugoslavia and that the organization of the federation must continue to be based on this principle.[64]

While Tito rejected the LCC's attempt to introduce the federalist state-building strand pursued during the war, he did not return to the Bolshevik strategy imposed in 1945. Despite his insistence upon adherence to the principles of democratic centralism, there was no major reversal of the decentralization within the LCY that had been set in motion in the previous decade. The most important institutional changes resulting in the federalization of the party were left intact; republican congresses continued to be held before the LCY congress and authority for appointment to central party organs remained in the hands of republican party leaders. At the same time, however, in an attempt to ensure the unity of the Communist Party and, therefore, the centralization of the state, Tito removed the genuinely popular Communist leaders in Croatia and Serbia after 1971 and appointed leaders who were loyal to him.

This compromise between the federalist and Bolshevik strategies appears to have offered the worst of both worlds. Croats and Serbs were unhappy because they had leaders who were unresponsive to their most fundamental political aspirations. At the same time, these republic party leaders began to use the extensive decision-making powers they had acquired by the reforms to pursue particularist interests, especially relating to the economy. This pattern of decision-making soon paralyzed the political system. Perhaps the most far reaching consequence of the events of 1971, however, was that they discredited any further attempt to resolve the Croat question, or the larger national question in Yugoslavia, within the framework of one party federalism established by the Partisan struggle.

De-Titoization and the Attack on the Partisan Resolution of the Croat Question

In the years after Tito's death in 1980, it soon became apparent that his attempts to manage and contain nationalist pressures within the framework of a one party state could only succeed as long as he lived. With Tito present, it was possible, though fraught with conflict and difficulty, to introduce more truly federal institutions while maintaining traditional party centralism. Once he was removed from the scene as enforcer of

---

64. *Journal of International Affairs* 1 (1972).

party discipline and ultimate arbiter of national conflicts, the institutional decentralization of the early 1970s permitted the release of strong centrifugal forces, and the system began to unravel.

None of this was readily apparent in the first few years after Tito's departure from the political scene, when the complicated mechanisms of collective leadership ensured the constant rotation of mostly conservative party leaders. Most of these men remained loyal to Tito's views, and the paralysis produced by the process of consensual decision-making ensured the temporary maintenance of the status quo. The elements of the federalist strategy adopted by Tito had their foes, however, especially among Serbs, who objected to the emasculation of the central party and governmental apparatus. Most importantly, Serbs opposed their loss of control over the two autonomous provinces in Serbia—Vojvodina and Kosovo—which had been granted virtual parity with the republics by the 1974 constitution. The outbreak of violence among the Albanian population (which now constituted approximately 90% of the population of the autonomous province) in Kosovo in 1981, and the mass exodus of Serbs and Montenegrins from this area, was the catalyst which prompted Serbs to attack the 1974 constitution and ultimately the entire foundation of the Yugoslav state. This attack had important ramifications for the question of Croatian statehood.

The resolution of the Croat question, and what was now called the Serb question, had always been inextricably linked; any attempt to achieve the national aims of one group necessarily involved the other because of their intermeshed population and often mutually exclusive national goals. Moreover, relations between these two groups was the pivotal factor of Yugoslav political life. Serbs and Croats residing in Serbia, Croatia, and Bosnia-Hercegovina constituted over half the population of Yugoslavia and inhabited almost two thirds of its territory. Hence, the emergence of the Serb question in the 1980s—for now it was Serbs who protested that they were oppressed and who sought to change the state arrangement—intimately involved the question of Croatia's status in the Yugoslav state.

For Serb intellectuals who first began to write and speak about the oppression of Serbs, the most obvious source of their grievances was the way in which the national question had been resolved during the Second World War. Consequently, they began to attack the CPY's role in the Partisan movement and especially its position on the national question. Several books and articles published in 1984 with the purported aim of "demystifying" the revolution reexamined the activities of non-Communist political and military forces during the war and the

Communists' treatment of them.[65] Before long, the activities of Tito himself and other illustrious Partisan leaders became the subject of critical inquiry. This process of de-Titoization, as it was quickly labeled by the Yugoslav press, soon called into question the entirety of Tito's and the Partisans' legacy.

Serbs complained foremost that the settlement of the national question in the wartime period had resulted in a "parcelization" of Serbia. Many Serbs felt that Tito had wanted to weaken Serbia in the new Yugoslav federation. Consequently, he had forced the reduction of Serbia to its pre-1912 borders.[66] The Partisans had further imposed the establishment of two autonomous provinces within these borders, while they rejected a similar arrangement in Croatia.[67] Moreover, the CPY had formed two new republics—Bosnia-Hercegovina, which had a large Serb population, and Montenegro, most of whose inhabitants considered themselves Serbs. The result of this arrangement was that Serbia was reduced in size and strength and that forty percent of its population was living in its autonomous provinces or outside its borders. And, Serbs claimed that in many of these republics Serbs were subject to harsh treatment and discrimination. For example, the Serb writer Vuk Drašković, charged that Croats were carrying out a policy of cultural genocide against Serbs in Croatia and that the equality for which Serbs had fought in the Partisan struggle had been robbed from them.[68]

The "parcelization" of Serbia may have been tolerable when a highly centralized state order was in effect and republic borders were virtually meaningless. But with the decentralization of political power to the republics after Tito's death, this arrangement became unacceptable. Consequently, many Serbs began to call for the reform or eradication of the 1974 constitution and a tightening of the federal system. When the Twelfth Party Congress in 1982 adopted a program of stabilization that did not endorse major change of the 1974 constitution, Serbs began to argue that stabilization could never succeed in the decentralized system that prevailed. Pressure to reform the 1974 constitution caused the LCY leadership to launch a discussion of the next party platform in 1984, a full year and a half before the Thirteenth Party Congress. This discussion did not resolve the impasse between those forces in Croatia and Slovenia

---

65. For example, see Veselin Djuretić, *Saveznici i jugoslovenska ratna drama* (Belgrade: 1985).

66. Kosta Čavoški, *Iz istorije stvaranja nove Jugoslavije* (London: 1987).

67. *Ibid.*

68. Alex N. Dragnich, "The Rise and Fall of Yugoslavia: The Omen of the Upsurge of Serbian Nationalism," *East European Quarterly* 23 2 (1989): 193.

who opposed major revision of the constitution and those Serbs who were pushing for recentralization. It did, however, provide the opportunity for an increasingly rancorous attack on the LCY and on fundamental aspects of the Yugoslav federal system.

If many Croats were opposed to attempts to recentralize the federal system, they were also wary of the process of de-Titoization launched by the Serbs. Croatia's internal political life was still greatly influenced by the aftermath of 1971, since most of the political leaders who had been placed in power by Tito retained their positions. The more moderate forces in the leadership, represented by LCC Secretary Mika Špiljak, came increasingly under fire from a group of hardliners gathered around a rising young politician, Stipe Šuvar. In the retrenched and conservative atmosphere that prevailed in Croatia, Šuvar attracted a group of mainly youthful supporters, who called for the recentralization and purification of the LCY. They also denounced vehemently what they claimed were the growing forces of nationalism in Croatia.[69] Nevertheless, while these two groups in Croatia may have disagreed on the need to centralize the party-state, they were both agreed on the dangers of de-Titoization.

Croat intellectuals and politicians were fully aware of the implications of the attacks on the Partisan legacy, both for Croatia's position in the federation and the status of Serbs residing in its territory. Consequently, they took a much more cautious approach to reexamining this question. Many Croats feared that this critical examination of the war was simply a veiled attack on Croats by trying to hold them all responsible for Ustasha massacres.[70] On the fifth anniversary of Tito's death, a professor of political science with close ties to the moderate political leadership wrote an article in the Zagreb weekly *Danas* in which he answered the charges made by Tito's critics.[71] Dušan Bilandžić insisted that those who asserted that "the CPY had deceived people in order to come to power" and that those who accused Tito of making a huge blunder with the promulgation of the 1974 constitution simply did not understand the Partisan or Tito's legacy. LCC documents in 1985 warned that the "united opposition" was calling for the "demystification of the revolution and recent history simply in order to demonstrate that self-management [had] outlived its usefulness."[72] By demanding de-Titoization and de-Kardeljization, the documents charged, the opposition was calling into question "the entire

---

69. The mouthpiece for these views was the Zagreb weekly *Polet*.

70. For example, see the article by religious affairs correspondent Nenad Ivanković, *Danas*, 4/9/85, 26-27.

71. *Danas*, 4/30/85, 4-11.

72. *Danas*, 6/11/85, 20-21.

ethical basis of Yugoslav society."[73] Špiljak similarly criticized the attacks
on the National Liberation Struggle in his speech to the LCC Tenth
Congress held just before the Thirteenth LCY Congress in June 1986. In a
thinly veiled warning to Serb proponents of de-Titoization, Špiljak
charged that incidents of "scholarly and political manipulation and
denigration of the revolution and its prominent personalities" were
simply a poor disguise for rehabilitating ideologies defeated in the war.[74]
Other Croat leaders like Milutin Baltić charged more bluntly that it was
"ridiculous" for Serbs to complain that they were oppressed.[75]

By the Thirteenth Party Congress in June 1986, the party and state
apparatus was largely paralyzed in the face of the country's worsening
economic problems and general sense of malaise. The decentralization of
political authority to republic party authorities had resulted in virtually
separate republic parties within the LCY which were unable to reach
agreement on pressing political and economic problems. As Serbs continued to demand fundamental reform of the system, liberal forces led by
the Slovenes began to press for an even greater loosening of the federation. The head of the LCY, the Montenegrin Vidoje Žarković, called for
an end to this deadlock by returning to the principles of the Partisan
movement, but his words went largely unheeded. In his opening remarks to the Congress, Žarković stated that confusion about the federal
system could only be clarified by looking to the National Liberation
Struggle. "[The Yugoslav federation] was created in the fire of the
National Liberation Struggle and the Socialist revolution as an expression of the desire of all of Yugoslavia's nations and nationalities,"
Žarković explained, and that "is why it can develop successfully only on
the basis from which it sprang...."[76]

This attempt to appeal to the founding myth of the revolution was a
last ditch effort, however, and it did not succeed. The fact that the
Congress was unable to issue anything more decisive than bland pronouncements about stabilization further discredited the federal system,
of which this paralysis appeared to be a symptom. The door was left
open for a major assault on the entire federal system by Slobodan
Milošević, who assumed the position of chairman of the Central
Committee of the League of Communists of Serbia (LCS) in May 1986.
Before long, Milošević began to lead the outcry against the "parceliza-

---

73. *Ibid.*
74. *Danas,* 5/20/86, 11.
75. *Danas,* 2/4/85, 6.
76. *Danas,* 7/1/86, 7.

tion" of Serbia and to join in accusations that the state arrangement imposed in 1945 had critically weakened Serbia.

By 1989, as preparations were being made for the next party congress, the wartime settlement of the Croat question had been seriously undermined. Serbs had come to feel that the arrangement of borders and republics worked out by the CPY during the war was tolerable, at best, under a more centralized political order than currently prevailed. Any further weakening of the federation, as Croats and Slovenes soon began to propose, must mean a reexamination of the "border question." Fearing that any redrawing of borders would lead to claims on their territory, most Croats opposed this challenge to the wartime settlement. But they were determined to achieve the kind of sovereignty they believed the revolution had promised, and failed to deliver. As the main players in the *maspok,* such as Franjo Tudjman, became the most important figures in Croat political life, they were determined to avoid the mistakes of 1971; if they couldn't achieve a loose federation within a more democratic Yugoslavia, then they would go it alone.

Epilogue: In Search of a New Solution

On January 22, 1990, after three days of rancorous debate, the Slovene delegation walked out of the Fourteenth Extraodinary Congress of the League of Communists of Yugoslavia. The Slovenes were angered by the continued refusal of the League of Communists of Serbia to endorse a federal model based upon autonomous republic and provincial party organizations. After a decade of deadlock, this struggle over the two federal models adopted by Communists during the formation of the Yugoslav party-state resulted in the destruction of the Communist Party itself. Although the LCY did not formally agree to relinquish its "leading role" until it met again briefly several months later in May, the Slovenes' dramatic exit effectively marked the end of forty-five years of rule by the Communist Party in Yugoslavia. In multiparty elections during the next several months, non-Communist governments came to power in four of the six republics of Yugoslavia.[77] For the first time since the Second

----

77. The Slovene Communist Party lost in elections held in April 1990 to the united opposition DEMOS. In the elections in Croatia in May 1990, the League of Communists of Croatia-Party of Democratic Change (LCC-PDC) lost to the CDC. In November 1990, the League of Communists of Bosnia-Hercegovina was defeated by the Moslem Party for Democratic Action. One month later the Macedonian Communists lost the election. The League of Communists of Serbia,

World War, the resolution of the Croat question, and the larger national question in Yugoslavia, lay in the hands of non-Communist as well as Communist political actors; the struggle over the shape (and even the existence) of the Yugoslav state entered a new phase.

With the elections in the spring of 1990, the Croat Democratic Community (CDC) became the most powerful political force in Croatia; its leader, Franjo Tudjman, was appointed president by the Sabor shortly thereafter.[78] The CDC, which had been dismissed as a right-wing and marginal group when it was founded in 1989, had grown rapidly in popularity during the past year as the authority of the LCC had begun to crumble.[79] Like the Croat Peasant Party before the Second World War, the Croat Democratic Community was endorsed by a wide spectrum of the population with diverse political views. For the vast majority of its adherents, however, the attainment of Croatian statehood was of paramount importance. During the election campaign, the CDC embraced several strands of the Croat national movement, from the Starčević variant in the nineteenth century to the Croat Peasant Party and the Communist Party of Croatia in the twentieth century. Although the third major political force of the twentieth century, the Ustasha, was initially omitted from public reference, it increasingly found a place under the CDC umbrella.[80]

In many ways, Tudjman's own background reflected this wide range of views. This son of a Croat Peasant Party official was already active in the Communist movement as a teenager before the war. During the

---

renamed the Socialist Party of Serbia, and the League of Communists of Montenegro both won the elections at the end of the year.

78. In the May elections in Croatia, the CDC won approximately 43% of the vote and in coalition with other center right parties won 205 of the 365 seats of the Sabor. The LCC-PDC won approximately 27% of the vote and in coalition with other leftist parties took 73 seats in the Sabor.

79. CDC leaders estimated that there were 50,000 CDC members at the end of 1989. By the spring of 1990 this figure had burgeoned to 250,000. The CDC program called upon the republic of Croatia to secede from the Yugoslav state if its population desired such a step. It also called for free elections, an independent judiciary, a free market economy. Some local branches also called for the restoration of the pre-1941 borders, which would return Bosnia-Hercegovina to Croat control.

80. In the spring of 1992, the CDC agreed to unite with the Croat National Committee (Hrvatski narodni odbor) which is the successor to an organization by the same name founded in 1950 by Branimir Jelić, an associate of Pavelić. Under the agreement, the CNC was to receive two places in the CDC Executive Committee. See *Danas*, 4/7/92, 7-10.

Second World War, he became a general in the Partisan army and was strongly committed to the resolution of the Croat question within the framework of a Yugoslav state. After the war, he became a historian, and was appointed director of the prestigious Institute for the History of the Workers' Movement in Croatia. Under his leadership, Institute publications began to explore sensitive national themes in the post-1918 historiography of Yugoslavia, especially pertaining to the Croat question. These activities earned Tudjman the censure of Communist Party officials, and in 1967 he was removed from his post as director of the Institute and expelled from the party.[81] Tudjman's activism increased, however, as he became a regular contributor to Matica Hrvatska's publication *Hrvatski tjednik*. His articles focusing on the Croat national movement and its struggles for Croatian statehood earned him the title of "historian of the Croat Spring."[82] They also earned him a prison sentence after Tito cracked down on the *maspok* in Croatia.[83] At this point, like many other participants in the events of 1971, he appears to have abandoned his Communist convictions, although he was not quick to embrace western liberal democracy. Both systems, he believed, had deprived the small nations of Europe of their ostensible right to national self-determination. Thereafter, the focus of his writings and political activities became the fulfillment of self-determination for Croatia.

When Tudjman and the CDC came to power in the spring of 1990, they were committed to achieving the goal of Croatian statehood. Indeed, it was their unswerving commitment to this task that accounted for their electoral success. While they appropriated the federalist strand of the Partisan movement in Croatia (Hebrang was now officially raised to the status of a Croat national leader), they were determined to change what they saw as the ultimate legacy of the Communist revolution—the thwarting of Croatian statehood and the squelching of the political forces

---

81. For example, *Putevi revolucije*, put out by IHRPH, touched on certain sensitive themes relating to the role of Croats in the Partisan movement. In 1967 IHRPH was one of several cultural and educational institutions that signed the "Declaration Concerning the Name and Position of the Croat Literary Language." This Declaration was denounced harshly by LCC officials who took steps to clean up nationalist elements in Croatia, particularly in the IHRPH and the Matica iseljenika Hrvatske.

82. For a description of Tudjman's intellectual evolution see Ivo Banac, "Svršimo s odiljanjem od Hrvatske na ljevici," *Globus*, 1/10/90, 4-5.

83. Tudjman was jailed for nine months for his role in the *maspok* and again from January 1980 to November 1984 for having expressed slanderous views about Yugoslavia to foreign journalists. He was banned from making public statements until 1989.

of the Croat national movement.[84] And, in contrast to Hebrang's staunch support for Communist Party rule, the CDC was committed to a multiparty, democratic system, though building democratic institutions was not as immediately important as the achievement of independence. In July 1990, the government took a major step toward independence when the Sabor adopted constitutional amendments declaring Croatia's sovereignty. Various independent governmental agencies were established, such as the independent Croatian news agency HINA, and the government officially adopted many of the symbols associated with Croatian history (some also associated with the Ustasha period).

In addition to effecting certain internal changes, Tudjman and the government took steps to give Croatian independence practical force by reorganizing the federation. In the summer of 1990, they began working on a plan in conjunction with Slovene leaders for rebuilding the Yugoslav state along confederal lines. In October, this plan was presented to federal authorities for formal consideration. The proposal incorporated many of the demands for constitutional revisions made by Matica Hrvatska in 1971. It called for the establishment of a loose federation of sovereign states based on the rights of voluntary association and secession. The new confederal institutions would include a parliament, a council of ministers, an executive committee and a confederal court; the parliament would perform a primarily consultative function and the council of ministers would make all decisions according to the principle of unanimity. Although the state would retain a monetary union and a common Yugoslav market, republics would have independent military forces and separate diplomatic missions abroad.

Fierce resistance to this proposal by virtually all political leaders in Serbia resulted in a definite drift among Croats in the next several months toward the idea of complete independence. The new Croatian constitution ratified on December 22, 1990, proclaimed the republic's right to secede from the Yugoslav state on the basis of a plebiscite within Croatia. After Slovenia announced it was taking steps to leave the federation within the next six months, Tudjman announced in February 1991 that Croats were ready to follow suit. As he put it in an address to the Sabor in March: "For political, demographic and economic reasons we can no longer accept any kind of relationship in which we are not mas-

---

84. The CDC has become increasingly hostile to the Partisan legacy in any form as the anti-communism of its adherents has increased. See *Danas*, 4/7/92, 7-10.

ters of our own destiny."[85] A clash with Serbia was simply a matter of time.

In addition to its efforts to change Croatia's relation to the larger Yugoslav state, Tudjman and the government moved quickly to reverse what was commonly viewed as another unacceptable legacy of the Partisan struggle—the predominance of Serbs in the police and security organs.[86] Reducing the number of Serbs in these organizations had been a main goal of Matica Hrvatska in 1971; the predominance of Serbs in the Partisan movement had also concerned Hebrang who believed it hindered attempts to attract Croats. In order to reduce the influence of the regular police, the government formed special police units composed of Croats. These "Guards" were charged with the task of keeping order in the "critical zones," those areas populated largely by Serbs. In October 1990, the government announced it was reducing by 60% the arms of the local police forces in these areas. Moreover, some Serbs who engaged in active opposition to the government or who held highly visible and prestigious posts were removed from their positions.[87]

These actions, and the steps being taken to loosen, if not sever, Croatia's connection to the Yugoslav state began to alarm many Serbs in Croatia. As in periods of the past, for example in 1944 and 1971, when Croats carved out a large measure of autonomy within the federation, Serbs began to seek explicit guarantees concerning their position in Croatia and a formal strengthening of their ties with Serbia. The vehicle for articulating their cause was the Serb Democratic Party (SDS), founded in the largely Serb-inhabited town of Knin in 1989. Shortly after the elections in the spring of 1990, the SDS members of the Sabor began to call upon the government to grant autonomous political status to regions of Croatia with a Serb majority. As at the end of the Second World War, when Serb Partisans had made similiar requests, Serb autonomy was vehemently rejected by the CDC government. Although the government agreed to consider granting these regions autonomous cultural status, it was not prepared to discuss political autonomy. Like Hebrang, and the LCC reformers, Croat leaders desired autonomy within the Yugoslav federation, but they were not prepared to grant it to any area within Croatia.[88]

---

85. *Radio Free Europe Reports*, 3/15/91, 28.

86. Croatia's regular police force at this time was approximately 60% Serb.

87. This was particularly the case in the Knin area after the August referendum.

88. The Croat government also began to struggle with autonomist forces in Istria at this time. A movement in Rijeka called the Front for the Autonomy of

In response to this refusal to consider political autonomy, SDS legisla-
tors withdrew from the Sabor. They accused Croat authorities of pursuing a policy of cultural genocide of Serbs after the Second World War,
and of depriving them of their civil rights. In mid-August 1990, the SDS
organized a referendum on independence in the Knin area. Although it
was banned by the Croatian government, SDS leaders claimed that Serbs
voted overwhelmingly to secede from Croatia if a confederal arrangement were adopted.[89] Skirmishes between Serbs and Croats (occasionally
involving the Yugoslav People's Army) in these areas escalated as local
Serb militias began to arm themselves. In October, the Serb National
Council, an unofficial parliament composed of Serbs in Croatia,
reiterated its declaration of autonomy of the previous July.[90] On
December 21, just days before the promulgation of the new Croat constitution, the Serb leaders announced the separation of the Serb
Autonomous Region (SAO) Krajina from Croatia.

Meanwhile, the Socialist Party of Serbia (formerly the League of
Communists of Serbia), which won the elections in December 1990,
began to turn its attention increasingly to the problem of Serbs in
Croatia.[91] The Socialist-dominated government, which had come to
power largely on the nationalist platform of its leader (and president of
the republic) Slobodan Milošević, was determined to reverse what it saw
as the Partisan legacy of "parcelizing" and weakening Serbia. The
nationalist mood of the population of Serbia, which had been ignited by
the situation in Kosovo, was further inflamed by what Serbs viewed as
the worsening situation of Serbs who lived outside of Serbia proper. The

---

Istria demanded that Rijeka be established as an independent city-state. Almost
all the municipal governments in Istria opposed the July 1991 constitutional
amendments which they saw as an attempt to centralize power. They also objected to the government's proposal to resettle some 20,000 Croats from Romania
to Istria. For a discussion of the CDC approach to this question see *Danas*,
11/27/90, 12.

89. Balloting for the referendum took place from August 19 to September 2
(voting also occured in Belgrade and Ljubljana). The ballots simply stated "For
Serb Autonomy, yes or no." Organizers explained that if Yugoslavia remained a
federation this would mean cultural autonomy; if it became a confederation then
it would mean territorial autonomy. *Radio Free Europe Reports*, 9/4/90.

90. The term Krajina means borderland and refers to the region of the military
frontier established by the Habsburgs. Krajina comprises approximately 15% of
the territory of Croatia and contains approximately 12% of its population.

91. The Socialist Party of Serbia won 48% of the votes which gave it 194 of the
250 seats in the National Assembly. Milošević himself received 65% of the vote in
the presidential elections in December.

question of Serbs residing within the traditional borders of Croatia had always been central to the Serb national movement. The movement sought to unite these Serbs to Serbia either by creating a unitary, highly centralized Yugoslav state or by establishing a Great Serbia which would incorporate these areas. Serbs had generally supported the more centralized, Bolshevik variant of state-building adopted by the Communist Party of Yugoslavia after the war, and in the decade after Tito's death Serb Communists had led the campaign to recentralize the state.[92] Although Milošević continued to declare officially that he was pursuing the goal of recentralizing the state (or at least preventing its further decentralization), he appeared increasingly to be looking toward the creation of a Great Serbia. When Croatia and Slovenia called for the creation of a confederal state in October 1990, Milošević insisted that the adoption of their proposal would result in Serbia's seceding from Yugoslavia and taking with it those areas of other republics populated by a majority of Serbs.

These statements, and the outpouring of support in Serbia for Serbs in Croatia, convinced many Croats that Milošević was simply trying to use Serbs in Croatia to overthrow the Croatian government, as he had two years previously in Montenegro and Vojvodina.[93] Tudjman and the government charged that "anti-bureaucratic guardists," as Milošević's supporters were called, were trying to undermine the legally constituted government of Croatia. Although this was probably a justifiable fear, it also gave the Croatian government an excuse to avoid making politically difficult concessions to Serb demands, concessions which might have reassured the Serbs.[94] Serb fears of a repeat of the massacres during the Second World War (and Serbs' increasingly frequent reference to them) infuriated Croats, who charged that they had been made to feel collectively guilty in Tito's Yugoslavia for the crimes of a relatively few Ustashas during the war.[95] When the Croatian government finally agreed

92. The extent of centralization should not be confused with extent of democracy, however, as many Serb democrats and opposition figures supported the goal of centralizing the state.

93. In 1988, supporters of Milošević called "anti-bureaucratic guards," engaged in street demonstrations that resulted in the resignations of the governments of Montenegro and Vojvodina.

94. During the spring of 1991, waves of panic began to ripple through the Serb community in Croatia as rumors of impending massacres spread. In several instances large numbers of Serbs crossed the border into neighboring Vojvodina and Serbia in an effort to escape these alleged crimes.

95. Both Serbs and Croats have deep grievances about how the Communists treated the question of historical guilt. Serbs charge that they were made to feel

in July 1991 to begin talks about the establishment of political autonomy for the predominantly Serb areas of Croatia, it was already too late to stop the fighting.

On June 25, 1991, Croatia declared its independence from the Yugoslav state.[96] Within days, fighting erupted in several places in the Krajina region between Serb irregulars and Croat police and national guard troops. The Communist state of Yugoslavia had ceased to exist; the second civil war (or a war between independent states, depending on one's perspective) in half a century had begun. To many observers, it appeared as if the horrible events of the Second World War were simply being replayed, with equal senselessness and ferocity. And, once again, contention between Serbs and Croats over the borders of their political units was at the heart of the matter. Even the vocabulary of the participants returned to that period as combatants and civilians alike referred to each other simply as Chetniks and Ustashas. As the last Partisan-built, Yugoslav institution, the Yugoslav People's Army, weighed in clearly on the side of the Serbs in August 1991, it became clear that no more forces existed which could restore the Partisan solution to the Croat question.

As the most basic aspects of the Communist approach to the Croat question unravelled, the fighting spread into Bosnia and Hercegovina. The CPY had attempted to put a halt to Serb and Croat wrangling over this area by creating a separate political unit. Communist Party authorities had further attempted to bolster the position of Bosnia-Hercegovina by declaring the third group inhabiting this republic, the Muslims, to be a nation. Nevertheless, when the Yugoslav state broke apart, the question of the status of Croats and especially Serbs in this new political unit resurfaced. Although the Partisan legacy had strengthened this republic's claim to statehood, it could not prevent both Serbs and Croats from reasserting their claims to portions of this territory.

The Croat question now begs for a new answer. The CPY attempted to resolve this problem within the framework of one-party federalism. Both

---

guilty for the "hegemonic" behavior of the Serb nation, particularly in the interwar period. According to them, this interpretation ignores the very significant state-building achievements of the Serbs.

96. In February 1991, the National Assemblies of Slovenia and Croatia passed a resolution calling for a peaceful, negotiated separation of Yugoslavia's six republics. They also passed constitutional amendments to their respective constitutions that gave republic law precedence over federal law. *Danas* stated at this time that "the second Yugoslavia [the Comunist federation established by Tito in 1945] will formally cease to exist on February 20." *Danas*, 2/19/91, cited in *Radio Free Europe Reports*, 3/15/91, 25.

the Bolshevik strategy, which called for a highly centralized state (and was therefore more generally acceptable to Serbs), and the federalist strategy, which decentralized power to regional party authorities (and was therefore more generally acceptable to Croats) ultimately proved unable to resolve the Croat question. Indeed, contention over these strategies contributed to the weakening of the League of Communists and the collapse of the party-state. The leaders of the South Slav nations must now grapple with the task of fundamentally reshaping the relation between nation and state established by the Communists during the Second World War.

Conclusion

Although the CPY declared the national question resolved in 1945, nationalism continued to affect the political development of the Yugoslav Socialist state. Conflict over the Croat question, which disappeared in the period of centralization and repression after the Second World War, reemerged with the introduction of political and economic reforms in the 1960s. At that time, Communists in Croatia attempted to revise significantly the federal model inherent in the Bolshevik strategy of state-building. Casting themselves as leaders of a popular national movement, they returned to the emphasis on Croatian institutions and interests the CPC had championed during the war. They advocated the reorganization of the state to allow for greater republican autonomy and attempted to confer legitimacy on this position by appealing to its roots in the Partisan struggle.

Although the circumstances of the two periods were different, there were some striking parallels between the strategy adopted by Communists in Croatia in 1944 and 1971 and the results of this strategy. First, and most importantly, the LCC's increasing emphasis on Croatian statehood caused considerable concern among the Serb population of Croatia, some of whom began to call for the establishment of an autonomous region of Serbs in Croatia. Serbs could point to an entirely different state-building strand from the revolution. For them, the National Liberation Struggle meant the imposition of a centralist system, based on "brotherhood and unity," in which borders did not matter much. The attempt by LCC liberals and Matica Hrvatska to call this legacy into question caused Serbs to seek new guarantees of their status in Croatia. Emphasis on Croatian statehood also began to create problems in Croatia's relations with its neighbors as questions about Croatia's borders and the status of Croats living in other republics resurfaced. Perhaps the most pressing problem the LCC federalist strategy faced was that it unleashed forces of nationalism in Croatia that party leaders could not control. Like CPP members loyal to Hebrang, Matica members were a potential source of support and strength for the LCC. But Matica Hrvatska also threatened to overwhelm the LCC, to dilute its organizational strength and to drag it in directions it did not want to go. Like CPC leaders in 1944, LCC leaders discovered that attempting to harness the unleashed forces of nationalism to a federalizing state-building strategy could be perilous indeed.

After Tito intervened in Croatia in 1971, he attempted to find a compromise to the two federal models embraced by the Bolshevik and federalist state-building strategies. He wanted to implement the political decentralization necessary for economic reform without threatening the unity and ultimate authority of the Communist Party. Hence, he endorsed the incorporation of many of the institutional reforms introduced in the sixties in the new constitution of 1974. At the same time, however, he attempted to maintain central party unity and control by removing the popular party leaders in Croatia (and Serbia) and appointing replacements loyal to him. This strategy of balancing the countervailing pressures of national autonomy and a unitary state succeeded only as long as he lived. After his death in 1980, the federalization of the LCY which Tito had sought to prevent accelerated. Opposition to this federalization, particularly among Serbs, resulted in an attack not only on the federal model championed by Croats, but on the entire settlement of the national question determined during the Second World War.

In the decade after Tito's death, both Serbs and Croats began to attack the alleged failures of the CPY to resolve the Croat and Serb questions during the formation of the Yugoslav Socialist state. Both Serbs and Croats felt betrayed by the legacy of the revolution because, in fact, there were two legacies. Croats pointed to the state-building strategy adopted by ZAVNOH, which they felt had been negated by the subsequent centralization of the party-state. After the events of 1971, many Communists in Croatia became convinced that their national aspirations could never be achieved within the framework of one-party federalism. Serbs felt betrayed by the legacy of the revolution because the "insignificance of borders" promised by the centralizing features of the Bolshevik state-building strategy was increasingly threatened by the federalization of the party and the resulting decentralization of the state. Therefore, Serbs demanded a redrawing of the borders of the political units established by the Communists. After the elections of 1989, both nations were determined to redress their grievances concerning the Communist resolution of the Croat question, and the wider national question in Yugoslavia. Yet, while the resolution of the Croat question during the Partisan struggle was rejected by both Serbs and Croats, the legacies of the war were not forgotten. Bitter memories of the terrible internecine violence of that period lurked just beneath the surface, making the search for a new resolution to the Croat and Serb questions an extremely difficult and painful process.

Conclusion

At the end of November 1945, the Communist-dominated Constituent Assembly proclaimed the establishment of the Socialist Federal Republic of Yugoslavia. In contrast to the previous Constituent Assembly in 1920, which the Communists had boycotted, the CPY carefully controlled and orchestrated every aspect of devising the new constitution. After struggling at times to survive in the interwar period, the CPY had been transformed during the wartime years from a marginal force in Yugoslav political life to the indiputable arbiter of Yugoslavia's postwar political development. There were two key elements to the CPY's remarkable accomplishments during the Second World War: its attention to building new political institutions and its use of nationalism in mobilizing the several nations of the interwar Yugoslav state. How the second element of the CPY's strategy affected the first has been the focus of this study.

An analysis of the CPY's approach to the Croat question reveals a complex picture of the effect of nationalism on the state-building activities of Yugoslav Communists. As this study demonstrates, nationalist pressures had a significant impact upon the CPY's state-building strategy and the institutions it built. Communists were not united in their approach to the Croat question or in their strategies for building new political institutions. Conflict over how to respond to Croat national sentiment and the organization of the state divided the Communist Party in the interwar years and continued to do so during the Second World War. Communists' failure to elicit Croat support for the resistance movement (and the CPY's political program) caused CPC leader Andrija Hebrang to modify the Bolshevik state-building strategy embraced by the CPY. Hebrang's federalist strategy placed the locus of political power in the regional party and state structures constructed during the war. This attempt to respond to Croat national sentiments by devising a different state-building strategy (though one within the framework of a one-party state) had profound implications for the evolution of the Yugoslav Socialist state. Although Tito imposed a centralized political order in 1945, conflict over the Bolshevik and federalist visions of the party-state was renewed during the reforms of the 1960s; it intensified in the decade after Tito's death as Serbs and Croats increasingly endorsed the federal model that adhered most closely to the traditional goals of their national movements. This conflict, and its accompanying political paralysis, contributed to the collapse of one-party rule in 1989.

In demonstrating how Communist leaders were influenced by nationalism in their state-building efforts, I do not mean to suggest that these Communists were nationalists themselves. Conflict over their state-building strategies was not usually motivated by Communists' nationalist convictions, at least not until relatively recently. In most instances, Communists were genuinely committed to the maintenance of a unified Yugoslav state based on one-party federal rule, and they denounced all forms of national chauvinism. Their overriding political goal was the proletarian revolution and the construction of a Socialist state, and they sought to use national sentiments to this end. For example, although Hebrang emphasized Croatian autonomy in order to draw support away from the CPP, he did not question the necessity for a unified Communist Party and construction of a unified Yugoslav state. However, as this study has demonstrated, Communists were not impervious to nationalist pressures in their attempts to achieve their political goals. The national ideologies and movements with which they competed for popular support caused them to pursue different political strategies and to adopt different approaches to constructing the state.

While conflict over the Croat question was the most serious political problem in the Kingdom of Serbs, Croats and Slovenes after 1918, the seeds of this conflict were sown long before this time. The crux of the conflict was a familiar one in Eastern Europe: the discontinuity between the borders of the preexisting political units (which in Yugoslavia had been subject to the political authority of different empires) and the dispositions of national populations. Serbs faced the problem of a large number of Serbs residing outside the borders of Serbia proper, especially in Croatia and Bosnia-Hercegovina, whom they wished to see united to a Serbian state. Croats faced the problem of a large population of Serbs residing within their historical lands and the difficulty of uniting their diverse regions in the face of strong (often irredentist) pressures from their neighbors. These different circumstances shaped the outlooks of both nations toward the construction of a South Slav state: Serbs mainly wanted an expansion of Serbia to incorporate all Serbs, though they were willing to consider including other South Slavs in this Serbian state; Croats possessed a range of views about a South Slav political arrangement, though the desire for a decentralized federal order was the predominant view. When the new state was organized along the centralized lines desired by Serbs, Croats quickly became disillusioned with the Yugoslav state.

The entrenched national identities and conflicting national ideologies of Serbs and Croats proved as difficult for the Communist Party of Yugoslavia in the interwar years as for non-Communist elites. While Serb and Croat political leaders were unable to develop any enduring strategy for elite accommodation and cooperation (or to encourage the popular endorsement necessary for such a strategy of elite cooperation to work), Communists battled over the political implications of this impasse. The CPY was torn by serious factional struggles over the Croat question, particularly in the first decade of its existence. Although their positions shifted over time, Communists in Croatia emphasized the importance of the national question. They more often advocated the introduction of a federal system (or the breakup of the Yugoslav state during the brief period from 1928 to 1934) and some form of cooperation with the Croat Peasant Party. When the Communist Party of Croatia was formed in 1937, it endorsed the CPY's federal program but adopted a different understanding of Communist interests based on conditions in Croatia. This tendency to devise political strategies and goals in response to the political pressures exerted by the Croat Peasant Party carried over into the Partisan struggle.

When war broke out, the CPY attempted to use its countrywide base and its federal program to mobilize Yugoslavia's national groups into the Communist-led Partisan movement and its political corollaries; these organizations would provide the framework for the new party-state and the foundation of the CPY's political power. However, the attempt to use nationalism to mobilize Croats into the Partisan movement met with little success during the first two years of the war. The CPY's federal program failed to assuage Croat fears about a unified Yugoslav state, and the vast majority of Croats remained politically loyal to the CPP. Consequently, when the CPY began to establish new federal and regional institutions in 1943, Hebrang sought to endow them with real authority; he also adopted important aspects of the CPP's political program in order to siphon off its support. In the division of power that evolved in the months after ZAVNOH's formation, the Croatian Council possessed a great deal more power than that envisioned under the Soviet model, making decisions on all aspects of social, political and economic policy without reference to AVNOJ as a higher political authority. Most importantly, Hebrang carved out an independent sphere of authority for the Communist Party of Croatia and began to establish that authority over all areas of Croatia, including the

traditionally autonomist Dalmatia. Since the centralization of authority in the Soviet type party-state was based upon a highly unified
party, this attempt to federalize the CPY had enormous implications
for the future distribution of power in the state.

Tito had no intention of allowing the federalization of the CPY,
however, and he remained as vehemently opposed to this idea as Lenin
had been. Other important CPY leaders were also firmly committed to
establishing a federal order based on the Soviet model. Consequently,
when the CPY's political position strengthened in 1945, it imposed a
Bolshevik state-building strategy which emphasized political centralization through a unitary Communist Party. This strategy meant
that there was no significant decentralization of political authority to
Croatia. It also meant that the CPY determined the number, size and
shape of the federal units without further debate within the
Communist Party (let alone public discussion or plebiscite). When discussion of the Croat question was reopened in later years, these decisions appeared even to many Communists to have been imposed arbi-
trarily and therefore illegitimately.

Although the CPY declared the Croat question resolved in 1945,
Croat dissatisfaction with the unitary state order remained. When
public discussion of the federal system began in the 1960s, the extent of
this dissatisfaction was revealed in Croatia. The nationalist pressure
exterted by Matica Hrvatska, particularly to reform the federal order,
caused LCC leaders to attempt to federalize the party and state structures and to seek legitimacy for this position in the "federalist" state-
building strategy pursued by Hebrang during the Second World War.
When Tito intervened and suppressed the *maspok*, many Communists in
Croatia became convinced that the solution to the Croat question could
not be achieved within the framework of one-party federalism.

The attempt of LCC reformers to champion Croatian sovereignty and
to decentralize political authority to regional authorities had a very
immediate impact on Serbs living in Croatia. These Serbs had not been
offered explicit guarantees of cultural or political autonomy after the
Second World War because the imposition of a highly centralized
political order and the emphasis on an overarching Yugoslav identity
appeared to make such arrangements unnecessary. However, the decentralization of political power enacted by the reforms and the LCC's
attempt to appeal to a different legacy of the revolution than the
"brotherhood and unity" that had been emphasized since the war
prompted Serbs to seek new political guarantees of their status in
Croatia. Serbs began to call for the establishment of cultural and even
political (territorial) autonomy. Although these demands were suppressed along with the *maspok* in 1971, they resurfaced with the disin-

tegration of LCY authority in the 1980s. After the collapse of one-party rule in 1989, as Croats first sought a fundamental restructuring of the federal system along confederal lines, and then to leave the state altogether, Serbs in Croatia protested that only a centralized Yugoslav state (or unification with Serbia) could protect their national interests. The tension that had been evident in the Communist solution to the Croat question, which was in fact two competing solutions, erupted into violent conflict.

After Tito's death in 1980, the CPY's "resolution" of the Croat question within the framework of one-party federalism began to unravel. Croats and Serbs increasingly endorsed the competing federal models, contained in the two state-building strategies pursued during the war, that adhered most closely to their traditional national goals. The centralized aspects of the Bolshevik federal model offered Serbs in Serbia proper and outside its borders the closest fulfillment of their national aims. Croats supported the federalist model which offered them more political autonomy and greater territorial unity. At the same time, dissatisfaction with the way in which the CPY had settled this question during the war increased as both Serbs and Croats objected to the legacy of the opposing state-building strand. As the legitimacy of the CPY's solution to the national question was undermined, so was the legitimacy of the Communist Party itself. Attempts to bolster the LCY's authority by appealing to the founding period of the Partisan struggle were hindered by the disputed legacy of this period. Ultimately, contention over the legacy of the CPY's approach to the national question during the Second World War paralyzed the party-state.

While both Serbs and Croats proclaimed the merits of the federalist and Bolshevik federal models, it is clear that neither one was capable of resolving the Croat question within the framework of one-party rule. The Bolshevik strategy was based on the ideal that Communist Party rule would create the class conditions for the disappearance of nationalism; meanwhile, Communists would foster an overarching Yugoslav identity that would replace the particular nationalisms of Yugoslavia's constituent national groups. While the first goal was utopian, the second proved unrealizable in the face of the entrenched national identities and ideologies of Yugoslavia's several nations. Moreover, the proponents of the Bolshevik strategy were not able to overcome the tension between the highly centralized party and the division of powers inherent in a federal system. While the Bolshevik strategy acknowledged and even legitimized national sentiments, it did not offer them any real political expression.

The federalist strategy also fell short of resolving the Croat question within the framework of one party federalism. Although it allowed for greater expression of national sentiments, it unleashed popular forces that threatened to undermine the basis of Communist party rule. Hebrang during the Second World War and the LCC liberals in 1971 attempted to present themselves as genuine leaders of the Croat national movement; but they were threatened by the specter of "real" national leaders from the Croat Peasant Party and Matica Hrvatska: This threat forced them to rely on coercion as well as cooptation. Perhaps most importantly, the federalist strategy could not offer a real solution to the Croat question unless it was based upon an agreement among all the republic party leaderships on the overall organization of the state. As we have seen, this agreement had been lacking since the inception of the Yugoslav state, and it was absent within the Communist Party itself. After Tito's death, strife within the LCY over the distribution of power among central and republic party and state organs resulted in serious political paralysis and a weakening of one-party rule.

With the collapse of communism in Yugoslavia, it is apparent that four decades of Communist Party rule were unable to mitigate conflict among Serbs and Croats over the organization of the state. While Yugoslavia's Communist leadership must be credited with some accomplishments in their efforts to resolve the national question in Yugoslavia, their solution was clearly not a permanent one. The attempts of Communist leaders to manage national aspirations within the framework of one-party federalism failed to create either a larger loyalty to the federal state or to respond to the desire for statehood of the state's constituent groups. Whether post-Communist political elites can resolve the Croat question more effectively remains to be seen; the events of the last few years do not leave much room for optimism. They may serve, however, as a warning of the potentially destructive impact of nationalism on the process of state-making in Eastern Europe and the former Soviet Union. In that case, an understanding of the legacy of the efforts of Communist elites to define the relationship between nation and state is of the utmost importance.

Abbreviations

AVNOJ	Antifascist Council of the People's Liberation of Yugoslavia (Antifašističko vijeće narodnog oslobodjenja Jugoslavije)
CDC	Croatian Democratic Community
CPC	Communist Party of Croatia
CPP	Croat Peasant Party
CPPP	Croat People's Peasant Party
CPY	Communist Party of Yugoslavia
CRPP	Croat Republican Peasant Party
IDP	Independent Democratic Party
LCC	League of Communists of Croatia
LCY	League of Communists of Yugoslavia
NDH	Independent State of Croatia (Nezavisna Država Hrvatska)
NKOJ	National Committee for the Liberation of Yugoslavia
NLF	National Liberation Front
PDC	Peasant-Democratic Coalition
PFY	Popular Front of Yugoslavia
PWP	Party of the Working People
PWPY	People's Workers' Party of Yugoslavia
SDS	Serb Democratic Party
ZAVNOH	Land Antifascist Council of the People's Liberation of Croatia (Zemaljsko antifašističko vijeće narodnog oslobodjenja Hrvatske)

Bibliography

Archival Sources

Arhiv Instituta za historiju radničkog pokreta Hrvatske, Zagreb
Fond: CK KPJ
        CK KPH
        Povjerenštva CK KPH
        Oblasni, okružni i kotarski komiteti KPH
        JNOF
        IO HSS
        HSS

Newspapers and Journals

Borba radnog naroda
Danas
Hrvatski tjednik
Naprijed
NIN
Proleter
Slobodni dom
Srpska riječ
Vjesnik radnog naroda

Books and Articles

Alexander, Stella. *Church and State in Yugoslavia since 1945.* Cambridge, England and New York: Columbia University Press, 1979.
Almond, Gabriel A. *Political Development: Essays in Heuristic Theory.* Boston: Little, Brown and Co., 1970.

Anderson, Perry. *Lineages of the Absolutist State*. Atlantic Highlands: Humanities Press, 1974.

Auty, Phyllis, and R. Clogg eds. *British Policy towards Wartime Resistance in Yugoslavia and Greece*. London, 1975.

Auty, Phyllis. *Tito: A Biography*. London: Longman Group Ltd., 1970.

Avakumović, Ivan. *History of the Communist Party of Yugoslavia*. Aberdeen, Scotland: Aberdeen University Press, 1964.

Babić, Nikola, ed. *AVNOJ i narodnooslobodilačka borba u Bosni i Hercegovini (1942-1943)*. Belgrade, 1974.

Bakarić, Vladimir. *Društvene klase, nacija i socijalizam*. Zagreb, 1976.

Bakarić, Vladimir. "Iz bilježnice Vladimira Bakarića." *Vjesnik*, July 27-28, 1975.

Bakarić, Vladimir. *Socijalistički samoupravni sistem i društvena reprodukcija*. 2 vols. Zagreb, 1974, 1978.

Bakarić, Vladimir. *To su bila čudesna vremena, dani herojstva*. Zagreb, 1971.

Balen, Šime. "Inicijativni odbor Zemaljskog antifašističkog vijeća narodnog oslobodjena Hrvatske." *Spomenica u čast dvadeset i pete godišnjice ZAVNOH-a*. Zagreb, 1969.

Banac, Ivo, ed. *War and Society in East Central Europe*. Brooklyn, New York: Atlantic Studies, 1983.

Banac, Ivo. *The National Question in Yugoslavia, Origin, History, Politics*. Ithaca, New York: Cornell University Press, 1984.

Banac, Ivo. *With Stalin Against Tito, Cominformist Splits in Yugoslav Communism*. Ithaca and London: Cornell University Press, 1988.

Barker, Elisabeth. *British Policy in South East Europe in the Second World War*. London: Macmillan Press Ltd., 1976.

Barker, Elisabeth. "British Wartime Policy towards Yugoslavia." *The South Slav Journal* 2 (April 1979).

Barry, Brian. *Sociologists, Economists and Democracy*. London: The MacMillan Company, 1970.

Basta, Milan. *Agonija i slom Nezavisne Države Hrvatske*. Belgrade, 1971.

Bedeski, Robert E. *State-Building in Modern China: the Kuomintang in the Prewar Period*. Berkeley: The University of California Press, 1981.

Belinić, Marko. *Put kroz život*. Zagreb, 1985.

Benigar, Aleksa *Alojzije Stepinac, hrvatski kardinal*. Rome, 1974.

Berend, Ivan, and Gyorgy Ranki. *Economic Development in Eastern Europe in the Nineteenth and Twentieth Centuries*. New York and London: Columbia University Press, 1974.

Bilandžić, Dušan. *Historija Socijalističke Federativne Republike Jugoslavije, Glavni Procesi*. Zagreb, 1978.

Bilandžić, Dušan, et al. *Komunistički pokret i socijalistička revolucija u Hrvatskoj*. Zagreb, 1969.

Blažević, Jakov. *Brazdama partije*. Zagreb, 1986.

Boban, Ljubo. "Britanija, Hrvatska i Hrvatska seljačka stranka 1939-1945 g." *Časopis za suvremenu povijest* 3 (1978).

Boban, Ljubo. *Maček i politika Hrvatske seljačke stranke, 1928-1941*. 2 vols. Zagreb, 1974.

Boban, Ljubo. "Položaj i držanje gradjanskih stranaka u Hrvatskoj 1944." *Narodnooslobodilačka borba i socijalistička revolucija u Hrvatskoj 1944.* Zagreb, 1976.

Boban, Ljubo. *Sporazum Cvetković-Maček.* Zagreb, 1965.

Boban, Ljubo. *Svetozar Pribićević u opoziciji 1929-1936.* Zagreb, 1973.

Bodrožć, Milica. "O nekim pitanjima politike Hrvatske seljačke stranke prema NOP u Hrvatskoj 1943 g." *Časopis za suvremenu povijest* 1 (1973): 33-50.

Breuilly, John. *Nationalism and the State.* New York: St. Martin's Press, 1982.

Bright, Charles, and Susan Harding, eds. *Statemaking and Social Movements.* Ann Arbor: The University of Michigan Press, 1984.

Burg, Steven. *Conflict and Cohesion in Socialist Yugoslavia: Political Decision Making since 1966.* Princeton: Princeton University Press, 1983.

Burks, Robert V. *The Dynamics of Communism in Eastern Europe.* Princeton: Princeton University Press, 1961.

Čalić, Dušan, and Ljubo Boban. *Narodnooslobodilačka borba i socijalistička revolucija u Hrvatskoj 1944 godine.* Zagreb, 1976.

Carnoy, Martin, *The State and Political Theory.* Princeton: Princeton University Press, 1984.

Cenčić, Vjenčeslav. *Enigma Kopinič.* 2 vols. Belgrade, 1983.

Četerdeset godina, zbornik sećanja aktivista jugoslovenskog revolucionarnog radničkog pokreta. 5 vols. Belgrade, 1960-1961.

Chlebowczyk, Jozef. *On Small and Young Nations in Europe: Nation Forming Processes in Ethnic Borderlands in East Central Europe.* Warsaw, 1980.

Clissold, Stephen. "Britain, Croatia and the Croat Peasant Party, 1939-1945." Unpublished article, 1979.

Clissold, Stephen. *Yugoslavia and the Soviet Union, 1939-1973: A Documentary Survey.* Oxford: Oxford University Press, 1975.

Clissold, Steven. *Whirlwind.* London: Cresset Press, 1949.

Cohen, Youseff. "The Paradoxical Nature of State-Making: The Violent Creation of Order." *American Political Science Review* (December 1981): 901-910.

Čolaković, Rodoljub et al., eds. *Pregled istorije Saveza komunista Jugoslavije.* Belgrade, 1963.

Čolaković, Rodoljub. *Kazivanje o jednom pokoljenju.* 3 vols. Sarajevo, 1968-1972.

Čolaković, Rodoljub. *Zapis iz oslobodilačkog rata.* 5 vols. Zagreb, 1947-1956.

Connor, Walker. "Nation-Building or Nation-Destroying." *World Politics* 24 (April 1972).

Connor, Walker. *The National Question in Marxist-Leninist Theory and Strategy.* Princeton: Princeton University Press, 1984.

Čulinović, Ferdo. *Dvadesetsedmi mart.* Zagreb, 1965.

Čulinović, Ferdo. *Jugoslavija izmedju dva rata.* Zagreb, 1961.

Čulinović, Ferdo. *Okupatorska podjela Jugoslavije.* Belgrade, 1970.

Čulinović, Ferdo. *Slom stare Jugoslavije.* Zagreb, 1958.

Čulinović, Ferdo. *Stvaranje nove jugoslavenske države.* Zagreb, 1959.

Čuvalo, Ante, *The Croatian National Movement, 1966-1972.* New York: Columbia University Press, 1990.

Damjanović, Pero, ed. *Peta zemaljska konferencija KPJ (19-23 oktobar 1940).* Belgrade, 1980.

Damjanović, Pero. *Tito pred temama istorije.* Belgrade, 1977.

Deakin, Frederick, W. "Britanija i Jugoslavija, 1941-1945." *Jugoslovenski istorijski časopis* (1963): 43-58.

Deakin, Frederick, W. *The Embattled Mountain.* Oxford, 1971.

Dedijer, Vladimir. *Dnevnik.* 3 vols. Belgrade and Sarajevo, 1970.

Dedijer, Vladimir. *Josip Broz Tito, Prilozi za biografiju.* Belgrade, 1953.

Dedijer, Vladimir. *Novi prilozi za biografiju Josipa Broza Tita.* 2 vols. Rijeka and Zagreb, 1982.

Dedijer, Vladimir. *Tito.* New York: Simon & Schuster, 1953.

Dedijer, Vladimir. *With Tito through the War.* London, 1951.

Despalatović, Elinor Murray. *Ljudevit Gaj and the Illyrian Movement.* New York: Columbia University Press, 1975.

Deutsch, Karl. *Nationalism and Social Communication: An Inquiry into the Foundations of Nationality.* New York: The Technology Press of MIT and John Wiley & Sons, Inc., 1953.

Djilas, Aleksa. *The Contested Country, Yugoslav Unity and Communist Revolution, 1919-1953.* Cambridge, Massachusetts and London, England: Harvard University Press, 1991.

Djilas, Aleksa. "The Foundations of Croatian Identity." *The South Slav Journal* 8 (1985).

Djilas, Aleksa. "The Illyrianist Movement and the Logic of the Yugoslav Idea." *The South Slav Journal* 10 (Spring 1987).

Djilas, Milovan. *Memoir of a Revolutionary.* New York: Harcourt Brace Jovanovich, 1973.

Djilas, Milovan. *Parts of a Lifetime.* New York: Harcourt Brace Jovanovich,1968.

Djilas, Milovan. *Vlast.* New York and London: Harcourt Brace Jovanovich, 1985.

Djilas, Milovan. *Wartime.* New York and London: Harcourt Brace Jovanovich, 1977.

Doder, Milenko. *Kopinič bez enigme.* Zagreb, 1986.

Donia, Robert J. *Islam under the Double Eagle: The Muslims of Bosnia and Hercegovina, 1878-1914..* New York: Columbia University Press, 1981.

Dragnich, Alex N. *The First Yugoslavia.* Stanford: Hoover Institution Press, 1983.

Drndić, Ljubo. "Klasni i nacionalni aspekti NOP-a Istre." *Dometi* 5-6-7 (1975).

Elazar, Daniel J. *Exploring Federalism.* University of Alabama Press, 1987.

Elazar, Daniel J., ed., *Federalism and Political Integration.* New York & London: Lanhan, 1984.

Enloe, Cynthia. *Ethnic Conflict and Political Development.* Boston: Little Brown & Company, 1973.

Enloe, Cynthia. *Police, Military and Ethnicity: Foundations of State Power.* New Brunswick, New Jersey: Transaction Books, 1980.

Evans, Peter B., Dietrich Reuschemeyer, and Theda Skocpol. *Bringing the State Back In.* Cambridge and New York: Cambridge University Press, 1985.

Feldman, Ana and Ljiljana Modrić. "Gradja KP Hrvatske 1941-1945. u Arhivu Instituta za historiju radničkog pokreta Hrvatske," *Časopis za suvremenu povijest* 3 (1975).

Gaži, Stjepan. "Beginning of the Croatian Peasant Party: A Historico-Political Survey." *Journal of Croatian Studies* 3-4 (1962-1963).

Gaži, Stjepan. *A History of Croatia.* New York, 1973.

Gaži, Stjepan. "Stjepan Radić: His Life and Political Activities (1871-1928)." *Journal of Croatian Studies* 24-25 (1973-1974).

Gellner, Ernest. *Nations and Nationalism.* Ithaca and London: Cornell University Press, 1983.

Gizdić, Drago. *Dalmacija 1941.* Zagreb, 1959.

Gizdić, Drago. *Dalmacija 1942.* Zagreb, 1959.

Gizdić, Drago. *Dalmacija 1943.* Zagreb, 1962.

Gizdić, Drago. *Dalmacija 1944-1945.* Zagreb, 1964.

Gligorijević, Branislav. *Demokratska stranka i politički odnosi u Kraljevini Srba, Hrvata i Slovenaca.* Belgrade, 1970.

Gligorijević, Branislav. *Parlament i političke stranke u Jugoslaviji, 1919-1920.* Belgrade, 1979.

Gravac, Igor. "O proučavanju struktura sudionika NOB-a i socijalističke revolucije u Hrvatskoj 1941-1945." *Časopis za suvremenu povijest* 2 (1974).

Gregorić, Pavle. *Narodnooslobodilački pokret u zapadnoj Slavoniji i Bjelovarskom okrugu u 1941 g.* Slavonski Brod, 1969.

Hamilton, Nora. *The Limits of State Autonomy: Post Revolutionary Mexico.* Princeton: Princeton University Press, 1982.

Hasanagić, Edib, ed. *Komunistička partija Jugoslavije, 1919-1941: Izabrani dokumenti.* Zagreb, 1959.

Hayes, Carlton J. H. *The Historical Evolution of Modern Nationalism.* New York: Russell & Russell, 1931.

Hehn, Paul N. *The German Struggle against Yugoslavia—Guerrillas in World War Two.* New York: Columbia University Press, 1979.

Hoptner, J.B. *Yugoslavia in Crisis, 1934-1941.* New York: Columbia University Press, 1962.

Horvat, Josip. *Ljudevit Gaj, njegov život, njegov doba.* Zagreb, 1975.

Horvat, Josip. *Politička povijest Hrvatske.* Zagreb, 1936.

Hronologija oslobodilačke borbe naroda Jugoslavije 1941-1945. Belgrade, 1964.

Huntington, Samuel. *Political Order in Changing Societies.* New Haven: Yale University Press, 1968.

Išek, Tomislav. *Djelatnost Hrvatske seljačke stranke u Bosni i Hercegovini do zavodjenja diktature.* Sarajevo, 1971.

Ivanković-Vonta, Zvonko. *Hebrang.* Zagreb, 1988.

Iveković, Mladen. *Hrvatska lijeva inteligencija, 1918-1945.* 2 vols. Zagreb, 1970.

Iveković, Mladen. *Nepokorena zemlja.* Zagreb, 1945.

Janjatović, Bosiljka. *Politika Hrvatske eljačke stranke prema radničkoj klasi.* Zagreb, 1983.

Janković, Dragoslav. *Jugoslovensko pitanje i Krfska deklaracija 1917 godine.* Belgrade, 1967.

Janković, Dragoslav. *Srbija i jugoslovensko pitanje 1914-1915*. Belgrade, 1973.

Jareb, Jare. *Pola stoljeća Hrvatske politike*. Buenos Aires: Knjižnica Hrvatske Revije, 1960.

Jareb, Jerome and Ivo Omrčanin, eds. "The End of the Croatian Army at Bleiburg Austria in May 1945 Acording to English Military Documents." *Journal of Croatian Studies* 18-19 (1977-1978).

Jelavich, Barbara, and Charles Jelavich. *The Establishment of the Balkan National States*. Seattle: University of Washington Press, 1977.

Jelić, Ivan. *Hrvatska u ratu i revoluciji 1941-1945*. Zagreb, 1978.

Jelić, Ivan. *Jugoslavenska socijalistička revolucija (1941-1945)*. Zagreb, 1979.

Jelić, Ivan. *Komunisti i revolucija. Studije iz povijesti komunističkog pokreta i revolucije u Hrvatskoj*. Zagreb, 1977.

Jelić, Ivan. *Komunistička partija Hrvatske, 1937-1945*. 2 vols. Zagreb, 1981.

Jelić, Ivan. "Tito i NOB u Hrvatskoj 1941 g." *Časopis za suvremenu povijest* (1984).

Jelić, Ivan. *Tragedija Kerestinca*. Zagreb, 1987.

Jelić, Ivan. *Uoči revolucije. Komunistički pokret u Hrvatskoj 1935-1941*. Zagreb, 1978.

Jelić-Butić, Fikreta. *Četnici u Hrvatskoj 1941-1945*. Zagreb, 1986.

Jelić-Butić, Fikreta. *Hrvatska seljačka stranka*. Zagreb, 1985.

Jelić-Butić, Fikreta. *Ustaše i Nazavisna Država Hrvatska 1941-1945*. Zagreb, 1977.

Johnson, Chalmers. *Peasant Nationalism and Communist Power*. Stanford: Stanford University Press, 1962.

Johnson, Chalmers, ed. *Change in Communist Systems*. Stanford: Stanford University Press, 1970.

Jones, William. *Twelve Months with Tito's Partisans*. Bedford, England: Bedford Press, 1946.

Jowitt, Kenneth. *Revolutionary Breakthrough and National Development*. Berkeley: University of California Press, 1971.

Jukić, Ilija. *The Fall of Yugoslavia*. New York and London: Harcourt Brace Jovanovich, 1974.

Kadić, Ante. "Vladimir Nazor." *Journal of Croatian Studies* 17 (1976): 64-73.

Kardelj, Edvard. *Razvoj slovenačkog nacionalnog pitanja*. Belgrade, 1960.

Kardelj, Edvard. *Borba za priznanje i nezavisnost nove Jugoslavije 1944-1957*. Ljubljana and Belgrade, 1980.

Kedourie, Elie. *Nationalism*. New York: Frederick A. Praeger, 1960.

Kisić-Kolanović, Nada. "Prilog proučavanju narodne vlasti u Hrvatskoj 1943-1945 g." *Časopis za suvremenu povijest* 2 (1979).

Klajkić, Dragan. *Dosije Hebrang*. Ljubljana and Belgrade, 1983.

Klajković, Vojmir. "Jugoslavenska vlada u emigraciji i saveznici prema pitanju Hrvatske, 1941-1944." Part 1, *Časopis za suvremenu povijest* 2-3 (1971).

Klajković, Vojmir. "Jugoslavenska vlada u emigraciji i saveznici prema pitanju Hrvatske 1941-1944." Part 2, *Časopis za suvremenu povijest* 1 (1973).

Klajković, Vojmir. "Jugoslovensko-britanski odnosi i Komintern 1941-1943 g." *Časopis za suvremenu povijest* 2 (1977).

Klajković, Vojmir. "Promena politike Velike Britanije prema Jugoslaviji u prvoj polovini 1943 g." *Jugoslovenski istorijski časopis* 2 (1963): 31-42.

Kobsa, Leopold. "O gledištima KPJ na nacionalno pitanje u Jugoslaviji u razdoblju izmedju dva svjetska rata." *Naše teme* (July 1969).

Kolar-Dimitrijević, Mira, ed. *Oslobodjenje Hrvatske 1945 godine*. Zagreb, 1986.

Kolar-Dimitrijević, Mira. "Put Stjepana Radića u Moskvu i pristup Hrvatske republikanske seljačke stranke u Seljačku internacionalu." *Časopis za suvremenu povijest* 3 (1972).

Končar, Ranko. "Problem autonomije Vojvodine u kontekstu odluke Drugog zasjedanja AVNOJ-a." *AVNOJ i narodnooslobodilačka borba u Bosni i Hercegovini*. Belgrade, 1974.

Konjević, Mile. "Formiranje i rad IO H(R)SS na oslobodjenom teritoriju 1943-1945." *Zbornik—Historijski Institut Slavonije* 7 (1975).

Konjević, Mile. "Konfrontacija baze i rukovodećeg aparata HSS u procesi diferencijacije." *Jugoslovenski istorijski časopis* 1 (1974).

Koštunica, Vojislav, and Kosta Čavoški. *Stranački pluralizam i monizam, Društveni pokreti i politički sistem u Jugoslaviji, 1944-1949*. Belgrade, 1983.

Krizman, Bogdan. *Ante Pavelić i ustaše*. Zagreb, 1978.

Krizman, Bogdan. *Jugoslavenske vlade u izbjeglištvu 1941-1943: Dokumenti*. Zagreb, 1981.

Krizman, Bogdan. *Korespondencije Stjepana Radića*. 2 vols. Zagreb, 1972-1973.

Krizman, Bogdan. "Napomene o nekim aspektima politike Hrvatske seljačke stranke u medjuratnom i ratnom razdoblju." *Časopis za suvremenu povijest* 3 (1978).

Krizman, Bogdan. *Pavelić izmedju Hitlera i Mussolinija*. Zagreb, 1980.

Krizman, Bogdan. *Raspad Austro-Ugarske i stvaranje jugoslavenske države*. Zagreb, 1977.

Krizman, Bogdan. "Stjepan Radić i Hrvatska pučka seljačka stranka u prvom svjetskom ratu." *Časopis za suvremenu povijest* 2 (1970).

Krizman, Bogdan. *Ustaše i Treći Reich*. Zagreb, 1983.

Krstulović, Vicko. *Jadranska orijentacija*. Zagreb, 1971.

Kulundžić, Zvonimir. *Atentat na Stjepana Radića*. Zagreb, 1967.

Kulundžić, Zvonimir, ed. *Stjepan Radić, politički spisi*. Zagreb, 1971.

Lasić, Stanko. *Sukob na književnoj ljevici*. Zagreb, 1970.

Lukač, Dušan. *Radnički pokret u Jugoslaviji i nacionalno pitanje 1918-1941*. Belgrade, 1972.

Maček, Vladko. *In the Struggle for Freedom*. New York: Robert Speller and Sons, Inc., 1957.

Maclean, Fitzroy. *Eastern Approaches*. London, 1949.

Maclean, Fitzroy. *The Heretic: The Life and Times of Josip Broz Tito*. New York: Harper & Bros., 1957.

Marić, Milomir. *Deca komunizma*. Belgrade, 1987.

Marjanović, Jovan. "Velika Britanija i Narodnooslobodilački pokret u Jugoslaviji 1941-1945." *Jugoslovenski istorijski časopis* 2 (1963): 31-42.

Matijević, Zlatko. "Hrvatska gradjanska politika izmedju dva rata u svjetlu jugoslavenske povijesne literature." *Časopis za suvremenu povijest* 1 (1980).

Matković, Hrvoje. "Stjepan Radić i Svetozar Pribićević u jugoslavenskoj politici od ujedinjenja do šestojanuarske diktature." *Jugoslovenski istorijski časopis* 4 (1969).

Matković, Hrvoje. *Svetozar Pribićević i Samostalna demokratska stranka do šestojanuarske diktature.* Zagreb, 1972.

Milatović, Mile. *Slučaj Andrije Hebranga.* Belgrade, 1952.

Milazzo, Matteo J. *The Chetnik Movement and the Yugoslav Resistance.* Baltimore and London: Johns Hopkins University Press, 1975.

Miletić, Antun. *Koncentracioni logor Jasenovac, 1941-1945.* Belgrade, 1986.

Minogue, K. R. *Nationalism.* London: B. T. Batsford, Ltd., 1967.

Moore, Barrington Jr. *The Origins of Dictatorship and Democracy: Lord and Peasant in the Making of the Modern World.* Boston: Beacon Press, 1966.

Moore, Barrington Jr. *Social Origins of Dictatorship and Democracy.* Boston: Beacon Press, 1982.

Morača, Pero, Dušan Bilandžić, and Stanislav Stojanović. *Istorija saveza komunista Jugoslavije.* Belgrade, 1977.

Morača, Pero. *Jugoslavija 1941.* Belgrade, 1971.

Morača, Pero. *Narodnooslobodilačka borba Jugoslavije 1941-1945.* Belgrade, 1971.

Motyl, Alexander J. *Will the Non-Russians Rebel? State, Ethnicity and Stability in the U.S.S.R..* Ithaca & London: Cornell University Press, 1987.

Narodnooslobodilačka borba i socijalistička revolucija u Hrvatskoj 1944 godine. Zagreb, 1976.

Nešović, Slobodan, ed. *Zakonodavni rad Pretsedništva Antifašističkog veća narodnog oslobodjenja Jugoslavije i Pretsedništva Privremene narodne skupštine Demokratske Federativne Jugoslavije (19 novembra 1944 - 27 oktobra 1945).* Belgrade, 1951.

Nešović, Slobodan, and Branko Petranović. *AVNOJ i revolucija.* Belgrade, 1983.

Nešović, Slobodan. *Stvaranje nove Jugoslavije 1941-1945.* Belgrade, 1981.

Nešović, Slobodan. *Diplomatska igra oko Jugoslavije 1941-1945.* Zagreb, 1977.

Pattee, Richard. *The Case of Cardinal Aloysius Stepinac.* Milwaukee: The Bruce Publishing Company, 1953.

Pavlowitch, Stevan. *Unconventional Perceptions of Yugoslavia, 1940-1944.* New York: Columbia University Press, 1985.

Pavlowitch, Stevan. *Yugoslavia.* New York: Praeger, 1971.

Perić, Ivan. *Ideje "masovnog pokreta" u Hrvatskoj.* Zagreb, 1974.

Perić, Ivan. *Suvremeni hrvatski nacionalizam.* Zagreb: August Cesarec, 1976.

Pešelj, Branko. "Serbo-Croatian Agreement of 1939 and American Foreign Policy." *Journal of Croatian Studies* 11-12 (1970-1971).

Petranović, Branko. *AVNOJ —revolucionarna smena vlasti, 1942-1945.* Belgrade, 1976.

Petranović, Branko. "Gradjanske stranke u Jugoslaviji 1944-1948 i njihov karakter." *Istorijski glasnik* 1 (1969).

Petranović, Branko. *Jugoslavenska vlada u izbeglištvu 1943-1945.* Zagreb, 1981.

Petranović, Branko. "O levim skretanjima KPJ krajem 1941 i u prvoj polovini 1942." *Zbornik za istoriju* 4 (1971).

Petranović, Branko. *Političke i pravne prilike za vreme Privremene vlade DFJ.* Belgrade, 1963.

Petranović, Branko. *Revolucija i kontrarevolucija.* Belgrade, 1983.

Petranović, Branko, and Vojislav Simović. *Istorija narodne vlasti.* Belgrade, 1979.

Pijade, Moša. *Izabrani govori i članci, 1941-1947.* Belgrade, 1948.

Pipes, Richard. *The Formation of the Soviet Union.* Cambridge: Harvard University Press, 1964.

Plenča, Dušan. *Medjunarodni odnosi Jugoslavije u toku drugog svetskog rata.* Belgrade, 1962.

Pleterski, Janko. *KPJ i nacionalno pitanje, 1919-1941.* Belgrade, 1971.

Pleterski, Janko. "Nacionalno pitanje u Jugoslaviji u teoriji i politici KPJ-KPS." *Jugoslovenski istorijski časopis* 1-2 (1969).

Pleterski, Janko. "Perspektiva federativnog uredjenja u novoj Jugoslaviji kao faktor narodnooslobodilačke borbe." *Časopis za suvremenu povijest* 3 (1973).

Pleterski, Janko. *Prvo opredeljenje Slovenaca za Jugoslaviju.* Belgrade, 1976.

Poulantzas, Nicos. "The Problem of the Capitalist State." *New Left Review* 58 (1969): 67-78.

Prnjat, Branko, ed. *War and Revolution in Yugoslavia 1941-1945.* Belgrade, 1985.

Purivatra, Atif. *Jugoslavenska muslimanska organizacija u političkom životu Kraljevine Srba, Hrvata i Slovenaca.* Sarajevo, 1974.

Ramet, Pedro. "Catholicism and Politics in Socialist Yugoslavia." *Religion in Communist Lands* 10 (3) 1982.

Ramet, Pedro. "From Strossmayer to Stepinac: Croatian National Ideology and Catholicism." *Canadian Review of Studies in Nationalism* 12 (1979).

Ramet, Pedro. *Nationalism and Federalism in Yugoslavia 1963-1983.* Bloomington: Indiana University Press, 1984.

Rastić, Marijan. *Izbor iz arhivske gradje Komunističke partije Jugoslavije i Komunističke partije Hrvatske za povijest 1941 g. u Hrvatskoj.* Zagreb, 1971.

Remington, Robin Alison. "Ideology as a Resource: A Communist Case Study," in *Nonstate Nations in International Politics,* Judy S. Bertelsen, ed.. New York: Praeger, 1977.

Revolucionarni radnički pokret u Zagrebu izmedju dva svjetska rata. Zagreb, 1968.

Ribar, Ivan. *Uspomene iz NORa.* Belgrade, 1961.

Ribar, Ivo Lola. *Govori i članci.* Belgrade, 1953.

Ribar, Ivo Lola. *Ratna pisma.* Belgrade, 1978.

Riker, William J. *Federalism, Origin, Operation and Significance.* Boston and Toronto: Little Brown & Company, 1964.

Roberts, Walter R. *Tito, Mihailović and the Allies, 1941-1945.* New Brunswick: Rutgers University Press, 1973.

Rothschild, Joseph. *East Central Europe between the Two World Wars.* Seattle and London: Washington University Press, 1974.

Rothschild, Joseph. *Ethnopolitics; a Conceptual Framework.* New York: Columbia University Press, 1981.

Rusinow, Dennison. *The Yugoslav Experiment 1948-1974.* Berkeley and Los Angeles: University of California Press, 1977.

Sadkovich, James J. *Italian Support for Croatian Separatism 1927-1937.* New York and London: Garland Publishing, Inc., 1987.

Schoplin, George. "The Ideology of Croatian Nationalism." *Survey* 19 (1) 1973.

Schurmann, Franz. *Ideology and Organization in Communist China*. Berkeley: University of California Press, 1968.

Šepić, Dragovan. *Italija, Saveznici i jugoslavensko pitanje 1914-1918*. Zagreb, 1976.

Šepić, Dragovan. *Vlada Ivana Šubašića*. Zagreb, 1981.

Seton-Watson, Hugh. *Eastern Europe between the Wars, 1918-1941*. Boulder, Colorado: Westview Press, 1986.

Seton-Watson, Hugh. *The East European Revolution*. New York: Praeger, 1956.

Seton-Watson, Hugh. *Nationalism and Communism, essays, 1946-1956*. New York: Frederick A. Praeger, 1965.

Seton-Watson, Hugh. *Nations and States, an enquiry into the origins of nations and the politics of nationalism*. Boulder, Colorado: Westview Press, 1977.

Seton-Watson, Robert W. "Yugoslavia and the Croat Problem." *Slavonic Review* 16 (1937): 102-112.

Shoup, Paul. *Communism and the Yugoslav National Question*. New York and London: Columbia University Press, 1968.

Sirotković, Hodimir. "Konstituiranje ZAVNOH-a." *Časopis za suvremenu povijest* 3 (1973).

Sirotković, Hodimir. "Osnivanje prve Narodne vlade Federalne Hrvatske." *Dometi* 5-6 (1975).

Sirotković, Hodimir. "Stvaranje federalne Hrvatske u NOBu." *Časopis za suvremenu povijest* 2-3 (1971).

Sjeverozapadna Hrvatska u NOB-u i socijalističkoj revoluciji, zbornik. Varaždin, 1976.

Smith, Anthony. *State and Nation in the Third World*. Brighton, England: Wheatsheaf Books, 1983.

Smith, Anthony. *Theories of Nationalism*. New York, Evanston, San Francisco and London: Harper & Row, 1971.

Spalatin, M.S. "The Croatian Nationalism of Ante Starčević, 1845-1871." *Journal of Croatian Studies* 16 (1975): 19-146.

Split u narodnooslobodilačkoj borbi i socijalističkoj revoluciji 1941-1945. Split, 1981.

Spomenica u čast dvadeset i pete godišnjice ZAVNOH-a. Zagreb, 1969.

Stepan, Alfred. *The State and Society: Peru in Comparative Perspective*. Princeton: Princeton University Press, 1978.

Stipetić, Zorica. "O pojmu lijeve inteligencije u Hrvatskoj u tridesetima godinama." *Časopis za suvremenu povijest* 1 (1979).

Stojkov, Todor. *Opozicija u vreme šestojanuarske diktature 1929-1935*. Belgrade, 1969.

Sugar, Peter and Ivo Lederer. *Nationalism in Eastern Europe*. Seattle and London: University of Washington Press, 1973.

Sugar, Peter, ed. *Ethnic Diversity and Conflict in Eastern Europe*. Santa Barbara, California: Clio, 1980.

Šuljak, Dinko. "Božidar Magovac—u vrtlogu podvale, spletke, i izdaje." *Hrvatska revija* 119 (September 1980): 416-430.

Supek, Ivan. *Krivovjernik na ljevici*. Bristol, England; BC Review, 1980.

Šuvar, Stipe, *Nacionalno i nacionalističko*. Split, 1974.

Tilly, Charles. *The Formation of National States in Western Europe*. Princeton: Princeton University Press, 1975.

Tito, Josip Broz. *Sabrana djela*. 16 vols. Belgrade, 1977-1980.

Tomasevich, Jozo. *Peasants, Politics and Economic Change in Yugoslavia*. Stanford, California: Stanford University Press, 1955.

Tomasevich, Jozo. *The Chetniks, War and Revolution in Yugoslavia 1941-1945*. Stanford, California: Stanford University Press, 1975.

Trumberger, Ellen. "A Theory of Elite Revolutions." *Studies in Comparative International Development* (Fall 1972): 191-201.

Tripalo, Miko. *Bez kompromisa u ostvarivanju samoupravnog socijalizma*. Zagreb, 1969.

Tripalo, Miko. *Hrvatsko proljeće*. Zagreb: Globus, 1989.

Tripalo, Miko. *S poprišta*. Zagreb, 1971.

Vlajčić, Gordana. *Jugoslavenska revolucija i nacionalno pitanje, 1919-1927*. Zagreb, 1974.

Vlajčić, Gordana. *Osma Konferencija zagrebačkih komunista*. Zagreb, 1976.

Vucinich, Wayne, ed. *Contemporary Yugoslavia, Twenty Years of Socialist Experiment*. Berkeley: University of California Press, 1969.

Vukmanović, Svetozar Tempo. *Revolucija koja teče*. Belgrade, 1971.

Wheare, K. C. *Federal Government*. New York: Oxford University Press, 1946.

Wheeler, Mark. *Britain and the War for Yugoslavia*. New York: Columbia University Press, 1980.

Zarić, Slobodan. *Revolucionarni omladinski pokret u Hrvatskoj 1941-1948*. Zagreb, 1980.

Zatezalo, Djuro. *Četvrta konferencija Komunističke partije za okrug Karlovca 1945*. Karlovac, 1985.

Zbornik dokumenata i podataka o narodnooslobodilačkom ratu jugoslovenskih naroda. vols. 1-13. Belgrade, 1949-1976.

Zemaljsko antifašističko vijeće narodnog oslobodjenja Hrvatske, Zbornik dokumenata 1943-1944. vols. 1-3. Zagreb, 1964-1975.

Živković Dušan. *Narodni front Jugoslavije, 1935-1945*. Belgrade, 1978.

About the Book and Author

This book explores the historical roots of the current conflict in Yugoslavia, providing a thorough background for an understanding of the entrenched antagonism between Serbs and Croats. Its particular focus is the Yugoslav Communist Party's attempts to resolve this problem in the process of remaking the state. Irvine's analysis fills a critical gap in the literature not only on Yugoslavia but also on the legacies of the Communist period for the current process of transition in Eastern Europe and the former Soviet Union.

Jill A. Irvine lived in Yugoslavia for several years and traveled extensively in Eastern Europe. She received her doctorate from Harvard University, where she was a fellow at the Russian Research Center. She is currently an assistant professor of political science at the University of Oklahoma.

Index